COLLECTIONS

A Harcourt Reading / Language Arts Program

Pathways to Adventure

TEACHER'S EDITION

SENIOR AUTHORS

Roger C. Farr • Dorothy S. Strickland • Isabel L. Beck

AUTHORS

Richard F. Abrahamson • Alma Flor Ada • Bernice E. Cullinan • Margaret McKeown • Nancy Roser
Patricia Smith • Judy Wallis • Junko Yokota • Hallie Kay Yopp

SENIOR CONSULTANT

Asa G. Hilliard III

CONSULTANTS

Karen Kutiper • Angelina Olivares • David A. Monti

Harcourt

Orlando   Boston   Dallas   Chicago   San Diego

Visit *The Learning Site!*
www.harcourtschool.com

Copyright © 2001 by Harcourt, Inc.

All rights reserved. No part of this publication may be reproduced or transmitted in any form or by any means, electronic or mechanical, including photocopy, recording, or any information storage and retrieval system, without permission in writing from the publisher.

Teachers using COLLECTIONS may photocopy copying masters in complete pages in sufficient quantities for classroom use only and not for resale.

HARCOURT and the Harcourt Logo are trademarks of Harcourt, Inc.

Acknowledgments appear in the back of this book.

Printed in the United States of America

ISBN 0-15-318934-7

1 2 3 4 5 6 7 8 9 10   030   2003 2002 2001 2000

Meet Our Authors!

Dr. Roger C. Farr

Chancellor's Professor and Director of the Center for Innovation in Assessment, Indiana University, Bloomington

RESEARCH CONTRIBUTIONS: Assessment, Portfolios, Reading-Writing Strategies, Staff Development

Dr. Dorothy S. Strickland

The State of New Jersey Professor of Reading, Rutgers University

RESEARCH CONTRIBUTIONS: Emergent Literacy, Linguistic and Cultural Diversity, Intervention, Phonics in Literature-based Curriculum, Integrated Language Arts, Assessment

Dr. Isabel L. Beck

Professor of Education and Senior Scientist at the Learning Research and Development Center, University of Pittsburgh

RESEARCH CONTRIBUTIONS: Beginning Reading, Reading Comprehension, Vocabulary, Phonics/Decoding Instruction, Critical Thinking, Technology

Dr. Richard F. Abrahamson
Professor of Education, University of Houston
RESEARCH CONTRIBUTIONS: Children's Literature, Strategic Reading, Reading Nonfiction

Dr. Alma Flor Ada
Director of Doctoral Studies in the International Multicultural Program, University of San Francisco
RESEARCH CONTRIBUTIONS: Bilingual Education, English as a Second Language, Family Involvement

Dr. Bernice E. Cullinan
Professor of Early Childhood and Elementary Education, New York University
RESEARCH CONTRIBUTIONS: Children's Literature, Emergent Literacy, Intervention, Integrated Language Arts

Dr. Margaret McKeown
Research Scientist at the Learning and Development Center, University of Pittsburgh
RESEARCH CONTRIBUTIONS: Reading Comprehension, Vocabulary

Dr. Nancy Roser
Professor, Language and Literacy Studies, University of Texas, Austin
RESEARCH CONTRIBUTIONS: Beginning Reading, Book Discussions, Early Childhood, Emergent Literacy, Phonics in Literature-based Curriculum, Reading Comprehension

Patricia Smith
Elementary Reading/Language Arts Coordinator, Cypress-Fairbanks School District, Houston, Texas, and Adjunct Professor of Education, University of Houston-Clear Lake
RESEARCH CONTRIBUTIONS: Early Literacy, Phonics, Technology

Dr. Judy Wallis
Language Arts Director, Spring Branch Independent School District, Houston, Texas
RESEARCH CONTRIBUTIONS: Integrated Language Arts, Reading Strategies

Dr. Junko Yokota
Associate Professor, Reading/Language Arts Department, National-Louis University, Evanston, Illinois
RESEARCH CONTRIBUTIONS: Multicultural Literature, Children's Literature

Dr. Hallie Kay Yopp
Professor, Department of Elementary Bilingual and Reading Education, California State University, Fullerton
RESEARCH CONTRIBUTIONS: Phonemic Awareness, Early Childhood

Senior Consultant

Dr. Asa G. Hilliard III
Fuller E. Callaway Professor of Urban Education, Department of Educational Foundations, Georgia State University, Atlanta
RESEARCH CONTRIBUTIONS: Multicultural Literature and Education

Consultants

Dr. Karen S. Kutiper
English/Language Arts Consultant, Harris County Department of Education, Texas
RESEARCH CONTRIBUTIONS: Early Literacy, Reader Response

Dr. David A. Monti
Professor, Reading/Language Arts Department, Central Connecticut State University
RESEARCH CONTRIBUTIONS: Flexible Grouping, Technology, Family Involvement

Angelina Olivares
Elementary Coordinator, Bilingual/ESL, Fort Worth Independent School District
RESEARCH CONTRIBUTIONS: Spanish Reading, English as a Second Language, Bilingual Education

Program Features

COLLECTIONS
A Harcourt Reading / Language Arts Program

Collections is a balanced, comprehensive program that provides the materials and support you need to help all your students become fluent, lifelong readers.

The foundation of **Collections** is research-based instruction and practice, organized in practical, easy-to-use lessons and components.

You will find the following features of effective reading instruction throughout the **Collections** program.

Literature

- **Wide reading** in a variety of **classic** and **contemporary works,** including realistic fiction, folktales, informational nonfiction, biography and autobiography, plays, and poems.

- Accessible, appropriate literature for **instructional-level reading.**

- Opportunities to self-select **trade books** for independent, sustained reading.

- Instruction in **setting purposes** for reading, **monitoring comprehension,** and using **reading strategies.**

- Instruction in distinguishing among different **genres** and **types of text.**

- Opportunities to **respond to literature** in ways that demonstrate comprehension, interpretation, and appreciation.

Where to Find It

- *Pathways to Adventure* Student Edition
- *Timeless Tales* Intervention Reader
- Reader's Choice Library
- Leveled Library
- Multi-Level Books
- Monitor Comprehension and Guided Reading

Oral Language

- Frequent listening opportunities to **develop vocabulary** and promote a **love of literature.**

- Oral reading and **retelling** activities, with assessment suggestions.

- Oral rereading to build **fluency** and **automatic word recognition.**

- Listening and speaking activities to help students **listen responsively** and **speak with expression,** appropriate volume and rate, and attention to phrasing and punctuation.

Where to Find It

- Listening to Literature
- Literature Cassettes
- Building Background and Concepts
- Building Literacy Skills

Word Identification

- **Decoding instruction,** appropriately sequenced and maintained through the grades.

- Opportunities to **apply decoding skills** during reading.

- Abundant **review and practice** activities.

- Multiple opportunities to read and reread, building **accuracy** and **fluency.**

Where to Find It

- Build Word-Identification Strategies
- Reviewing Word-Identification Strategies
- Decoding Long Words and Word Study activities
- Decoding/Phonics Minilessons

Writing

- Direct instruction that emphasizes major **writing forms, purposes,** and **processes** and that connects reading to writing.

- Helpful suggestions to improve **organization** and **elaboration.**

- Systematic **grammar** and **spelling** instruction to develop proficiency in the conventions of writing.

- Frequent opportunities to **respond to literature** through writing.

- **Test preparation** to equip students for success on standardized and state tests.

Where to Find It

- Writing, Grammar, and Spelling lessons
- Building Literacy Skills
- Grammar and Spelling Practice Books
- Cross-Curricular Connections
- Test Prep

Program Features

Vocabulary

- Direct instruction in word **meanings** and **usage.**

- Systematic vocabulary **introduction, review,** and **practice.**

- Strategies for confirming meaning and pronunciation through **syntax, context, references,** and **resources.**

- Instruction in word parts such as **prefixes, suffixes,** and **root words.**

- Engaging activities and lessons using **synonyms, antonyms, homophones, homographs, specialized vocabulary,** and **cross-curricular words.**

- Ongoing vocabulary development through **extensive reading** and **listening.**

Where to Find It

- Introducing Vocabulary
- Reviewing Vocabulary Words
- Extending Vocabulary
- Vocabulary Skill Lessons
- Develop Vocabulary Through Listening

Comprehension

- Carefully organized instructional plan that includes **preteaching** the skill before reading, **applying** the skill during reading, and **reinforcing** and **practicing** the skill after reading.

- **Systematic instruction** that builds through the grades, with each tested skill introduced, retaught, reviewed at least twice, and maintained after testing and in subsequent grades as appropriate.

- Ongoing **strategy instruction** to help students gain meaning from text and build independence.

- Questions and activities to build **critical-thinking** skills.

- Retelling and **summarizing** activities to assess comprehension.

- **Test preparation** to equip students for success on standardized and state tests.

Where to Find It

- Skill lessons in both the *Teacher's Edition* and *Student Edition*
- Using Reading Strategies, Preteach the Strategy, Return to the Strategy
- Monitor Comprehension
- Comprehension Cards
- Mission: Comprehension™ Skills Practice CD-ROM
- Test Prep
- Test Tutor on *The Learning Site!* **www.harcourtschool.com**

Collections Assessment Options

**The chart below gives a brief overview of the
assessment resources that are available in *Collections*.**

Formal Assessments

For placement and assessment	Level	Purpose
Kindergarten and Grade 1 Reading Inventory	K–1	To diagnose early literacy skills and assist in group placement
Placement and Individual Inventory Teacher's Guide	2–6	To diagnose individual students; to make placement decisions
At the theme level		
Reading and Language Arts Skills Assessment *Reading Skills Assessment*	1 2–6	To measure progress; to diagnose
Holistic Reading Assessment	1–6	To obtain a global picture of reading comprehension
Reading/Writing Performance Assessment	1–6	To measure progress in reading comprehension and writing
At the selection level		
Selection Comprehension Tests	1–6	To monitor vocabulary and comprehension
Throughout the year		
Emergent Literacy in Kindergarten	K	To assess early literacy skills
Portfolio Assessment Teacher's Guide	1–6	To provide tips on starting, maintaining, and evaluating portfolios
At mid-year and end-of-year		
Mid-Year and End-of-Year Reading and Language Arts Skills Assessment	1	To provide a cumulative evaluation of skills development
At mid-year and end-of-year		
Reading Skills Assessment	2–6	To provide a cumulative evaluation of skills development

Informal Assessments

Teacher's Edition

- ✔ Assessment suggestions for each theme
- ✔ Assessment notes at "point of use" throughout the lessons
- ✔ Informal inventories/running records
  Grade 1: 2 per theme, 12 per grade
  Grade 2–6: 1 per theme, 6 per grade

- ✔ Writing Rubrics
- ✔ Self-assessment strategies

- ✔ Test Prep notes for skills lessons, writing, and grammar

Leveled Library (Primary/Intermediate Library)

- ✔ Benchmark Books for Evaluation
- ✔ Running records for trade books

Program Features

Contents

Contents

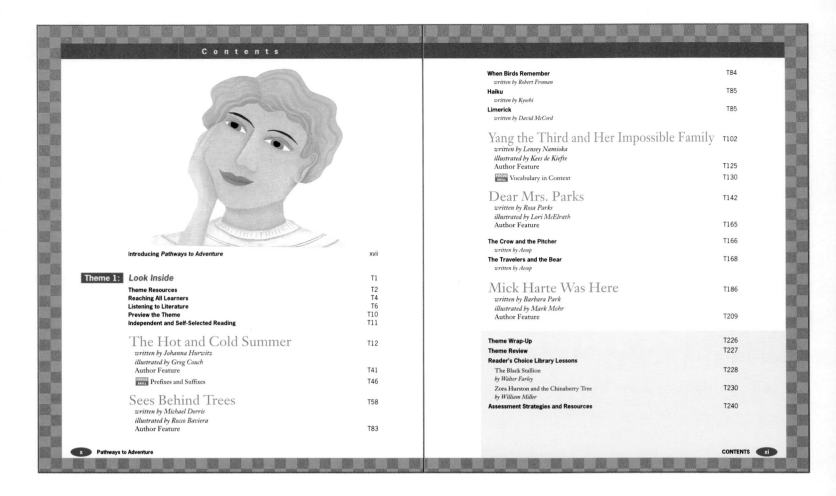

Contents

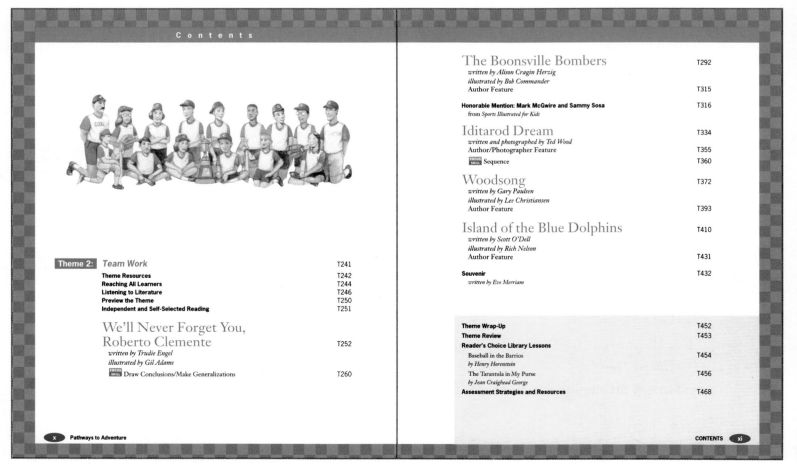

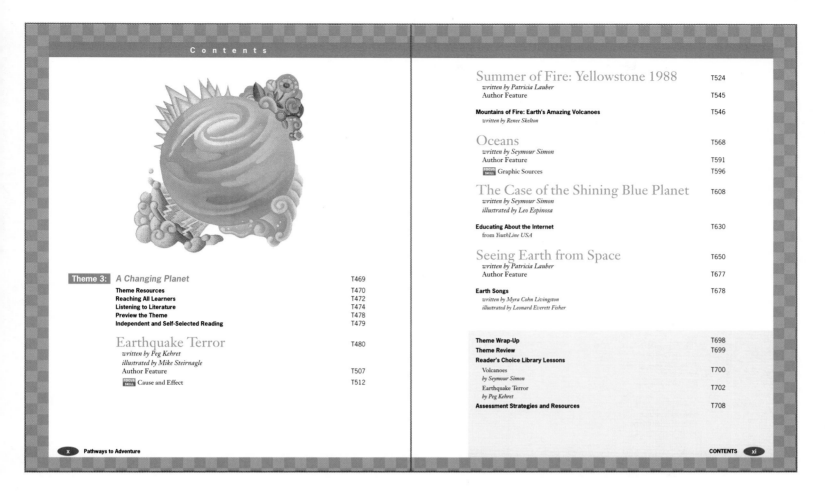

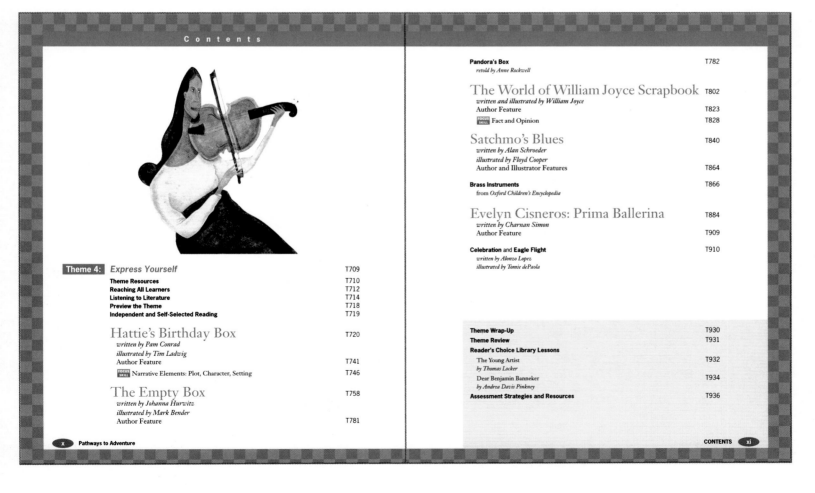

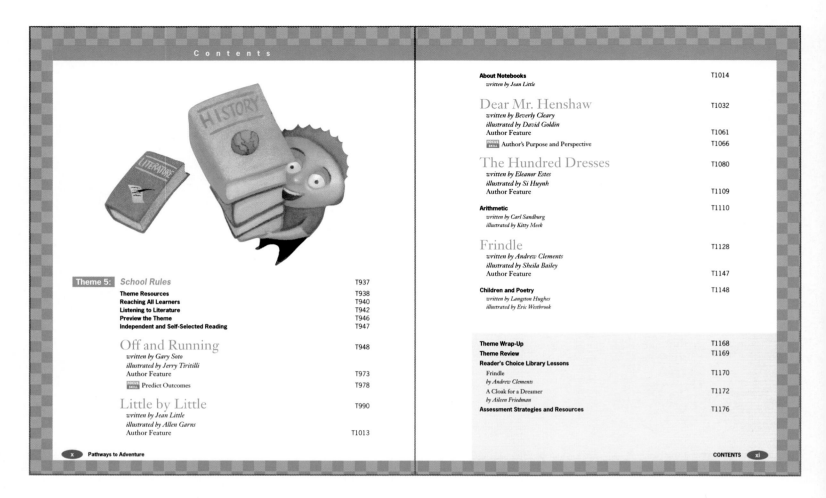

Reference Materials

■ *Reteach Lessons*

Reference Materials

- ## *Comprehension Cards*

- ## *Activity Cards*

- ## *School-Home Connection*

- ## *Additional Reading*

Introducing the Book

Invite students to discuss the title, *Pathways to Adventure*, and the cover illustration. Ask what the title might mean. Then discuss what is happening in the cover illustration.

You may want to share the following information about the cover artist:

Murray Kimber, born in Lethbridge, Canada, began creating oil paintings during his final year at the Alberta College of Art & Design. In addition to producing illustrations for international companies, he has illustrated two children's books. The first, *Josepha: A Prairie Boy's Story*, has won numerous awards, including one of Canada's highest honors, the *Governor General's Award for Children's Illustration*. In 1997 Murray Kimber closed his studio in Canada and moved to Mexico, where he has dedicated more of his time to producing personal works. He and his wife, Kari, live in the city of Cholula.

Predicting What's Inside

Discuss the letter to the reader. Have students read the letter on page 3 of the *Student Edition*. Invite volunteers to tell about adventures that they have experienced or read about. Discuss how reading is like going on an adventure.

Examine the organization of the book. Ask students to preview the table of contents on pages 4–15. Help them understand the organization of the book by pointing out the six theme titles. Explain that the *Student Edition* contains excerpts from many books as well as shorter pieces, such as poems and magazine articles. Have students look at the selection titles and the book covers and make predictions about what they will be reading.

Examine the information at the end of the book. Have students find the Glossary and the Index of Titles and Authors, beginning on page 626. As students locate each section, ask them how these parts of the book might be useful to them. Pages A2 and A6 contain information about introducing students to the Glossary and the Index.

COLLECTIONS

A Harcourt Reading / Language Arts Program

PATHWAYS TO ADVENTURE

SENIOR AUTHORS

Roger C. Farr • Dorothy S. Strickland • Isabel L. Beck

AUTHORS

Richard F. Abrahamson • Alma Flor Ada • Bernice E. Cullinan • Margaret McKeown • Nancy Roser
Patricia Smith • Judy Wallis • Junko Yokota • Hallie Kay Yopp

SENIOR CONSULTANT

Asa G. Hilliard III

CONSULTANTS

Karen S. Kutiper • David A. Monti • Angelina Olivares

Harcourt

Orlando   Boston   Dallas   Chicago   San Diego

Visit *The Learning Site!*
www.harcourtschool.com

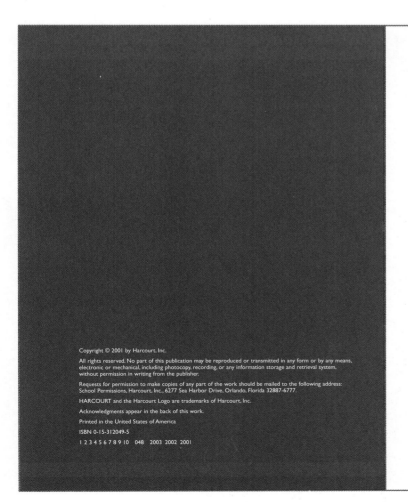

Dear Reader,

Everyone loves to take part in an adventure—whether it's exploring an exciting place, playing a new instrument, or joining a team. But as you may know from reading a good book or listening to friends, learning about the experiences of others can also be a thrill.

Prepare to share adventures from all over the world—from high above Earth's atmosphere to the powerful oceans below, from Alaska's snowy wilderness to cities and schools just like yours. You will read stories developed in the minds of imaginative writers and adventures experienced by real people in real places. In **Pathways to Adventure,** you will meet brave characters, including some American heroes, who either seek a challenge or are faced with one unexpectedly. Maybe you will find that someone else's adventure is like one of your own! Come travel with us in search of excitement, surprise, and adventure.

Sincerely,

The Authors
The Authors

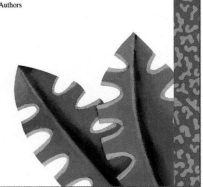

Look Inside

Theme

Contents

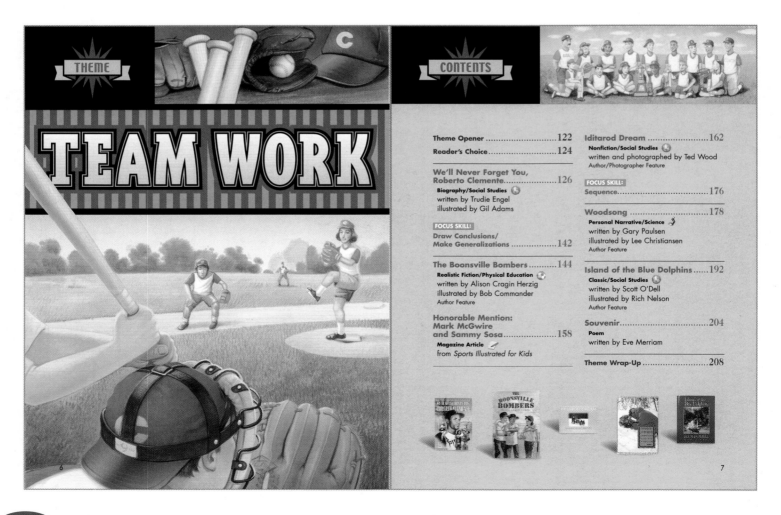

THEME

CONTENTS

TEAM WORK

THEME
A CHANGING PLANET

Contents

Theme
Express Yourself

Contents

THEME
SCHOOL RULES

CONTENTS

THEME
AMERICAN ADVENTURE

CONTENTS

Using Reading Strategies

Introduce the Concept

Discuss with students what they do when they read. They may mention things that they do before, during, or after reading. Ask questions such as these: **What do you do to get yourself ready to read? What do you do when you don't understand something you are reading? What do you do when you come to a word you don't know?** Make a list on the board of students' answers. Tell students that they have named some good reading *strategies*. Explain that a strategy is a plan for doing something well.

EXPLAIN STRATEGIES GOOD READERS USE Have students read pages 16–17. Explain that these are the strategies they will be focusing on as they read the selections in this book. Discuss with students a brief explanation of each strategy:

- **Use Prior Knowledge** Think about what you already know about the topic and the kind of selection you are reading. For example, if you are reading an information book about tornadoes, think of what you already know about tornadoes. Think of what you know about information books, too. Using prior knowledge can help you set a purpose for reading—for example, to learn more about tornadoes.

- **Make and Confirm Predictions** Think about what might happen next in a story. Read to find out whether you are right. Make new predictions as you read.

- **Adjust Reading Rate** Think about the type of selection you are reading. A selection that has a lot of facts and details, such as a selection about volcanoes, may have to be read more slowly than a story about a character your age.

- **Self-Question** Have you ever found that you have questions as you are reading? Learn to ask yourself good questions as you read. This will help you check your understanding and focus on important ideas in the selection.

- **Create Mental Images** Sometimes, picturing in your mind what you are reading can help you understand and enjoy a selection. Pay attention to descriptive details.

- **Use Context to Confirm Meaning** After you read an unfamiliar or difficult word, ask yourself whether what you read makes sense in the sentence and whether it fits what is happening in the selection. By paying attention to the words around unfamiliar words, you can learn many new words and become a stronger reader.

- **Use Text Structure and Format** Find clues to meaning by looking at how the author organized the information. Look at headings and captions.

- **Use Graphic Aids** Sometimes a selection has graphic aids, such as pictures, graphs, charts, diagrams, maps, or time lines. These often show important information that can help you understand the selection.

- **Use Reference Sources** Use other books such as dictionaries and encyclopedias to help you understand unfamiliar words and ideas. You can also use them to check or confirm what you think something means.

- **Read Ahead** If you are having trouble understanding something in a selection, such as who a certain character is, don't give up. Keep on reading. The meaning may become clearer when you have more information.

- **Reread** If something doesn't make sense, you may have missed an important point. Try reading the passage again or going back to an earlier part of the selection.

- **Summarize and Paraphrase** Tell or list the main points of the selection or the main things that happened. Restate the text in your own words. This will help you understand and remember what you read.

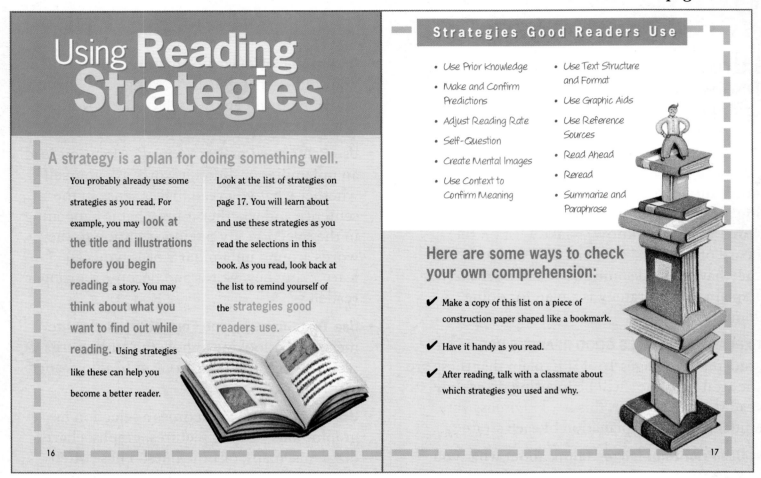

Using Reading Strategies

MONITOR COMPREHENSION Distribute copies of Thinking About My Reading and My Reading Log, pages A25–A26. Have each student begin a personal reading portfolio. Students can use the forms to record how they choose self-selected books, the strategies they use during reading, and other reading behaviors.

STRATEGY BOOKMARK Have students make a bookmark from a sheet of heavy paper and write the strategies on the bookmark. Invite students to decorate their bookmarks. As they read, they should refer to the bookmark to help remind them of the strategies they can use.

READING NOTEBOOK Explain to students that they should keep a reading notebook to record their responses to selections and to monitor their progress as readers. They may use a spiral-bound notebook or sheets of paper stapled together. In the notebook, they should create sections to write about which strategies work best for them and to develop their own plans for reading different kinds of selections. You may want to have them record how long they read each day. They should also set aside a section of the notebook for a vocabulary log, where they will list new or interesting words they come across in their reading.

Look Inside

In this theme, **students will learn about the process of self-discovery. They will read and listen to selections about young people who discover their strengths and abilities while growing up. Through these selections, students will be encouraged to look within themselves and examine their own unique attributes.**

Theme Resources

The following resources can help you provide regular, frequent opportunities for every student to read and listen to literature as well as to practice and reinforce skills.

INSTRUCTIONAL-LEVEL READING

STUDENT EDITION: PATHWAYS TO ADVENTURE

"The Hot and Cold Summer,"
pages 22–41

"Sees Behind Trees," pages 46–61

"When Birds Remember," "Haiku," and "Limerick," pages 62–63

"Yang the Third and Her Impossible Family," pages 66–79

"Dear Mrs. Parks," pages 84–97

"The Crow and the Pitcher" and "The Travelers and the Bear," pages 98–101

"Mick Harte Was Here," pages 104–117

EASY READER:
TIMELESS TALES

"A Fish Tale" pages 6–11

"The Quiver" pages 14–20

"The Audition" pages 22–27

"Lessons from Barbara Jordan" pages 30–36

"That Day Last Week" pages 38–44

 All selections are available on *Literature Cassettes 1* and *2*.

INDEPENDENT/SELF-SELECTED READING

READER'S CHOICE LIBRARY

Zora Hurston and the Chinaberry Tree by William Miller

The Black Stallion by Walter Farley

TAKE-HOME BOOKS

Lonely No More

Fire from Ice

Kwan's Big Performance

Dear Grandma

Taking Chances

See also Independent and Self-Selected Reading, page T11, and the Leveled Library.

LISTENING SELECTIONS

READ ALOUD TO STUDENTS

LISTENING TO LITERATURE

"The Emperor and the Kite" by Jane Yolen,
  pages T6–T9

TECHNOLOGY CONNECTIONS

***Mission: Comprehension™
Skills Practice* CD-ROM**
Prefixes and Suffixes;
Vocabulary in Context

Videocassettes
A Talk with Johanna Hurwitz
©1997, Library Video
Company, 20 min.
*Marsalis on Music: Sousa to
Satchmo* ©1995, Library Video
Company, 55 min.

Student activities:
Building Background, Bonus
Words, Author Information,
Skills Activities, Test Tutor,
Computer Station Activity
Cards

Teacher resources:
Link Bank, Graphic Organizers,
Multi-Level Resources

Visit *The Learning Site!*
www.harcourtschool.com

Reaching All Learners

Customizing Instruction

To help you keep all students working individually or in small groups while you provide direct instruction, try some of these flexible grouping strategies.

During...	Some students can...
Introducing Vocabulary	• Play a word game with a partner in the Vocabulary Station. • Use a thesaurus to find synonyms for a vocabulary word.
Preteaching the Skill	• Preview the selection and write a prediction about it. • Read the selection with a partner and work on one or more of the Response Activities.
Writing/Grammar/Spelling	• Read a Leveled Library book. • Work on pages in their *Spelling Practice Books*. • Complete a Building Literacy Skills activity.

Theme Project

THE INSIDE STORY   Talk with students about this section's theme, Look Inside. Have them brainstorm questions they might ask adults about experiences the adults had when growing up that helped them become who they are today.

Pairs of students can then choose appropriate questions to use in an interview with an adult family member, friend, or neighbor; an adult in your school; or possibly a community leader. Students may, with the permission of their subjects, record the interviews or else take notes during the interviews and later record their impressions. Have the class share and categorize the interviews and then create an oral history collection.

INQUIRY PROJECTS
Throughout this theme, you will see several opportunities for **Inquiry Projects.** Suggestions can be found on pages T57, T101, T141, T185, and T225.

> **MATERIALS**
> ■ paper
> ■ pencils
> ■ clipboard (optional)
> ■ cassette recorder and tape

Exploring Affixes

You can build on students' existing vocabulary to help them make discoveries about language structure and incorporate new words into their vocabulary.

Begin by listing affixes, such as *trans-*, *thermo-*, *-graph*, and *-oid*. Have students brainstorm and list words they know that contain each of the affixes. Through discussion, lead students to identify similarities in meaning that will help them determine the meaning of each affix.

Once students have established the correct meanings, you may want to suggest additional words and have students use a dictionary to find other words that contain the affixes. Encourage students to explore how some meanings may have changed over time.

Provide opportunities for students to practice using their expanding vocabulary through creative writing assignments, discussions, and worksheets. For example, you might ask students to use ten of their words in a science fiction story.

Creative Writing Motivators

How do you support your students in finding new and creative ideas for their writing? Comparing notes with your fellow teachers is one way to discover fresh ideas and techniques that may work for you. Start a file of ideas that you have found effective so you can share them with colleagues and provide your students with a variety of activities. Here are some that you might like to try:

■ **READ ALOUD** Choose award-winning contemporary literature or a classic that will capture your students' imagination. As you read aloud, guide your students to appreciate plot development and literary language. Students might then extend the story or write their own stories with similar plots.

■ **PHOTO FILE** Begin a file of interesting pictures from old magazines. Invite students to select a picture to write about. For example, the picture might illustrate the setting, the characters, or a story event.

■ **WORD PUZZLE** Use vocabulary words or words on a theme such as a current topic in science or social studies to create a word puzzle. Have students locate the words in the puzzle and then write a story that includes those words.

REACHING ALL LEARNERS **MULTI-AGE CLASSROOMS**

The grade-level themes in **Collections** are based on universal themes that align across all grades in the same order. This order facilitates theme-based learning in multi-age environments and combination classrooms. The universal theme for Look Inside is *Self-Discovery*.

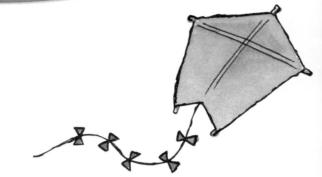

READ ALOUD TO STUDENTS

The Emperor and the Kite

by Jane Yolen

GENRE: FOLKTALE

Selection Summary: The emperor's youngest daughter is so tiny that no one pays much attention to her. When the emperor is seized by plotters and held prisoner in a tower, the tiny princess uses her kite to send him food and eventually to help him escape. From that time on, the emperor keeps her by his side and never again neglects any person, great or small.

AUTHOR PROFILE

Jane Yolen has written more than 150 books, many for children but some for adults and young adults as well. She has taught children's literature at Smith College and served on the board of directors of the Society of Children's Book Writers and Illustrators. She says that she began as a journalist and poet and started writing children's books "by accident."

Once in ancient China there lived a princess who was the fourth daughter of the emperor. She was very tiny. In fact she was so tiny her name was Djeow Seow (GEE•OW SHEE•OW), which means "the smallest one." And, because she was so tiny, she was not thought very much of—when she was thought of at all.

Her brothers, who were all older and bigger and stronger than she, were thought of all the time. And they were like four rising suns in the eyes of their father. They helped the emperor rule the kingdom and teach the people ways of peace. Even her three sisters were all older and bigger and stronger than she. They were like three midnight moons in the eyes of their father. They were the ones who brought food to his table. But Djeow Seow was like a tiny star in the emperor's sight. She was not even allowed to bring a grain of rice to the meal, so little was she thought of. In fact she was so insignificant, the emperor often forgot he had a fourth daughter at all.

1. How do you feel about Djeow Seow? Do you think the author intends for you to feel this way? Explain.

And so, Djeow Seow ate by herself. And she talked to herself. And she played by herself, which was the loneliest thing of all. Her favorite toy was a kite of paper and sticks.

Every morning, when the wind came from the east past the rising sun, she flew her kite. And every evening, when the wind went to the west past the setting sun, she flew her kite. Her toy was like a flower in the sky. And it was like a prayer in the wind.

In fact a monk who passed the palace daily made up a poem about her kite.

> *My kite sails upward,*
> *Mounting to the high heavens.*
> *My soul goes on wings.*

But then he was a monk, and given to such thoughts. As for Princess Djeow Seow, she thanked him each day for his prayer. Then she went back to flying her toy.

But all was not peaceful in the kingdom, just as the wind is not always peaceful. For the wind can trouble the waters of a still pond. And there were evil men plotting against the emperor.

They crept up on him one day when he was alone, when his four sons were away ruling in the furthermost parts of the kingdom and his three daughters were down in the garden. And only Princess Djeow Seow, so tiny she seemed part of the corner where she sat, saw what happened.

2. Why does the author say that the emperor was alone when the evil men crept up on him?

The evil men took the emperor to a tower in the middle of a wide, treeless plain. The tower had only a single window, with an iron bar across the center. The plotters sealed the door with bricks and mortar once the emperor was inside.

Then they rode back to the palace and declared that the emperor was dead. When his sons and daughters heard this, they all fled to a neighboring kingdom where they spent their time sobbing and sighing. But they did nothing else all day long.

All except Djeow Seow. She was so tiny, the evil men did not notice her at all. And so, she crept to the edge of the wide, treeless plain. And there she built a hut of twigs and branches.

Every day at dawn and again at dark, she would walk across the plain to the tower. And there she would sail her stick-and-paper kite. To the kite string she tied a tiny basket filled with rice and poppyseed cakes, water chestnuts and green tea. The kite pulled the basket high, high in the air, up as high as the window in the tower. And, in this way, she kept her father alive.

So they lived for many days: the emperor in his tower and the princess in a hut near the edge of the plain. The evil men ruled with their cruel, harsh ways, and the people of the country were very sad.

One day as the princess prepared a basket of food for her father, the old monk passed by her hut. She smiled at him, but he seemed not to see her. Yet as he passed, he repeated his prayer in a loud voice. He said:

> *My kite sails upward,*
> *Mounting to the high heavens.*
> *My emperor goes on wings.*

The princess started to thank him. But then she stopped. Something was different. The words were not quite right. "Stop," she called to the monk. But he had already passed by. He was a monk, after all, and did not take part in things of this world.

And then Djeow Seow understood. The monk was telling her something important. And she understood.

3. What do you think the monk was telling Djeow Seow? What do you think she will do?

Each day after that, when she was not bringing food to her father, Djeow Seow was busy. She twined a string of grass and vines, and wove in strands of her own long black hair. When her rope was as thick as her waist and as high as the tower, she was ready. She attached the rope to the string of the stick-and-paper kite, and made her way across the treeless plain. When she reached the tower, she called to her father. But her voice was as tiny as she, and her words were lost in the wind.

ACCESS PRIOR KNOWLEDGE
Use these suggestions to help students make connections between the selection and what they know:

- Explain that the story students are going to hear is a folktale. Have students tell what a folktale is and then name other folktales they know.
- Tell students that this folktale is from China. You may want to have students locate China on a map or globe and tell what they know about that country.

SET A PURPOSE FOR LISTENING
Have students use what they know about folktales to set a purpose for listening. (to be entertained; possibly to interpret the lesson that the tale teaches) Remind students that this story is a folktale. Point out that some folktales are universal—they deal with themes and situations that could take place anywhere. As students listen, ask them to think of changes that would be needed to set this tale in Europe, Asia, or North America. Have them also decide on their main purpose for listening.

STRATEGY REMINDER

Concentrate on the Speaker
Discuss with students why they should pay close attention to your tone of voice as you read. Guide them to understand that your tone will help convey the feelings of characters in the story. Have students state what feelings the tone has conveyed.

LISTENING STRATEGIES
- **Concentrate on the Speaker**
- Separate Fact from Opinion
- Keep an Open Mind
- Self-Question
- Create Mental Images

Listen Responsively   You can use the questions in the margins to assess students' understanding and appreciation. You can also look for nonverbal cues such as facial expressions that indicate surprise, pleasure, or other emotions at appropriate points in the story.

Develop Vocabulary Through Listening   As you read, have students listen for words that appeal to the senses, including colorful adjectives and vivid verbs. Have students discuss how these words helped to create mental images.

Tip for Reading Aloud   Before reading, tell students to listen for the author's use of figurative language. Read comparisons and descriptive language expressively and with emphasis to help students recognize and appreciate them.

At last, though, the emperor looked out and saw his daughter flying her kite. He expected the tiny basket of food to sail up to his window as it had done each day. But what should he see but the strand of vines and grass and long black hair. The wind was raging above, holding the kite in its steely grip.

And the princess was below, holding tight to the end of the rope.

4. What do you predict will happen next? What story clues help you make your prediction?

Although the emperor had never really understood the worth of his tiniest daughter before, he did now. And he promised himself that if her plan worked she would never again want for anything, though all she had ever wanted was love. Then he leaned farther out the tower window and grasped the heavy strand. He brought it into his tower room and loosened the string of the kite. He set the kite free, saying, "Go to thy home in the sky, great kite." And the kite flew off toward the heavens.

Then the emperor tied one end of the thick strand to the heavy iron bar across the window, and the other end stretched all the way down to Djeow Seow's tiny hands.

The emperor stepped to the window sill, slipped under the iron bar, saluted the gods, and slid down the rope. His robes billowed out around him like the wings of a bright kite. When his feet reached the ground, he knelt before his tiny daughter. And he touched the ground before her with his lips. Then he rose and embraced her, and she almost disappeared in his arms.

With his arm circling her, the emperor said, "Come to thy home with me, loyal child." He lifted the tiny princess to his shoulders and carried her all the way back to the palace.

At the palace, the emperor was greeted by wild and cheering crowds. The people were tired of the evil men, but they had been afraid to act. With the emperor once again to guide them, they threw the plotters into prison.

And when the other sons and daughters of the emperor heard of his return, they left off their sobbing and sighing, and they hurried home to welcome their father. But when they arrived, they were surprised to find Djeow Seow on a tiny throne by their father's side.

5. Why did the emperor want Djeow Seow to rule with him?

To the end of his day, the emperor ruled with Princess Djeow Seow close by. She never wanted for anything, especially love. And the emperor never again neglected a person—whether great or small. And, too, it is said that Djeow Seow ruled after him, as gentle as the wind and, in her loyalty, as unyielding.

Responding to the Literature

WRITE A HAIKU

Reread for students the original version of the monk's poem on page T6. Explain that the poem is a haiku, a form of poetry that originated in Japan. A haiku consists of three lines of five, seven, and five syllables. It presents a clear picture, often of an object or animal. Have students observe their own environment, perhaps outside the classroom window, and write their own haikus.

DESIGN A KITE

Tell students that kites come in a great variety of shapes, sizes, colors, and designs. Ask students to design a special new kite for Djeow Seow to replace the one her father set free during his rescue from the tower.

EXTEND VOCABULARY

Have students use colorful adjectives and vivid verbs from the story to write a poem about a kite flying in the wind. Encourage them to use comparisons like those the author uses in the story.

DISCUSS THE SELECTION

1 **What lesson does this folktale teach?** (Possible responses: Small people can do important things. Never neglect a person, whether great or small.) CRITICAL: RETURN TO PURPOSE/INTERPRET THEME

2 **Why do you think this tale has been passed down and retold over many years?** (Possible response: It is a simple story that people enjoy hearing, with a message that listeners can relate to.) METACOGNITIVE: EXPRESS PERSONAL OPINIONS/MAKE JUDGMENTS

RETELL/SUMMARIZE

Have students record story events in a cause-effect chart. For example, Djeow Seow's small size causes the plotters to overlook her. Tell students they can ask you to reread a part of the story if they are unsure about the relationships of events. Have them use the cause-effect chart to summarize the story.

18   19

Preview the Theme

DISCUSS THE THEME CONTENTS   Have students examine the table of contents for this theme, Look Inside. Ask students to name the genres of the selections listed there, as well as any titles or authors that are familiar to them. Then ask students to predict what the selections might have in common.

QUICKWRITE

Ask students to list in their journals or Reading Notebooks several reasons why it is important for young people to think about who they are, what they can do, and what makes them special. They can add to their ideas as they progress through the theme.

BEGIN AN ONGOING GRAPHIC ORGANIZER   Have students begin creating a graphic organizer that will help them record discoveries that characters in this theme make about themselves. You may want to keep the organizer on a computer, a chart, or a bulletin board. Students can return to it periodically during the theme to add information.

Who Looked Inside	What the Character or Characters Learned

Reader's Choice

The Black Stallion
by Walter Farley
REALISTIC FICTION
Alec learns about survival and friendship on a desert island with a majestic, wild creature—a black stallion.
Award-Winning Author
READER'S CHOICE LIBRARY

Zora Hurston and the Chinaberry Tree
by William Miller
BIOGRAPHY
Inspired by her mother, a young and curious Zora discovers that her dreams have no limits.
Notable Social Studies Trade Book
READER'S CHOICE LIBRARY

The Hot and Cold Summer
by Johanna Hurwitz
REALISTIC FICTION
Best friends Rory and Derek are planning their best summer ever. Will their plans and friendship survive when a girl comes to visit for the summer?
Texas Bluebonnet Award; Parents' Choice

Kids Explore the Gifts of Children with Special Needs
by Westridge Young Writer's Workshop
BIOGRAPHY
Written by kids, this book features 10 individuals with disabilities who beat the odds. Learn from people whose experiences may be different from our own.

Yang the Youngest and His Terrible Ear
by Lensey Namioka
REALISTIC FICTION
Yingtao and his friend come up with a plan to save the Yang's musical reputation.
Award-Winning Author

20   21

Independent and Self-Selected Reading

Zora Hurston and the Chinaberry Tree by William Miller EASY
The Hot and Cold Summer by Johanna Hurwitz EASY

Yang the Youngest and His Terrible Ear by Lensey Namioka AVERAGE

The Black Stallion by Walter Farley CHALLENGING
Kids Explore the Gifts of Children with Special Needs by Westridge Young Writers Workshop CHALLENGING

PREVIEW READER'S CHOICE BOOKS Ask a student to read aloud the book titles. Have volunteers predict what some of the books may be about. INFERENTIAL: MAKE PREDICTIONS

CHOOSE TRADE BOOKS Students may use the following questions to help them choose books to read:

- Have I enjoyed reading other books of this type?
- Do the title and cover make the book seem interesting?
- Can I learn something new by reading this book?

MONITOR COMPREHENSION Distribute Thinking About My Reading, page A25, and have students complete it to monitor their own comprehension.

TRADE BOOK LESSON PLANS See the Reader's Choice Library lesson plans on pages T228–T231. For more detailed lessons, see the *Leveled Library Teacher's Guide*.

"The Hot and Cold

THEME
Look Inside

GENRE
Realistic Fiction
- The **setting** could be a real place.
- The **characters** and **events** are like people and events in real life.

CROSS-CURRICULAR CONNECTIONS

- **SOCIAL STUDIES:** Emergency Services
- **SCIENCE:** Parrot Facts

FOCUS STRATEGY USE PRIOR KNOWLEDGE

- **Before Reading:** Strategy Reminder on page T21
- **During Reading:** Apply the Strategy on pages T24, T36
- **After Reading:** Return to the Strategy on page T45

FOCUS SKILL PREFIXES AND SUFFIXES

- **Before Reading:** Introduce the Skill on pages T20–T21
- **During Reading:** Apply the Skill on pages T26, T28, and T38
- **After Reading:** Practice the Skill on pages T46–T47 (*Student Edition*, pages 44–45)

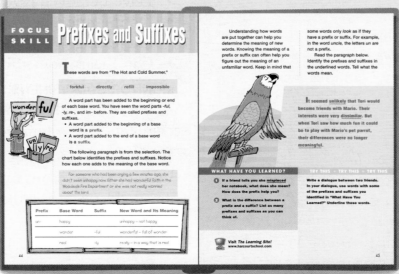

▲ **Student Edition, pages 44–45**

As students read "The Hot and Cold Summer," they will see that it is important to keep an open mind when meeting someone new.

Selection Summary

When a girl named Bolivia comes to visit their neighbors for the summer, Rory and Derek are determined not to let her spoil their plans. In fact, they decide not to speak to her at all. Then Bolivia's pet parrot escapes, and the whole neighborhood becomes involved in trying to capture it. Along the way, the boys begin to discover that Bolivia may be a more interesting person than they thought she would be.

Author Profile

Johanna Hurwitz has been making up stories since she was a little girl. She told her first stories to her little brother and later made up stories for her children. Before she began writing them down, however, she worked as a children's librarian in schools and in public libraries, including the New York Public Library in New York City. Among the many awards that Johanna Hurwitz has won are the Texas Bluebonnet Award and other state awards for books chosen by children.

REACHING ALL LEARNERS

BELOW-LEVEL READERS

EASY READER
"A Fish Tale," pp. 6–13. Reinforces selection vocabulary and these additional words from "The Hot and Cold Summer":
suspicion investigate hovered
See *Timeless Tales Intervention Reader Teacher's Guide*, pages 2–7.

CASSETTE
"The Hot and Cold Summer" is available on *Literature Cassette 1*.

CHALLENGE

LEVELED LIBRARY
Beetles, Lightly Toasted by Phyllis Reynolds Naylor.
CHALLENGING

INQUIRY PROJECTS
See page T57. Have students pose questions about topics such as parrots or types of trees. They can then do research to answer their questions.

THE HOT AND COLD SUMMER

Skills and Strategies

Reading

Listening

Speaking

Viewing

Vocabulary

authority
souvenir
incredible
vow
commotion
exhausted

DAY 1

BUILDING BACKGROUND AND CONCEPTS T18

INTRODUCING VOCABULARY T19
Transparency 1
Practice Book p. 1

PRETEACHING SKILLS
Before Reading
✔ **FOCUS SKILL** Prefixes and Suffixes (Introduce) T20–T21
Transparency 2
FOCUS STRATEGY Use Prior Knowledge T21

PREREADING STRATEGIES T22

READING THE SELECTION T22–T41
 Literature Cassette 1
Author Information T41

ALTERNATIVE SELECTION
Easy Reader: "A Fish Tale"

NOTE: Students may begin reading the selection on Day 2.

DAY 2

LITERARY RESPONSE T40
Return to the Predictions/Purpose
Appreciating the Literature

THINK ABOUT IT T40

RETELL AND SUMMARIZE T41
Practice Book p. 2

DECODING/PHONICS
Vowel Diphthongs: /ou/ou, ow (Maintain) T25

REREADING FOR FLUENCY
Readers Theatre T44

LITERATURE RESPONSE
Extend the Story T44

INTERVENTION STRATEGIES FOR BELOW-LEVEL READERS T45
FOCUS STRATEGY Return to the Strategy

Language Exploration

	DAY 1	DAY 2
Writing	**Expressive Writing:** Personal Narrative Connect Writing to Reading T50	Teach/Model T50 Analyze the Model *Transparency 3* *Language Handbook p. 54*
Grammar	**Declarative and Interrogative Sentences** Teach/Model T52 *Transparency 5* *Language Handbook pp. 94–95*	Extend the Concept T52 *Grammar Practice Book p. 7*
Daily Language Practice	1. **How was you're vacation.** (your; vacation?) 2. **we went swimming in our pool?** (We; pool.)	1. **was yesterday's picnic fun.** (Was; fun?) 2. **Everyone eight plenty of food** (ate; food.)
Spelling	**Words with Short Vowels** master ahead build front meant bread ready busy quit mother above does Pretest/Self-Check T54 *Transparency 6*	Teach/Model T54 *Practice Book p. 6* Handwriting Tip

---

KEY

✔ Tested Skills

■ **Management Option:** See Managing the Classroom, page T16, for ongoing independent activities.

 Reaching All Learners: Support for "A Fish Tale," an alternative selection, appears on *Timeless Tales Intervention Reader Teacher's Guide* pp. 2–7.

READING AND RESPONDING

DAY 3

EXTENDING SKILLS & STRATEGIES

DAY 4

EXTENDING SKILLS & STRATEGIES

DAY 5

RESPONSE ACTIVITIES
Create a Flyer T42
Make a Speech T42
■ Recording Station
Write Etiquette Rules T42
■ Publishing Station
Role-Play a Scene T42

Selection Comprehension Test

ORAL LANGUAGE
Phone Conversation T44

VIEWING
Perspective in Art T44
Activity Card 1, R10

INDEPENDENT READING
Reader's Choice Library:
Frindle T17

Reader's Choice Library Book ▶

DECODING/PHONICS
After Reading
✔ **FOCUS SKILL** Prefixes and Suffixes (Introduce)
T46–T47
Practice Book pp. 3–4
🖳 *Mission: Comprehension™ Skills Practice CD-ROM*

VOCABULARY T48–T49
Reviewing Vocabulary Words
Extending Vocabulary

TAKE-HOME BOOK
Lonely No More T48

CROSS-CURRICULAR CONNECTIONS
Social Studies: Emergency Services T56

Take-Home Book ▶

STUDY AND RESEARCH SKILLS
Book Parts (Maintain) T29

CROSS-CURRICULAR CONNECTIONS
Science: Parrot Facts T57
Activity Card 2, R10
FOCUS SKILL Apply Prefixes and Suffixes

INQUIRY PROJECTS T57
Research

SELF-SELECTED READING T17
• *Aldo Peanut Butter*
• *Lily's Crossing*
• Leveled Library Book: *Beetles, Lightly Toasted*

Leveled Library Book ▲

Writing Prompts T50
Prewrite and Draft T51
Transparency 4
🖳 *ClarisWorks for Kids®*

Revise T51

Assessment T51
Student Self- and Peer Assessment
Scoring Rubric

Oral Review/Practice T53
Grammar Practice Book p. 8

Apply to Writing T53
Practice Book p. 5

Cumulative Review T53
Grammar Practice Book p. 9

---

1. **Derek and Rory. Finally met Lucette**
   (Rory finally; Lucette.)
2. **did you think that Lucette was a baby.**
   (Did; baby?)

1. **Rory looked up and saw a bright green parrot abuve his head** (above; head.)
2. **Did he use a piece of bred to get the parrot's attention.** (bread; attention?)

1. **Edna's mothir helped catch Lucette**
   (mother; Lucette.)
2. **unfortunately, Lucette was not yet reddy to return home.** (Unfortunately; ready)

Spelling Strategies T55
Apply to Writing
Spelling Practice Book p. 10

Spelling Activities T55
Spelling Practice Book p. 11

Posttest T55

Managing the Classroom

While you provide direct instruction to individuals or small groups, other students can work on ongoing activities like the ones below.

Listening Station

OBJECTIVE

To listen to music mentioned in the selection

MATERIALS

- cassette or CD player
- tape or CD of *Carmen* by Georges Bizet
- tape or CD of John Denver's "Take Me Home, Country Roads"

Students may enjoy listening to and comparing recordings of the two pieces of music mentioned in the selection.

Publishing Station

OBJECTIVE

To compile and publish an etiquette book

MATERIALS

- paper
- blank books
- art materials

Students might like to compile their etiquette rules for the Mind Your Manners activity on page T42 into a book of etiquette for students their age. Have students illustrate the book, perhaps with humorous drawings.

Recording Station

OBJECTIVE

To rehearse a speech

MATERIALS

- audiocassettes
- cassette recorder

As students work on their speeches for the Live and Learn activity on page T42, encourage them to record themselves and listen to the tapes to determine how they can improve their speeches. Students might also ask a classmate to listen to the tape and offer advice.

Map and Stamp Station

OBJECTIVE

To learn about other countries

MATERIALS

- world map
- globe
- other maps
- foreign stamps glued onto index cards
- geography puzzles

Have students use the resources in the Map and Stamp Station to learn more about the countries that Bolivia lists on page 28 of "The Hot and Cold Summer."

Note: For more options, see pages T42–T43, T44–T45, and T56–T57.

GUIDED READING

Multi-Level Books

EASY

The Adventures of Ali Baba Bernstein
by Johanna Hurwitz. Avon, 1995.
REALISTIC FICTION: SELECTION AUTHOR

A Llama in the Family
by Johanna Hurwitz. Scholastic, 1996. REALISTIC FICTION: SELECTION AUTHOR

EASY READER: TIMELESS TALES
"A Fish Tale," pp. 6–13. REALISTIC FICTION: FRIENDSHIP

TAKE-HOME BOOK
Lonely No More
REALISTIC FICTION: NEW COMMUNITIES

AVERAGE

Aldo Peanut Butter
by Johanna Hurwitz. Puffin, 1992.
REALISTIC FICTION: SELECTION AUTHOR

My Brother Louis Measures Worms and Other Louis Stories
by Barbara Robinson. HarperCollins, 1990.
REALISTIC FICTION: FAMILY LIFE

The Cold and Hot Winter
by Johanna Hurwitz. William Morrow, 1988.
REALISTIC FICTION: SELECTION AUTHOR

READER'S CHOICE LIBRARY
Frindle
by Andrew Clements. REALISTIC FICTION: FRIENDSHIP

See the **Reader's Choice Library lesson plan** on pages T1170–T1171.

CHALLENGING

Dog Days
by Colby Rodowsky. Farrar, Straus & Giroux, 1990. REALISTIC FICTION: SUMMER/NEW FRIENDS

Lily's Crossing
by Patricia Reilly Giff. Delacorte, 1997.
HISTORICAL FICTION: NEW FRIENDS

Hobie Hansen, You're Weird
by Jamie Gilson. William Morrow, 1987.
REALISTIC FICTION: SUMMER/NEW FRIENDS

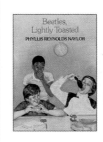

LEVELED LIBRARY BOOK
Beetles, Lightly Toasted
by Phyllis Reynolds Naylor.
REALISTIC FICTION: FAMILY LIFE

Building Background and Concepts

See *ESL Manual* pages 2–7. You may want to introduce these additional words and phrases:

rare (page 24)
edge away (page 24)
topmost (page 31)
fiddled with (page 36)

OTHER BACKGROUND-BUILDING IDEAS

 A Talk with Johanna Hurwitz (Good Conversation Series) © 1997, Library Video Company, 20 min.

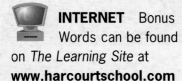 **INTERNET** Bonus Words can be found on *The Learning Site* at **www.harcourtschool.com**

Access Prior Knowledge

Discuss being a newcomer. Ask students how it feels to be a visitor in a strange place and how a newcomer hopes to be treated. (Possible responses: might feel shy, unsure, hopeful; hopes to be accepted and treated kindly)

Develop Concepts

Build a web using vocabulary words. Have students begin a web about introducing a visitor to others in a neighborhood. Ask questions to encourage them to add vocabulary words to the web: **How would you get your neighbors together? Would you create a big commotion?** Highlight indicates vocabulary.

find out if he or she is an authority on something

maybe have a picnic or other gathering

don't create a big commotion

introducing a visitor

ask about a hobby, interest, or special souvenir

make a vow to be friendly and helpful

don't let visitor get exhausted

Tell students that "The Hot and Cold Summer" is a story about two boys and how they act toward someone who is visiting their neighborhood.

BONUS WORDS

Introduce names for objects. If necessary, introduce the following names for useful objects found in "The Hot and Cold Summer": *ear plugs, attaché case, transistor radio.*

ear plugs

attaché case

transistor radio

Introducing Vocabulary

Build Word Identification Strategies

Decode familiar patterns.

Display Transparency 1, or copy it on the board, and have volunteers read the dialogue aloud. Remind students that they can often use familiar patterns to help them figure out an unfamiliar word. Model decoding the word *commotion*:

> **MODEL** When I look carefully at this word, I see that part of it looks like the familiar word *motion*. The first syllable is also familiar from words like *common* and *complete*. I can pronounce the parts of the word together to see if it sounds like a word I know.

As students decode the other vocabulary, encourage them to confirm the meanings by asking questions like **Does it look right? Does it sound right? Does it make sense?**

CHECK UNDERSTANDING

Practice other vocabulary strategies. Have students answer questions with sentences that show what the vocabulary words mean. MEANINGFUL SENTENCES

- **Which word means the opposite of *energetic*?** ANTONYM
- **How can someone become an authority on a subject?** EXPLANATION
- **Which word is a synonym for *promise* or *pledge*?** SYNONYM
- **Would you expect to read about incredible events in realistic fiction or in a tall tale?** PRIOR KNOWLEDGE
- **Which word comes originally from the Latin word *subvenire*, meaning "to come up; to come to mind"? How does this meaning relate to the meaning of the vocabulary word?** WORD ORIGIN
- **What might a commotion look and sound like?** DESCRIPTION

QUICKWRITE

READING NOTEBOOK Give students a few minutes to list names of people whom they consider to be experts and the subject on which each person is an *authority*. Students might list authors, experts they have seen on TV or in other media, or people they know.

VOCABULARY

"What's all the **commotion**?"
"Sarah's cat is up a tree."
"Cats climb trees all the time."
"Oh, I suppose you're an **authority** on cats."
"No, but I bet I can get it to come down."
"How?"
"Put a blanket on the ground. Then wait until the cat is **exhausted** and comes down to get some sleep."
"It's **incredible** how silly you can be. I should make a **vow** never to listen to you."
"Go right ahead. But when the cat comes down, don't ask me to give you the blanket for a **souvenir**!"

Teaching Transparency 1

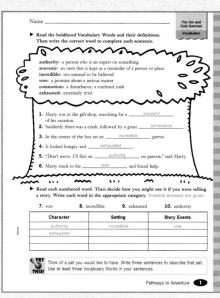

▲ **Practice Book, page 1**

The Hot and Cold Summer   **T19**

Prefixes and Suffixes

BEFORE READING

SKILL TRACE

INTRODUCE	
• Before Reading:	T20–T21
• During Reading:	T26, T28, T38
• After Reading:	T46–T47
Reteach	R2
Review 1	T81
Review 2	T163
Test	Theme 1
Maintain	T273

OBJECTIVE:

To use prefixes and suffixes for independent decoding of words

Preview the Literature

Preview the selection and discuss the genre.

Invite students to look at the illustrations and tell where the story takes place. (in a suburban neighborhood) Then have them read silently *Student Edition* pages 22 and 23.

Ask: **Does the introduction seem to tell about events that could really happen?** Explain that stories about events that could really happen are called *realistic fiction*.

Introduce the Skill

Discuss prefixes and suffixes.

Remind students that some words are formed by adding a prefix or a suffix to a base word. Display Transparency 2, or copy it on the board. Have volunteers read aloud the definition of a prefix, the example, and the two sentences that follow. Then have students tell the meanings of the prefix and of the new word. (Possible responses: "again"; "read again") Follow the same procedure with the information on a suffix. (Possible responses: "person who is or does"; "person who reads")

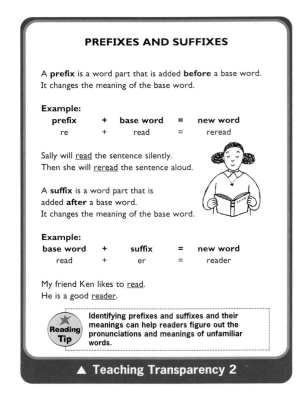

PREFIXES AND SUFFIXES

A **prefix** is a word part that is added **before** a base word. It changes the meaning of the base word.

Example:

prefix	+	base word	=	new word
re	+	read	=	reread

Sally will <u>read</u> the sentence silently.
Then she will <u>reread</u> the sentence aloud.

A **suffix** is a word part that is added **after** a base word. It changes the meaning of the base word.

Example:

base word	+	suffix	=	new word
read	+	er	=	reader

My friend Ken likes to <u>read</u>.
He is a good <u>reader</u>.

Reading Tip
Identifying prefixes and suffixes and their meanings can help readers figure out the pronunciations and meanings of unfamiliar words.

▲ Teaching Transparency 2

Model the Thinking

Model identifying prefixes and suffixes.

Read aloud and discuss with students the Reading Tip on Transparency 2. Then use the introduction on *Student Edition* page 23 to model for students how to identify a base word and suffix:

> MODEL **In the first sentence of the introduction, I read about a surprise visitor. I know that the suffix *-or* means "a person who is or does," so the word *visitor* means "a person who visits."**

DURING/AFTER READING

- Apply the Skill, pages T26, T28, T38
- Practice the Skill, pages T46–T47

PRETEACH THE STRATEGY

FOCUS STRATEGY ## Use Prior Knowledge ⭐

Encourage students to monitor their comprehension.

Tell students that they can use what they already know about a subject to help them understand what they read. Point out that in reading the introduction they discovered that this story is realistic fiction. Since it seems to be about young people and events that could really happen, they can use their own knowledge and experience to decide how characters might act or how a situation might turn out.

- Apply the Strategy, pages T24, T36
- Return to the Strategy, page T45

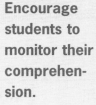 *See the Strategy Builder copying masters, pages A40–A45.*

STRATEGIES GOOD READERS USE

- **Use Prior Knowledge** FOCUS STRATEGY
- Make and Confirm Predictions
- Adjust Reading Rate
- Self-Question
- Create Mental Images
- Use Context to Confirm Meaning
- Use Text Structure and Format
- Use Graphic Aids
- Use Reference Sources
- Read Ahead
- Reread
- Summarize and Paraphrase

Prereading Strategies

PREVIEW AND PREDICT

If students have not yet previewed the selection, have them look at the illustrations and read the title and introduction on pages 22 and 23. Encourage them to make predictions about the story. Remind them that a realistic fiction story includes a setting, characters, a problem, and a solution that are believable. Then have students begin a prediction chart for "The Hot and Cold Summer." Explain that they can revise or confirm predictions and make new predictions about story events as they read. See *Practice Book* page 2.

Prediction Chart	
What I Predict Will Happen	**What Actually Happens**
Derek and Rory will decide to talk to Bolivia after all.	

SET PURPOSE

Read to Enjoy Have students set a purpose for reading "The Hot and Cold Summer." Remind them that one purpose for reading is to enjoy a story. If students have difficulty setting a purpose, offer this suggestion:

> MODEL **I learned from my preview that the two boys have decided not to speak to Bolivia. I will enjoy finding out whether something happens to make them change their minds.**

The Hot And Cold Summer
by Johanna Hurwitz
illustrated by Greg Couch

Texas Bluebonnet Award

22

Options for Reading

DIRECTED READING Use the **Monitor Comprehension** questions to check students' comprehension. Support students reading below or on level by using the **Guided Reading** strategies on pages T24, T26, T28, T30, T32, and T36. WHOLE CLASS/SMALL GROUP

COOPERATIVE READING Have students reading on or above level use *Comprehension Card 1* (p. R7) to focus on **characters** in the story. INDEPENDENT/SMALL GROUP

INDEPENDENT READING Have students reading on or above level read independently at their own pace. Encourage them to add to their prediction charts as they read. INDIVIDUAL/ WHOLE CLASS

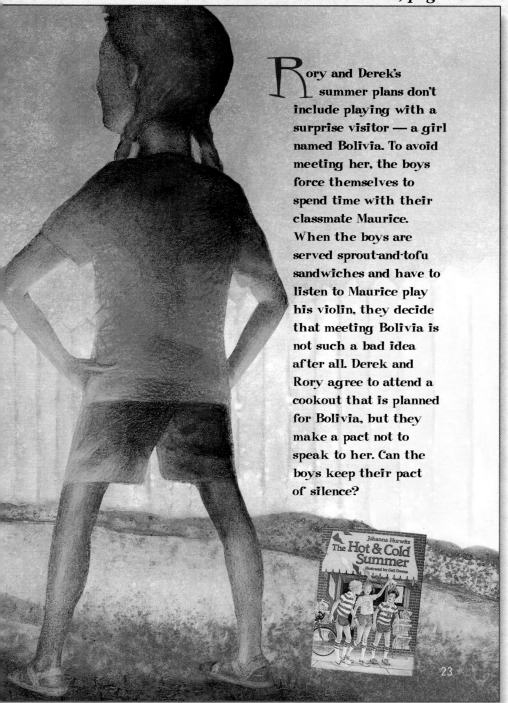

Rory and Derek's summer plans don't include playing with a surprise visitor — a girl named Bolivia. To avoid meeting her, the boys force themselves to spend time with their classmate Maurice. When the boys are served sprout-and-tofu sandwiches and have to listen to Maurice play his violin, they decide that meeting Bolivia is not such a bad idea after all. Derek and Rory agree to attend a cookout that is planned for Bolivia, but they make a pact not to speak to her. Can the boys keep their pact of silence?

23

SKILLS IN CONTEXT

Informal Assessment

INTERVENTION STRATEGIES

REACHING ALL LEARNERS

MODIFIED INSTRUCTION Have students read the title, "The Hot and Cold Summer," and the introduction. Ask what they see on the first two pages. Discuss these selection words:

emerge   intention   stunned

onlookers   suspicion

Tell students to read through page 29 to find out what happens at the cookout.

EASY READER Students may read "A Fish Tale," found on pages 6–13 in *Timeless Tales.* See *Timeless Tales Intervention Reader Teacher's Guide,* pages 2–7.

"The Hot and Cold Summer" is available on *Literature Cassette 1.*

Monitor Comprehension

❶ Why do Derek and Rory think they should get something in compensation for Bolivia? (Possible responses: because they don't want to meet her; because they think that having her around might interfere with their summer plans) INFERENTIAL: DRAW CONCLUSIONS

❷ Do you think the boys will go with Bolivia to see Lucette? Why or why not? (Possible response: no; because they don't want to be friends with Bolivia or do things with her) INFERENTIAL: MAKE PREDICTIONS

Guided Reading

STRATEGIES GOOD READERS USE

FOCUS STRATEGY **Use Prior Knowledge** Students may have difficulty telling why Derek and Rory think they deserve compensation. In a small group, discuss using prior knowledge:

MODEL **I know from the introduction that the boys don't expect to like Bolivia. I also know that sometimes if I do something I don't want to do, I will give myself some kind of reward, or compensation. The story says that the cake, hamburgers, and root beer are compensation for Bolivia.**

Derek and Rory grinned at one another. The cake, the hamburgers, and the bottle of root beer that was waiting on the table were the least that they should get in compensation for Bolivia. The boys waited, knowing the two girls would emerge from behind the Golding's hedge at any moment.

Sure enough, the hedge parted and first Mr. and then Mrs. Golding and then a redheaded girl walked into the Dunn's yard. "This is Bolivia!" said Mrs. Golding proudly. She said it in the same way she often introduced a new type of cookie or cake, as if Bolivia was something she had created in her kitchen. Rory took a quick look and then shifted his gaze. He didn't want to appear interested. He noticed, however, that he had been right about one thing. Bolivia was several inches taller than he was.

"Hi, Bolivia. Welcome to Woodside!" said Mr. Dunn. "I'm just putting on the hamburgers. How do you like yours?"

"I like mine well done," said Bolivia.

"Fine," said Mr. Dunn. "So do Rory and Derek." He turned to the boys, who were trying to edge away from the guest of honor. Derek's mother grabbed him. "Bolivia, this is Derek. He and Rory will be your friends this summer."

Neither boy said anything.

"How's Lucette settling in?" asked Mrs. Dunn. Rory realized for the first time that Bolivia's little sister hadn't come to the barbecue.

"She's fine. At first she was very quiet, but just before we left the house she said her first word to me. She knows ten words. It's so exciting," said Mrs. Golding.

Bolivia turned to Rory and Derek. "I couldn't bring Lucette to the barbecue because the smoke might be bad for her," she explained. "Do you want to come to my aunt's house and see her?"

These were the first words Bolivia spoke directly to the boys.

24

SOCIAL STUDIES

BOLIVIA Students may be interested to learn that Bolivia is the name of a country in South America. Some of the highest peaks in the Andes mountain range are found in Bolivia, as well as the highest large navigable lake in the world, Lake Titicaca. Students may also find it interesting that the country took its name in 1825 to honor Simón Bolívar, a great leader in the nation's war for independence. You may want to point out that Bolivia in "The Hot and Cold Summer" is a person named for a country that was in turn named for a person.

SKILLS IN CONTEXT · T25

DECODING/PHONICS

SKILL TRACE	
Introduce	Grade 2
Maintain	T25

Vowel Diphthongs: /ou/*ou, ow*

TEACH/MODEL

Have students locate the following words on page 24: *proudly, however,* and *house.* Write the words on the board, and have students pronounce them. Then ask a volunteer to underline the letters that stand for the vowel sound /ou/ in each word. *(ou, ow, ou)* Point out that knowing that the letters *ou* and *ow* may stand for this sound can help students figure out how to pronounce unfamiliar words.

PRACTICE/APPLY

Write the following words on the board and have students pronounce them: *trousers, coward, flounder, bounce, allowance, trowel, lounge, endowment.* As students continue reading the selection, encourage them to pause occasionally to look for and write down additional words in which the letters *ou* or *ow* stand for the /ou/ sound.

ou	ow
proudly	however
house	town
mouths	allowed
thousand	now
sprouts	towel
around	vow
sounded	down
about	crowded
ground	
cloud	
outside	

CHALLENGE

FIGURATIVE LANGUAGE Have students reread the first three sentences of the second paragraph on page 24. Discuss the comparison the author uses to describe the way Mrs. Golding says, "This is Bolivia!" Then encourage students to read the line aloud as they think Mrs. Golding might have said it.

REACHING ALL LEARNERS

Monitor Comprehension

❶ Why does Derek say "Gobble, gobble"? (Possible response: He is making a joke because Bolivia mentions turkey, and that is the sound turkeys make.) CRITICAL: INTERPRET CHARACTERS' MOTIVATIONS

❷ How did understanding prefixes and suffixes help you read the words *forkful*, *refill*, **and** *luckily*? (Possible response: suffix *-ful*, meaning "filled with," added to *fork*; prefix *re-*, meaning "again," added to *fill*; suffix *-ly* meaning "in a way that is," added to *lucky* after changing *y* to *i*)

FOCUS SKILL INFERENTIAL: PREFIXES AND SUFFIXES

Guided Reading

STRATEGIES GOOD READERS USE

Reread If students have difficulty understanding why Derek says "Gobble, gobble," use prompts such as these to remind them to use a rereading strategy:

- **Think about the meaning of the word** *gobble*.
- **Go back and reread the last few sentences before Derek says "Gobble, gobble."**
- **Look for a reference that might explain why he says that.**

Rory shook his head no. Derek also shook his head.

"Don't be shy," said Mr. Golding. "Go meet Lucette."

Rory shook his head again.

"You fellows are missing something really special," said Mrs. Dunn as she removed the plastic wrap from the salads.

Rory couldn't understand his mother. Why should he get excited over someone else's baby sister? He didn't care that Lucette had said her first word. Edna had known a lot of words by the time she was two. What was so special about Lucette?

Derek leaned toward Rory and whispered, "If we keep our mouths full of food, we can't talk."

Rory grinned. If his mother had told him once, she had told him a thousand times not to talk with food in his mouth.

"Right." He nodded.

The boys picked up paper plates. "Can we start eating?" asked Rory.

"If you're so hungry that you can't wait, go ahead," said Mrs. Dunn. Both boys piled their plates with potato salad and cole slaw.

Bolivia picked up a plate, too.

Edna pulled on Bolivia's skirt. "I made the cole slaw," she said.

"No kidding," said Bolivia.

"I made the potato salad, too," said Edna.

"The burgers are ready," called Mr. Dunn.

The three older children went to get their meat.

"You know," Bolivia said, turning to Rory and Derek, "last summer I was in Israel with my parents. They make hamburgers out of turkey there."

It was hard to imagine turkey hamburgers, although Rory thought they probably would be better than vegetable burgers with sprouts.

"Gobble, gobble," said Derek.

"What?" asked Bolivia.

26

SCIENCE

PLASTIC WRAP Point out that Mrs. Dunn had used plastic wrap to keep the salads fresh. Tell students that the first plastic products, developed in about 1860, were made mostly from vegetable matter (derived from cotton, oat hulls, seeds, or starches), or from coal. Today most plastics are petroleum-based. Many types of plastics are used for a wide variety of purposes in homes and industry. Encourage students to note different types and uses for plastics in their homes and at school.

"Gobble, gobble," he repeated.

Rory kicked Derek. His friend wasn't exactly speaking to Bolivia, but it was close.

Derek got the message. He stuffed his mouth with potato salad.

"Do you like my potato salad?" asked Edna.

"Rory, tell Bolivia about Woodside. This is her first visit here," Mr. Dunn called from his position at the grill.

Rory shoveled in a large forkful of potato salad and turned to his father, pointing to his mouth.

"There's a lot of things to do around here," said Mrs. Curry, since neither of the boys were speaking. "There's the town pool." She turned to Derek. "Which are the days when the public library is showing free movies for kids?" she asked.

Derek took an enormous bite out of his hamburger and shrugged his shoulders.

Rory licked some ketchup off his fingers and went back to refill his plate. Luckily he was very hungry after the lunch at Maurice's house.

"You like my cole slaw?" asked Edna.

"Where else have you traveled with your parents?" asked Mrs. Dunn.

27

REACHING ALL LEARNERS

ESL

BODY LANGUAGE To avoid speaking, Rory and Derek use body language to communicate. Have students act out the first three sentences on page 26, with either you or a student reading aloud the words that Mr. Golding speaks. Discuss the idea that shaking one's head is a way of saying *no* without using words. Then call attention to and discuss these examples of body language on page 27: when Rory kicks Derek, when Rory points to his mouth, and when Derek shrugs his shoulders. Have students express in English what the character is communicating.

Monitor Comprehension

❶ Is Rory right in thinking that Bolivia knows that he and Derek don't want her around? How do you know? (Possible responses: yes; because they don't speak to her and have refused her invitations; because she ends up playing with little Edna and then leaves without saying anything to them)
CRITICAL/METACOGNITIVE: INTERPRET STORY EVENTS

❷ How does knowing about suffixes help you understand the last sentence on page 29? (Possible response: The word *endlessly* has two suffixes: *-less*, meaning "without," and *-ly*, meaning "in a certain way or manner." The sentence means that the summer stretches before them as if it has no end.) **FOCUS SKILL** INFERENTIAL: PREFIXES AND SUFFIXES

Guided Reading

STRATEGIES GOOD READERS USE

Self-Question If students have difficulty deciding whether Bolivia is getting the boys' message, they may need to use a self-questioning strategy. Model it for them:

⬭MODEL **When I read about the way Rory and Derek are acting, I ask myself these questions: How would I feel in Bolivia's place? What would I think if people didn't speak to me and didn't want to come to my house when I invited them?**

Good, thought Rory. Let the grown-ups keep Bolivia busy talking. She sounded like a geography book, listing all the foreign countries where she'd been: Israel, Egypt, Mexico, France, Spain. . . .

After a little while, Bolivia turned to the boys again. "Would you like to come over tomorrow and play with Lucette?" she asked. "We could teach her some new words. I'll let you feed her if you like."

Girls really have no idea what boys like to do, Rory thought. What boy in his right mind would want to sit around playing nursery school with a little baby? He shook his head no.

"How about you?" asked Bolivia, turning to Derek.

"No," said Derek. Then realizing what he had done, he pushed another forkful of potato salad into his mouth.

Bolivia sat down on the ground next to Edna. She began playing "This little piggy went to market" on the little girl's bare toes. It was probably the eighty thousandth time that someone had played that baby game with Edna, but still she laughed and laughed.

Rory moved away, taking Derek with him.

"Boys, don't rush off," shouted Mrs. Curry. "We're going to cut the cake soon."

28

MUSIC

CARMEN Ask students what they think Derek means when he says, "I've heard enough of that *Carmen*." You may want to explain that *Carmen* is a famous opera by the French composer Georges Bizet. First performed in 1875, it has since become one of the most popular operas of all time. The story is set in Seville, Spain, and the opera is loved for its romantic atmosphere and exotic music.

Bolivia was not going to scare them off the cake, Rory decided. Especially since it had chocolate frosting. So the boys moved back to the center of activity. Mrs. Golding was busy discussing something with the two mothers. Mr. Golding, the neighborhood authority when it came to cars, was talking to Mr. Dunn and Mr. Curry about motors.

Rory saw Bolivia go through the hedge back to the Golding's house. Maybe she had to use the bathroom, he thought. But just maybe, she was getting the message that he and Derek didn't want her around.

With Bolivia gone, at least for a few minutes, the boys could stop eating and rest. It was hard work keeping your mouth stuffed with food.

"What should we do tomorrow?" asked Derek.

"Let's go to the pool," said Rory. "Mrs. Golding never signs up for a pool card and so Bolivia won't be allowed in."

"What if it rains?" asked Derek.

Rory looked up at the sky. It was still light and there wasn't a single cloud. "It won't rain," he said. "But if it does, we'll go over to Maurice's again."

"Okay," said Derek. "But if we go, I'm taking ear plugs with me. I've heard enough of that *Carmen*."

Rory stuck his hand into his pocket and pulled out a sprout from the sandwich he had disposed of earlier in the day. "A souvenir of the first afternoon hiding from Bolivia," he said, presenting it to Derek.

"This is just the beginning of July," said Derek. "Do you realize how many more days there are till she goes home?"

"As many days as there were sprouts in that sandwich," said Rory, sighing.

"It's going to be a long, long summer," agreed Derek.

At any other time, the thought of a long, long summer would have filled the boys with delight. But now it stretched endlessly before them.

29

INTERVENTION STRATEGIES

MODIFIED INSTRUCTION If students cannot summarize what happens at the cookout, model a summary for them:

MODEL **Derek and Rory watch Bolivia <u>emerge</u> from behind the neighbor's hedge. Their <u>intention</u> is to keep their mouths filled with food so they won't have to speak to Bolivia. She invites them to come to her aunt's house to meet Lucette, but they refuse. After Bolivia leaves, Derek and Rory make plans for the next day, which include avoiding Bolivia.**

Then help students set a purpose for reading through page 35. (to find out whether the boys succeed in avoiding Bolivia)

STUDY AND
RESEARCH SKILLS

SKILL TRACE	
Introduce	Grade 4
Maintain	T29

Book Parts

TEACH/MODEL

Ask a volunteer to reread the first paragraph on page 28. Point out that a geography book is a type of textbook that teaches about countries of the world. Model recalling parts of a textbook:

MODEL **I know that a textbook has a table of contents that tells how the book is organized and names the main parts. The table of contents is located at the front of the book.**

Prompt students to name and describe other important parts of a textbook. Record responses on the board.

Parts of a Textbook

Book Part	Description	Location
Table of contents	names main parts of book	in front of book
Glossary	small dictionary of words used in the text	in back of book
Pictures	photographs to help reader visualize content	wherever needed
Captions	tell reader how pictures are related to text	under, above, or beside pictures
Typographic cues (headings, etc.)	ways to make important information stand out	throughout text

PRACTICE/APPLY

Have students locate and identify book parts in their social studies textbook or another textbook.

Monitor Comprehension

1 **Why does Rory suggest calling the ambulance or the police?**
(Possible responses: He still thinks Lucette is a baby; he is worried about Lucette; he thinks about what he would do if his sister Edna fell out of a window.) CRITICAL: INTERPRET STORY EVENTS

2 **At what point did you begin to suspect that Lucette is not Bolivia's baby sister?** (Responses will vary but might include that students began to suspect when Bolivia says she saw Lucette go out the window, when Mr. Golding says he sees Lucette in the mimosa tree, or when Bolivia talks about Lucette walking on her arm and flying around the room.) INFERENTIAL: DRAW CONCLUSIONS

Guided Reading
STRATEGIES GOOD READERS USE
Use Context to Confirm Meaning
Students may not recognize the word *ambulance* when they read it. Ask the following questions to help them use context to confirm the meaning:

• **What does Rory think has happened?**
• **Who would you call if someone was injured?**
• **How can you use this context to help you figure out the meaning of *ambulance*?**

The morning after the barbecue, Derek and Rory met outside at nine-thirty. The boys wore their trunks under their clothes and each had a towel and a sandwich. Mrs. Dunn called after them, "Ask Bolivia to go with you," but Rory pretended not to hear. He had no intention of knocking on the Goldings' door. Anyway, Bolivia wouldn't have a membership card to the pool yet. And Rory didn't know if she had a bike. He didn't want to go anywhere with that girl and especially not if he had to go on foot. He looked around and was relieved that she was not in sight. He glanced up at the window of Bolivia's room and for a second, he thought he saw one of the curtains move. But then all was still again. It was probably just a little breeze.

"Let's get going," he said to Derek, who had been checking the air in his tires. "We want to make our getaway while the coast is clear."

Suddenly the boys heard a shriek.

"Help, help! Lucette has escaped!"

Derek and Rory looked at each other. What was the big fuss? Had Bolivia's little sister climbed out of her playpen or something?

Bolivia stuck her head out of the upstairs window. "Have you seen Lucette?" she called.

The boys shook their heads. How could little Lucette manage the heavy door? "She's got to be inside the house," said Derek.

"No. I saw her go out the window," Bolivia shouted.

Rory dropped his bike in surprise. How could the baby get out the window?

"Go around the back," demanded Bolivia. "I'll come and look with you. She must be in one of the trees."

Derek and Rory stood stunned. Had Bolivia lost her senses? If the baby had fallen out the window, she would be lying on the ground. It was impossible that she would land in a tree.

Mrs. Golding came running out of the house. "Should we

30

SCIENCE

MIMOSAS Have students recall the kind of tree that Lucette perched in. (a mimosa tree) Explain that the mimosa includes about 400 species of trees, shrubs, and herbs. Tell students that the leaves of many types of mimosas are so sensitive that they droop when touched even slightly. In fact, one type of mimosa plant is a shrub called the touch-me-not.

call the fire department?" she asked her niece.

"Call an ambulance or the police," said Rory. His heart was beating loud. He knew how he would have felt if Edna had fallen out the window.

Mr. Golding had gone out the back door. "I see her. I see her," he called from the backyard. "She's in the Dunns' mimosa tree."

Rory ran to the back of his house followed by Derek, Bolivia, and Mrs. Golding. He couldn't see any baby in the tree. "Where is she?" he shouted to Mr. Golding. He wondered if she had fallen out the window and then climbed the tree. It seemed incredible. He and Derek had been trying to climb that tree for years.

"It's all my fault." Bolivia was crying. "I opened the door so she could walk on my arm, and the next thing I knew she was flying around and around the room."

"She must be scared in a new place," said Mrs. Golding, putting her arm around her niece. "Don't cry. We'll all help catch her."

"I'll get a ladder," said Mr. Golding.

Rory watched as the old man leaned his ladder against the side of the tree.

"Hey, look at that!" shouted Derek.

Rory looked where his friend was pointing. On the very topmost branch of the mimosa tree was a large green bird with a blue-and-red head.

"It's a parrot!" he shouted. He had never seen one before except in the encyclopedia, but there was no mistaking that size or color.

"Of course it's a parrot," Bolivia shouted at him. "What did you think Lucette was? An elephant?

31

CHALLENGE

REACHING ALL LEARNERS

LOOKING BACK Have students recall what Rory sees when he glances up at Bolivia's window as he and Derek are about to leave for the pool. (a curtain moving) Discuss students' ideas about why the author included that detail. You may want to introduce the term *foreshadowing* and explain that authors sometimes give hints about events that happen later in the story.

Monitor Comprehension

❶ What else besides their vow of silence keeps Rory and Derek from admitting they thought Lucette was a baby? (Possible responses: embarrassment; feel silly and don't want to admit their error)
INFERENTIAL: DETERMINE CHARACTERS' EMOTIONS

❷ Why is Mr. Golding red in the face? (Possible responses: He keeps moving the ladder to follow Lucette; the effort makes him warm and causes his face to get red.) LITERAL/ INFERENTIAL: CAUSE-EFFECT

Guided Reading

STRATEGIES GOOD READERS USE
Use Context to Confirm Meaning
Students who have difficulty explaining why Mr. Golding is red in the face may not be using context to confirm the meaning of *exertion*. Guide them by using prompts such as the following:

- **Reread from the beginning of the paragraph to recall what Mr. Golding is doing that might cause his face to look red.**
- **Pay attention to the words that follow the word *exertion* in the sentence.**
- **How does the context help you confirm the meaning of *exertion*?**

It wasn't only their vow of silence that kept Rory and Derek from admitting they had thought Lucette was a baby.

While they were shouting, the bird flew from the mimosa tree to the maple.

No sooner had the ladder been put in place there than the bird flew over the hedge and into the next yard, landing in a locust tree. Mr. Golding looked red in the face from the exertion of moving the ladder back and forth.

"Let me help," called Mr. Dunn, coming from the house. Twice a week, even during the summer, he took classes in school administration so that he might someday become a principal. Now he forgot his courses as he dropped his attaché case with his papers and books and ran toward Mr. Golding.

32

SOCIAL STUDIES

BECOMING A PRINCIPAL Call attention to the last paragraph on page 32. Ask students what Mr. Dunn is doing in order to become a school principal. (taking classes in school administration twice a week, even during the summer) Ask whether students have ever thought about how someone becomes a school principal. You may want to designate a student or students to interview your own school principal on that subject and report back to the class.

33

ESL

REACHING ALL LEARNERS

USE PICTURES   You may want to have students point out and say the names of these items shown in the illustration on pages 32–33: parrot, ladder, bike or bicycle.

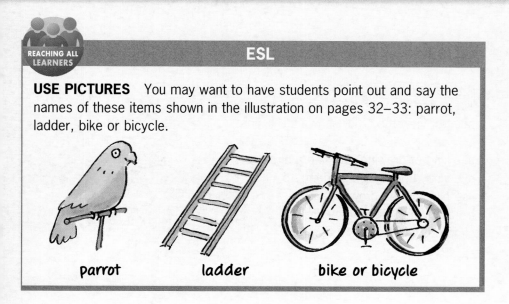

parrot   ladder   bike or bicycle

Monitor Comprehension

1 **How would you describe Rory's and Derek's emotions during the events described on page 35? How does the author show you these emotions?** (Possible response: The boys are excited and eager to help. Derek calls to Lucette and asks Bolivia what Lucette likes to eat. Both boys forget about the swimming pool, chase around the hedges, and rush home to get fruit.) INFERENTIAL: DETERMINE CHARACTERS' EMOTIONS

2 **What does Mrs. Dunn mean when she says, "This isn't working"?** (Possible response: Using fruit to get Lucette to come down isn't working because Lucette is still flying around.) INFERENTIAL: REFERENTS

ILLUSTRATOR'S CRAFT

BIRD'S-EYE VIEW Ask students to describe the illustration on page 34 and to tell from whose point of view the artist shows the scene. (from Lucette's point of view) Talk about why this kind of drawing is called a bird's-eye view. Encourage students to use clues in the drawing and from the story to identify the characters in the illustration.

"Hello there. Hello there," shrieked Lucette as she flew from tree to tree.

"Hello there, yourself!" Derek called back. He looked at Rory. Rory hadn't told him not to speak to a bird.

Mrs. Dunn came outside, followed by Edna. The little girl began jumping up and down. "I see her!" she shouted. "Catch her! Catch her!"

"Hello there!" Lucette called down to them.

"I'm going to call the fire department," Mr. Golding said. "They have taller ladders, and we have an awful lot of trees around here for Lucette to investigate."

"Hello there!" Edna called up to the bird.

Mrs. Dunn put her arms around Bolivia. "Don't worry. We won't let her get away." She comforted the girl as Lucette flew into the branches of one tree and then another. The swimming pool was forgotten as Rory and Derek chased in and out of the hedges, keeping their eyes on the bird.

"Could we get her down with some food?" asked Derek when he stopped to catch his breath. "What does she like to eat?"

"Fruit," said Bolivia.

Everyone rushed home except the two men with the ladder. Rory brought back some grapes. Derek had an apple. "Hello there!" shouted Edna, waving a banana for Lucette.

They made a pile of all the fruit in the Golding yard. Lucette hovered in the air above it for a moment, but she didn't land.

"What else does she like?" asked Mrs. Dunn. "This isn't working."

Mr. Dunn climbed down the ladder as the bird flew off once again. "None of my courses in running a school have prepared me for a morning like this," he said, wiping the sweat off his forehead.

In the distance they could hear approaching sirens. The fire department was on its way.

35

INTERVENTION STRATEGIES

MODIFIED INSTRUCTION   Guide students in summarizing the story so far.

- Derek and Rory ignore Bolivia at the cookout.
- The next morning, they see Bolivia at her window.
- She shouts that Lucette has escaped.
- Derek and Rory are <u>stunned</u> to find out that Lucette is a talking parrot.
- Everyone tries to help catch Lucette as she flies from tree to tree.

Help students set a purpose for reading to the end of the selection on page 40. (to find out whether Lucette is captured and whether Derek and Rory speak to Bolivia)

Monitor Comprehension

❶ Why do you think Bolivia is smiling? (Possible responses: because she is enjoying all the excitement; because she is not really worried about Lucette; because Lucette is having a good time) INFERENTIAL: INTERPRET CHARACTERS' EMOTIONS

❷ Do you think Lucette will be caught? Why or why not? (Possible responses: yes; because she seems quite tame and has not flown away; because she swoops lower when she hears the radio; because the author describes the events in a light and humorous tone that seems to suggest a happy ending) INFERENTIAL: MAKE PREDICTIONS

Guided Reading

STRATEGIES GOOD READERS USE

FOCUS STRATEGY **Use Prior Knowledge** If students do not make the connection between the light tone of the story and the likelihood of a happy outcome, model using prior knowledge:

MODEL **The author writes this scene with humor. The characters are having a good time. I know from my reading experiences that cheerful and amusing stories usually end happily. I think this story will have a happy ending and that Lucette will be returned safely to Bolivia.**

Dogleg Lane was filled with onlookers. People driving by got out of their cars to see what was happening. Neighbors came out of doors. Three large fire trucks pulled up in front of the Golding house. The firemen, wearing their helmets and tall boots, leaped off the trucks dragging ladders and long hoses with them.

"My vegetables could use a little water," said Mr. Dunn from where he was stationed.

"There's no fire," shouted Mrs. Golding. "It's a bird in the tree."

"Birds belong in trees," said one of the firemen, not yet understanding that Lucette was a pet bird who belonged in a cage.

"Hello there. Hello there!" Lucette greeted the new arrivals. She seemed to be having a great time.

Rory looked over at Bolivia. She was smiling. She looked like she was having a great time, too. For someone who had been crying a few minutes ago, she didn't seem unhappy now. Either she had wonderful faith in the Woodside Fire Department or she was not really worried about the bird.

"Music!" Bolivia remembered suddenly. "Lucette loves country music."

Derek ran into his house and came out with the little transistor radio he had gotten on his last birthday. He fiddled with the dials, looking for a station that played country music.

"That's good," shouted Bolivia. "Leave it there."

Derek stood holding his radio at full volume and looking up at Lucette.

"Hello there," shouted the bird, swooping lower.

Strains of "Country Roads" came over the radio. The neighbors that had crowded around began to sing and clap their hands in time to the music.

36

MUSIC

JOHN DENVER Ask whether students are familiar with the song "Country Roads" by John Denver, also known by the title "Take Me Home, Country Roads." Tell students that when John Denver toured mainland China in 1992, he was surprised to learn that "Country Roads" was the most famous Western song in China. He once said, "Music does bring people together; it allows us to experience the same emotions." John Denver was killed in a plane crash in 1997.

Informal Assessment

FOCUS SKILL **PREFIXES AND SUFFIXES**

To assess whether students are using prefixes and suffixes effectively to help them decode words, ask the following questions:

- **When you come across unfamiliar words in this story, do you look for prefixes and suffixes?**
- **What example can you give of a word with a prefix or suffix on page 36? How does the prefix or suffix affect the meaning of the word?**

Further instruction on prefixes and suffixes can be found on pages T46–T47.

REACHING ALL LEARNERS

CHALLENGE

ANALYZE CHARACTERS Discuss whether students think Rory and Derek are equally committed to their plan to ignore Bolivia. Students may say that Derek seems more likely to slip up and speak to Bolivia. He is actively helping to recapture Lucette, while Rory seems to be evaluating the situation. Encourage students to make predictions about what might happen with regard to the boys' vow of silence.

Monitor Comprehension

1 **How does your knowledge of prefixes and suffixes help you understand what Bolivia does and says when she notices Rory standing nearby listening?**
(Possible responses: the word *hastily*, formed by adding the suffix *-ly*, to mean "in a hasty way"; the word *overexcited*, formed by adding the prefix *over-*, to mean "excited too much") **FOCUS SKILL** INFEREN-
TIAL: PREFIXES AND SUFFIXES

2 **What details in the story might lead Rory to suspect that Bolivia planned the whole morning?**
(Possible responses: seeing the curtain move; Bolivia's reaction to the commotion; Bolivia's statement that Lucette comes when Bolivia calls her) INFERENTIAL:
DRAW CONCLUSIONS

3 **After reading the ending of the story on page 40, do you think Derek and Rory will become friends with Bolivia? Why or why not?** (Possible responses: yes; because they are interested in learning more about the parrot; because they will see now that Bolivia is a clever and interesting person) INFERENTIAL: MAKE
PREDICTIONS

38

SCIENCE

THE DOPPLER EFFECT   Point out that the author says the fire trucks disappeared with their sirens wailing. Ask whether students have ever noticed that sounds such as a siren's wail or a train's whistle seem higher in pitch as they approach and lower in pitch as they move away. Explain that this change in pitch, called the Doppler effect, occurs because sound waves grow longer or shorter as the source of the sound moves in relation to the observer.

Mrs. Golding began introducing Bolivia to the people that she recognized. Bolivia smiled at everyone. She was really enjoying this commotion very much, Rory decided.

"Can your parrot do any tricks?" asked one of the onlookers.

"She knows ten words, and she can play dead, and she comes flying to my arm when I call her," said Bolivia proudly.

She noticed Rory standing nearby listening and added hastily, "But she won't come now. She's in a new place and she's overexcited by all the people."

The firemen got a call on their radio. There was a real fire somewhere. As quickly as they arrived, they disappeared with their sirens wailing. "We'll come back later if you still need us," one of the men called back as they departed.

Lucette seemed to be getting tired. She wasn't flying so much. She sat in the Curry's maple tree and looked around her.

"Who's my bird?" shouted Bolivia.

"Lucette. Lucette," the bird answered.

"Hey, she knows her name!" shouted Derek.

Rory was as excited by the bird as Derek. But he also had a strong suspicion that the whole morning had been planned by Bolivia. The more he thought about it, the more certain he was that she had opened the cage and the window on purpose. She had probably seen him through her window as he waited for Derek and she had decided to mess up the morning for them.

"I've got her. I've got her," shouted Mr. Dunn in triumph, as he slowly came down the ladder.

"Hello there!" Lucette greeted all the people in the yard. Everyone burst into applause and ran to get a closer look at the bird. The Goldings looked exhausted and relieved that this first emergency was over. Mr. Dunn handed Lucette over to Bolivia, looking very pleased with himself. It wasn't every morning that he climbed into trees to catch a bird.

"I feel like Tarzan," he said to Mrs. Dunn.

39

INTERVENTION STRATEGIES

REACHING ALL LEARNERS

MODIFIED INSTRUCTION Help students summarize the story:

- The story begins at the cookout, where Derek and Rory stuff their mouths with food so they don't have to talk to Bolivia.
- The next day, Bolivia's pet parrot, Lucette, gets out and flies all around while everyone tries to catch her and a crowd of onlookers gathers.
- Rory has a strong suspicion that Bolivia had Lucette escape on purpose. After Lucette is captured, Derek is excited, and he asks Bolivia a lot of questions about the parrot, forgetting his promise to Rory not to speak to Bolivia.

Literary Response

RETURN TO THE PREDICTIONS/PURPOSE

Were your predictions about this story confirmed? Discuss with students whether their purpose for reading was met.

APPRECIATING THE LITERATURE

Do you think the author succeeded in creating realistic characters? Explain. (Possible response: Yes; the characters act and think much like boys and girls this age.)

Think About It

❶ Why might Bolivia be happy that Lucette got away? (Possible responses: She got to meet her neighbors; everyone saw Lucette and had a good time; she may be able to become friends with Derek and Rory.)
CRITICAL: LITERARY ANALYSIS

❷ What mistaken idea did the boys have about Lucette? Why might they have made this mistake? (Possible response: They thought Lucette was Bolivia's baby sister; she has a girl's name and they are told that she speaks ten words.) CRITICAL: LITERARY ANALYSIS

❸ What went wrong with Derek and Rory's plan not to speak to Bolivia, and what did they learn from what happened? (Possible responses: They spoke to her because they were curious about Lucette. They learned not to judge people before getting to know them.) INFERENTIAL: SUMMARIZE/ THEME CONNECTION

Derek just couldn't keep from asking Bolivia questions. "Where did you get her?" he wanted to know. "How many words can she say? Could she learn my name?" He was thrilled that Lucette was this clever bird and not the baby sister he and Rory had expected.

"You naughty girl," Bolivia scolded her pet. "I'm going to put you into your cage right now." She looked at Derek and said, "This has been a tiring morning for her. But tomorrow you can come over and help me clean her cage and feed her. Maybe I can teach her to say your name," she offered.

"Super," said Derek, not remembering until the words were out of his mouth that he had promised Rory he would never, ever speak to Bolivia.

Think About It

❶ Why might Bolivia be happy that Lucette got away?

❷ What mistaken idea did the boys have about Lucette? Why might they have made this mistake?

❸ What went wrong with Derek and Rory's plan not to speak to Bolivia, and what did they learn from what happened?

40

Meet the Author
Johanna Hurwitz

What influenced you to become a writer?

Books have been a part of my life as long as I can remember. My father owned a secondhand bookstore. Even though he eventually gave up the store, he never gave up the books. Every room of our house was filled with books. No wonder everyone in our family loved to read! I especially liked to read series books. That might be the reason why I've continued to write about the characters in *The Hot and Cold Summer*.

Where do you get ideas for your books?

My own children, who are now grown up, sparked many of my ideas when they reported on activities at school and with their friends. Other ideas come from students I meet on visits to schools and libraries. Anything can happen in my books because everything in them comes from real life.

Where do the characters from *The Hot and Cold Summer* come from?

I really met someone who had a daughter named Bolivia. As soon as I heard that name, I knew it was perfect and I would have to "borrow" it for a book. Derek and Rory are based on my own son and his friends, boys I see in my neighborhood. Boys that age do not want to talk to girls or fuss over babies, and they will do anything to avoid it.

41

ABOUT THE AUTHOR

JOHANNA HURWITZ has traveled across the United States and to countries such as Portugal, Nicaragua, and the African nations of Morocco and Mozambique. She says that she has made many friends on these trips and has discovered new ideas to write about. Discuss what students think the author means when she says that anything can happen in her books because everything in them comes from real life. (Possible response: Real people have a wide variety of experiences, which she uses as a source of ideas.)

 INTERNET Additional author information can be found on *The Learning Site* at **www.harcourtschool.com**

Informal Assessment

RETELL

Have students retell the story in their own words. Monitor whether the student

☐ relates events in sequence.

☐ includes story elements such as characters, setting, and plot.

☐ uses phrases, language, or vocabulary from the text.

☐ understands relationships in the text—for example, recognizes cause-and-effect relationships.

SUMMARIZE

Encourage students to summarize the story by recalling important story events. Students can refer to the prediction chart they completed while reading. See also *Practice Book* page 2.

ONE-SENTENCE SUMMARY Have students use their completed prediction charts to write a sentence that summarizes "The Hot and Cold Summer."

Name _____

▶ Complete the prediction chart for "The Hot and Cold Summer." In the first column, write predictions you make as you read the story. In the second column, write what actually happens. Possible responses are given.

What I Predict Will Happen	What Actually Happens
Derek and Rory will decide to talk to Bolivia after all.	Derek and Rory talk to Bolivia.
The boys will avoid meeting Lucette.	The boys do meet Lucette.
Lucette will be a very smart little girl.	Lucette turns out to be a parrot.
Mr. Golding will rescue Lucette from the tree.	Mr. Dunn rescues Lucette from the tree.

▶ Use your prediction chart to write a one-sentence summary of "The Hot and Cold Summer."

Possible response: While trying to catch Bolivia's pet parrot, Derek and Rory discover that Bolivia is an interesting person after all.

2 Pathways to Adventure

▲ **Practice Book, page 2**

Activity Choices

LIVE AND LEARN

Make a Speech Remind students to identify their audience and their purpose for giving the speech. Encourage them to use information from the story as well as their predictions about what might happen after the day of Lucette's escape. CRITICAL: REFLECT INTERPRETATIONS

LUCETTE ON THE LOOSE

Create a Flyer Provide a bulletin board or other area where students can post their completed flyers to share with classmates. CREATIVE: ART

MIND YOUR MANNERS

Write Etiquette Rules You may want to have students work in pairs or small groups. Suggest that they discuss how they would like to be treated by others in social situations and then write their rules based on their discussion. CRITICAL: CONNECT TO PERSONAL EXPERIENCES

HELLO THERE!

Role-Play a Scene Give students an opportunity to share their scenes with classmates. You might also arrange for students to perform their skits for people in your school who appear as characters in the scenes. CREATIVE: DRAMA

Response Activities

Live and Learn

MAKE A SPEECH Imagine that when Rory goes back to school, his teacher asks him to give a short speech on the topic "Experience Is the Best Teacher." Rory decides to talk about what he learned from the experience of meeting Bolivia. Prepare the speech you think Rory might give, using an outline or notes on index cards to organize the main ideas. Then deliver the speech to your classmates.

Lucette on the Loose

CREATE A FLYER Imagine that Lucette has flown away. Create a flyer that Bolivia can post around the neighborhood to help find her missing pet. Use art materials or computer software to create a flyer that will catch people's attention. Be sure to include all the information that people will need to identify Lucette and return her to Bolivia.

42

SCHOOL-HOME CONNECTION

The activities on the copying master on page R15 provide opportunities for students and family members to work together. You may want to assign some or all of the activities as homework during the week.

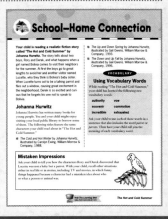

TEST TUTOR Family members can help students prepare for standardized or state tests on *The Learning Site* at **www.harcourtschool.com**

Copying Master, page R15 ▶

Mind Your Manners

WRITE ETIQUETTE RULES When Rory and Derek first met Bolivia, they knew they were not being polite to her. How should you act when you are introduced to someone? Write some rules of etiquette, or good manners, for young people to follow when they meet other people that are about the same age.

Hello There!

ROLE-PLAY A SCENE What might happen if a talking parrot like Lucette flew into a window of your school? With a small group, role-play the scene that you imagine. You can role-play not only yourselves and the parrot but also others who might become involved, such as your teacher and principal. If you wish, make your scene funny.

43

Assessment

SELECTION COMPREHENSION TEST

To evaluate comprehension, see pages 1–3.

INFORMAL ASSESSMENT

PERFORMANCE ASSESSMENT Student work for the Live and Learn activity may be used for performance assessment of selection comprehension.

PORTFOLIO OPPORTUNITY

Students may want to add their flyers for the Lucette on the Loose activity to their portfolios.

REACHING ALL LEARNERS

INTERVENTION STRATEGIES

FINDING STORY INFORMATION Some students may need help identifying appropriate information to use in their flyers. Provide these page numbers for locating information from the story:

name and type of bird	bottom of page 31
description of bird	bottom of page 31
what bird likes to eat	middle of page 35
name of street where bird escaped	top of page 36
tricks bird can do	top of page 39

Building Literacy Skills

Readers Theatre

Groups of students can read scenes from "The Hot and Cold Summer" as a Readers Theatre. You may want to assign students more than one role so as to include all the characters in a scene. Students should sit facing the audience and read their parts expressively. READING/LISTENING

Extend the Story

Point out that the characters in "The Hot and Cold Summer" attend the barbecue one day and that Lucette escapes the next day. Ask students to imagine what might happen the day after that and to write a sequel to the story. Before beginning, students may want to reread the end of the story on *Student Edition* page 40. WRITING

Phone Conversation

Suppose Bolivia's parents have called to see how she likes Woodside. Have students role-play conversations between Bolivia and her parents. Suggest that they have Bolivia describe story events and her feelings about them, while her parents ask questions and comment on Bolivia's experiences. SPEAKING/LISTENING

Tips for Speakers
• Use appropriate language.
• Speak clearly.
• Describe your ideas and feelings.

Tips for Listeners
• Identify the speaker's tone and mood.
• Note details.
• Compare your interpretation with the speaker's.

Perspective in Art

The artist uses perspective in a dramatic way in the illustrations for "The Hot and Cold Summer." Have students analyze several illustrations and then use the same techniques to create their own drawings. Activity Card 1 on page R10 guides students to analyze perspective. VIEWING/REPRESENTING

▶ Perspective in Art   ACTIVITY CARD 1

Perspective is the art of drawing or painting objects on a flat surface in such a way that they appear to have depth and distance. You can learn about perspective by looking at the illustrations for "The Hot and Cold Summer." Then you can draw your own picture.

1. Look at the illustration on pages 22–23 of "The Hot and Cold Summer."
   ■ The figure of Bolivia is much larger than the figures of the two boys. Her shadow towers over them.
   ■ Larger objects appear to be closer. Smaller objects appear to be farther away.
   ■ Why might the artist have chosen to draw the picture this way?
2. Look at the illustration on pages 32–33.
   ■ Why is the parrot so much larger than the people on the ground?
   ■ To see the scene from this angle, where would you have to be?
3. Now look at the illustration on pages 36–37.
   ■ Compare the sizes of Derek (holding the radio) and the parrot.
   ■ Notice the sizes of the firefighters and other elements.
   ■ To see the scene from this angle, where would you have to be?
4. Compare the illustration on pages 38–39 with those on pages 32–33 and 36–37. How are the illustrations alike and different?
5. Now draw a picture of your own. Decide from what angle you want to show the scene. Use perspective to create a feeling of depth and distance.

Activity Card 1 ▶

REACHING ALL LEARNERS

Intervention Strategies for Below-Level Readers

RETURN TO THE STRATEGY

Reinforce Comprehension

FOCUS STRATEGY **Apply the Use Prior Knowledge strategy.** Talk with students about how using reading strategies helps them better understand what they read. Remind students that the focus strategy for reading "The Hot and Cold Summer" is Use Prior Knowledge. Discuss the strategy by asking questions such as these:

- **How does using what you already know help you understand this story?**
- **What kinds of information do you recall that help you understand what you read?**

Have students practice this strategy as they reread a section of "The Hot and Cold Summer." As students silently reread pages 35 and 36, have them note instances when they used prior knowledge to understand what they read and to predict what would happen next. Have them record this information in a chart.

Page	How Prior Knowledge Helped
35	I know that the fire department uses tall ladders to get cats out of trees. Knowing this, I can predict that they will try to get Lucette out of the tree.

LANGUAGE EXPLORATION

Proper Nouns

Discuss common nouns and proper nouns. Have students recall the difference between common and proper nouns. Ask them to reread the third paragraph on page 24 and identify three proper nouns. (Bolivia, Woodside, Mr. Dunn) Then have students name the proper nouns used in the story for these common nouns that are things: opera, month, parrot, fire department, song. (Carmen, July, Lucette, Woodside Fire Department, "Country Roads") Have them search the selection to find proper nouns for the common nouns listed in the chart.

Common Nouns	Proper Nouns
People	**People**
children	Derek, Rory, Bolivia, Edna, Maurice
grown-ups	Mr. Golding, Mrs. Golding, Mr. Dunn, Mrs. Dunn, Mrs. Curry, Mr. Curry
movie character	Tarzan
Places	**Places**
town	Woodside
country	Israel, Egypt, Mexico, France, Spain
street	Dogleg Lane

SKILL TRACE

INTRODUCE	
• Before Reading:	T20–T21
• During Reading:	T26, T28, T38
• After Reading:	T46–T47
Reteach	R2
Review 1	T81
Review 2	T163
Test	Theme 1
Maintain	T273

OBJECTIVE:

To use prefixes and suffixes for independent decoding of words

REACHING ALL LEARNERS

ESL

Help students understand the meaning of the prefix *un-* by having them draw a happy face and an unhappy face and by covering something and then uncovering it.

CHALLENGE

Discuss adding prefixes and suffixes to Greek and Latin root words. For example, *predict* is formed by adding the prefix *pre-*, meaning "before," to the root *dict*, meaning "to say." The word *visible* is formed by adding the suffix *-ible*, meaning "able," to the root *vis*, meaning "to see."

RETEACH See page R2 for a lesson in multiple modalities.

TECHNOLOGY

The *Mission: Comprehension™ Skills Practice* **CD-ROM** provides additional practice with reading comprehension and focus skills.

FOCUS SKILL # Prefixes and Suffixes

AFTER READING

Return to the Concept

Extend the thinking.

Encourage students to recall prefixes and suffixes they identified while reading "The Hot and Cold Summer." Explain that it is important for students to look for a base word they recognize in order to understand a word with a prefix or suffix. Some words look as if they have a prefix or suffix, but the letters are part of the word.

refill = re- ("again") *+ fill*
regular = regular (does not have a prefix)
sailor = sail + -or ("person that is or does")
mirror = mirror (does not have a suffix)

Model the thinking.

Have students read page 44 in the *Student Edition*. Discuss the examples in the chart and how the prefix or suffix changes the meaning of each base word. You may want to use this model:

> MODEL **Adding the prefix *un-* to the word *happy* forms a new word that means "not happy." In this case, the prefix gives the new word an opposite meaning from the base word.**

Summarize.

Ask students to tell how recognizing prefixes and suffixes helped them understand the selection.

Guided Practice

Have students make judgments.

Have students read page 45. Help them determine the meanings of the underlined words. Then guide them to use the underlined words to create a chart like the one on page 44.

Test Prep

These tips can help students answer test items on prefixes and suffixes:

• A prefix is added to the beginning of a base word.
• A suffix is added to the end of a base word.
• Adding a prefix or a suffix creates a new word with a different meaning.

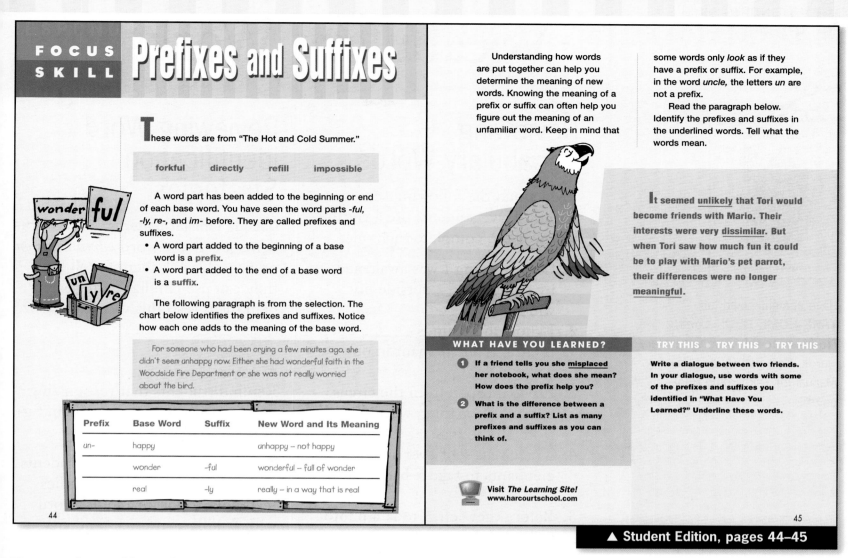

FOCUS SKILL — Prefixes and Suffixes

These words are from "The Hot and Cold Summer."

| forkful | directly | refill | impossible |

A word part has been added to the beginning or end of each base word. You have seen the word parts *-ful*, *-ly*, *re-*, and *im-* before. They are called prefixes and suffixes.

- A word part added to the beginning of a base word is a **prefix**.
- A word part added to the end of a base word is a **suffix**.

The following paragraph is from the selection. The chart below identifies the prefixes and suffixes. Notice how each one adds to the meaning of the base word.

> For someone who had been crying a few minutes ago, she didn't seem unhappy now. Either she had wonderful faith in the Woodside Fire Department or she was not really worried about the bird.

Prefix	Base Word	Suffix	New Word and Its Meaning
un-	happy		unhappy – not happy
	wonder	-ful	wonderful – full of wonder
	real	-ly	really – in a way that is real

Understanding how words are put together can help you determine the meaning of new words. Knowing the meaning of a prefix or suffix can often help you figure out the meaning of an unfamiliar word. Keep in mind that some words only *look* as if they have a prefix or suffix. For example, in the word *uncle*, the letters *un* are not a prefix.

Read the paragraph below. Identify the prefixes and suffixes in the underlined words. Tell what the words mean.

It seemed <u>unlikely</u> that Tori would become friends with Mario. Their interests were very <u>dissimilar</u>. But when Tori saw how much fun it could be to play with Mario's pet parrot, their differences were no longer <u>meaningful</u>.

WHAT HAVE YOU LEARNED?

1. If a friend tells you she <u>misplaced</u> her notebook, what does she mean? How does the prefix help you?

2. What is the difference between a prefix and a suffix? List as many prefixes and suffixes as you can think of.

TRY THIS • TRY THIS • TRY THIS

Write a dialogue between two friends. In your dialogue, use words with some of the prefixes and suffixes you identified in "What Have You Learned?" Underline these words.

Visit *The Learning Site!* www.harcourtschool.com

44 / 45

▲ Student Edition, pages 44–45

Practice/Apply

Have students apply the skill. Have students answer the questions and complete the activities on page 45.

WHAT HAVE YOU LEARNED?

1. **Possible response:** She means that she put it in the wrong place. The prefix *mis-* means "wrong."

2. **Possible response:** A prefix is at the beginning of a word. A suffix is at the end of a word. Lists will vary.

INTERNET Students can use the Prefixes and Suffixes activities on *The Learning Site* at **www.harcourtschool.com**

TRY THIS

Before students begin writing their dialogues, you may want to suggest that they brainstorm words with the prefixes and suffixes that they identified. Looking over the words may help students think of a topic for the dialogue.

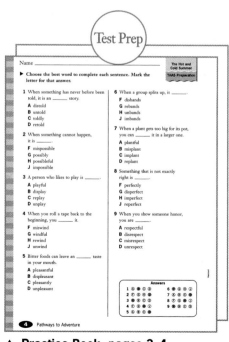

▲ **Practice Book, pages 3–4**

The Hot and Cold Summer **T47**

Lonely No More

by Emily Hutchinson
illustrated by Mark Jarmin

Have students read the
TAKE-HOME BOOK *Lonely No More* to reinforce vocabulary words. See also *Guided Reading Manual for Take-Home Books,* page 2.

Vocabulary Workshop

Reviewing Vocabulary Words

Read aloud the following sentence frames. Have students use a vocabulary word to complete each one.

1. One morning I was awakened by a huge _____ outside my window. *(commotion)*
2. I know this sounds _____ , but there was an elephant in our yard. *(incredible)*
3. It had escaped from the circus, and the poor thing was _____ from all the fuss. *(exhausted)*
4. The circus sent over an _____ on elephants to take it back. *(authority)*
5. Before they left, I took a photo to keep as a _____ . *(souvenir)*
6. I also made a _____ to keep an open mind when people tell stories that sound impossible. *(vow)*

Reviewing Word Identification Strategies

Decode familiar patterns. Have students locate the word *administration* on page 32. Ask them to tell how they can use familiar patterns to help them read this word. (recognize familiar syllables such as *ad* as in *admit*, *min* as in *minute*, the blend *str* as in *strong*, the syllable *tion* as in *motion*) Remind students that recognizing familiar patterns can help them figure out unfamiliar words.

Words in Textbooks Have students look through their social studies textbooks to locate and list words with familiar patterns. Students should also indicate the patterns and explain how and why they are familiar.

Extending Vocabulary

NAMES OF FOODS

Word Origins   The names of many of the foods mentioned in "The Hot and Cold Summer" have interesting origins. For example, tell students that the hamburger is named for the city of Hamburg in Germany, where the ground beef patty originally known as "Hamburg steak" was invented.

Create a chart.   Ask students to begin a chart of food names and their origins like the one shown here. Have students look through the selection to find food names and then look up the origins in a dictionary or word history reference.

Food Word	Origin
hamburger	Named for Hamburg, Germany, where it was invented
potato	Spanish *batata*, originally from Taino language of the Greater Antilles and Bahamas
salad	*salar* ("to salt"), from Latin *sal*, meaning "salt"
cole slaw	Dutch *koolsla*, from *kool* ("cabbage") + *sla* ("salad")
ketchup	Malay *kechap* ("fish sauce")
sandwich	Named after John Montagu, 4th Earl of Sandwich, who had the idea in about 1762 of putting slices of cold beef between pieces of toast
cookie	Dutch *koekje* ("little cake")

FOOD FOR THOUGHT

Reference Sources/Online or Print Dictionaries

Have students brainstorm names of other foods they like to eat. Then have them use an online or print dictionary that includes etymologies to look up the names of these foods and discover where the food names came from.

Expressive Writing

PERSONAL NARRATIVE

Connect Writing to Reading

Remind students that the excerpt from "The Hot and Cold Summer" describes how Derek and Rory meet Bolivia. Explain that a personal narrative is written in the first person and it tells about something that happened in the narrator's life. Ask students how a personal narrative would be different from the selection. (Possible response: A personal narrative would not be fictional, and it would be written in the first person.)

Teach/Model

Display Transparency 3. Tell students that they will be reviewing a model of a personal narrative. They will then write personal narratives of their own.

STUDENT MODEL: PERSONAL NARRATIVE

A personal narrative describes an experience or event from the writer's life. It is written in the first person. Here is a personal narrative written by a student.

Would I Be a Bobcat?

The most exciting day of my life was the day I tried out for the Bobcats, the basketball team at my school. I woke up when it was still dark outside, and I got ready for school. Then I practiced dribbling on the sidewalk with my dad and my sister. We even ran around my parents' cars in the driveway and pretended they were players on the other team.

All day long at school, I couldn't sit still. Even science, my favorite class, seemed to last forever. Finally, it was time to go to the gym!

One by one, everybody who was trying out got to take a turn at dribbling, passing, guarding, and shooting baskets. I was nervous when my turn came. I did pretty well at most things, but when I tried to dribble, the ball kept rolling away from me. I was sure I wouldn't make the team because of that, but the coaches said it was something we could work on in practice. I was going to be a Bobcat!

▲ **Teaching Transparency 3**

ANALYZE THE MODEL

- Audience—readers of school newspaper
- Writer's task—write about trying out for the basketball team

FOCUS ON ORGANIZATION

- The first sentence tells what the personal narrative is about.
- Beginning, middle, and final events are told in time order.
- There is one paragraph for each part of the day: in the morning before school, during the school day, at the tryout.

FOCUS ON ELABORATION

- Writer includes interesting details, such as dribbling with dad and sister, pretending cars in driveway were players on other team, and taking turns at specific skills during tryouts.
- Writer's feelings about the events are shown through expressive statements such as *the most exciting day of my life* and narrator's behavior, such as getting up and ready for school so early.

TECHNOLOGY

Students may use a word processing program such as *ClarisWorks for Kids®* to plan and write their personal narratives.

 Writing Prompts

Choose one of the following:

A Assign a prompt, for example:
Write a personal narrative about how facing a difficulty helped you discover something about yourself. Describe events in time order, and use the first-person point of view. Include specific details.

B Have students write a personal narrative about a topic of their own choosing.

Prewrite and Draft

Have students list several possible topics for a personal narrative and then choose one. Students may use a graphic organizer such as the one on Transparency 4 to help them organize the events. Remind students to use paragraphs to show the organization of the narrative.

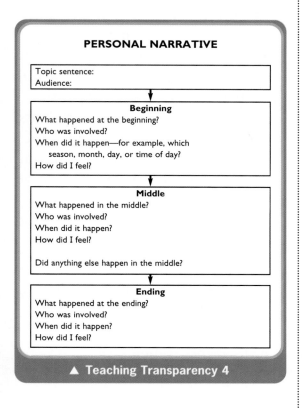

PERSONAL NARRATIVE

Topic sentence:
Audience:

Beginning
What happened at the beginning?
Who was involved?
When did it happen—for example, which
    season, month, day, or time of day?
How did I feel?

Middle
What happened in the middle?
Who was involved?
When did it happen?
How did I feel?

Did anything else happen in the middle?

Ending
What happened at the ending?
Who was involved?
When did it happen?
How did I feel?

▲ Teaching Transparency 4

Revise

Have students work in pairs or small groups to discuss their personal narratives. Suggest the following questions to help students work together constructively:

- **Is the narrative written from the first-person point of view, using the pronouns *I*, *me*, and *my*?**
- **Does the narrative have a clear beginning, middle, and ending?**
- **Are specific details included to describe the events?**
- **Are time-order words included to make the sequence of events clear?**
- **Are the writer's feelings about the events clearly shown?**

After students have discussed each other's writing, have them revise their own personal narratives.

SCORING RUBRIC FOR SUGGESTED PROMPT

4 Advanced
The narrative has an appropriate title and a clear beginning, middle, and ending. Signal words and phrases help identify the order of events. The narrative is written in the first person and contains specific details and vivid descriptive words that make clear the writer's feelings about the events.

3 Proficient
The title is appropriate, and the narrative has a beginning, a middle, and an ending. A few time-order words are used to link events. The writer maintains the first person point of view. The narrative contains some details that describe the events, and the writer uses some techniques to show feeling.

2 Basic
The title does not reflect the content of the narrative. The narrative has a beginning, a middle, and an ending, but events are not clearly linked by time-order words. There are few descriptive details, and the writer has difficulty maintaining the first person point of view. The writer's feelings are not clearly shown.

1 Below Basic
The personal narrative is missing a title, or the title does not reflect the content of the story. The narrative lacks a clear topic. Only one or two events are included, and the order is not clear. There is little or no detail, and the story is not told from the first person point of view. The language is not interesting.

Declarative and Interrogative Sentences

SKILL TRACE

INTRODUCE	T52–T53
Review	T73

Language Handbook, pages 94–95

ESL

Ask questions such as the following, and prompt students to answer in complete sentences. Then invite students to ask you the same questions or others of their choice. Write a question and answer on the board to demonstrate end punctuation.

Do you have a pet?

How long have you had your pet?

What is your favorite time of year?

What do you like to do then?

Teach/Model

DAILY LANGUAGE PRACTICE

1. **How was you're vacation.** (your; vacation?)
2. **we went swimming in our pool?** (We; pool.)

INTRODUCE THE CONCEPT Use sentences 1–3 on Transparency 5 as you discuss these points:

- A **sentence** expresses a complete thought. It names someone or something and tells who the person is or what the person or thing does.
- Begin every sentence with a capital letter and end it with an end mark.
- A **declarative sentence** makes a statement.
- An **interrogative sentence** asks a question.

Have students rewrite items 4 and 5 to make them complete sentences.

DECLARATIVE AND INTERROGATIVE SENTENCES

1. The neighbors planned a picnic.
   (declarative; voice falls)
2. Who was the special guest?
   (interrogative; voice rises)
3. Is Lucette a colorful bird?
   (interrogative; voice rises)
4. trying to find Lucette
   (Possible response: The girl was trying to find Lucette.)
5. what the bird eats
   (Possible response: I don't know what the bird eats.)
6. the three men were talking about car motors
   (The three men were talking about car motors.)
7. rory didn't think it would rain
   (Rory didn't think it would rain.)
8. will we cut the cake soon
   (Will we cut the cake soon?)

▲ **Teaching Transparency 5**

Extend the Concept

DAILY LANGUAGE PRACTICE

1. **was yesterday's picnic fun.** (Was; fun?)
2. **Everyone eight plenty of food** (ate; food.)

BUILD ORAL LANGUAGE Read aloud sentences 1–3 on Transparency 5 without showing them. Ask students which sentences are declarative and which are interrogative. Read the sentences aloud again. Ask students whether your voice rises or falls at the end of each sentence. Point out that when spoken aloud, declarative sentences end with a falling pitch. Questions usually end with a rising pitch.

Show the transparency, and have students read sentences 6–8 silently. Have volunteers correct the sentences orally as you correct them on the transparency.

Name _____

Declarative and Interrogative Sentences

Skill Reminder
- A sentence is a group of words that expresses a complete thought.
- A declarative sentence is a statement and ends with a period.
- An interrogative sentence is a question and ends with a question mark.

▶ Write *sentence* if the word group is a sentence. If it is not a sentence, add words to turn it into a sentence. In items 1, 4, and 5, responses will vary; possible responses are given.
1. Glanced up at the window. not a sentence: Rory glanced up at the window.
2. The boys saw a bird. sentence
3. Was it sitting on a branch? sentence
4. How did Lucette? not a sentence: How did Lucette get free?
5. Where was? not a sentence: Where was the parrot?

▶ Rewrite each sentence correctly, using capital letters and end marks. Then write *declarative* or *interrogative* to tell what kind of sentence it is.
6. everyone began to applaud Everyone began to applaud. declarative
7. what was the big fuss What was the big fuss? interrogative
8. has anyone seen Lucette Has anyone seen Lucette? interrogative
9. the bird flew from tree to tree The bird flew from tree to tree. declarative

Declarative and Interrogative Sentences   GRAMMAR PRACTICE BOOK 7

▲ **Grammar Practice Book, page 7**

DAY 3 Oral Review/Practice

DAILY LANGUAGE PRACTICE

1. **Derek and Rory. Finally met Lucette** (Rory finally; Lucette.)

2. **did you think that Lucette was a baby.** (Did; baby?)

SENTENCE CHALLENGE Divide the class into two teams. A student on Team A makes a statement in the form of a declarative sentence. A student on Team B then transforms that sentence into an interrogative sentence. Each correctly formed interrogative sentence scores 1 point. After every student has had a turn, have teams switch roles. The team that scores more points wins.

▲ Grammar Practice Book, page 8

DAY 4 Apply to Writing

DAILY LANGUAGE PRACTICE

1. **Rory looked up and saw a bright green parrot abuve his head** (above; head.)

2. **Did he use a piece of bred to get the parrot's attention.** (bread; attention?)

QUESTION AND ANSWER Have students work in pairs to develop a news conference held by Bolivia after Lucette's rescue. One student should write interrogative sentences for the reporters to ask. The second student should write declarative sentences for Bolivia's answers.

Test Prep

Share these pointers about sentences as students prepare for language tests:
- In a declarative sentence, other words may occasionally come before the subject: *Suddenly the bird spoke.*
- Interrogative sentences can often be recognized by word order: *Is it lost?*

▲ Practice Book, page 5

DAY 5 Cumulative Review

DAILY LANGUAGE PRACTICE

1. **Edna's mothir helped catch Lucette** (mother; Lucette.)

2. **unfortunately, Lucette was not yet reddy to return home.** (Unfortunately; ready)

SENTENCE COMPLETION Write the following sentence frames on the board. Have students copy and complete each sentence. Remind students to add capital letters and end punctuation where needed.
(Possible responses are given.)

1. robert and Tina _____ the salad for the barbecue

2. _____ used fresh lettuce and ripe tomatoes

3. Who _____ the hamburgers

4. _____ summer your favorite time of year

(1. Robert and Tina made the salad for the barbecue. 2. They used fresh lettuce and ripe tomatoes. 3. Who cooked the hamburgers? 4. Is summer your favorite time of year?)

▲ Grammar Practice Book, page 9

SPELLING

Words with Short Vowels

SPELLING WORDS

1. master
2. ahead*
3. build
4. front*
5. meant
6. bread
7. ready
8. busy*
9. quit
10. mother*
11. above
12. does

BONUS WORDS

13. advantage
14. business
15. sweater
16. plastic*

*Words appearing in "The Hot and Cold Summer." Additional story words that follow the generalizations are *another, other, hamburger, quickly, dead, forehead, sweat,* and *back.*

STUDENT-CHOSEN WORDS

17. _____
18. _____
19. _____
20. _____

INTERVENTION

REACHING ALL LEARNERS

Encourage less-proficient spellers to find Student-Chosen Words by looking for words with short vowels that they have misspelled in their own writing.

DAY 1 Pretest/Self-Check

ADMINISTER THE PRETEST. Say each word, and then use it in a Dictation Sentence. (See Day 5.) Help students self-check their pretests using the list at the top of Transparency 6.

OPEN SORT Have students think of ways to sort the Spelling Words. For example, they might sort words according to number of syllables or by parts of speech. Ask volunteers to share their categories and lists.

WORDS WITH SHORT VOWELS

Spelling Words

1. master	5. meant	9. quit
2. ahead	6. bread	10. mother
3. build	7. ready	11. above
4. front	8. busy	12. does

Short *a*	Short *e*	Short *i*	Short *u*
master	ahead	build	front
	meant	busy	mother
	bread	quit	above
	ready		does

- **Short *a*** can be spelled *a.*
- **Short *e*** can be spelled *ea.*
- **Short *i*** can be spelled *u, i,* or *ui.*
- **Short *u*** can be spelled *o, oe,* or *o-e.*

▲ Teaching Transparency 6

DAY 2 Teach/Model

CLOSED SORT Display the top part of Transparency 6, or write the information on the board. Ask students to copy the chart and write each Spelling Word where it belongs.

Read the words *master* and *advantage.* Ask students what vowel sound is the same in both. (short *a*) Have a volunteer circle the letter that stands for this sound. Repeat with *ahead* and *bread,* then *build* and *busy,* and then *front* and *does.* Uncover and discuss the generalizations.

Handwriting Tip

Remind students to keep the joining stroke high when joining *o* to other letters; otherwise, an *o* could look like an *a.*

_____

o a

Name _____

▶ Write the Spelling Word that means the opposite of each word.

1. begin — quit
2. behind — ahead
3. idle — busy
4. below — above
5. back — front
6. destroy — build

▶ Write the Spelling Word that rhymes with each word.

7. tent — meant
8. sled — bread or ahead
9. faster — master
10. buzz — does
11. steady — ready
12. another — mother

SPELLING WORDS
1. ahead
2. build
3. front
4. busy
5. quit
6. above
7. master
8. meant
9. bread
10. ready
11. mother
12. does

Handwriting Tip: Take care to make a clear loop when you write the letter *e.* Otherwise, your *e* might look like an *i.* Practice writing these Spelling Words.

13. meant — meant
14. bread — bread
15. ready — ready
16. does — does

6 Pathways to Adventure

▲ Practice Book, page 6

VISUALIZING   Remind students that some vowel sounds can be spelled in different ways. Write the word *ready*, correctly spelled, on the board. Tell students to look at the word carefully and take a mental picture of it. Then erase the word and write the following words on the board:

ready   redy   reddy

Ask a volunteer to tell which word is spelled correctly. (*ready*) Repeat for the word *does*, using the spellings *does*, *duz*, and *dus*.

Apply to Writing

Have students check spellings of vowel sounds as they proofread their writing. Ask them to keep in mind that a short vowel sound may be spelled with more than one letter.

WORD CROSSES   Have students make word crosses, using some of the Spelling Words. They begin by writing one word and continue by using a letter in that word to begin the next word. Words may run either horizontally or vertically.

CROSSWORD PUZZLE   Have students turn their word crosses into a crossword puzzle by drawing an outline on graph paper. Show them how to add numbers and write clues for the words in their puzzle. When they have finished, they can exchange papers with a classmate and solve each other's puzzles.

Assess students' progress, using the Dictation Sentences.

DICTATION SENTENCES

1. **master**   The dog obeyed its **master**.
2. **ahead**   She ran **ahead** of the others in the race.
3. **build**   Let's **build** a tree fort!
4. **front**   The display is at the **front** of the room.
5. **meant**   I **meant** to get milk at the store.
6. **bread**   He spread the **bread** with jelly.
7. **ready**   Are you **ready** to go on the hike?
8. **busy**   I was too **busy** to answer the phone.
9. **quit**   We can **quit** work at noon.
10. **mother**   My **mother** taught me how to sew.
11. **above**   The kite flew high **above** us.
12. **does**   He **does** chores at home every day.

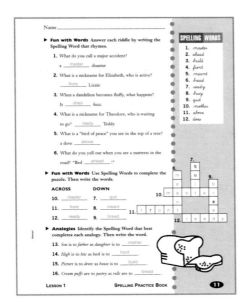

▲ Spelling Practice Book, page 10

▲ Spelling Practice Book, page 11

Cross-Curricular Connections

MULTI-AGE CLASSROOMS

Students who have more experience using the Internet can help classmates use online search engines to locate appropriate Web sites for the Emergency Services activity.

CHALLENGE

Students may expand their independent research for the Parrot Facts activity by locating other reference books or online sources that include information about parrots.

SOCIAL STUDIES

Emergency Services

MATERIALS

- a computer with Internet access
- local phone directory
- newsletters or other sources of information about emergency services in your community
- paper
- pencils

CREATE A PAMPHLET In "The Hot and Cold Summer," Mr. Golding calls the fire department to help catch Lucette. Before Rory realizes that Lucette is a bird, he suggests calling an ambulance or the police. Have small groups of students use the Internet, a local phone book, and other available resources to research emergency services in their own community. Students can then use the information to create a pamphlet to tell citizens about these services.

READING ELECTRONIC TEXTS/VIEWING/WRITING

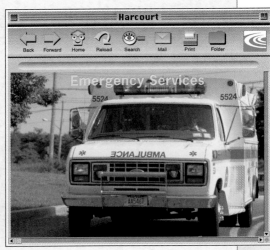

Parrot Facts

MATERIALS
- encyclopedia in print, on CD-ROM, or online
- paper
- pencils

RESEARCH PARROTS In "The Hot and Cold Summer," Rory and Derek are fascinated by Bolivia's parrot. Students can use encyclopedias either in print, on CD-ROM, or online to research parrots and create a fact sheet. Activity Card 2, page R10, gives suggestions for carrying out this activity.

FOCUS SKILL After students have completed their research, discuss how their ability to recognize prefixes and suffixes helped them understand words they encountered in their research. READING REFERENCE SOURCES/ WRITING

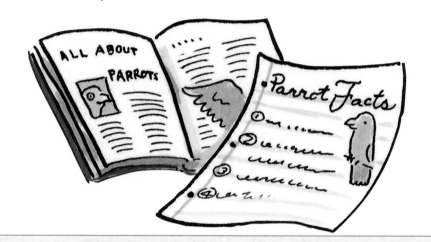

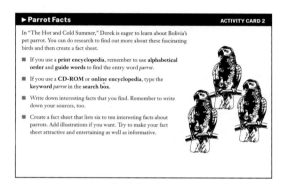

▶ **Parrot Facts** ACTIVITY CARD 2

In "The Hot and Cold Summer," Derek is eager to learn about Bolivia's pet parrot. You can do research to find out more about these fascinating birds and then create a fact sheet.

■ If you use a **print encyclopedia**, remember to use **alphabetical order** and **guide words** to find the entry word *parrot*.

■ If you use a **CD-ROM** or **online encyclopedia**, type the **keyword** *parrot* in the **search box**.

■ Write down interesting facts that you find. Remember to write down your sources, too.

■ Create a fact sheet that lists six to ten interesting facts about parrots. Add illustrations if you want. Try to make your fact sheet attractive and entertaining as well as informative.

▲ **Activity Card 2**

Inquiry Projects

"The Hot and Cold Summer" is a rich source of topics and ideas for inquiry. Have students brainstorm possible research topics and organize the ideas in a diagram. Students can use some of the resources shown here to help them begin their own inquiry projects.

"The Hot and Cold Summer"		
Countries	**Trees**	**Music**
Israel Egypt Mexico France Spain	mimosa locust maple	opera country music

RESOURCES

A Llama in the Family
by Johanna Hurwitz.
Scholastic, 1996.
EASY

The Cold and Hot Winter
by Johanna Hurwitz.
William Morrow, 1988.
AVERAGE

READER'S CHOICE LIBRARY
Frindle
by Andrew Clements.
AVERAGE

Dog Days
by Colby Rodowsky.
Farrar, Straus & Giroux, 1990. CHALLENGING

"Sees Behind Trees"

THEME
Look Inside

GENRE
Historical Fiction

- The **setting** is a real time and place in the past.
- The **characters** may include actual historical figures but also may be fictional.
- It may include some **events** that really happened and some that are made up.

CROSS-CURRICULAR CONNECTIONS

- **SOCIAL STUDIES:** Special Names
- **ART:** Native American Dwellings

FOCUS STRATEGY **USE PRIOR KNOWLEDGE**

- **Before Reading:** Preteach the Strategy on page T67
- **During Reading:** Apply the Strategy on pages T70, T74, T80
- **After Reading:** Return to the Strategy on page T89

FOCUS SKILL **CHARACTER DEVELOPMENT**

- **Before Reading:** Introduce the Skill on pages T66–T67
- **During Reading:** Apply the Skill on pages T72, T76
- **After Reading:** Practice the Skill on pages T90–T91

COMPANION SELECTION

- "When Birds Remember"
Haiku Poem
Limerick Poem
Genre: Poetry

Teachers' Choice
SLJ Best Book
Booklist Editors' Choice
Notable Trade Book for the Language Arts

▲ **Student Edition, pages 62–63**

As students read "Sees Behind Trees," they will learn that although everyone does not have the same talents and abilities, each person has worth and value.

Selection Summary

Walnut, a young Native American boy, has been unable to learn to shoot a bow accurately. After his uncle realizes that the problem is the boy's poor eyesight, his mother gives up trying to teach him to shoot. Instead, she asks him every day to describe the things he "sees" with his sharpened sense of hearing. To be recognized as a grown-up and to be given a grown-up name, Walnut and the other boys his age must demonstrate skill with the bow. Walnut is sure he will fail. To his surprise, however, there is a new test this year to find a person "with the ability to see what can't be seen." Walnut is the only boy able to pass, thus earning his grown-up name, Sees Behind Trees, and a special place among his people.

Author Profile

Michael Dorris was born in Louisville, Kentucky, and grew up in Kentucky and Montana. In addition to writing fiction for young people, he wrote notable works of adult fiction and nonfiction, articles, poems, short stories, reviews, and songs. His work won many awards, including the Scott O'Dell Award for Historical Fiction for his first young-adult novel, *Morning Girl*. Michael Dorris founded the Native American Studies Program at Dartmouth College and coauthored *A Guide to Research on North American Indians*.

REACHING ALL LEARNERS — BELOW-LEVEL READERS

EASY READER
"The Quiver" pp. 14–21. Reinforces selection vocabulary and these additional words from "Sees Behind Trees":

criticize   ordinary   blurry

See *Timeless Tales Intervention Reader Teacher's Guide*, pages 8–13.

CASSETTE
"Sees Behind Trees" and the accompanying poems are available on *Literature Cassette 1*.

CHALLENGE

READER'S CHOICE LIBRARY
The Black Stallion by Walter Farley.

INQUIRY PROJECTS
See page T101. Encourage students to pose questions about topics related to "Sees Behind Trees" such as the senses or Native American rites and then carry out research to answer them.

SUGGESTED
LESSON PLANNER

SEES BEHIND TREES

Skills and Strategies

Reading

Listening

Speaking

Viewing

Vocabulary
quiver
tread
moss
sternly
exaggerate
compose

BUILDING BACKGROUND AND CONCEPTS T64

INTRODUCING VOCABULARY T65
Transparency 7
Practice Book p. 7

PRETEACHING SKILLS
Before Reading
✔ **FOCUS SKILL** Character Development (Introduce) T66–T67
Transparency 8
FOCUS STRATEGY Use Prior Knowledge T67

PREREADING STRATEGIES T68

READING THE SELECTION T68–T83
 Literature Cassette 1
Author Information T83

ALTERNATIVE SELECTION
Easy Reader: "The Quiver"

NOTE: Students may begin reading the selection on Day 2.

LITERARY RESPONSE T82
Return to the Predictions/Purpose
Appreciating the Literature

THINK ABOUT IT T82

RETELL AND SUMMARIZE T83
Practice Book p. 9

REREADING FOR FLUENCY
Dramatization T88

LITERATURE RESPONSE
Journal Entry T88

**INTERVENTION STRATEGIES
FOR BELOW-LEVEL READERS** T89
FOCUS STRATEGY Return to the Strategy
Language Exploration

COMPANION SELECTIONS
"When Birds Remember,"
"Haiku," "Limerick" T84–T85

Writing	**Expressive Writing: Descriptive Paragraph** Connect Writing to Reading T94	Teach/Model T94 Analyze the Model *Transparency 10* *Language Handbook pp. 46–48*
Grammar	**Imperative and Exclamatory Sentences** Teach/Model T96 *Transparency 12* *Language Handbook pp. 94–96*	Extend the Concept T96 *Grammar Practice Book p. 10*
Daily Language Practice	1. **People has different abilitys.** (have; abilities.) 2. **Practice helps us, develop are abilities.** (us develop our)	1. **What did Walnut and his mothar practice every morning.** (mother; morning?) 2. **Walnut wants to kwit target practice** (quit; practice.)
Spelling	**Words with Long *a*, *e*, and *i*** stayed brain thief meat flight style delighted daily breathe meanwhile believes tonight Pretest/Self-Check T98 *Transparency 13*	Teach/Model T98 *Practice Book p. 14* Handwriting Tip

KEY

✔ **Tested Skills**

■ **Management Option:** See Managing the Classroom, page T62, for ongoing independent activities.

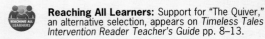 **Reaching All Learners:** Support for "The Quiver," an alternative selection, appears on *Timeless Tales Intervention Reader Teacher's Guide* pp. 8–13.

DAY 3
READING AND RESPONDING

RESPONSE ACTIVITIES
Design a T-Shirt T86
Role-Play a Situation T86
Design a Project T86
 Computer Station
T62
Write a Review T86

Selection Comprehension Test

DECODING/PHONICS
Vowel Variant: /ô/ (Maintain) T79

ORAL LANGUAGE
Describe What You Hear T88
Activity Card 3, R11

VIEWING
Overlapping T88

INDEPENDENT READING
Reader's Choice Library:
The Black Stallion T63

**Reader's Choice
Library Book** ▶

DAY 4
EXTENDING SKILLS & STRATEGIES

LITERARY CONCEPTS
After Reading
✔ **FOCUS SKILL** Character Development (Introduce)
T90–T91
Transparency 9
Practice Book pp. 10–11

DECODING/PHONICS
✔ Prefixes and Suffixes (Review) T81
Practice Book p. 8

VOCABULARY T92–T93
Practice Book p. 12
■ Vocabulary Station

TAKE-HOME BOOK
Fire from Ice T92

CROSS-CURRICULAR CONNECTIONS
Social Studies: Special Names T100
Activity Card 4, R11
■ Publishing Station
FOCUS SKILL Apply Character
Development

Take-Home Book ▶

DAY 5
EXTENDING SKILLS & STRATEGIES

GRAMMAR
Declarative and Interrogative Sentences
(Review) T73

CROSS-CURRICULAR CONNECTIONS
Art: Native American Dwellings T101

INQUIRY PROJECTS T101
Research

SELF-SELECTED READING T63
• *Morning Girl*
• *The Indian School*
• *Buffalo Hunt*

Writing Prompts T94 Prewrite and Draft T95 *Transparency 11* *The New Kid Pix®*	Revise T95	Assessment T95 Student Self- and Peer Assessment Scoring Rubric
Oral Review/Practice T97 *Grammar Practice Book* p. 11	Apply to Writing T97 *Practice Book* p. 13	Cumulative Review T97 *Grammar Practice Book* p. 12
1. Walnut listens to the sounds. In the trees abuve his head. (sounds in; above) **2. Dus he hear more than the other boys.** (Does; boys?)	**1. Listen to the birds bild their spring nests** (build; nests.) **2. What a beautiful moon tonite?** (tonight!)	**1. All the boys staid in the clearing!** (stayed; clearing.) **2. Walnut was delited with the results of the trial?** (delighted; trial.)
Spelling Strategies T99 Apply to Writing *Spelling Practice Book* p. 12	Spelling Activities T99 *Spelling Practice Book* p. 13	Posttest T99

Visit *The Learning Site!*
www.harcourtschool.com

Managing the Classroom

While you provide direct instruction to individuals or small groups, other students can work on ongoing activities like the ones below.

Computer Station

OBJECTIVE

To use the Internet to learn more about products for the visually impaired

MATERIALS

- computer with Internet access

Students who are working on the Using Other Senses activity on page T86 may want to learn more about products available for the visually impaired. Suggest that they list or book-mark helpful Web sites for classmates to explore.

Visit *The Learning Site!*
www.harcourtschool.com

Vocabulary Station

OBJECTIVE

To explore words borrowed from other languages

MATERIALS

- reference books on word origins
- unabridged dictionary
- pencils
- paper

Students can use reference books for the Native American Words activity on page T93. Have them make a chart to classify words according to the language from which they were borrowed. Invite them to share their findings.

Borrowed Words	Origin of Words
caucus hominy prairie	Native American languages
chowder levee	French
rancho tortilla	Spanish

Publishing Station

OBJECTIVE

To publish results of research on famous people

MATERIALS

- paper
- bookbinding materials

Students can combine their biographical sketches from the Special Names activity on page T100 into a booklet. They can group sketches into categories such as Political Figures, Athletes, and People in the Arts.

Research Station

OBJECTIVE

To research Native American rituals or ceremonies

MATERIALS

- encyclopedias
- nonfiction books about Native Americans
- library pass

Have students research Native American rituals or ceremonies that mark the transition from childhood to young adulthood. Students can then record in a notebook what they learn and they can raise new questions for further investigation.

Note: For more options, see pages T86–T87, T88–T89, and T100–T101.

GUIDED READING

Multi-Level Books

EASY

Anasazi by Leonard Everett Fisher. Atheneum, 1997. NON-FICTION: NATIVE AMERICANS

EASY READER: TIMELESS TALES "The Quiver" pp. 14–21.

HISTORICAL FICTION: TEAMWORK

TAKE-HOME BOOK

Fire from Ice

REALISTIC FICTION: NATIVE AMERICAN

LEVELED LIBRARY BOOK

Sees Behind Trees by Michael Dorris.

HISTORICAL FICTION: SELECTION AUTHOR

AVERAGE

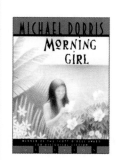

Morning Girl by Michael Dorris. Hyperion, 1994.

HISTORICAL FICTION: SELECTION AUTHOR

Clambake: A Wampanoag Tradition by Russell M. Peters. Lerner, 1992. NONFICTION: NATIVE AMERICANS

Kids Explore the Gifts of Children with Special Needs by Westridge Young Writers Workshop. John Muir, 1994.

NONFICTION: SPECIAL NEEDS

READER'S CHOICE LIBRARY

And Then What Happened, Paul Revere? by Jean Fritz. NONFICTION: HISTORICAL AMERICAN

See the **Reader's Choice Library lesson plan** on pages T1414–T1415.

CHALLENGING

American Indian Children of the Past by Victoria Sherrow. Millbrook Press, 1997. NONFICTON: NATIVE AMERICANS

Buffalo Hunt by Russell Freedman. Holiday House, 1988.

NONFICTION: NATIVE AMERICANS

READER'S CHOICE LIBRARY

The Black Stallion by Walter Farley.

REALISTIC FICTION: COMING OF AGE

See the **Reader's Choice Library lesson plan** on pages T228–T229.

Building Background and Concepts

ESL

See *ESL Manual* pages 8–13. You may want to introduce these additional words and phrases:

give in (page 49)
odd (page 52)
make his way (page 54)
trial (page 55)
light on his feet (page 59)
passed (page 59)

OTHER BACKGROUND-BUILDING IDEAS

INTERNET Bonus Words and additional background ideas can be found on *The Learning Site* at **www.harcourtschool.com**

Access Prior Knowledge

Discuss listening. Ask students to suggest times when they might make a special effort to listen carefully. (Possible responses: when someone is giving directions or important information; when someone is speaking very quietly; when you are trying to hear a faint sound or a sound in the distance) Discuss the idea that a person might also concentrate on listening if he or she were in a dark place and having difficulty seeing. Suggest that students close their eyes and try to identify sounds they hear around them.

Develop Concepts

Make a predict-o-gram using vocabulary words. Have students complete a predict-o-gram that shows how each vocabulary word might be used in the story. Help them understand the meaning of any vocabulary word that is unfamiliar to them. Ask students to think about what each word might have to do with the setting, characters, problem, story events, or solution. Some words may be under more than one category. Have students provide support for their choices. Highlight indicates vocabulary.

Predict-o-Gram				
Setting	**Characters**	**Problem**	**Events**	**Solution**
moss	tread	exaggerate	exaggerate	compose
	sternly		quiver	

Explain that "Sees Behind Trees" is a story about a Native American boy who faces a great challenge.

BONUS WORDS

Introduce nature words. You may want to introduce to students these words that are mentioned in "Sees Behind Trees" that have to do with nature: *reed, clamshell, grapevine, hummingbird, gourds, hickory, trout.*

clamshell

gourds

hickory tree

trout

Introducing Vocabulary

Build Word Identification Strategies

Decode familiar patterns.

Display Transparency 7, and have volunteers read aloud the paragraph. Remind students that they may be able to figure out a word they don't know by looking for familiar patterns. Model using the strategy to decode the word *exaggerate*:

> (MODEL) **I notice that this word begins with the letters *ex*, like other words I know, such as *extra* and *excellent*. I also see that it ends in a pattern that I have seen in other words, such as *imitate* and *narrate*. The second *g* is followed by the vowel *e*, so I will try the soft sound for *g*. When I break the word into syllables and say it aloud, *ex/ag/ger/ate*, it sounds like a word I know.**

As students decode the other vocabulary, encourage them to confirm their pronunciations by asking questions like **Does the word sound right? Does it make sense?**

CHECK UNDERSTANDING

Practice other vocabulary strategies. Have students answer questions with sentences that show what the vocabulary words mean. MEANINGFUL SENTENCES

- **Why might a teacher speak sternly to a student?** EXAMPLE
- **What does moss look like?** DESCRIPTION
- **What word has a meaning similar to *footstep*?** SYNONYM
- **What word means the opposite of *fluster* or *disturb*?** ANTONYM
- **Why would a person carry a quiver?** EXPLANATION
- **Which word comes from the Latin word *exaggerare*, meaning "to heap up"? How does that meaning relate to the meaning of the vocabulary word?** WORD ORIGIN

QUICKWRITE

READING NOTEBOOK Have students write one or two sentences describing a time when it would be acceptable for a speaker or writer to *exaggerate*, and one or two sentences describing a situation when a speaker or writer should be careful not to *exaggerate*.

VOCABULARY

The boy moves through the forest carrying his arrows in a **quiver**. He listens carefully for the **tread** of a deer or the scurrying of a squirrel or rabbit. He notices that nothing has disturbed the **moss** growing on the log. His elders have taught him to use his senses well. More than once he has been **sternly** reminded that his life may depend on his paying close attention to every sound and movement in the forest. He knows that his elders do not **exaggerate**. So, if he begins to feel nervous or excited, he will quickly **compose** himself. Silently, he watches and listens and sniffs the air.

▲ **Teaching Transparency 7**

Name _____

▶ As you read each sentence, use context clues to determine the meaning of the boldfaced Vocabulary Word. Then, use the words to complete each analogy.

Kaitlyn's **tread** was so silent that nobody knew she was near.
Nick did not **exaggerate** how steep and rugged the hiking trail would be.
Kim noticed **moss** growing on the tree trunks and rocks.
The leader of the hike spoke commands **sternly** to keep everyone in order.
The archer pulled an arrow from the **quiver** on his back.
Before he drew the bowstring, he took a deep breath to **compose** himself.

1. *Happily* is to *gladly* as *strictly* is to _____ sternly
2. *Stir up* is to *excite* as *calm down* is to _____ compose
3. *Soil* is to *flower* as *tree trunk* is to _____ moss
4. *Hand* is to *touch* as *foot* is to _____ tread
5. *Paper* is to *briefcase* as *arrow* is to _____ quiver
6. *Whisper* is to *shout* as *understate* is to _____ exaggerate

▶ Read each definition. Write the correct word on the line.

7. in a strict manner _____ sternly
8. to overstate _____ exaggerate
9. way of walking _____ tread
10. tiny, flowerless plants _____ moss
11. to calm oneself _____ compose
12. a case for arrows _____ quiver

TRY THIS! Choose one Vocabulary Word. If the word is a noun, write three adjectives that could be used to describe it. If the word is a verb, write three adverbs that could be used to describe it. If the word is an adverb, write three verbs it could describe.

Pathways to Adventure **7**

▲ **Practice Book, page 7**

Sees Behind Trees **T65**

OBJECTIVE:

To understand how an author develops characters

Preteach
FOCUS SKILL Character Development

BEFORE READING

Preview the Literature

Preview the selection and discuss the genre.

Have students look at the illustrations and tell what they show about the characters. (They are Native Americans.) Then ask students to read silently the first three paragraphs on *Student Edition* page 48. Ask: **Do the story and illustrations seem to tell about a character, setting, and events that actually existed in the past?** Remind students that stories of this type are called *historical fiction*.

Introduce the Skill

Discuss character development.

Tell students that the way an author develops a character is called character development. Understanding a character's traits and personality helps readers understand and make predictions about his or her actions. Display Transparency 8 and have volunteers read aloud the introduction and the chart. Discuss the examples; then refer to "The Hot and Cold Summer." Ask students how those characters are developed.

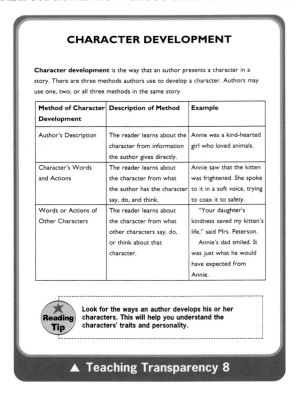

CHARACTER DEVELOPMENT

Character development is the way that an author presents a character in a story. There are three methods authors use to develop a character. Authors may use one, two, or all three methods in the same story.

Method of Character Development	Description of Method	Example
Author's Description	The reader learns about the character from information the author gives directly.	Annie was a kind-hearted girl who loved animals.
Character's Words and Actions	The reader learns about the character from what the author has the character say, do, and think.	Annie saw that the kitten was frightened. She spoke to it in a soft voice, trying to coax it to safety.
Words or Actions of Other Characters	The reader learns about the character from what other characters say, do, or think about that character.	"Your daughter's kindness saved my kitten's life," said Mrs. Peterson. Annie's dad smiled. It was just what he would have expected from Annie.

Reading Tip ★ Look for the ways an author develops his or her characters. This will help you understand the characters' traits and personality.

▲ Teaching Transparency 8

Model the Thinking

Model recognizing character development.

Read aloud and discuss with students the Reading Tip on Transparency 8. Then use the introduction and the first three paragraphs of the story on *Student Edition* page 48 to model recognizing character development.

 **I can tell that this story is told in the first person. That means that one of the characters is telling the story. From the character's own thoughts and actions, I think that this character doesn't see very well. I can also tell something about the mother from this character's thoughts, because the character thinks that the mother's voice sounds anxious and that she looks worried.**

Tell students that they will learn much more about the main character, who narrates the story, as well as other characters, as they continue reading.

DURING/AFTER READING

- Apply the Skill, pages T72, T76
- Practice the Skill, pages T90–T91

PRETEACH THE STRATEGY

FOCUS STRATEGY Use Prior Knowledge ★

Encourage students to monitor their comprehension.

Tell students that they can often use their own knowledge and experiences to help them understand a story. Ask volunteers how using their own experiences can help them when they are reading. (Possible response: Having been in a similar situation or having had the same feelings as a character can help you understand what is happening or why the character speaks or acts in a certain way.)

- Apply the Strategy, pages T70, T74, T80
- Return to the strategy, page T89

 See the Strategy Builder copying masters, pages A40–A45.

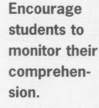

STRATEGIES GOOD READERS USE

- **Use Prior Knowledge** FOCUS STRATEGY
- Make and Confirm Predictions
- Adjust Reading Rate
- Self-Question
- Create Mental Images
- Use Context to Confirm Meaning
- Use Text Structure and Format
- Use Graphic Aids
- Use Reference Sources
- Read Ahead
- Reread
- Summarize and Paraphrase

Prereading Strategies

PREVIEW AND PREDICT

If students have not yet previewed the selection, they can look at the illustrations and read the title and the first three paragraphs on page 48. Ask them to make predictions. Point out that historical fiction is set in a real time and place in the past and may include actual historical figures and events as well as fictional ones. Have students begin a character development chart for "Sees Behind Trees." See *Practice Book* page 9.

Character Development Chart		
Character	What I Learned About This Character	How I Learned the Information
Walnut	trying to learn to shoot a bow; can't see well	character's own thoughts and actions
Walnut's mother	concerned about narrator; tries to help him	character's words and actions; narrator's thoughts

SET PURPOSE

Read to Appreciate the Writer's Craft

Ask students to set a purpose for reading. Remind them that one purpose for reading is to appreciate the writer's craft. If students have difficulty setting a purpose, offer this suggestion:

MODEL **In my preview, I noticed the author's interesting way of writing. For example, the narrator says the mother's voice snapped in his ear as loudly as the string of his bow. I'll read to enjoy the author's colorful use of language.**

46

Options for Reading

DIRECTED READING Use the **Monitor Comprehension** questions to check students' understanding. The **Guided Reading** strategies on pages T70, T72, T74, T76, and T80 provide support for students reading below or on level. WHOLE CLASS/SMALL GROUP	**COOPERATIVE READING** Students reading on or above level can focus on **author's craft** by using *Comprehension Card 6* (page R9). INDEPENDENT/SMALL GROUP 	**INDEPENDENT READING** As students read the selection silently, have them add information to their character development charts. After reading, use the questions on page T82 to stimulate discussion. INDIVIDUAL/WHOLE CLASS

SEES BEHIND TREES

by Michael Dorris

illustrated by Rocco Baviera

Teachers' Choice
SLJ Best Book
Booklist Editors' Choice
Notable Trade Book for
the Language Arts

47

SKILLS IN CONTEXT

Informal Assessment

INTERVENTION STRATEGIES

MODIFIED INSTRUCTION Have students read the title, "Sees Behind Trees," and tell what they see in the illustrations on pages 46–49. Discuss these story words:

sash embarrass ability dense

Ask students to read through page 51 to find out whether the boy learns to shoot the bow.

EASY READER Students may read **"The Quiver,"** found on pages 14–21 in *Timeless Tales*. See *Timeless Tales Intervention Reader Teacher's Guide*, pages 8–13.

"Sees Behind Trees" and the accompanying poems are available on *Literature Cassette 1*.

Monitor Comprehension

❶ Why is it so important for Walnut to learn to shoot a bow?
(Possible response: In his culture a boy must learn this skill to become a man.)
LITERAL/INFERENTIAL: CAUSE-EFFECT

❷ What do you think Walnut means when he says that his name "was tired, pounded into flour" in his mother's mouth?
(Possible response: When his mother says his name, it sounds over-used because she has said it so often.)
INFERENTIAL: UNDERSTAND FIGURATIVE LANGUAGE

❸ When Walnut says "Now we had to solve the problem," what problem does he mean? (Possible response: the fact that he has difficulty seeing things unless they are very close to him) INFERENTIAL: IMPORTANT DETAILS

Guided Reading

STRATEGIES GOOD READERS USE

FOCUS STRATEGY **Use Prior Knowledge** If students have difficulty understanding the author's use of figurative language, discuss in a small group how using prior knowledge to interpret the meaning can help.

MODEL **Walnut says that his name is tired, pounded into flour. I know that flour is made by grinding wheat until the grains are small. I think Walnut means that his name is like pounded grains because his mother has said it many times.**

"**T**RY HARDER. TRACK IT with your eye before you shoot."

My mother's anxious voice snapped in my ear as loudly as the string of my bow.

"Track what?" I asked for the third time this morning. Before me all I could see was the familiar blur of green and brown that meant I was outside in the forest on a sunny day. Then, by squinting, I could sense something coming toward me, smell the familiar pemmican scent of berries mixed with dried meat, recognize the tread of moccasins I had heard a thousand times before. Gradually one blurry image began to stand out from all the others and an instant later it turned into my approaching mother. When she was close enough for me to touch, I could tell from her face and from the tenseness of her body that she was worried.

"This," she said, shaking the clump of moss that she held in one hand. In the other were the four arrows I had already shot, which she dropped at my feet. "When I throw the moss in the air, imagine its flight and then aim where you think it will be by the time your arrow meets it. It's not so hard, and every boy must learn how to do it before he can become a man."

A rumbling noise came from my stomach and my mother smiled her I've-got-an-idea smile. "Think of the moss as your breakfast," she suggested. "Imagine it is a corn cake, hot from the ashes, soooo delicious."

48

SOCIAL STUDIES

NATIVE AMERICAN INFLUENCES Point out the words *pemmican* and *moccasins* on page 48. Explain that Native Americans traditionally made pemmican by drying deer meat, pounding it into a paste with melted fat and fruit, and forming the mixture into loaves or cakes. Pemmican is nutritious and doesn't easily spoil, so it is now made as a survival food. Explain that the English word *moccasin* is from the Algonquian language and describes shoes or boots similar to the moccasins made and worn by Native Americans.

pemmican ▶   moccasins ▶

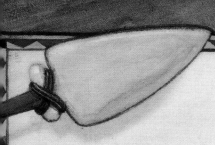

I could almost taste it on my tongue, feel its crunch as I bit down, smell the sweet fullness it would bring. "Couldn't I eat first, just this once?" I pleaded. "I'm sure I could find the moss in the sky if I weren't so hungry."

For a moment I thought my mother would give in, and I leaned toward her, blinking as though a steaming golden corn cake would appear in her hand to replace the straggly plant. But all that changed was my mother's expression.

"Walnut." My name in her mouth was tired, pounded into flour. "You know the rule: you must find the target before breakfast can find you."

I nodded. If that was the rule, I wouldn't eat for a long time. We had faced this matter of what I couldn't see many times before— when my mother would point to something I couldn't locate or throw a ball I couldn't catch—

but it had never before been such serious business. Now we couldn't just act as though nothing was wrong. Now we had to solve the problem. We had struggled with it every morning since, three days ago, my mother had decided it was time to teach me, her oldest child, how to use a bow and arrow. I had never once succeeded and I knew that sooner or later she would give up, make some excuse, and feed me. But it would not be soon.

"Maybe if you made your eyes smaller?" My mother encouraged me by bringing her cheeks so close to her forehead that she looked like a dried onion, and I made the mistake of laughing.

"Today . . . ," my mother said in the same voice she had used when I was younger and she told me not to play with sharp knives. She picked up an arrow from the ground and sternly held it out for me to take. She walked back toward the place where she threw the moss into the air. "Today, we will *not* surrender." Before I could object she had

49

REACHING ALL LEARNERS

ESL

UNUSUAL WORDS   Call attention to the way Walnut describes his mother's smile on pages 48–49. Point out to students that the word before *smile* consists of four words with hyphens between them. Ask students to show how they might give an I've-got-an-idea smile if they had a good idea. Then point out the spelling of the word *soooo* on page 49. Tell students that the word *so* is sometimes spelled with extra *o*'s to show that the speaker is drawing out the word. Pronounce *soooo* in a drawn-out way, and then have students do the same.

Monitor Comprehension

1 **Why does Walnut say that laughing at his mother is a mistake?** (Possible response: She is serious about what she is saying.) INFERENTIAL: DRAW CONCLUSIONS

2 **What did you learn about Walnut from his thoughts about the many other things he can do?** (Possible response: He has many skills and talents, including a good memory and keen senses of smell and hearing.) **FOCUS SKILL** INFERENTIAL: CHARACTER DEVELOPMENT

3 **How does Brings the Deer feel about Walnut? How do you know?** (Possible response: He cares about him. Walnut describes his voice as gentle and understanding. Brings the Deer's words and actions show that he wants to help Walnut.) **FOCUS SKILL** INFERENTIAL/ METACOGNITIVE: CHARACTER DEVELOPMENT

Guided Reading

STRATEGIES GOOD READERS USE

Summarize and Paraphrase If students have difficulty telling what they learned about Walnut, discuss how summarizing and paraphrasing can help them understand what they read. Ask these questions:

- **What are the main things Walnut thinks about?**
- **How would you describe what Walnut is able to do without changing the meaning?**

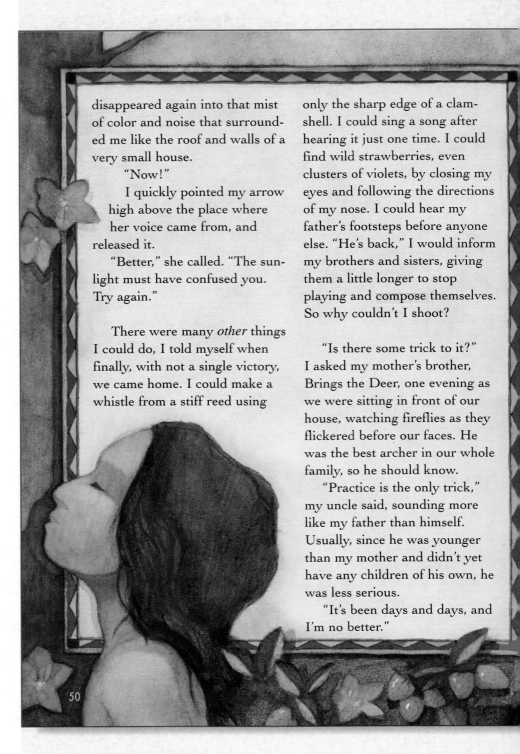

disappeared again into that mist of color and noise that surrounded me like the roof and walls of a very small house.

"Now!"

I quickly pointed my arrow high above the place where her voice came from, and released it.

"Better," she called. "The sunlight must have confused you. Try again."

There were many *other* things I could do, I told myself when finally, with not a single victory, we came home. I could make a whistle from a stiff reed using only the sharp edge of a clamshell. I could sing a song after hearing it just one time. I could find wild strawberries, even clusters of violets, by closing my eyes and following the directions of my nose. I could hear my father's footsteps before anyone else. "He's back," I would inform my brothers and sisters, giving them a little longer to stop playing and compose themselves. So why couldn't I shoot?

"Is there some trick to it?" I asked my mother's brother, Brings the Deer, one evening as we were sitting in front of our house, watching fireflies as they flickered before our faces. He was the best archer in our whole family, so he should know.

"Practice is the only trick," my uncle said, sounding more like my father than himself. Usually, since he was younger than my mother and didn't yet have any children of his own, he was less serious.

"It's been days and days, and I'm no better."

50

AUTHOR'S CRAFT

SIMILES Have students recall why Walnut laughs at the face his mother makes. (She looked like a dried onion.) Explain that the author is describing Walnut's mother's face by comparing it with something different, a dried onion. Then have students locate the passage on page 50 that describes how the mist of color and noise around him feels to Walnut. (like the roof and walls of a very small house) Discuss the comparison and how the author's use of figurative language helps readers understand how Walnut feels.

"Maybe . . ." Brings the Deer's tone was gentler, more understanding. "Maybe your bowstring is not tight enough?" He reached over to where it rested by my leg and tested it. "No, it seems all right. Maybe you're closing your eyes at the last moment before you shoot? *I* did that myself when I first started."

I shook my head.

"Maybe . . . How many fingers am I holding up?"

I tipped my head. The dusky light was dim, but I could still see my own hands, balled into fists. "Fingers?"

"How many?"

I couldn't tell how many arms he was holding up, much less fingers. "Three?" I guessed.

"How many now?"

"Two?"

"Now?"

"Five?"

There was a silence. "Walnut, I was holding up no fingers at all."

"I knew that," I said, though it wasn't true. "I was making a joke."

But Brings the Deer didn't laugh.

The next morning when my mother woke me for shooting practice, we went to a new part of the forest. That was only the first odd thing.

"Put down your bow and sit on this rock," my mother said, patting a large flat stone at the base of a pine tree. Then, from her sack she brought out a tightly woven sash, placed it over my eyes, and tied it with a length of grapevine.

51

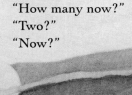

SKILLS IN CONTEXT

GRAMMAR

SKILL TRACE	
Introduce	T52–T53
Review	T73

Declarative and Interrogative Sentences

TEACH/MODEL

Ask students to tell what kind of a sentence this is: *He was the best archer in our whole family, so he should know.* (declarative) Remind them that a declarative sentence makes a statement and ends with a period. Next, read aloud this sentence: *"How many fingers am I holding up?"* Model how to identify the kind of sentence it is:

MODEL **When I read "How many fingers am I holding up?" I see that the sentence is asking something and ends with a question mark. This tells me it is an interrogative sentence.**

PRACTICE/APPLY

Have students look through the story to identify examples of each type of sentence.

REACHING ALL LEARNERS

INTERVENTION STRATEGIES

MODIFIED INSTRUCTION Help students summarize the story so far: Walnut tries to shoot the moss with his arrow, but each time he misses. He thinks about other things that he can do well and wonders why he can't shoot. He asks his mother's brother, Brings the Deer, about it. Brings the Deer suggests a few reasons and then he asks Walnut to tell him how many fingers he is holding up.

Help students set a purpose for reading through page 55. (to find out whether Brings the Deer will be able to help Walnut)

Monitor Comprehension

1 **Why might Walnut have pretended he was joking with Brings the Deer?** (Possible responses: He is embarrassed. He doesn't want Brings the Deer to know that he can't see how many fingers his uncle is holding up.)
CRITICAL: INTERPRET CHARACTER'S MOTIVATIONS

2 **Why does Walnut's mother tie the sash over his eyes?** (Possible responses: so he can concentrate on the sounds and smells; so he will use just his ears and nose) INFERENTIAL: DRAW CONCLUSIONS

3 **What does Walnut's mother mean when she tells him to look with his ears?** (Possible response: to describe by listening instead of by looking) CRITICAL: AUTHOR'S CRAFT/INTERPRET IMAGERY

Guided Reading

STRATEGIES GOOD READERS USE

FOCUS STRATEGY **Use Prior Knowledge** If students cannot explain why Walnut might have pretended he was joking, use these prompts to help them apply their own knowledge of similar situations:

• **Think about a time when you or someone you know tried to turn a serious situation into a joke.**

• **How did you feel? Do you think Walnut might feel the same way?**

"What are you doing?" I wanted to know.

"Shhh," she said. "Describe this place to me."

"But I've never been here before and I can't see."

"Shhh," she said again. "Look with your ears."

At first, there was nothing to hear—just . . . forest. But the longer we didn't talk, the more separate parts announced themselves: the hush of a brook just behind me and, farther beyond that, the rush of a river. The buzz of a beehive on a tree not far over to my right. The beat of a hummingbird's wings as it dove in and out of a cluster of . . . what was that smell? . . . *roses* near where my mother—who, I could tell, had just oiled her hair this morning—sat.

"Don't move," I said as I heard her prepare to shift her weight. "It's only a hummingbird."

52

SCIENCE

HUMMINGBIRDS Have students recall the kind of bird that Walnut hears. (hummingbird) Invite students to tell what they know about hummingbirds. You may want to share the following information:

• The smallest of all types of birds are in the hummingbird family. Many species are less than 3 inches (8 cm) long.
• Hummingbirds have long tongues that they use to reach inside flowers to feed on nectar and insects.
• Hummingbirds are the only birds able to fly backward.

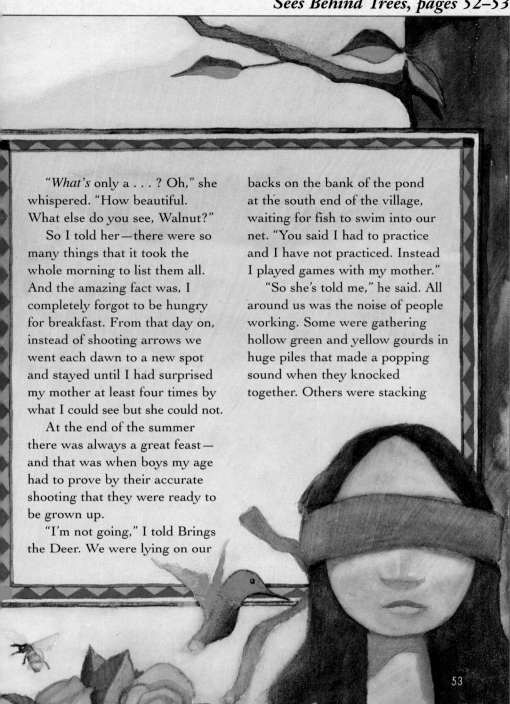

"*What's* only a . . . ? Oh," she whispered. "How beautiful. What else do you see, Walnut?"

So I told her—there were so many things that it took the whole morning to list them all. And the amazing fact was, I completely forgot to be hungry for breakfast. From that day on, instead of shooting arrows we went each dawn to a new spot and stayed until I had surprised my mother at least four times by what I could see but she could not.

At the end of the summer there was always a great feast— and that was when boys my age had to prove by their accurate shooting that they were ready to be grown up.

"I'm not going," I told Brings the Deer. We were lying on our backs on the bank of the pond at the south end of the village, waiting for fish to swim into our net. "You said I had to practice and I have not practiced. Instead I played games with my mother."

"So she's told me," he said. All around us was the noise of people working. Some were gathering hollow green and yellow gourds in huge piles that made a popping sound when they knocked together. Others were stacking

53

CHALLENGE

POETIC LANGUAGE   Call attention to the paragraph on page 53 in which Walnut begins to describe the forest, beginning with the words *At first . . . .* Ask students to think about how the author uses sound devices, such as rhyme, alliteration, and onomatopoeia, to make the passage seem poetic and lyrical. Point out the subtle rhyme of *hush* and *rush*; the alliteration of *rush* and *river*, and of *buzz*, *beehive*, and *beat*; and the fact that *hush*, *rush*, and *buzz* are also onomatopoeic.

" . . . the rush of a river "
▲ alliteration

Monitor Comprehension

1 **How does the author show how Walnut feels about the feast?** (Possible response: through Walnut's words) **FOCUS SKILL** INFERENTIAL: CHARACTER DEVELOPMENT

2 **What is Brings the Deer talking about when he says his sister did not exaggerate? How do you know?** (Possible response: She did not exaggerate about Walnut's hearing. He says this after Walnut hears his father and Brings the Deer does not.) INFERENTIAL/METACOGNITIVE: DRAW CONCLUSIONS

3 **How do you think Walnut will feel about having to do an extra, harder trial?** (Possible response: more discouraged than he is already) INFERENTIAL: MAKE PREDICTIONS

Guided Reading

STRATEGIES GOOD READERS USE

Reread To help students figure out what Brings the Deer means, suggest that they reread. Use this model:

(MODEL) **It doesn't make sense that Brings the Deer would be talking about the feathers, so I go back and reread. Walnut's father has arrived and Walnut heard him, but Brings the Deer did not. Walnut's mother must have told her brother about Walnut's hearing, and that's what he is talking about.**

firewood—I could hear them stumbling up with their arms full, dropping the load with a rolling crash, and then the even tap-tap-tap of setting the logs straight. Even Brings the Deer was replacing the old bluebird feathers on his fancy headband with new ones. From off to one side I picked up the rich hickory smell of stewing venison.

"My father will be ashamed." My best friend Frog was, I knew, even now out somewhere practicing his aim. I didn't know why he was nervous—he told me that he had been able to shoot moss out of the air on his very first try.

"Have you asked him?"

"Who, Frog?" Had even Brings the Deer heard of Frog's talent?

"Your father. Have you talked to him about this?"

"No, but . . . he's coming now."

Brings the Deer stood up and looked all around. "Where?"

"On the other side of the pond," I told him, just as my father called our names.

"Walnut? Brings the Deer? Where are you?"

"I see him now," said my uncle. "Over here," he yelled.

While we waited for my father—he walked like a beaver, his feet flat and wide apart—to make his way over to us, Brings the Deer sat next to me and shook his head. "It's amazing," he laughed, and admired the design of the new feathers. "My sister did not exaggerate."

Before I could say anything, my father burst from the rest of the colors around us and sat down on my stomach.

"Ah," he sighed, and stretched his arms. "A dry, comfortable seat at last."

"I can't breathe!" I tried to shove him off me, but he was too heavy.

"How very strange," my father said to Brings the Deer. "I thought I heard my son speak from inside my own body."

"Yes," Brings the Deer replied. "It's what a bird must feel when she sits on her nest after the chicks hatch."

"I am sinking into the mud," I muttered, and poked my father beneath his ribs with my finger.

54

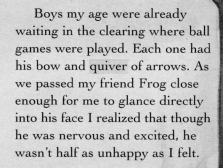

Why was he being so playful, as if I were still a very little boy?

"What's this? What's this?" he cried, cocking his head and jumping up. "Walnut, what are you doing down there? Come home quickly. The contests are going to start early."

"Father . . . ," I began. How I hated to embarrass him.

"No time for talking. This year there is going to be an extra trial, *much* harder."

"Harder than hitting a target?" I might as well stay in the mud instead of cleaning up.

Boys my age were already waiting in the clearing where ball games were played. Each one had his bow and quiver of arrows. As we passed my friend Frog close enough for me to glance directly into his face I realized that though he was nervous and excited, he wasn't half as unhappy as I felt.

55

REACHING ALL LEARNERS

INTERVENTION STRATEGIES

MODIFIED INSTRUCTION Model summarizing the story to this point:

MODEL Walnut's guess about how many fingers Brings the Deer is holding up is wrong. The next morning Walnut's mother ties a <u>sash</u> over his eyes and asks him what he hears. Every morning they do this. It is almost time for the yearly feast, when the boys Walnut's age must show they can shoot their bows. Walnut doesn't want to go because he can't shoot. He is afraid he will <u>embarrass</u> his father.

Help students set a purpose for reading to the end of the story. (to find out what happens at the feast)

Monitor Comprehension

1 **How does Walnut feel when he gets to the clearing? How do you know? Does this confirm your prediction about how he would feel about the new trial?** (Possible responses: unhappy, worried, having no hope of success; says he might as well stay in the mud, realizes he is much more unhappy than Frog, worries that his mother will be criticized)
INFERENTIAL/METACOGNITIVE: DETERMINE CHARACTERS' EMOTIONS/CONFIRM PREDICTIONS

2 **How does the author help you imagine the sound of the weroance's voice?** (Possible response: describes it as slow and booming, from deep within her body, like the sound of a horn or a drum) CRITICAL: AUTHOR'S CRAFT/APPRECIATE LANGUAGE

3 **What do you predict the new contest might be? What information are you using to make your prediction?** (Possible response: It will have something to do with using senses other than sight; the weroance says they need someone who can see what can't be seen.) INFERENTIAL: MAKE PREDICTIONS

56

WORD STUDY

WEROANCE   Have students use context to tell what *weroance* means. (most important person) Explain that the Powhatan people of Virginia used *weroance* as a name for their chiefs. Among other Native American peoples, the word may have meant "leading man in a tribe," "a king or great lord," or "a woman queen." Scholars believe that *weroance* may have come from *wilaw,* meaning "rich, valuable, precious" and *antesi,* meaning "exist, get along, have such a manner of life."

wilaw + antesi = weroance

The flat afternoon sun made the colors of the earth and rocks as bright as if they were wet. There was no wind to stir the branches of the trees and give me an excuse for missing my shots. The sky was the pale, shiny blue of a trout's scale.

Brings the Deer gave my arm a squeeze and then went over to join the crowd of adults and small children watching in the shade nearby. I was sure my mother must be among them. I wondered what she was thinking. When people learned she hadn't taught me how to shoot, they might criticize her. Ay-yah-yah.

The weroance, our most important person, the expert on hunting, stood nearby. She raised her hands for quiet, and when everyone was still, she spoke in the slow, booming voice she saved for the most solemn moments. It seemed to come from deep within her body, to be blown through a horn of shell, to rattle like the skin of a hand drum.

"Sometimes," she said, "the people need someone to do the impossible. As necessary as hunting is, as necessary as growing and harvesting plants, sometimes we need even more than those tasks can provide. We need someone with the ability to see what can't be seen. And we won't have the regular contest until someone passes this new one."

There was a silence, then all the boys around me began to whisper to one another.

"What does she mean?" worried one.

"How can they expect us to do that?" another demanded. "Isn't it enough that our mothers have taught us how to shoot moss from the sky?"

"So," the weroance went on steady as the beat of a large bird's wings, "the first test will be for . . . "

57

ESL

EXPRESSING EMOTIONS Point out the word *Ay-yah-yah* on page 56. Explain to students that different cultures may use different words to represent sounds that people make when they are unhappy or upset about something. The author uses this word to show how Walnut would feel if people criticized his mother. Have students pronounce the word in an expressive way. Tell students that words also express happy sounds, such as *ha-ha* in English. Ask students to share words for happy sounds in their first language.

DECODING/PHONICS

SKILL TRACE	
Introduce	Grade 2
Maintain	T79

Vowel Variant: /ô/

TEACH/MODEL

Write the following sentences on the board:

Boys my age were <u>already</u> waiting in the clearing where <u>ball</u> games were played.

When people learned she hadn't <u>taught</u> me how to shoot, they might criticize her.

Have volunteers read the sentences aloud and identify the vowel sound they hear in the three underlined words. (/ô/) Point out that the /ô/ sound can be spelled with *a* followed by *l* or *ll* and can also be spelled *augh*. Then write this sentence on the board:

I thought the audience would yawn.

Have students identify three words with the /ô/ sound spelled three different ways. (*thought, ough; audience, au; yawn, aw*) Remind them to try the /ô/ sound when they are trying to decode words with these letter patterns.

PRACTICE/APPLY

Have students record the words with the /ô/ sound in a chart like the one below. Challenge them to find ten more words with the same sound and record those words in the appropriate columns.

al, all	au	augh	ough	aw
already	audience	taught	thought	yawn
ball	(cause)	(caught)	(brought)	(awful)
(although)	(fault)	(naughty)	(bought)	(crawl)
(small)				

Monitor Comprehension

① **How are the children's names different from the adults' names?**
(Possible response: The children have short names like Walnut and Frog. The adults have names that tell something about them.) INFERENTIAL: COMPARE AND CONTRAST

② **Were your predictions about the new contest confirmed? Why do you think the weroance decides to have this contest?** (Possible response: because she knows that Walnut will not pass the shooting test but has a special ability) INFERENTIAL/CRITICAL: CONFIRM PREDICTIONS/INTERPRET STORY EVENTS

③ **Do you think the weroance will give Walnut a grown-up name? If so, what name might it be?**
(Possible response: yes; perhaps Sees Behind Trees, the title of the story) INFERENTIAL: MAKE PREDICTIONS/SPECULATE

Guided Reading

STRATEGIES GOOD READERS USE

FOCUS STRATEGY **Use Prior Knowledge** If students have difficulty suggesting a name for Walnut, help them use prior knowledge. Ask these questions:

• In the story, how do children get their grown-up names?
• What can Walnut do that might earn him a grown-up name?
• In your experience, do story titles often refer to things that are very important in the story?

I missed what she said because something fell at my feet. I looked down—it was the sash and a length of grapevine. My mother must have tossed it.

"See behind *trees*?" Frog repeated the weroance's words, and the boy next to me looked toward the forest uncertainly.

But I knew what to do. I tied the sash around my eyes and remained very still. The wind made fingers through the trees and I used them to feel my way in each direction. My mind flew the way a hawk must fly, skimming over all that was ordinary, alert for a dart of something out of place. I paid no attention to the rustle of leaves or the rain of a waterfall. Those expected sounds—those sounds I knew from all my morning games with my mother—I put to one side, and waited.

What was that? A dead branch snapped. A rock, slightly closer, tumbled down a hill. A breath was drawn in.

"Who will begin?" The weroance interrupted my ears. "You," she said.

And Frog tried, without much hope, "I see a raccoon. He is asleep in the bough of a tree."

"You," she said. Another voice, Sleeps Late, no more confident, answered. "I see a . . . spiderweb, strung on the brambles of a mulberry bush."

"Now you," she said, but this time there was no reply. "You. Walnut."

58

CULTURAL CONNECTIONS

NAMES Point out that in many Native American cultures children are given names that reflect special abilities or that have to do with their family. In many other cultures, names are given to honor elders or deceased family members. Have students discuss how people in their cultures get their names.

I thought so hard that my head felt tight between my ears. I was afraid to make a mistake in front of so many people, but then I pretended it was my mother asking me to listen, curious and interested as she had been every morning.

"A man is coming from the south," I said. "He is light on his feet but has a limp. He is not young, for he must breathe hard to climb. He is . . ." I stopped talking, shut my eyes even behind my blindfold, and concentrated. There was no mistaking it. "He is laughing! It is Gray Fire!"

I heard people turning to look behind me, whispering among themselves. I could almost *feel* them looking to see if I was right. That part of the forest was dense, the paths overgrown and winding.

"There!" Brings the Deer's voice was loud above the rest. "It is, it *is* Gray Fire!" The weroance's brother! He had been given his name because he was so quiet he could pass through the village like smoke.

Strong hands untied the vine that bound the sash around my eyes. My father's hands. They lingered for just an instant on my hair. I'm sure no one else but me noticed.

"This part of the contest is over," the weroance announced. "Each boy except the one who passed must now prove himself with a bow in order to earn the right to his grown-up name."

"And what of the boy who passed?" my mother called out from where she stood. "What about my Walnut?"

"When a boy passes the test he is no longer a boy," the weroance answered. "He no longer wears a boy's name."

59

INTERVENTION STRATEGIES

MODIFIED INSTRUCTION   Help students summarize the story:

- Walnut can't shoot a bow because he has trouble seeing. He has the <u>ability</u> to hear and smell things better than others.
- He is afraid that he will not pass the test that proves he is ready to be grown up and that he will not be given a grown-up name.
- A new test is included this year—one that only Walnut can pass. He alone hears Gray Fire coming through the <u>dense</u> forest. He receives his grown-up name, Sees Behind Trees.

Discuss the idea that this story demonstrates that each person has his or her own special abilities.

SKILLS IN CONTEXT

DECODING/PHONICS
TESTED SKILL

Prefixes and Suffixes

SKILL TRACE	
Introduce	T20, T46
Reteach	R2
Review 1	T81
Review 2	T163
Test	Theme 1
Maintain	T273

TEACH/MODEL

Point out the word *uncertainly* on page 58. Explain that it contains two word parts—the prefix *un-*, which means "not," and the suffix *-ly*, which means "in that way." Ask students to speculate on the meaning of *uncertainly*. Model the thinking:

> MODEL   **When I'm not sure what a word means, I can use the prefix and suffix to help figure it out. When I put the meanings of *un-* + *certain* + *-ly* together, I figure out that *uncertainly* means "in a way that is not certain."**

PRACTICE/APPLY

Have students find other words in the story with *un-* and *-ly*. (*slightly, untied*) Remind them to be sure the letters at the beginning or end of a word are really a prefix or suffix.

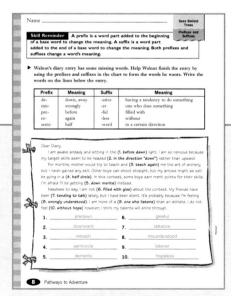

▲ **Practice Book, page 8**

Literary Response

RETURN TO THE PREDICTIONS/PURPOSE

Were your predictions about the characters and events in "Sees Behind Trees" confirmed? If you changed your predictions, at what point did you revise them? Discuss with students whether their purpose for reading was met.

APPRECIATING THE LITERATURE

Were you satisfied with the ending of the story? Why or why not?
(Responses will vary.)

Think About It

1 **What important lesson do the boys learn when Walnut receives his new name?** (Possible responses: What you can do is more important than what you can't do. Everyone has something to contribute.) INFERENTIAL: SUMMARIZING/THEME CONNECTION

2 **What does this story say about people's different strengths?** (Possible responses: that everyone has different talents and abilities; that we should look for and value people's different strengths) CRITICAL: PERSONAL RESPONSE

3 **Why do you think there is an extra trial at the feast this year?** (Possible response: Walnut's mother or uncle may have told the weroance about his talent.) CRITICAL: LITERARY ANALYSIS

Everyone stopped what they were doing to hear what she would say next. I turned the sash in my hand, the sash my mother had woven. It was soft to the touch, as if it had been made from silky moss.

"Sees Behind Trees," the weroance pronounced, "is now a young man."

Think About It

1 What important lesson do the boys learn when Walnut receives his new name?

2 What does this story say about people's different strengths?

3 Why do you think there is an extra trial at the feast this year?

60

About the Author
Michael Dorris

Michael Dorris was a member of the Modoc Indians on his father's side of the family. He said, "I lived on a reservation part of the time when I was a child, so I knew my Indian relatives. That part of my background was front and center." He also read a lot when he was young. He said, "The thing I like about reading is that it puts you in charge. You can stop and start, you can reread something, and you can imagine what the characters and places look like. When you read, you're a participant in the story. When you're watching television, you're not."

61

Informal Assessment

RETELL
Have each student retell the story. Monitor whether the student

☐ includes the story elements.

☐ evaluates the author's perspectives, intent, or craft in creating the text.

☐ uses phrases, language, or vocabulary from the text.

☐ shows understanding of characters' feelings and actions.

SUMMARIZE
Ask students to summarize the story by completing the character development chart. See *Practice Book* page 9.

ONE-SENTENCE SUMMARY   Have students use their completed character development chart to write a brief summary statement of "Sees Behind Trees."

▲ **Practice Book, page 9**

ABOUT THE AUTHOR

MICHAEL DORRIS celebrated his Native American heritage in his writings for young people and adults, but the many and varied awards he received show that his characters and themes are universal. He was a professor at Dartmouth College for many years, served as a consultant to several television stations, and appeared on radio and television programs. Discuss the opinion Michael Dorris expressed about the pleasure of reading compared to watching television. Ask whether students agree with his comments, and why or why not.

 INTERNET   Additional author information can be found on *The Learning Site* at **www.harcourtschool.com**

Companion Selection

INTRODUCE THE POEMS

Ask students what special ability Sees Behind Trees developed. (to listen carefully; to hear things that no one else heard) Then tell students that they are going to read three poems about sounds. Have students look at pages 62–63 and tell what they notice about the poems. (The first one has an unusual shape. All are short.)

APPRECIATING THE POEMS

Have students read the poems silently several times in order to understand their meaning and to appreciate their forms. Then reread the poems aloud to students, and ask the following questions:

① **What shapes do the words form in "When Birds Remember"?**

(Possible responses: a tree; a flock of birds flying away) INFERENTIAL: POET'S CRAFT/IMPORTANT DETAILS

② **In what ways are these poems similar to and different from each other?** (Possible responses: "When Birds Remember" and "Limerick" are both about birds and they contrast sound and silence. "When Birds Remember" and "Haiku" both describe sounds. All three are about listening.)

INFERENTIAL: COMPARE AND CONTRAST

REREADING FOR A PURPOSE

Have students do a choral reading of "When Birds Remember." Encourage them to read sound words, such as *cheeping* and *squeaking*, in a way that calls each sound to mind and to read the words *sudden silence* in hushed voices.

LISTENING/SPEAKING/READING

▼ POETRY

Sounds of Nature
Three Poems

SHAPE POEM
When Birds Remember
by Robert Froman
lettering by Ray Barber

Birds in a tight cloud flying off on an important errand they had almost forgotten about.

Sudden Silence

Birds scattered in a tree top cheeping twiting fluttering scratching fluttering twitching clucking twittering squeaking fidgeting. chirping whistling flitting rustling Pecking trilling

62

POET'S CRAFT

POETRY FORMS Discuss with students the three types of poems on these pages. Have them identify each type of poem. Students should recognize that a shape poem or concrete poem may be shaped like an object and that the shape is part of the poem's meaning. A haiku is a form of Japanese poetry that presents a clear image in very brief form. A limerick consists of five lines and is usually humorous. Lines 1, 2, and 5 rhyme with each other. Lines 3 and 4 are shorter and also rhyme with each other.

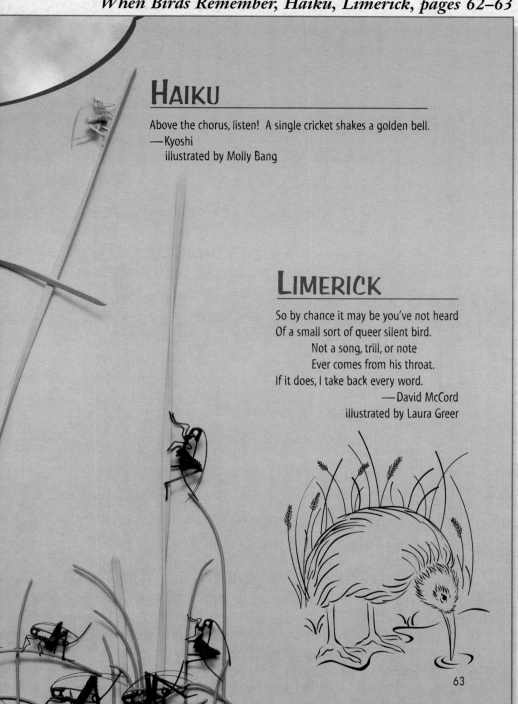

HAIKU

Above the chorus, listen! A single cricket shakes a golden bell.
—Kyoshi
illustrated by Molly Bang

LIMERICK

So by chance it may be you've not heard
Of a small sort of queer silent bird.
Not a song, trill, or note
Ever comes from his throat.
If it does, I take back every word.
—David McCord
illustrated by Laura Greer

63

My Notes

ABOUT THE POETS

ROBERT FROMAN has written more than twenty books, mostly about science and mathematics. "When Birds Remember" appeared in his second book of poetry for young readers. He says that the poems in this book "began as a sort of free-wheeling haiku" and grew from there into the shapes of things.

SYLVIA CASSEDY and **KUNIHIRO SUETAKE** have translated many haiku from Japanese, including this one by **KYOSHI**. They suggest that you read haiku very slowly. "As you let each phrase add to the scene developing in your mind, a haiku will seem like a gem that breaks into hundreds of sparkling fragments of light when held against the sun."

Activity Choices

A NEW NAME

Design a T-Shirt   After students have sketched their designs, you may want to provide large sheets of paper that they can cut in the shape and size of actual T-shirts. String a clothesline across the room to display the completed T-shirts.
CREATIVE: ART

A FRIEND IN NEED

Role-Play a Situation   To help students focus on situations in which keen senses of hearing and smell would be particularly helpful, suggest that they think of times when it might be difficult or impossible to see where one is going or to use the sense of sight to figure out something.   CREATIVE: DRAMA

USING OTHER SENSES

Design a Product   Students might work in pairs or small groups on this project. Some may be interested in using reference materials or the Internet to research products that are already available to people with varying levels of visual impairment.   CREATIVE: WRITING

MAKING CONNECTIONS

Write a Review   Encourage students to discuss the poems with classmates. Partners might take turns reading the poems aloud while the other person listens with his or her eyes closed.
CRITICAL/CREATIVE: CONNECT IDEAS ACROSS TEXTS/WRITING

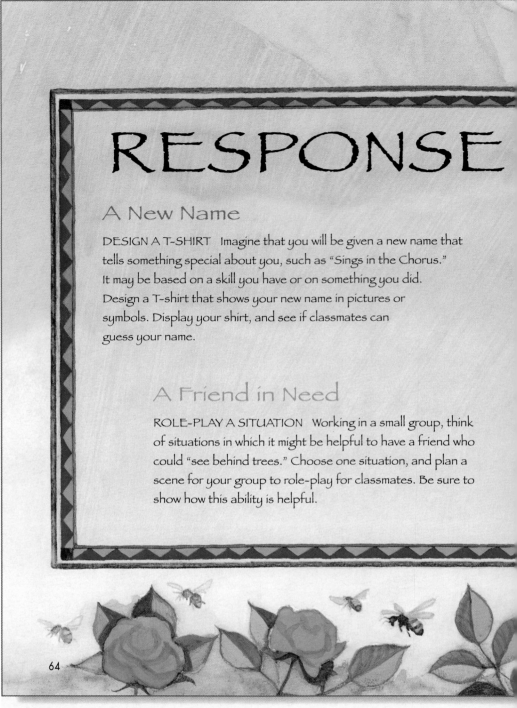

RESPONSE

A New Name

DESIGN A T-SHIRT   Imagine that you will be given a new name that tells something special about you, such as "Sings in the Chorus." It may be based on a skill you have or on something you did. Design a T-shirt that shows your new name in pictures or symbols. Display your shirt, and see if classmates can guess your name.

A Friend in Need

ROLE-PLAY A SITUATION   Working in a small group, think of situations in which it might be helpful to have a friend who could "see behind trees." Choose one situation, and plan a scene for your group to role-play for classmates. Be sure to show how this ability is helpful.

64

SCHOOL-HOME CONNECTION

Suggest that students work together with family members to complete the activities on the copying master on page R16. If you want, some or all of the activities may be assigned as homework during the week.

Copying Master, page R16 ▶

ACTIVITIES

Using Other Senses

DESIGN A PRODUCT Design a new product to help people who cannot see well. Your invention should allow people to use senses other than sight to do something they cannot see well enough to do. Write a brief description of your product, and include diagrams or sketches.

Making Connections

WRITE A REVIEW Suppose that Walnut read the three poems, "Haiku," "When Birds Remember," and "Limerick." What might he say about these poems? From his point of view, write one or more sentences about each poem, expressing his thoughts about it.

65

REACHING ALL LEARNERS

INTERVENTION STRATEGIES

HELP A FRIEND Some students may need help completing the Using Other Senses activity. Have students think about these ideas:

- Suppose you had a friend who couldn't see well enough to shoot a bow but who could hear very well. Can you think of something else your friend might have trouble doing, besides shooting a bow?
- How could you help your friend do something that might be difficult for him or her?
- Write or draw to show how you could help your friend.

Building Literacy Skills

REREADING FOR FLUENCY

Dramatization

Assign pairs or small groups of students to reread and dramatize scenes from "Sees Behind Trees." For example, two students can play the roles of Walnut and his mother in the first scene of the story. Two students can play the roles of Walnut and Brings the Deer in the scene where they are lying by the pond. After each pair or group presents its scene, have the class compare the dramatized version with the text version.

LISTENING/SPEAKING/

READING

WRITING

Journal Entry

Ask students to speculate about the meaning of the name *Brings the Deer* and why that person might have been given that name. Students may want to look back at page 51 of the story for a clue. Then have students write a journal entry that Brings the Deer might have written on the day he got his grown-up name. WRITING

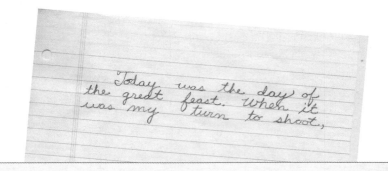

ORAL LANGUAGE

Describe What You Hear

Tell students to sit with their eyes closed for a few minutes and listen to the sounds around them. They should not only try to identify the sounds but also think about the qualities of each sound and how they could describe these sounds to others. Have students take turns describing to classmates the sounds they heard, using expressive adjectives and verbs to convey a vivid impression. Students can refer to Activity Card 3, page R11.

LISTENING/SPEAKING

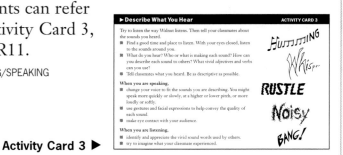

Activity Card 3 ▶

VIEWING

Overlapping

Call attention to the illustration of the boys standing in line on page 57. Point out that each figure overlaps, or partially covers, the next figure in the line. Suggest that students take some time to look around them to confirm that objects and people in real life are frequently seen this way, with one thing overlapping another. Then have students draw their own pictures using the overlapping technique. VIEWING/REPRESENTING

REACHING ALL LEARNERS

Intervention Strategies for Below-Level Readers

RETURN TO THE STRATEGY

Reinforce Comprehension

FOCUS STRATEGY **Apply the Use Prior Knowledge strategy.** Discuss with students the idea that using strategies while they read can help them better understand what they are reading. Remind students that the focus strategy for reading "Sees Behind Trees" is Use Prior Knowledge. Ask students:

• **How can your knowledge of people and events help you make sense of what you read?**
• **How can your knowledge about stories and how they are written help you better understand what you read?**

Suggest that students practice using this strategy as they silently reread the second complete paragraph on page 50 of "Sees Behind Trees." Have them use a chart like the one below to help them understand how the mother's voice sounds and how the mist of color and noise feels to Walnut.

What I Read	What I Know (Prior Knowledge)
Walnut's mother uses the same voice she used when he was younger and she told him not to play with sharp knives.	Mothers sometimes speak sternly to their children when the children do something dangerous.
The mist of color and noise surrounds Walnut like the roof and walls of a very small house.	Being in a small house can make a person feel uncomfortable, closed in on all sides, without enough room to move freely.

LANGUAGE EXPLORATION

Homographs

Discuss words that are spelled alike. Have students locate *bow* (first paragraph, page 48), *dove* (third paragraph, page 53), and *wind* (second paragraph, page 56) in the story. Have them pronounce each word and tell what it means. Explain that *b-o-w* can also be pronounced to rhyme with *cow*. Ask students what this word means. Explain that two words that are spelled the same but are pronounced differently and have different meanings are called **homographs**. Discuss the homographs *bow* and *bow*, *dove* and *dove*, *wind* and *wind*. Students can record the pronunciations and meanings of these homographs in a chart. Ask them to think of other homographs and add them to the chart.

Word	Rhyming Word	Meaning
bow	go	what you use to shoot arrows
bow	cow	to bend at the waist
dove	stove	went into the water, or moved as if diving into water
dove	love	a kind of bird
wind	pinned	moving air
wind	find	to turn something around and around

OBJECTIVE:

To understand how an author develops characters

REACHING ALL LEARNERS

CHALLENGE

Encourage students to read other stories and identify the ways in which the author develops characters. Then have them write their own stories using all three methods of character development.

INTERVENTION

Show students pictures of people engaged in various activities. Ask what students can tell about the people from what they see in the pictures.

RETEACH See page R3 for a lesson in multiple modalities.

FOCUS SKILL
Character Development

AFTER READING

Return to the Concept

Extend the thinking.

Encourage students to tell how and what they learned about the characters in "Sees Behind Trees." Record their ideas on a chart.

Character	How Developed	What I Learned
Walnut	his words, thoughts, and actions words and actions of other characters	He has trouble seeing. He worries he will embarrass his family. He can hear and smell better than others.
Walnut's mother		
Brings the Deer		

Work with students to add information about Walnut's mother and Brings the Deer to the chart.

Model thinking about character development.

Have students read the section of the story in which Walnut's father arrives, beginning with the words *Before I could say anything* at the bottom of page 54 through the end of page 55. Ask how the author develops the character of Walnut's father. You may want to model the thinking:

MODEL **Walnut describes how his father teases him. From his description of his father's actions, I can tell that his father has a sense of humor. I also know from what Walnut says that his father was playful when Walnut was a little boy, so I think his father is the kind of parent who enjoys spending time with his child.**

Test Prep

These tips can help students answer items on character development.

• Pay attention to the words, actions, and thoughts of the characters.
• Watch for clues to a character's traits and personality.

Guided Practice

Discuss character development.

Explain that in "Sees Behind Trees" the author does not provide direct information about the characters because the story is told from Walnut's point of view. Point out that while the reader knows what Walnut is thinking, he or she can't know what other characters are thinking because Walnut can observe the other characters' actions and words but not their thoughts. Write the diagram to the right on the board or use Transparency 9. Work with students to list information about Brings the Deer that they learned while reading the story and to determine how the author developed the character.

Summarize.

Ask students to discuss how understanding character development helped them better understand the meaning of the story.

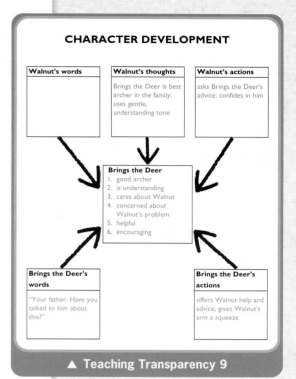

▲ Teaching Transparency 9

Practice/Apply

LET'S WATCH A MOVIE

PERFORMANCE ASSESSMENT   Invite students to think of a scene from a favorite movie that helps the viewer understand more about a character. Have students describe the movie scene and analyze the ways the scriptwriter developed the character. Point out that a scriptwriter faces special challenges because characters on screen must be developed through actions and words. The only way the scriptwriter can convey a character's thoughts is by having the character speak them aloud. COMPARE FORMS/WRITING

THE CHARACTER GAME

Have students work in small groups to make simple game spinners with three sections labeled (1) Direct Information, (2) Information from the Character, (3) Information from Other Characters. Have students prepare a set of cards for character traits such as honesty, sense of humor, helpfulness, jealousy, self-confidence, cleverness, and selfishness. Students take turns picking a card at random, spinning the pointer, and then giving an example of how an author might use the method shown on the spinner to present the trait on the card. LISTENING/SPEAKING/WRITING

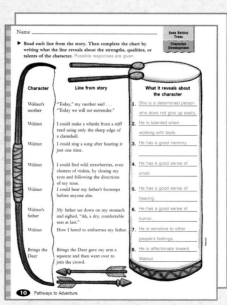

▲ Practice Book, pages 10–11

Sees Behind Trees   T91

Vocabulary Workshop

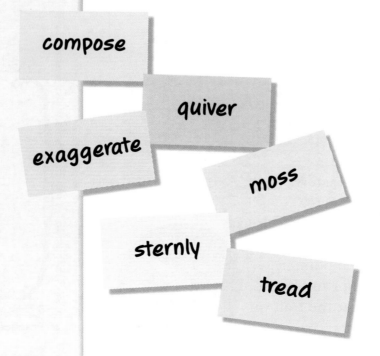

Fire from Ice
by Josh Craig
illustrated by Eric Velasquez

Have students read the
TAKE-HOME BOOK
Fire from Ice to reinforce
vocabulary words. See also
*Guided Reading Manual for
Take-Home Books*, page 3.

Reviewing Vocabulary Words

Read aloud the following sentence
frames. Have students use a vocabulary word or hold up the correct
word card to complete each one.

1. The rocks near the stream were
   covered with soft green _____.
   (moss)
2. The father spoke _____ to his
   son when the boy made too
   much noise. *(sternly)*
3. The father told the boy to _____
   himself and pay attention.
   (compose)
4. The boy talked more softly then
   and walked with a lighter _____.
   (tread)
5. The father took an arrow from
   his _____ and shot at the paper
   target. *(quiver)*
6. The boy did not _____ when he
   told people his father was a good
   archer. *(exaggerate)*

compose

quiver

exaggerate

moss

sternly

tread

Reviewing Word Identification Strategies

Decode familiar patterns. Have students look back at page 49 and
locate the word *expression*. Ask students to identify familiar patterns
they see in this word and to mention some other words they know
with the same patterns. (Possible
responses: first syllable *ex* as in *excellent*
and *extra*; last syllable *ion* as in *direction*
and *confusion*) Have students divide
the word into syllables and pronounce it. (ik•spresh´ən) Remind
them that recognizing familiar patterns can help them figure out unfamiliar words. Have students
identify familiar patterns in the
words below that may help them
pronounce and decode them.

confession	illustrate
inheritance	obscurity
expiration	perception
perspective	explosive

Science Words Have students look
through science textbooks to find
additional examples of words with
familiar patterns. (Possible responses:
extinction, survival, hibernate, germi-
nate, magnetism, conductive, investigate)
Call on volunteers to read their
words aloud and to identify the
familiar pattern or patterns in each
word.

Extending Vocabulary

Metaphors

Reread with students Walnut's description on page 58 of what happened when he tied the sash around his eyes: *The wind made fingers through the trees and I used them to feel my way in each direction.* Ask students to explain this sentence and to describe the picture it creates in their minds. Explain that the author uses figurative  language to compare the wind to fingers moving through the trees and also to compare Walnut's thoughts to fingers moving and searching. Explain that this type of comparison, which is made without the use of signal words such as *like* or *as*, is called a **metaphor.**

Create metaphors. Have students create metaphors by making comparisons that complete sentences. Use the following sentences:

His voice was _____.

My feet were _____.

The water was _____.

Her hair was _____.

Reference Sources/Print and Online Encyclopedias

Recall with students the Native American words *pemmican* and *moccasins* in "Sees Behind Trees" that have been borrowed by the English language. Discuss the idea that every language acquires new words when speakers come into contact with speakers of other languages and "borrow" words from them. Have students use encyclopedias, both print and online, to locate other English words that have been borrowed from Native American languages or from other languages. Suggest that students look up information on topics such as *language, English language, American English,* and *Native American languages.*

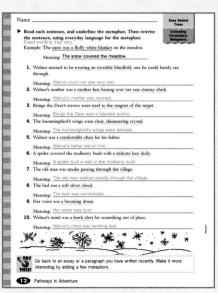

▲ **Practice Book, page 12**

Sees Behind Trees **T93**

Expressive Writing

DESCRIPTIVE PARAGRAPH

Connect Writing to Reading

Explain that descriptive writing uses words that appeal to the five senses to tell what something looks, tastes, smells, sounds, or feels like. Ask students to reread the third paragraph of "Sees Behind Trees." Ask what sense words the writer uses to describe the woods. (Possible responses: sight—*familiar blur of green and brown*; smell—*pemmican*; sound— tread of moccasins; touch—*tenseness of body*) Explain that learning to write descriptions will help students understand and appreciate the descriptions they read.

Teach/Model

Display Transparency 10. Explain that it shows a model of a descriptive paragraph. Tell students that this will help them write their own descriptive paragraphs.

**STUDENT MODEL:
DESCRIPTIVE PARAGRAPH**

In a descriptive paragraph, the writer uses sense words to tell how something looks, tastes, smells, sounds, or feels. Here is a descriptive paragraph a fifth grader wrote to a friend about baking cookies.

topic sentence	*Yesterday I baked cookies for the first time ever. I mixed the dough with my hands, and it felt soft and squishy. It also felt*
details and sense words	*grainy because of the sugar. The chocolate chips looked like shiny little buttons as I poured them into the yellow dough. I formed tiny balls of dough the size of cherries and baked the cookies for ten minutes. Soon the whole*
comparisons	*house smelled like a bakery. The soft, sweet cookies seemed to melt in my mouth!*

▲ **Teaching Transparency 10**

ANALYZE THE MODEL

- Audience—a friend
- Writer's task—describe what it was like to bake cookies

FOCUS ON ORGANIZATION

- Topic sentence tells what the paragraph describes
- Details are presented in a logical order

FOCUS ON ELABORATION

- Experience is described through details that appeal to the senses. (touch—*soft and squishy, grainy*; sight—*bright, yellow*; taste—*sweet*; smell—*like a bakery*)
- Writer uses comparisons to sharpen the description. (*chips looked like shiny little buttons; tiny balls of dough the size of cherries; smelled like a bakery*)
- Verbs (*mixed, poured, formed*) also help reader picture what is happening.

Writing Prompts

Ⓐ Assign a prompt, for example:
Describe your favorite food. Include sensory details and comparisons to help your reader understand why you like the food so much.

Ⓑ Have students write a descriptive paragraph about a topic of their own choosing. Students should include sensory details and comparisons.

TECHNOLOGY

Students may use a word processing program such as *The New Kid Pix*® to write and illustrate their descriptive paragraphs.

Prewrite and Draft

Have students brainstorm a list of possible topics for a descriptive paragraph. Tell them to write a topic sentence to identify the subject they will describe. Students may use a web such as the one on Transparency 11 to record their topic sentence and sensory details.

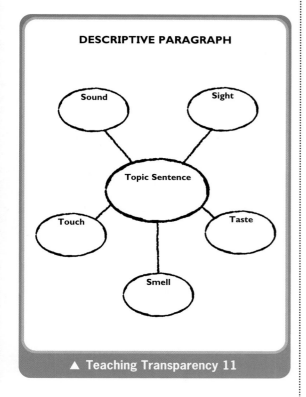

DESCRIPTIVE PARAGRAPH

Sound

Sight

Topic Sentence

Touch

Taste

Smell

▲ Teaching Transparency 11

Revise

Students can work in pairs or small groups to discuss their descriptive paragraphs. Provide the following questions to help students work constructively:

- **Does the first sentence clearly state what will be described?**
- **Are details provided that appeal to the senses?**
- **Are comparisons used to make the details more vivid?**
- **Are the details presented in a logical order?**
- **How does the paragraph make you feel about the topic? Why?**

After students have discussed each other's writing, have them revise their own descriptive paragraphs. Remind them to check for spelling errors by using a dictionary or an electronic spell checker.

SCORING RUBRIC FOR SUGGESTED PROMPT

4 Advanced
The descriptive paragraph opens with a topic sentence that clearly tells what will be described. The writer includes many specific sensory details, all relevant to the topic and arranged in a logical order. The writer makes interesting and appropriate comparisons and has a clear sense of audience and purpose.

3 Proficient
The descriptive paragraph opens with a topic sentence that tells what will be described. There are several sensory details, but not all the appropriate senses are included. The details are arranged in a logical order, however. A precise or vivid comparison is used. The writer is aware of the audience and purpose.

2 Basic
A topic sentence is provided, but it is not very interesting. The writer includes sensory details but addresses only one or two of the appropriate senses. The organization is not clear. There may be a comparison, but it does not work well. The audience would wonder about the purpose of the paragraph.

1 Below Basic
The topic sentence is missing or off the topic. There are few details and little sensory description. The paragraph rambles, and the details stray from the topic. The writer loses sight of the purpose and audience.

Imperative and Exclamatory Sentences

SKILL TRACE	
INTRODUCE	T96–T97
Review	T123

**Language Handbook,
pages 95–96**

REACHING ALL LEARNERS

ESL

Have students insert the word
What or *How* at the beginning of
the following sentence frames:

_____ nervous the boys were
before the contest! (*How*)

_____ a good listener Walnut was!
(*What*)

_____ a proud day it was for
Walnut! (*What*)

Invite students to offer their own
examples of similar sentences.

DAY 1 — Teach/Model

DAILY LANGUAGE PRACTICE
1. **People has different abilitys.** (have;
abilities.)
2. **Practice helps us, develop are abilities.**
(us develop our)

INTRODUCE THE CONCEPT Use sentences 1–3 on Transparency 12 as
you discuss the following points:

- An **imperative sentence** gives a
command or makes a request. The
subject is *you* (understood). The sentence ends with a period.
- An **exclamatory sentence**
expresses strong feeling. It ends
with an exclamation point.

Have students tell what kind of sentence each is. Then have them
rewrite sentences 4 and 5 correctly.

**IMPERATIVE AND EXCLAMATORY
SENTENCES**

1. Track the ball with your eye. (imperative)

2. How blurry it looks! (exclamatory)

3. Find the target before breakfast. (imperative)

4. meet me at the bus stop (Meet me at the bus stop.)

5. what a beautiful day it is (What a beautiful day it is!)

6. Walk slowly in the forest (Walk slowly in the forest.)

7. Keep your eyes and ears open (Keep your eyes and ears
open.)

8. How blue the sky is (How blue the sky is!)

▲ **Teaching Transparency 12**

DAY 2 — Extend the Concept

DAILY LANGUAGE PRACTICE
1. **What did Walnut and his mothar practice every morning.** (mother; morning?)
2. **Walnut wants to kwit target practice**
(quit; practice.)

BUILD ORAL LANGUAGE Display
Transparency 12. Have volunteers
read sentences 6–8 aloud and correct the sentences orally as you correct them on the transparency.

Explain that a sentence can be both
exclamatory and imperative. Say
aloud an example, such as *Watch
out!* Invite students to offer other
examples, saying them with strong
feeling.

Name _____

Imperative and
Exclamatory
Sentences

Skill Reminder

- An imperative sentence is a command or a request. Most
imperative sentences end in a period. The subject of an imperative sentence
is you (understood).
- An exclamatory sentence expresses strong feeling and ends in an
exclamation point.

▶ Rewrite each of the sentences below to make it an imperative sentence with the
subject you understood. Use capital letters and end marks correctly.

1. I want you to sit on the rock.   Sit on the rock.

2. I want you to listen carefully.   Listen carefully.

3. I want you to look with your ears.   Look with your ears.

4. I do not want you to move.   Do not move.

5. I want you to tell what you see.   Tell what you see.

▶ Rewrite each sentence correctly, using capital letters and end marks.
Then write whether the sentence is imperative or exclamatory.

6. how soft the brook sounds
How soft the brook sounds! exclamatory

7. do not wade into the river now
Do not wade into the river now. imperative

8. what lovely roses those are
What lovely roses those are! exclamatory

9. how beautiful that bird is
How beautiful that bird is! exclamatory

10. put down your bow
Put down your bow. imperative

11. describe this place
Describe this place. imperative

10 GRAMMAR PRACTICE BOOK   Imperative and Exclamatory Sentences

▲ **Grammar Practice Book, page 10**

DAILY LANGUAGE PRACTICE

1. **Walnut listens to the sounds. In the trees abuve his head.** (sounds in; above)

2. **Dus he hear more than the other boys.** (Does; boys?)

CHANGING KINDS OF SENTENCES

Say a declarative sentence from the story, such as "I see a raccoon." Have a volunteer change the sentence to form either an imperative or an exclamatory sentence: "See the raccoon." "The raccoon is huge!" The volunteer then gives a sentence for another student to change, and play continues.

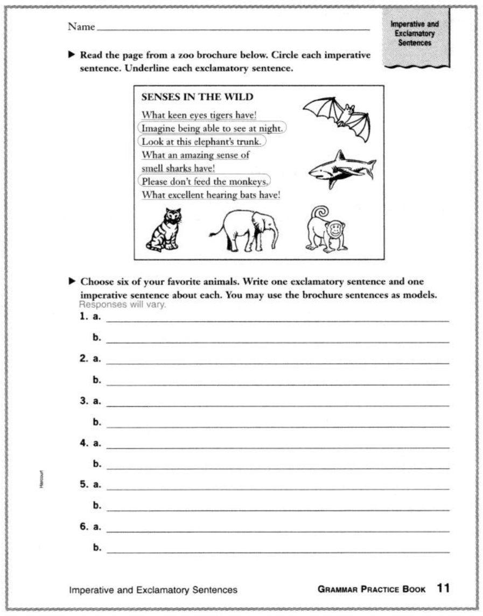

[Worksheet image]

Name _____

Imperative and Exclamatory Sentences

▶ Read the page from a zoo brochure below. Circle each imperative sentence. Underline each exclamatory sentence.

SENSES IN THE WILD
What keen eyes tigers have!
Imagine being able to see at night.
Look at this elephant's trunk.
What an amazing sense of smell sharks have!
Please don't feed the monkeys.
What excellent hearing bats have!

▶ Choose six of your favorite animals. Write one exclamatory sentence and one imperative sentence about each. You may use the brochure sentences as models.
Responses will vary.
1. a. _____
   b. _____
2. a. _____
   b. _____
3. a. _____
   b. _____
4. a. _____
   b. _____
5. a. _____
   b. _____
6. a. _____
   b. _____

Imperative and Exclamatory Sentences   GRAMMAR PRACTICE BOOK 11

▲ Grammar Practice Book, page 11

DAILY LANGUAGE PRACTICE

1. **Listen to the birds bild their spring nests** (build; nests.)

2. **What a beautiful moon tonite?** (tonight!)

DIARY ENTRY Have pairs of students develop a diary entry that Walnut, Frog, or Sleeps Late might have written about the contest. The entry should include at least three of the four kinds of sentences: declarative, interrogative, imperative, and exclamatory.

Test Prep

To help prepare students for language tests, point out these variations of imperative and exclamatory sentences:

- In most imperative sentences *you* (understood) is the subject. However, an imperative sentence may have a stated subject. *Sit down. You sit down.*
- In some exclamatory sentences, the subject and verb are not stated. *What a wonderful day (it is)!*

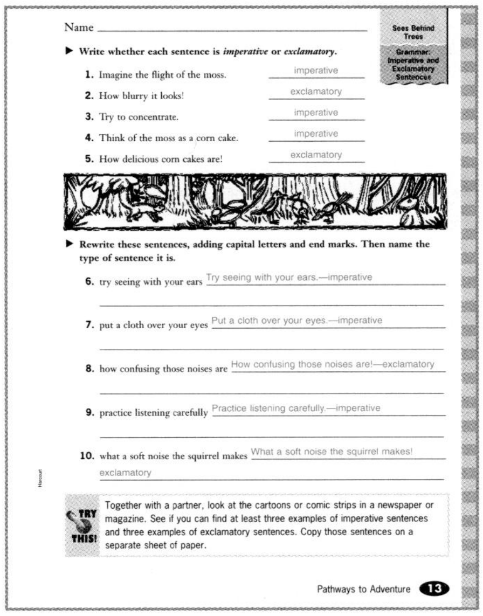

[Worksheet image]

Name _____

Sees Behind Trees

Grammar: Imperative and Exclamatory Sentences

▶ Write whether each sentence is *imperative* or *exclamatory*.

1. Imagine the flight of the moss.   imperative
2. How blurry it looks!   exclamatory
3. Try to concentrate.   imperative
4. Think of the moss as a corn cake.   imperative
5. How delicious corn cakes are!   exclamatory

▶ Rewrite these sentences, adding capital letters and end marks. Then name the type of sentence it is.

6. try seeing with your ears   Try seeing with your ears.—imperative
7. put a cloth over your eyes   Put a cloth over your eyes.—imperative
8. how confusing those noises are   How confusing those noises are!—exclamatory
9. practice listening carefully   Practice listening carefully.—imperative
10. what a soft noise the squirrel makes   What a soft noise the squirrel makes!—exclamatory

TRY THIS! Together with a partner, look at the cartoons or comic strips in a newspaper or magazine. See if you can find at least three examples of imperative sentences and three examples of exclamatory sentences. Copy those sentences on a separate sheet of paper.

Pathways to Adventure **13**

▲ Practice Book, page 13

DAILY LANGUAGE PRACTICE

1. **All the boys staid in the clearing!** (stayed; clearing.)

2. **Walnut was delited with the results of the trial?** (delighted; trial.)

SENTENCE COMPLETION After reminding students of the four types of sentences, write the following incomplete sentences on the board. Have students rewrite the sentences by putting one word in each blank and adding the appropriate end mark.

1. _____ an exciting competition that was (What; was!)
2. _____ me about your favorite competition (Tell; competition.)
3. _____ the forest always filled with sound (Is/Was; sound?)
4. _____ didn't the other boys hear the sounds (Why; sounds?)

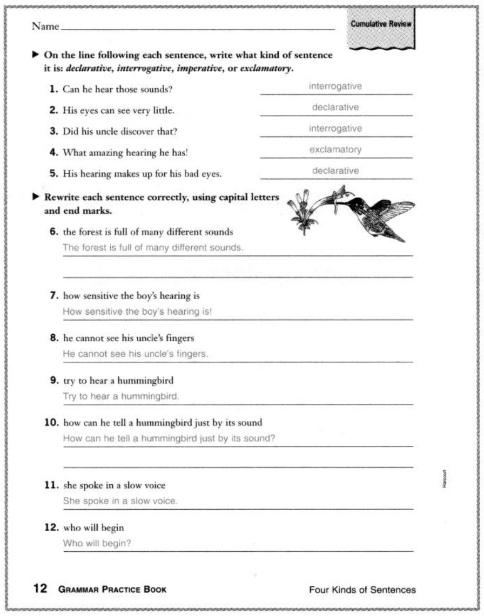

[Worksheet image]

Name _____

Cumulative Review

▶ On the line following each sentence, write what kind of sentence it is: *declarative, interrogative, imperative,* or *exclamatory.*

1. Can he hear those sounds?   interrogative
2. His eyes can see very little.   declarative
3. Did his uncle discover that?   interrogative
4. What amazing hearing he has!   exclamatory
5. His hearing makes up for his bad eyes.   declarative

▶ Rewrite each sentence correctly, using capital letters and end marks.

6. the forest is full of many different sounds
   The forest is full of many different sounds.
7. how sensitive the boy's hearing is
   How sensitive the boy's hearing is!
8. he cannot see his uncle's fingers
   He cannot see his uncle's fingers.
9. try to hear a hummingbird
   Try to hear a hummingbird.
10. how can he tell a hummingbird just by its sound
    How can he tell a hummingbird just by its sound?
11. she spoke in a slow voice
    She spoke in a slow voice.
12. who will begin
    Who will begin?

12 GRAMMAR PRACTICE BOOK   Four Kinds of Sentences

▲ Grammar Practice Book, page 12

SPELLING

Words with Long *a*, *e*, and *i*

SPELLING WORDS

1. stayed*
2. brain
3. thief
4. meat*
5. flight
6. style
7. delighted
8. daily
9. breathe
10. meanwhile
11. believes
12. tonight

BONUS WORDS

13. increased
14. explained
15. slightly
16. payment

*Words appearing in "Sees Behind Trees." Additional story words following the generalizations are *aim*, *waiting*, *raised*, *remain*, *pleaded*, *sunlight*, *tight*, and *fireflies*.

STUDENT-CHOSEN WORDS

17. _____
18. _____
19. _____
20. _____

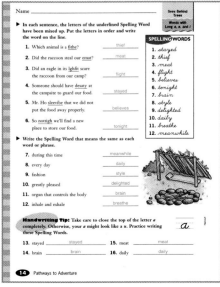

REACHING ALL LEARNERS

INTERVENTION

Less-proficient spellers can add easier Student-Chosen Words that follow the generalizations—such as *may*, *leaf*, and *high*—to their weekly spelling lists. Have students use these words in their writing activities.

DAY 1 **Pretest/Self-Check**

ADMINISTER THE PRETEST. Say each word, and then use it in a Dictation Sentence. (See Day 5.) Help students self-check their pretests using the list at the top of Transparency 13.

OPEN SORT Have students look for ways to sort the Spelling Words. For example, they might sort them according to number of syllables or according to the word ending. Ask volunteers to share their categories and sorted lists.

WORDS WITH LONG *a*, *e*, AND *i*

Spelling Words

1. stayed	5. flight	9. breathe
2. brain	6. style	10. meanwhile
3. thief	7. delighted	11. believes
4. meat	8. daily	12. tonight

Long *a*	Long *e*	Long *i*
way	**field**	**light**
stayed	thief	flight
	believes	delighted
		tonight
paint	**seat**	**type**
brain	meat	style
daily	breathe	
	meanwhile	

- The long *a* sound can be spelled *ay* or *ai*.
- The long *e* sound can be spelled *ie* or *ea*.
- The long *i* sound can be spelled *igh* or *y-e*.

▲ **Teaching Transparency 13**

DAY 2 **Teach/Model**

CLOSED SORT Display Transparency 13, or write the information on the board. Have students copy the chart and write each Spelling Word where it belongs.

Have a volunteer read the words *stayed* and *daily*. Ask what vowel sound is in both words. (long *a*) Circle the letters that stand for this sound. (*ay* and *ai*) Repeat the procedure, using *thief* and *meat*. Then have students read the generalizations to confirm their conclusions.

 Handwriting Tip

Remind students not to loop the letter *i*. Otherwise, the *i* could look like an *e*.

$$i$$

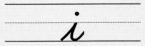

Name _____

▶ In each sentence, the letters of the underlined Spelling Word have been mixed up. Put the letters in order and write the word on the line.

1. Which animal is a *fithe*?   thief
2. Did the raccoon steal our *emat*?   meat
3. Did an eagle in its *lghft* scare the raccoon from our camp?   flight
4. Someone should have *deaty* at the campsite to guard our food.   stayed
5. Mr. Ho *sleevibe* that we did not put the food away properly.   believes
6. So *nottigh* we'll find a new place to store our food.   tonight

▶ Write the Spelling Word that means the same as each word or phrase.

7. during this time   meanwhile
8. every day   daily
9. fashion   style
10. greatly pleased   delighted
11. organ that controls the body   brain
12. inhale and exhale   breathe

SPELLING WORDS
1. stayed
2. thief
3. meat
4. flight
5. believes
6. tonight
7. brain
8. style
9. delighted
10. daily
11. breathe
12. meanwhile

Handwriting Tip: Take care to close the top of the letter *a* completely. Otherwise, your *a* might look like a *u*. Practice writing these Spelling Words.

13. stayed _____stayed_____   15. meat _____meat_____
14. brain _____brain_____   16. daily _____daily_____

14 Pathways to Adventure

▲ **Practice Book, page 14**

DAY 3 — Spelling Strategies

GUESSING AND CHECKING Remind students that the same vowel sound can be spelled more than one way. Write the following on the board:

r __ __   str __ __ ght

Say the words *ray* and *straight*, and ask students to guess the letters that spells the long *a* sound in each word. Have students check a dictionary to see if they are right. Call on volunteers to fill in the correct letters. Repeat the process, using *brief* and *leave* for long *e*, and *might* and *style* for long *i*.

✏ Apply to Writing

Have students work together to peer-edit a piece of writing. Have them check for the letter combinations that spell the long *a*, *e*, and *i* sounds and correct misspellings.

▲ Spelling Practice Book, page 12

DAY 4 — Spelling Activities

SPIDERS Divide the class into two teams for a spelling game whose object is to be the first team to draw a complete spider. Tell the first player on one team a Spelling Word. If the player spells it correctly, he or she may draw one part of the spider on the board. Alternate between the teams until one team has completed a spider:

GUESS THE RHYME Have students list words that rhyme with some of the Spelling Words and then use their lists to write short rhymed verses. Invite students to read their verses aloud, leaving out the last rhyming word, and to see if their classmates can supply the word. For example, *My cat likes any kind of meat. When she catches a rat, she thinks it's a* _____ (treat).

▲ Spelling Practice Book, page 13

DAY 5 — Posttest

Assess students' progress, using the Dictation Sentences.

DICTATION SENTENCES
1. **stayed**   We **stayed** to help clean up after the party.
2. **brain**   The **brain** is protected from injury by the skull.
3. **thief**   The **thief** left fingerprints at the crime scene.
4. **meat**   Members of the cat family eat mostly **meat**.
5. **flight**   My **flight** was delayed for two hours.
6. **style**   Do you like the latest clothing **style**?
7. **delighted**   Ann was **delighted** when she won first prize.
8. **daily**   Learning to play an instrument requires **daily** practice.
9. **breathe**   It became difficult to **breathe** when smoke filled the room.
10. **meanwhile**   **Meanwhile**, let's wait outside for the taxi.
11. **believes**   No one **believes** that tall tale.
12. **tonight**   There will be a full moon **tonight**.

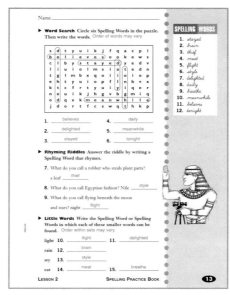

Sees Behind Trees   **T99**

Cross-Curricular Connections

REACHING ALL LEARNERS

ESL

Have students ask family members if they know of any famous people from their country of origin who are known by special names because of their talents or something they accomplished.

CHALLENGE

Students may work with a partner or in a small group to interview classmates about the Native American dwellings they constructed. Then they can develop a guidebook to the different types of dwellings included in the class exhibit.

MATERIALS

- print and online encyclopedias
- a computer with Internet access
- paper
- pencils

> ▶ **Special Names**   ACTIVITY CARD 4
>
> "Sees Behind Trees" is Walnut's new name, given to honor his special ability. Famous people in many fields have been known by names that tell something about their talents or accomplishments. Follow these steps to research a famous person and write a biographical sketch.
>
> 1. Choose one of these people to write about.
>
>   Simón Bolívar (El Liberador, The Liberator)   Richard I (the Lion-Hearted)
>   Florence Nightingale (Lady with the Lamp)   William Cody (Buffalo Bill)
>   Harriet Tubman (Moses _or_ the Moses of Her People)   Andrew Jackson (Old Hickory)
>   Martha Jane Canary (Calamity Jane)   Chris Evert (the Ice Maiden)
>
> 2. Use print and online encyclopedias and other references to research the person by both the real name and the special name.
> 3. Answer these questions: **Why is this person famous? How did this person acquire his or her special name?**
> 4. Take notes on your research and write down your sources.
> 5. Use your information to write a biographical sketch. Include the person's real name and special name, why the person was given the special name, and other interesting facts about the person's life.

▲ **Activity Card 4**

SOCIAL STUDIES

Special Names

WRITE A BIOGRAPHICAL SKETCH   In "Sees Behind Trees," Walnut receives a new name that reflects his special ability. Gray Fire and Brings the Deer also have names that tell something special about them. Students can use print and online encyclopedias and the Internet to research historical figures and others in fields such as sports and the arts who have been known by special names because of their talents or accomplishments. Students can then write a brief biographical sketch of the person they have chosen, telling how that person acquired a special name and whether the name fits.

Activity Card 4, page R11, will help students plan and conduct their research for this activity; it also includes a list of suggested subjects.

Students may want to combine their completed biographical sketches into a booklet. For suggestions, see Managing the Classroom, page T62.   READING REFERENCE

SOURCES/WRITING/INQUIRY

FOCUS SKILL Discuss with students how their understanding of character development might help them write their biographical sketch of a famous person.

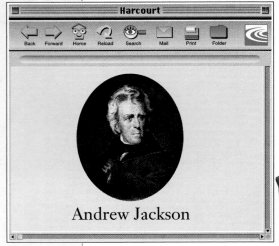

Andrew Jackson

Native American Dwellings

MATERIALS
- encyclopedias
- books on Native Americans that contain information on types of dwellings
- art materials, such as: heavy paper, markers, paint, brushes, glue, and tape
- scrap materials

CONSTRUCT A MODEL Call attention to the dwellings shown on page 51 of "Sees Behind Trees." Tell students that Native American peoples in different regions constructed different types of dwellings, depending on their needs and the materials available. Have small groups of students use encyclopedias and other reference books to find information about and pictures of various types of Native American dwellings. Each group can then choose one type of dwelling and construct a model. Students should also write a description telling what the Native American people or peoples used this type of dwelling for, the geographical location where they lived, what materials they used, and other relevant details.

Remind students that

- reference books usually have an index in the back with topics arranged in alphabetical order.
- print encyclopedias usually have an index in a separate volume.
- guide words at the tops of encyclopedia pages show at a glance what topics are found on those pages. READING REFERENCE

SOURCES/WRITING/INQUIRY

Inquiry Projects

"Sees Behind Trees" can be a springboard for inquiry into many related topics and ideas. Brainstorm topics that students want to learn more about, and have them organize their responses in a web. Students can use some of the resources below to begin their inquiry projects.

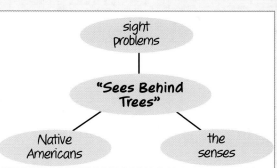

RESOURCES

Anasazi by Leonard Everett Fisher. Atheneum, 1997. EASY

Clambake: A Wampanoag Tradition by Russell M. Peters. Lerner, 1992. AVERAGE

Kids Explore the Gifts of Children with Special Needs by Westridge Young Writers Workshop. John Muir, 1994. AVERAGE

Buffalo Hunt by Russell Freedman. Holiday House, 1988. CHALLENGING

"Yang the Third and Her

THEME
Look Inside

GENRE
Realistic Fiction

■ The **setting** could be a real place, usually contemporary.

■ The **characters** and **events** are like people and events in real life.

CROSS-CURRICULAR CONNECTIONS

■ **SOCIAL STUDIES:** Summer Camp Directory

■ **MUSIC:** Presenting the Classics

FOCUS STRATEGY **SELF-QUESTION**

■ **Before Reading:** Preteach the Strategy on page T111

■ **During Reading:** Apply the Strategy on pages T114, T118

■ **After Reading:** Return to the Strategy on page T129

Lensey Namioka

Yang the Third and Her Impossible Family

The companion to
Yang the Youngest and His Terrible Ear

Illustrated by Kees de Kiefte

Parents' Choice

FOCUS SKILL VOCABULARY IN CONTEXT

■ **Before Reading:** Introduce the Skill on pages T110–T111

■ **During Reading:** Apply the Skill on pages T114, T118, T120

■ **After Reading:** Practice the Skill on pages T130–T131 (*Student Edition*, 82–83)

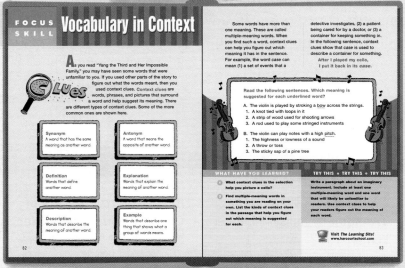

▲ **Student Edition, pages 82–83**

As students read "Yang the Third and Her Impossible Family," they will see that being part of a family means accepting family members for who they are.

Selection Summary

Yingmei, or Mary, as she has decided to call herself, and her family have recently immigrated to Seattle from China. Mary wants to be friends with the popular Holly Hanson. She also wants her family, especially her mother, to learn American ways and stop embarrassing her. Mary believes she can reach both goals when she volunteers her mother to be Holly's piano accompanist for an orchestra tryout. The results are not what Mary anticipates. When Holly and her mother come to the Yang house for a practice session, Mary learns a valuable lesson about family loyalty and compassion.

Author Profile

Lensey Namioka was born in Beijing, China, in 1929 and moved to the United States with her family when she was nine. Namioka had to struggle with many of the problems that Mary's character faces in the story as she adapts to a foreign culture. Like the Yang family, Namioka's family was musically talented. But she preferred reading. Namioka later became a mathematics instructor. She thinks her math background gives a thrifty quality to her writing. She doesn't like to waste a word.

REACHING ALL LEARNERS
BELOW-LEVEL READERS

EASY READER
"The Audition," pp. 22–29. Reinforces selection vocabulary and these additional words from "Yang the Third and Her Impossible Family":

pianist   flatter   blunders

See *Timeless Tales Intervention Reader Teacher's Guide,* pages 14–19.

CASSETTE
"Yang the Third and Her Impossible Family" is available on *Literature Cassette 1.*

CHALLENGE

Music by Carolyn Grimshaw. World Book, 1996. CHALLENGING

INQUIRY PROJECTS
See page T141. Have students pose questions about selection-related topics such as Chinese customs or chamber music and carry out research to answer them.

YANG THE THIRD AND HER IMPOSSIBLE FAMILY

Skills and Strategies

Reading

Listening

Speaking

Viewing

Vocabulary

audition
sonata
accompanist
accompaniment
grimaced
simultaneously

BUILDING BACKGROUND AND CONCEPTS T108

INTRODUCING VOCABULARY T109
Transparency 14
Practice Book p. 15

PRETEACHING SKILLS
Before Reading
✔ **FOCUS SKILL** Vocabulary in Context (Introduce) T110–T111
Transparency 15
FOCUS STRATEGY Self-Question T111

PREREADING STRATEGIES T112
READING THE SELECTION T112–T125
Literature Cassette 1
Author Information T125

ALTERNATIVE SELECTION
Easy Reader: "The Audition"

NOTE: Students may begin reading the selection on Day 2.

LITERARY RESPONSE T124
Return to the Predictions/Purpose
Appreciating the Literature

THINK ABOUT IT T124

RETELL AND SUMMARIZE T125
Practice Book p. 17

REREADING FOR FLUENCY
Readers Theatre T128

LITERATURE RESPONSE
New Ending T128

INTERVENTION STRATEGIES FOR BELOW-LEVEL READERS T129
FOCUS STRATEGY Return to the Strategy

Language Exploration

Writing	**Expressive Writing: Realistic Story** Connect Writing to Reading T134	Teach/Model T134 Analyze the Model *Transparency 16* *Language Handbook pp. 38–39*
Grammar	**Complete and Simple Subjects** Teach/Model T136 *Transparency 18* *Language Handbook pp. 98–101*	Extend the Concept T136 *Grammar Practice Book p. 13*
Daily Language Practice	1. **What beautiful music I heard tonite?** (tonight!) 2. **The violinist played. With a powerful, smooth style.** (played with)	1. **Breath evenly when you sing** (Breathe; sing.) 2. **Dayly practice will improve any musician's skill!** (Daily; skill.)
Spelling	**Words with Long *o* and Long *u*** soul　smoke　move　clue fruits　lose　chase　stole prove　produce　juice　drove Pretest/Self-Check T138 *Transparency 19*	Teach/Model T138 *Practice Book p. 22* Handwriting Tip

---

KEY

✔ **Tested Skills**

■ **Management Option:** See Managing the Classroom, page T106, for ongoing independent activities.

 Reaching All Learners: Support for "The Audition," an alternative selection, appears on *Timeless Tales Intervention Reader Teacher's Guide* pp. 14–19.

READING AND RESPONDING

DAY 3

EXTENDING SKILLS & STRATEGIES

DAY 4

EXTENDING SKILLS & STRATEGIES

DAY 5

RESPONSE ACTIVITIES
Listen to Music T126
■ Art Station
Write an Advice Column T126
Make a Phrase Book T126
Draw a Diagram T126

Selection Comprehension Test

LITERARY CONCEPTS
✔ Character Development T115
Practice Book p. 16

ORAL LANGUAGE
Take the Hot Seat T128
Activity Card 5, R12

VIEWING
Special Lettering T128

INDEPENDENT READING
Reader's Choice Library:
Baseball in the Barrios T107

Reader's Choice Library Book ▶

COMPREHENSION
After Reading
✔ **FOCUS SKILL** Vocabulary in Context (Introduce) T130–T131
Practice Book pp. 18–19
 Mission Comprehension™ Skills Practice CD-ROM

GRAMMAR
Imperative and Exclamatory Sentences (Review) T123

VOCABULARY T132–T133
Reviewing Vocabulary Words
Extending Vocabulary
Practice Book p. 20

TAKE-HOME BOOK
Kwan's Big Performance T132

CROSS-CURRICULAR CONNECTIONS
Social Studies: Summer Camp Directory T140
Activity Card 6, R12

Take-Home Book ▶

CROSS-CURRICULAR CONNECTIONS
Music: Presenting the Classics T141
■ Publishing Station
✔ **FOCUS SKILL** Apply Vocabulary in Context

INQUIRY PROJECTS T141
Research

SELF-SELECTED READING T107
• *Yang the Second and Her Secret Admirers*
• *The Facts and Fictions of Minna Pratt*
• *The Laziest Boy in the World*

Writing Prompts T134 Prewrite and Draft T135 *Transparency 17*  ClarisWorks for Kids®	Revise T135	Assessment T135 Student Self- and Peer Assessment Scoring Rubric
Oral Review/Practice T137 *Grammar Practice Book* p. 14	Apply to Writing T137 *Practice Book* p. 21	Cumulative Review T137 *Grammar Practice Book* p. 15
1. **Holly beleeves that dogs are more important than music** (believes; music.) 2. **Meanwile, Mary thinks just the opposite,** (Meanwhile; opposite.)	1. **Mary choze to help holly with her audition.** (chose; Holly) 2. **Holly, wanted to proov that she could play the violin.** (Holly wanted; prove)	1. **The two families. Drov to the audition.** (families drove) 2. **Mary's mother, believes that music is good for the sol.** (mother believes; soul.)
Spelling Strategies T139 Apply to Writing *Spelling Practice Book* p. 14	Spelling Activities T139 *Spelling Practice Book* p. 15	Posttest T139

Visit The Learning Site!
www.harcourtschool.com

Managing the Classroom

While you provide direct instruction to individuals or small groups,
other students can work on ongoing activities like the ones below.

Vocabulary Station

OBJECTIVE

To create a crossword puzzle with a music theme

MATERIALS
- paper
- pencil
- dictionary

Have students create a crossword puzzle with a music theme. Answers could name musicians, musical instruments, musical compositions, and so on. Students can refer to the story for musical words and use a dictionary to develop clues.

Publishing Station

OBJECTIVE

To create a book of biographical sketches of classical composers

MATERIALS
- paper
- pencils
- three-hole punch
- binders

Have students write and illustrate their biographical sketches of classical composers for the Presenting the Classics activity on page T141. They can then collect their biographies in a class book.

Art Station

OBJECTIVE

To interpret music through art

MATERIALS
- paper
- crayons, markers, or paints

After students have listened to different compositions for the Musical Opinions activity on page T126, have them select the piece that had the greatest effect on them. Then have them illustrate how the music makes them feel.

Learning Log

OBJECTIVE

To record facts and details about music

MATERIALS
- notebooks or folders
- pencils

Provide students with a list of topics related to both classical and contemporary music and the print resources to research these topics. Have students select a topic from the list, and tell them to record what they learn in their Reading Notebooks.

Note: For more options, see pages T126–T127, T128–T129, and T140–T141.

REACHING ALL LEARNERS

Multi-Level Books

EASY

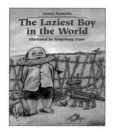

The Laziest Boy in the World by Lensey Namioka. Holiday House, 1998. REALISTIC FICTION: SELECTION AUTHOR

EASY READER: TIMELESS TALES "The Audition" pp. 22–29 REALISTIC FICTION: MUSIC

TAKE-HOME BOOK **Kwan's Big Performance** REALISTIC FICTION: MUSIC

LEVELED LIBRARY BOOK **The Violin Man** by Maureen Brett Hooper. HISTORICAL FICTION: MUSICAL INSTRUMENT

AVERAGE

Yang the Youngest and His Terrible Ear by Lensey Namioka. Yearling, 1994. REALISTIC FICTION: SELECTION AUTHOR

Immigrant Girl: Becky of Eldridge Street by Brett Harvey. Holiday House, 1987. HISTORICAL FICTION: IMMIGRATION

READER'S CHOICE LIBRARY **Baseball in the Barrios** by Henry Horenstein NONFICTION: TRADITIONS

See the **Reader's Choice Library lesson plan** on pages T454–T455.

CHALLENGING

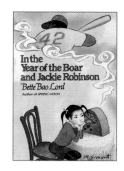

In the Year of the Boar and Jackie Robinson by Bette Bao Lord. HarperCollins, 1987. REALISTIC FICTION: ASIAN CULTURE

The Facts and Fictions of Minna Pratt by Patricia MacLachlan. HarperCollins, 1988. REALISTIC FICTION: YOUNG MUSICIAN

READER'S CHOICE LIBRARY **The Young Artist** by Thomas Locker. REALISTIC FICTION: CREATIVITY

See the **Reader's Choice Library lesson plan** on pages T932–T933.

Building Background and Concepts

See *ESL Manual* pages 14–19. You may wish to introduce these additional words and phrases:

tryout (page 68)
under the impression (page 73)
stage fright (page 74)
in spite of (page 78)

OTHER BACKGROUND-BUILDING IDEAS

VIDEO   Marsalis on Music: Sousa to Satchmo ©1995, Library Video Company, 55 min.

INTERNET   Bonus Words can be found on *The Learning Site* at **www.harcourtschool.com**

Access Prior Knowledge

Discuss ways people find to fit in.

Ask students what challenges a student coming from another region or country might face in a new school. (Possible responses: trying to understand and speak the language; becoming accepted) Ask students how new students might try to fit in at a new school. Lead students to suggest that they might make friends and demonstrate their talents by joining academic clubs, sports teams, or drama and music groups.

Develop Concepts

Build a web using vocabulary words.

Have students begin a web about musical tryouts. Ask questions that encourage them to add vocabulary to the web: **A person with musical talent might try out for a musical group. Where would he or she go for the tryout? What might someone need to make his or her tryout better?**

Highlight indicates vocabulary.

Then explain that "Yang the Third and Her Impossible Family" is about a Chinese girl who tries to help a friend with her musical audition and discovers something about herself and her family.

BONUS WORDS

Introduce musical words.   If necessary, introduce the following words related to music found in "Yang the Third and Her Impossible Family": *cello, viola, bow, orchestra, violin, score.*

cello   *violin*   *score*

Introducing Vocabulary

Build Word Identification Strategies

Decode using structural analysis.

Display Transparency 14, and have volunteers read the paragraph aloud. Remind students that they can sometimes figure out new words by looking for familiar prefixes, suffixes, and base words. Model using structural analysis to decode the word *accompanist*.

> **MODEL** I see that this word ends with the suffix *-ist*, which means "one who does." I recognize the base word *company*. I can put together what I know to pronounce this word. I know from the context that it has something to do with music. I can guess that it means "one who plays music in company with or for someone else."

As students decode the other vocabulary, encourage them to confirm the pronunciation and meaning by referring to their glossaries or dictionaries.

CHECK UNDERSTANDING

Practice other vocabulary strategies. Have students answer questions with complete sentences that show what the vocabulary words mean.

MEANINGFUL SENTENCES

- **What might people do at an audition for a play or a concert?**
  PRIOR KNOWLEDGE
- **Is a sonata something you're likely to hear an orchestra play?**
  EXAMPLE
- **What does an accompanist do?** EXPLANATION
- **If a person grimaced, what was he or she probably feeling?**
  DESCRIPTION
- **If two things happen *simultaneously*, in what order do they occur?** EXPLANATION
- **Why might a musician want accompaniment?** PRIOR KNOWLEDGE

QUICKWRITE

READING NOTEBOOK Invite students to write about a time when they *grimaced*. Remind them to describe how they were feeling at the time.

VOCABULARY DEFINED

audition a tryout to test the ability of an actor or musician

sonata a musical composition, usually in several movements or sections

accompanist a person who plays music to support the main part

accompaniment music played to support the main part

grimaced expressed pain, annoyance, or disgust

simultaneously happening at the same time

VOCABULARY

Anna waited nervously. In a few minutes she would try out for the State Youth Orchestra. "You have no reason to worry," she told herself. "You know you're ready for this **audition**. You've played this **sonata** hundreds of times." It was a good speech, but it didn't stop Anna from worrying. And where was her brother David, her **accompanist**? Would he show up on time to play piano **accompaniment** for her? Anna **grimaced**. Then she smiled. Just as her name was called, David appeared by her side. **Simultaneously** they reached out and took each other's hands. "Show them how the violin was meant to be played," David said as they walked on stage. So Anna did.

▲ Teaching Transparency 14

▲ Practice Book, page 15

Yang the Third and Her Impossible Family **T109**

SKILL TRACE	
INTRODUCE	
• Before Reading:	T110–T111
• During Reading:	T114, T118, T120
• After Reading:	T130–T131
Reteach	R4
Review 1	T157
Review 2	T199
Test	Theme 1
Maintain	T423

OBJECTIVE:

To use context clues
to understand the
meaning of words

Preteach
FOCUS SKILL
Vocabulary in Context

BEFORE READING

Preview the Literature

Preview the selection and discuss the genre.
Invite students to read the title and look at the illustrations to tell who and what the story might be about. (two girls; their families; music) Then have them silently read *Student Edition* page 67. Ask: **Does the story seem to be about events that could really happen?** Explain that stories about events that could really happen are called *realistic fiction*.

Introduce the Skill

Discuss vocabulary in context.
Explain to students that using **context clues** as they read will help them figure out the meanings of unfamiliar words or words that have more than one meaning or pronunciation. Display Transparency 15, and have a volunteer read aloud the explanation of *context*. Guide students through the paragraph, and have them determine the meanings of the underlined words. Ask them to explain how they used context clues to figure out the meanings of these words.

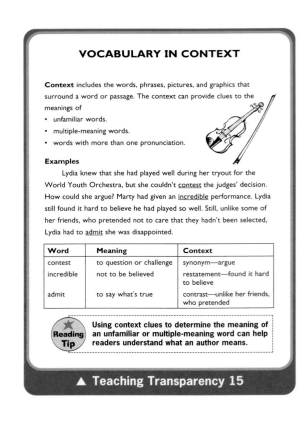

VOCABULARY IN CONTEXT

Context includes the words, phrases, pictures, and graphics that surround a word or passage. The context can provide clues to the meanings of
• unfamiliar words.
• multiple-meaning words.
• words with more than one pronunciation.

Examples

Lydia knew that she had played well during her tryout for the World Youth Orchestra, but she couldn't <u>contest</u> the judges' decision. How could she argue? Marty had given an <u>incredible</u> performance. Lydia still found it hard to believe he had played so well. Still, unlike some of her friends, who pretended not to care that they hadn't been selected, Lydia had to <u>admit</u> she was disappointed.

Word	Meaning	Context
contest	to question or challenge	synonym—argue
incredible	not to be believed	restatement—found it hard to believe
admit	to say what's true	contrast—unlike her friends, who pretended

Reading Tip Using context clues to determine the meaning of an unfamiliar or multiple-meaning word can help readers understand what an author means.

▲ Teaching Transparency 15

Model the Thinking

Model using context to determine word meaning.

Read aloud and discuss with students the Reading Tip on Transparency 15. Then use the passage on the transparency to model for students how to use context clues to determine the meaning of *contest*, a multiple-meaning word.

 **I know the word *contest* has a couple of meanings: "a competition" or "to question or challenge." The accent is on the first syllable for a noun and on the second syllable for a verb. I read that Lydia "couldn't contest the judges' decision." Then I read the next sentence: "How could she argue?" One meaning of *argue* is "to challenge." When I put this information together, I know that in this passage *contest* is a verb that means "to question or challenge."**

DURING/AFTER READING

- Apply the Skill, pages T114, T118, T120
- Practice the Skill, pages T130–T131

PRETEACH THE STRATEGY

 Self-Question ⭐

Encourage students to monitor their comprehension.

Explain that students can monitor their comprehension by asking and answering their own questions about characters and events in a story. Model how self-questioning can help readers:

 When I ask myself questions about a story that I'm reading, I make sure that I'm paying attention to the important elements in the story.

- Apply the Strategy, pages T114, T118
- Return to the Strategy, page T129

 See the Strategy Builder copying masters, pages A40–A45.

STRATEGIES GOOD READERS USE

- Use Prior Knowledge
- Make and Confirm Predictions
- Adjust Reading Rate
- **Self-Question** FOCUS STRATEGY
- Create Mental Images
- Use Context to Confirm Meaning
- Use Text Structure and Format
- Use Graphic Aids
- Use Reference Sources
- Read Ahead
- Reread
- Summarize and Paraphrase

Prereading Strategies

PREVIEW AND PREDICT

If students have not yet previewed the selection, have them look at the illustration and read the story title on pages 66 and 67. Ask them to make predictions about the story. Remind them that a realistic fiction story has characters and events that are like people and events in real life. Have students begin a story map for "Yang the Third and Her Impossible Family." See *Practice Book* page 17.

STORY MAP

```
┌──────────────────┐   ┌──────────────────┐
│   Characters     │   │     Setting      │
│  Yang the Third  │   │                  │
└────────┬─────────┘   └────────┬─────────┘
         │                      │
         └──────────┬───────────┘
              ┌──────────────┐
              │   Problem    │
              │              │
              └──────┬───────┘
                     ▼
              ┌──────────────┐
              │Important Events│
              │              │
              └──────┬───────┘
                     ▼
              ┌──────────────┐
              │   Solution   │
              │              │
              └──────────────┘
```

SET PURPOSE

Read to Enjoy Ask students to set a purpose for reading "Yang the Third and Her Impossible Family." Remind them that one purpose for reading is to enjoy a selection. If students have difficulty setting a purpose for reading the story, offer this suggestion:

> MODEL **I think I'll enjoy finding out about Yang the Third and why her family is impossible.**

66

Options for Reading

DIRECTED READING Use the **Monitor Comprehension** questions to check students' comprehension. The **Guided Reading** strategies on pages T114, T116, T118, and T122 will benefit students reading below or on level. WHOLE CLASS/SMALL GROUP	**COOPERATIVE READING** Have students reading on or above level use *Comprehension Card 1* (p. R7) to focus on **characters**. INDEPENDENT/SMALL GROUP 	**INDEPENDENT READING** Encourage students to note in their Reading Notebooks how they respond to the events and characters in the selection, especially to how Mary's attitudes change as the story progresses. INDIVIDUAL/WHOLE CLASS

Yang the Third and Her Impossible Family

by Lensey Namioka
illustrated by Kees de Kiefte

Though they now live in Seattle, Washington, Yingmei's family still follows many Chinese customs, such as referring to the children by their birth order: Eldest Brother, Second Sister, Third Sister, and Fourth Brother.

Yingmei (Third Sister) wants to become an American more than anything else. To accomplish this —

• She changes her name to Mary.
• She keeps a list of American words and phrases.
• She accepts a kitten from Holly Hanson, the most popular girl at school, even though it is forbidden.

Yingmei tries very hard, but she can't control everything that happens. In particular, she can't prevent her family members from saying and doing things that embarrass her in front of her new friends.

Parents'
Choice

67

REACHING ALL LEARNERS

INTERVENTION STRATEGIES

MODIFIED INSTRUCTION Ask students to read the title and describe what they see in the pictures on pages 66 through 69. Discuss these story words:

**rehearsal   mistake
friendship   uncomfortable**

Then have students read to page 69.

EASY READER Students may read **"The Audition,"** found on pages 22–29 in **Timeless Tales.** See **Timeless Tales Intervention Reader Teacher's Guide,** pages 14–19.

"Yang the Third and Her Impossible Family" is available on *Literature Cassette 1.*

Monitor Comprehension

1 **What are Holly's two problems and how does Mary try to help?**
(Possible response: Holly's accompanist for an important tryout is sick, and Holly doesn't really want to try out. Mary suggests that her mother play the accompaniment.) INFERENTIAL: SUMMARIZE

2 **Why is Mrs. Hanson doubtful about Mary's offer?** (Possible response: Mrs. Yang has made social mistakes in the past.) INFERENTIAL: SPECULATE

3 **Explain how you used context to determine the meanings of these words: *rehearsal* and *swerved*.**
(Students should explain how they used surrounding text to determine meaning.)
FOCUS SKILL INFERENTIAL: VOCABULARY IN CONTEXT

Guided Reading

STRATEGIES GOOD READERS USE

FOCUS STRATEGY **Self-Question** If students have difficulty understanding why Mrs. Hanson is doubtful about Mary's offer, work with a small group to remind students to ask themselves questions about the characters as they read.

MODEL **When I read page 69, I ask myself why Mrs. Hanson does not immediately accept Mary's offer. I recall that the introduction explains that Mary's family makes social mistakes. Mrs. Hanson seems to really care about Holly's audition, so she is worried that Mrs. Yang will do something embarassing.**

I tried to squeeze my left leg behind my cello case in the backseat. It was a week after Kim's birthday party, and we were on the way to a rehearsal of the All-City Orchestra. The best players from the Seattle elementary schools had been selected to form a citywide orchestra, which rehearsed once a week.

Holly and I had been chosen from our school; so had Kim. The rehearsals were held in an auditorium across town from our neighborhood, so Mrs. Hanson and Mrs. O'Meara took turns driving the three of us to the rehearsals.

It was nice of Mrs. Hanson and Mrs. O'Meara to include me. My cello was only half-size, but it still took up a lot of room, and I had a struggle fitting it in the car.

"What time is your tryout on Wednesday, Holly?" asked Mrs. Hanson, who was driving that week. "I have to make sure I can get time off to take you over."

Holly was silent for a moment. "I might have to call it off. The accompanist is sick, and I'm not sure she'll be able to play."

Mrs. Hanson turned her head sharply to look at Holly. The car swerved, and she got it back into the lane before she spoke again. "But that's awful! You've been practicing the piece for ages! And it's too late for you to prepare some unaccompanied piece! Why didn't you tell me earlier?"

"It's not the end of the world, Mom," muttered Holly.

"Can't your music teacher find another accompanist?" asked Mrs. Hanson. "There must be other pianists around!"

"It's a hard piece, that Brahms. We won't be able to get anybody ready by Wednesday."

I could see the tendons on Mrs. Hanson's neck. It occurred to me that *she* was the one who was really bothered, not Holly.

A brilliant idea suddenly hit me. "Mrs. Hanson, my mother can play the accompaniment for Holly's tryout."

68

▌MUSIC

CHAMBER MUSIC Holly's tryout is for the Junior Chamber Orchestra. Chamber music was originally composed to be performed in the rooms, or chambers, of homes. It was therefore written for a limited number of musicians who usually played stringed and wind instruments. Sometimes a piano or harpsichord was included. The string quartet, one of the most common chamber music groups, is made up of two violinists, a viola player, and a cello player.

We had arrived at the auditorium. Mrs. Hanson stopped the car and slowly turned to look at me. "Are you sure? She can't stop if she makes a mistake, you know. It would ruin Holly's piece."

Mother might do a lot of embarrassing things, but if there was one thing I felt confident about, it was her musical ability. "My mother has played a lot of chamber music with other people, so she never loses the beat even if she makes a mistake."

"Thank you for the offer, Mary," Mrs. Hanson said. But she still looked doubtful.

It might be mean of me, but I hoped Holly's accompanist would stay sick. This was a chance for Mother to get on Mrs. Hanson's good side for a change. Holly would be grateful to me for saving her audition.

Halfway through the rehearsal we had a break. Holly came to the cello section and made her way to my stand. "Can I talk to you for a minute, Mary?"

I could tell that she was unhappy about something. "Sure, Holly," I said. "What's wrong?"

She absently ran her finger across the horsehair of her viola bow, and some of the resin flew up in a fine powder. "It's about your mother accompanying me for the tryout," she said finally. "I don't really care about getting in to the Junior Chamber Orchestra, you know. My mom wants me to join, because it's such a select group and they have a summer camp on Orcas Island."

69

INTERVENTION STRATEGIES

MODIFIED INSTRUCTION Help students summarize what has happened so far.

MODEL **Mary and Holly both play in the All-City Orchestra. On the way to a _rehearsal_, Holly says that the accompanist for her tryout for the Junior Chamber Orchestra is sick. Mary suggests that her mother accompany Holly, but Mrs. Hanson is worried that Mrs. Yang will make a _mistake_ and mess up Holly's tryout.**

Help students set a purpose for reading through page 73. (to find out if Mrs. Hanson accepts Mary's offer)

SKILLS IN CONTEXT

LITERARY CONCEPTS
TESTED SKILL

Character Development

SKILL TRACE	
Introduce	T66, T90
Reteach	R3
Review 1	T115
Review 2	T203
Test	Theme 1
Maintain	T307

TEACH/MODEL

Ask students to describe Mary. (self-conscious, worried, eager to please) Have students provide information from the story to support their characterization. Remind them that a story character is developed through

- the author's description of the character.
- the character's own actions, words, and thoughts.
- other characters' actions, words, and thoughts.

Model recognizing character development.

MODEL **I learn about Mary from her thoughts, how she acts, and what she says. She worries about her family being accepted by Mrs. Hanson and feels they have to try extra hard to prove they are good at something.**

PRACTICE/APPLY

As students read, have them fill in a chart with these headings to track the development of Mary: *Character, What I Learned About Her,* and *How I Learned It.*

▲ Practice Book, page 16

Monitor Comprehension

1 **What do you learn about Fourth Brother during his talk with Mary?** (Possible response: He is concerned about Mary's feelings and wants to help her feel accepted.) INFERENTIAL: DETERMINE CHARACTERS' TRAITS

2 **How do you know that Mary is upset by her encounter with the Sylvesters?** (Possible responses: She worries that the Sylvesters might get a dog that will attack the kitten; she compares herself to a juggler she once saw.) METACOGNITIVE: DETERMINE CHARACTERS' EMOTIONS

3 **Why is Mary finding it difficult to ask her mother to play for Holly?** (Possible responses: Mary thinks that if her mother plays for Holly, she may risk losing Holly's friendship; Mary might be worrying that her family will embarrass her again.) INFERENTIAL: SUMMARIZE

Guided Reading

STRATEGIES GOOD READERS USE

Use Context to Confirm Meaning Ask students to read the fourth paragraph on page 70, which begins *On the way home, . . .* If they misread a word, use a prompt similar to the following to help them focus on the context:

- **You said _____. Would it make sense for Mrs. Hanson to say that here?** SEMANTIC CUES
- **You said _____. Does that sound right?** SYNTACTIC CUES

A summer camp where people just made music! It sounded like heaven. Playing in the All-City Orchestra was fun, but being in the Junior Chamber Orchestra would be a real privilege. I tried not to feel envious. "I'd give anything to join something like that! Is it very expensive?"

Holly nodded. "It costs a bundle, but my dad will pay for it. In fact he's one of the main supporters of the orchestra. But frankly, I'd rather have the money for something else — like raising purebred dogs."

She grimaced as she looked around the rehearsal hall. I didn't know what to say. Were we really that different? Did she really think purebred dogs are more important than music?

On the way home, Mrs. Hanson seemed more friendly. "Your mother is a professional pianist, isn't she? Maybe I *will* ask her to play for Holly's tryout if the regular accompanist can't make it, Mary."

I looked at Holly and saw that she was gently shaking her head. If I asked Mother to play the accompaniment, Holly might get mad and wouldn't let me be her friend anymore. After I had worked so hard to get this far with her!

Then I thought of Mother. I thought of how many social blunders she had been making. If she got to play in Holly's tryout, the Hansons would find out what a good pianist she was and respect her a lot more.

It was hard to decide. So I just mumbled something.

"Fine!" Mrs. Hanson said cheerfully. "I'll give your mother a call tomorrow."

It was nice that Fourth Brother cared about my feelings...

70

WORD STUDY

MUSIC WORDS WITH *-IST*: Point out the word *pianist* on page 70, and remind students that the suffix *-ist* means "one who does something." Ask students what a *pianist* does. (plays the piano) Point out that the final *o* in *piano* was dropped before the suffix was added. Then have students add the suffix *-ist* to these words to make each one tell about someone who plays that instrument: *violin, harp, clarinet.*

piano (- o) + ist = pianist

violin + ist = violinist

As Mrs. Hanson dropped me at our house, I ran into Mr. and Mrs. Sylvester. "We saw that kitten again, Mary," said Mr. Sylvester. "It seems to hang around a lot. I wonder if it's a stray. Maybe we can take it home."

"I don't want a cat, Benny," said Mrs. Sylvester. "Cats are stuck-up animals, and they care only about themselves. I want another dog. I want a beagle like Jenny!"

Her voice quavered a little, and I knew she still missed their dog.

"Now, now, Denny," said Mr. Sylvester. "We'll find a beagle just like Benny one of these days."

When I went in the house, Fourth Brother was making himself a peanut butter and jelly sandwich in the kitchen.

"I thought you didn't like peanut butter," I said.

"I knew you were embarrassed because I was always eating bean sprouts for lunch," he said. "So I thought I'd try to get used to peanut butter."

It was nice that Fourth Brother cared about my feelings. He took a big bite of the sandwich. "Anyway, I couldn't find anything else to eat," he mumbled.

I remembered why I wanted to talk to him. "Did you hear what the Sylvesters said? They saw Rita again!"

Fourth Brother licked the peanut butter from the roof of his mouth and swallowed. Then he said, "It's okay as long as she comes when I play the dinner signal."

"But if Mrs. Sylvester gets another dog, it might tear Rita to pieces!"

"We'll have to talk her out of it," said Fourth Brother.

That was easy enough to say. But what could we do if the Sylvesters finally found a beagle to replace Jenny?

71

Monitor Comprehension

1 **How do you know that music is important to the Yangs? What might this have to do with the reason Mary and her brother are hiding Rita?** (Possible response: They discuss music at dinner, and instruments and music are all over the living room. A kitten might damage the music or the instruments.) METACOGNITIVE: DRAW CONCLUSIONS

2 **Explain how you used context to determine the meanings of these words:** *distract* **and** *fetched*. (Responses will vary.) **FOCUS SKILL** INFERENTIAL: VOCABULARY IN CONTEXT

Guided Reading

STRATEGIES GOOD READERS USE

FOCUS STRATEGY **Self-Question** If students cannot identify the connection between the hidden kitten and the Yang family's musical interests, remind them to ask themselves questions that help them connect what they know to the events in the story. Suggest that they ask questions like the following:

- **What do I know about the way kittens behave?**
- **What do I know about musical instruments and sheet music?**
- **What does Mary say her living room looks like?**

Mother's face turned pink, I could tell she was pleased.

I had too many things to worry about. Rita kept escaping from the basement. Having Mother accompany Holly might ruin my friendship with her. And my family kept disgracing themselves in public.

Once I saw a juggling act in China. A girl balanced three plates simultaneously by spinning them at the ends of three chopsticks. I felt like that juggler. At any minute, one of the plates might fall and smash into bits.

Mrs. Hanson called Tuesday night when we were having dinner. I answered the phone. "Mary," she said, "do you still think your mother could play the accompaniment tomorrow for Holly's audition?"

I felt torn. If I said yes, I risked losing Holly's friendship. But if she didn't want to be in the orchestra, why couldn't she just play badly at the audition? Maybe she was too proud. She didn't want her mother to see that she wasn't good enough or that she wasn't trying hard.

From where I stood in the hallway, I could see into the dining room. Mother was bringing in a stir-fried dish, and after setting it down, she wiped her forehead.

"I know it's very short notice," Mrs. Hanson was saying. "Hello? Are you still there, Mary?"

I cleared my throat. "Yes, Mrs. Hanson. I'm sure my mother would be able to do it. Can you bring the music over tonight?"

Mrs. Hanson breathed a sigh of relief. "Thank you, Mary. I'll be over as soon as I can."

"Well, we're still having supper . . . ," I told her.

"Of course, of course!" she said quickly. "I'll come at eight, shall I?"

72

SCIENCE/MUSIC

PITCH AND KEY Mrs. Yang refers to the Brahms viola sonata as *the one transposed from a violin sonata.* When a composition is *transposed,* it is rewritten at a different pitch — a different highness or lowness. You can play something higher or lower than it is written by going up or down an octave — eight notes. You can also transpose music by going up or down less than an octave. When this happens, the key of the music changes.

It was strange to hear Mrs. Hanson sounding so anxious to please. I told her that eight o'clock was fine, then walked slowly back to the dining room table.

The family looked at me curiously. "What was that about?" asked Father.

"Mother," I said in a rush, "Mrs. Hanson needs a pianist to play the accompaniment for Holly's tryout. It's a Brahms viola sonata. She's bringing over the music tonight at eight. Can you do it?"

Mother's face turned pink. I could tell she was pleased. "Why, yes, I think I can. Is that the one transposed from a violin sonata?"

I didn't know, but Father and Eldest Brother did. For the rest of the meal, we discussed the piece and whether Mother could play it at such short notice.

Mother wasn't the only one who looked happy. Father said it was about time people learned how good Mother was, while Eldest Brother and Second Sister both beamed and nodded agreement.

Fourth Brother was the only one who didn't look completely happy. "I hope Mrs. Hanson doesn't mention Rita," he said to me as the two of us cleared the table.

I had forgotten about Rita! Mrs. Hanson was under the impression that we had already told my family about her. I had to prevent Mrs. Hanson from saying something.

Mrs. Hanson and Holly arrived promptly at eight. Mrs. Hanson looked around at our living room. I had given up trying to neaten the room, and there were music stands all over. My cello leaned against the sofa, and next to it was an open case containing Elder Brother's violin. Heaps of sheet music were piled on the stands, on the sofa, and on the floor. To walk across the room, you had to negotiate carefully between piles.

"Goodness, you have a lot of music!" Mrs. Hanson exclaimed. "If you had the kitten in here . . ."

I knew what she was going to say next, and I had to head her off. Before I could do anything, there was a clatter behind me. Fourth Brother had acted first: He had knocked over a couple of music stands.

73

Informal Assessment

INDIVIDUAL READING INVENTORY

Have students read aloud the bracketed passage on page 72. For this passage, you may wish to focus on the following:

Number of words read: _104_

Number of meaning-based miscues: ———

Number of symbol/sound miscues: ———

Number of self-corrections: ———

A complete guide to keeping and interpreting individual reading inventories, including recording forms to monitor students' progress throughout the year, appears on pages A27–A35.

INTERVENTION STRATEGIES

MODIFIED INSTRUCTION   Help students summarize what happens after Mrs. Hanson calls Mary:

⟨MODEL⟩ **Mary is afraid she might lose Holly's friendship if her mother agrees to accompany Holly, and Mrs. Yang does. When Holly arrives with Mrs. Hanson, Mary and her brother keep Mrs. Hanson from talking about the kitten they are hiding. As Mrs. Yang and Holly get ready to practice, Holly looks uncomfortable. When they begin to play, Mary starts to worry about Holly.**

Then help students set a purpose for reading through page 77. (to find out how Mary's opinions of her family and Holly change)

Monitor Comprehension

❶ How does the author help you understand the meaning of *fatal* **on page 74?** (Possible responses: *Fatal* means "deadly" or "doomed." One clue is the synonym *lifeless*; another is the explanation that Holly's *heart wasn't in the music.* Because Holly doesn't seem interested in her music, everyone seems concerned that she may not do well at her tryout.) **FOCUS SKILL** INFERENTIAL: VOCABULARY IN CONTEXT

❷ What does Mary mean on page 75 when she says, ". . . nobody was fooled"? (Possible responses: Everyone, including Mrs. Hanson and Holly, recognizes that Holly doesn't enjoy playing the viola. Holly does everything technically right but has no feeling for the music. Holly isn't fooling anyone into thinking that she really wants to play.) CRITICAL: INTERPRET STORY EVENTS

As I helped him set the stands up again, he whispered to me, "You'll have to think of something else to distract her."

"As I was saying—," Mrs. Hanson began again.

"Mother," I interrupted desperately, "we haven't tuned the piano for some time. Do you think that will bother Holly?"

Mother walked over to the piano and played a blurringly fast chromatic scale across the keyboard. "It should do well enough." She turned to Mrs. Hanson. "Have you got the music?"

At last that took Mrs. Hanson's mind from Rita—for the time being. She fetched the music and handed it to Mother.

Mother looked at the score. "My husband thought it might be this sonata. I've accompanied him on it—in a different key, of course." She sat down at the piano and looked at Holly. "Shall we try it?"

Holly looked uncomfortable—the first time I had ever seen her really uncomfortable. Slowly, she took out her viola and tuned it. "I'm getting stage fright," she muttered, looking around at the circle of eyes.

"Then it would be good practice for the real audition," said Mrs. Hanson with a nervous laugh.

We moved aside piles of instruments and music and found seats. Holly and Mother began.

After a few bars, I began to worry—but not about Mother. There was nothing wrong with her piano playing. She had played the piece before, after all.

The problem was Holly. She had obviously been well taught. Her bowing was correct, her fingering neat, and her pitch true. She seemed to be following the score carefully, obeying all the dynamics signs. But there was something lifeless about her playing— and that was fatal.

74

My family and I looked around at one another, and I saw the same conclusion in everybody's eyes. Even Fourth Brother, who can't tell "Old MacDonald Had a Farm" from "Mary Had a Little Lamb," seemed to know from the expression on Holly's face that her heart wasn't in the music.

At the end we all clapped politely, but nobody was fooled. "I told you I had stage fright," Holly said in a low voice.

Mrs. Hanson swallowed. "You'll get over it by tomorrow, darling," she said, and the forced smile on her face was painful to see. She turned to Mother. "Thank you very much, Mrs. Yang. You played beautifully."

"Oh, no, I was simply awful!" said Mother. She knew she had done well, but for a Chinese it would be very rude to agree.

"You're a marvelous pianist, really!" insisted Mrs. Hanson.

Mother again disagreed. "I'm very poor. You must not flatter me."

"No, no!" said Mrs. Hanson. "I'm not trying to flatter you."

Holly looked impatient. "Mom, we'd better go."

75

Informal Assessment

FOCUS SKILL **VOCABULARY IN CONTEXT**

To assess whether students are using context to figure out the meanings of unfamiliar words or multiple-meaning words, ask these questions:

- **The word *poor* has more than one meaning. What meanings can this word have? How can you figure out what *poor* means on page 75?**

- **What does *flatter* on page 75 mean? What clues can you use to determine its meaning?**

Further instruction on Vocabulary in Context can be found on pages T130–T131.

REACHING ALL LEARNERS

CHALLENGE

WHAT ARE THEY THINKING? Ask students to imagine what is going on in the minds of the Yangs, Mrs. Hanson, and Holly as Holly plays the viola in the Yangs' living room. Have students draw a cartoon to illustrate this story event. The cartoon should include thought or speech balloons that express the thoughts and feelings of each character.

Monitor Comprehension

1 **Should Mrs. Hanson have realized that the Yangs weren't insulting her and Holly? Explain your response.** (Possible responses: Yes; the Yangs have been very kind. Mrs. Yang smiles broadly when she says "Yes!" Mrs. Hanson knows that they have recently moved from China, where customs are different.) CRITICAL: MAKE JUDGMENTS

2 **What does the confusion between *yes* and *no* teach Mary? Why do you think the author included this event in the story?** (Possible response: Learning English is not just a matter of understanding meanings of words—people must also know when to use them; the author may want readers to understand how difficult it can be for people to adjust to a new culture.) CRITICAL: RECOGNIZE AUTHOR'S PURPOSE

Guided Reading

STRATEGIES GOOD READERS USE

Use Prior Knowledge If students have trouble identifying the author's purpose, discuss how using prior knowledge can help.

MODEL **When the Hansons giggled over Mary's confusion with *yes* and *no*, I felt bad for the Yangs. I think the author wanted me to feel bad to help me recognize how difficult it can be for people to learn the ways of a new culture.**

"Of course, darling," Mrs. Hanson said quickly. She turned to Mother. "Holly has to get a good night's rest. We don't want her to go to the audition all tired and sleepy, do we?"

"Yes!" said Mother, smiling broadly.

Mrs. Hanson blinked. "I mean, we wouldn't want Holly to fail the audition!"

"Yes, yes!" said Mother.

The rest of the Yangs agreed. "Yes," we all said earnestly.

Mrs. Hanson and Holly stared at us. I could tell that something was wrong, but I didn't know what it was. Finally Mrs. Hanson turned abruptly and walked to the front door. "Good night!" she said curtly. Opening the door, she walked out, followed by Holly.

I went after them, determined to find out what the matter was.

"Uh—did my mother say something funny again just now?" I asked when I had caught up with the Hansons.

Mrs. Hanson stopped. "Well, it just sounded awfully strange, what all of you said. I could hardly believe my ears!"

I didn't know what she was talking about. "What did we say? What sounded strange?"

"It sounded like you wanted me to fail the audition!" said Holly.

It was my turn not to believe my ears. "We said no such thing!"

"I said we wouldn't want Holly to fail the audition," Mrs. Hanson said slowly, very slowly. "Then your family said yes—every single one of you!"

"Of course we said yes!" I cried indignantly. "We agreed with you completely! We certainly don't want Holly to fail the audition!"

The three of us stood frozen and looked at one another. To a passerby, we must have looked like three store dummies.

Suddenly Mrs. Hanson began to laugh. "Yes! We have no bananas!" she sang in a high, cracked voice.

She had gone completely mad! Maybe the anxiety over Holly's audition had driven her out of her mind. I looked at Holly. But she was laughing as well. "It's an old song my grandma used to sing," she told me.

76

AUTHOR'S CRAFT

"YES! WE HAVE NO BANANAS" The song title "Yes! We Have No Bananas" helps the Hansons understand the Chinese use of *yes* to show agreement. The author also uses this as a way to help readers understand the confusion between a typical American response, explained by Holly, and the typical Chinese response, explained by Mary.

Mrs. Hanson turned to me, still laughing. "You all said yes because you agreed with me, just like in the song 'Yes! We Have No Bananas.'"

I still didn't understand. "Was that wrong?"

Holly tried to explain. "In English, you'd say, 'No, we wouldn't want Holly to fail the audition.'"

I had thought that learning English was just a matter of memorizing a lot of new words and phrases. It is much more complicated than that. Even knowing when to say yes or no is tricky!

I turned slowly away and started for home. I'd have a lot to write in my notebook tonight. Behind my back, I heard Mrs. Hanson and Holly giggling and softly singing, "Yes! We have no bananas today!"

Suddenly I felt I had to say something. I turned again and caught up with the Hansons. "Mrs. Hanson," I said, "we're new in this country, and we can't do everything right immediately. I hope you'll try to be patient."

Without waiting for her to reply, I turned to Holly. "When you picked up your viola for the first time, you probably played a few sour notes. I bet your teacher didn't break down laughing."

By now both Mrs. Hanson and Holly had sobered. "You're quite right, Mary," Mrs. Hanson said quietly. "We should have been more understanding."

I turned slowly away and started for home. I'd have a lot to write in my notebook tonight.

77

INTERVENTION STRATEGIES

MODIFIED INSTRUCTION Discuss how Mary's feelings toward the Hansons and toward her own family change in the story.

- At first, Mary seems to be in awe of the Hansons. At the same time, she is embarrassed by her own family's social mistakes.
- Mary questions how different she and Holly are after Holly says she'd rather raise dogs than go to music camp.
- When Mary hears and sees Holly play, she realizes that Holly does not care about music.
- When Mary hears the Hansons giggling behind her back, she realizes how unfeeling they can be, and she defends her family.

SKILLS IN CONTEXT

GRAMMAR

SKILL TRACE	
Introduce	T96–T97
Review	T123

Imperative and Exclamatory Sentences

TEACH/MODEL

Ask students to identify an exclamatory sentence on page 76 and tell how they know it is exclamatory. (Possible response: "We said no such thing!" It expresses Mary's strong feelings about Mrs. Hanson's comments. It ends with an exclamation point.) Point out this sentence on page 77: "I hope you'll try to be patient." Explain that this sentence can be rewritten as an imperative sentence. Model rewriting the sentence.

> MODEL An imperative sentence gives a command. The subject is *you* (understood). I will rewrite the sentence this way: *Try to be patient.* Most imperative sentences end with a period. Once in a while, an imperative sentence is also an exclamation and ends with an exclamation point.

PRACTICE/APPLY

Have students rewrite the following declarative and interrogative sentences as imperative sentences:

I wish you would play that piece again.
(Play that piece again.)

You can put your violin over here.
(Put your violin over here.)

Will you help me clean up the room?
(Help me clean up the room.)

Do you want to feed the cat?
(Feed the cat.)

Then ask students to look for examples of exclamatory sentences in the selection. Have them explain how they recognized that the sentences are exclamatory.

Literary Response

RETURN TO THE PREDICTIONS/PURPOSE

Were your predictions about the story confirmed? Discuss with students whether their purpose for reading was met.

APPRECIATING THE LITERATURE

What do you think about the way Mary's feelings toward her family change at the end of the story?
(Responses will vary.)

Think About It

1 **Why does Mary want her mother to accompany Holly on the piano at the audition?** (Possible response: Her mother is an accomplished pianist, and Mary thinks that if her mother accompanies Holly, it will make up for the social mistakes her mother has made.) INFERENTIAL: SUMMARIZE

2 **Do you think Mary is right to tell Mrs. Hanson and Holly how their laughter makes her feel? Why or why not?** (Responses will vary.) CRITICAL: EXPRESS PERSONAL OPINIONS

3 **Why do you think the author included the description of the juggling act that Mary saw in China?** (Possible response: because it is an interesting and dramatic way to show how Mary is feeling) CRITICAL: LITERARY ANALYSIS/THEME CONNECTION

She looked at Holly. "You should apologize, too."

Holly murmured something. Her face didn't show much expression, so I couldn't tell how she felt.

As I walked home, I thought about how unfair I had been to my family all these months. I thought they had been impossible, because they didn't make more of an effort to learn American ways.

But I am actually one of them: In spite of my list of new words and my careful study of American ways, I still make mistakes, just like the rest of the family.

I had blamed Mother more than the rest, because she had made the most embarrassing mistakes. I should have remembered that she had to spend all her time cooking and feeding us. She didn't have time to meet a lot of Americans and learn the customs of this country.

I had been ashamed of Mother. Now I was more ashamed of myself.

Think About It

1 Why does Mary want her mother to accompany Holly on the piano at the audition?

2 Do you think Mary is right to tell Mrs. Hanson and Holly how their laughter makes her feel? Why or why not?

3 Why do you think the author included the description of the juggling act that Mary saw in China?

78

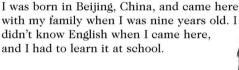

Meet the Author
Lensey Namioka

Was your family musical like the Yangs?

I'd say so. My father has composed music, and my sister is a professor of musicology, so they had very good "ears." But not me! Once, my sister hid my violin exercise book. She confessed years later that she just couldn't take listening to me practice anymore! Still, my family was supportive of other things I did.

What were some of the other things you did?

Actually, I liked playing the piano. It was really only the violin that I disliked. I hated tuning it up! I preferred reading. I was a real bookworm. After I found the public library, it became my home away from home.

What else in the story comes from your own life?

I was born in Beijing, China, and came here with my family when I was nine years old. I didn't know English when I came here, and I had to learn it at school.

Was it hard to learn English?

It wasn't as bad as it sounds. Kids learn fast, and I had good friends.

79

ABOUT THE AUTHOR

LENSEY NAMIOKA loved reading and making up adventure stories as a child. When she started writing children's books, she naturally wrote adventure stories. Later she based her work on her own childhood experiences. Namioka often places her main characters in humorous situations, reinforcing her belief that humor is the best vehicle an author has for conveying an important message.

INTERNET Additional author information can be found on *The Learning Site* at **www.harcourtschool.com**

Informal Assessment

RETELL

Have each student retell the story in his or her own words. Check to make sure that the student

☐ relates the main ideas and relevant details in sequence.

☐ provides a sentence that summarizes the main idea of the story.

☐ includes story elements: the main characters, the setting, the story problem, the solution.

☐ relates text to relevant experiences.

SUMMARIZE

Ask students to summarize the story by recalling key story elements. Students can refer to the story map they completed while reading. See also *Practice Book* page 17.

ONE-SENTENCE SUMMARY Have students use their completed story maps to write a one-sentence summary of "Yang the Third and Her Impossible Family."

▲ **Practice Book, page 17**

Activity Choices

MUSICAL OPINIONS

Listen to Music   Provide students with recordings of a variety of orchestral titles. Include examples of orchestral music such as symphonies, concertos, and suites. You may also want to include chamber music titles. CRITICAL: REACT CRITICALLY/ORGANIZE INFORMATION

GOOD ADVICE

Write an Advice Column   Suggest that students look through age-appropriate magazines to read examples of advice column letters and responses for style and content. CREATIVE: WRITING/USE TECHNOLOGY

WHAT DOES IT MEAN?

Make a Phrase Book   Invite students whose first language is not English to share the words, phrases, and expressions that have caused them the most difficulty while learning English. Engage the whole class in a discussion of why these words, phrases, and expressions are sometimes difficult to understand. CREATIVE: WRITING

MUSICAL RESEARCH

Draw a Diagram   Work as a class to brainstorm and list a variety of musical instruments. You might also wish to display examples of diagrams in which parts are marked and labeled. CREATIVE: ILLUSTRATING; CRITICAL: USE MULTIPLE SOURCES

Response

Musical Opinions

LISTEN TO MUSIC With a small group, listen to an audiotape or a CD of orchestra music. Discuss what you like or dislike about the music, and compare it to the kinds of music you listen to most often. Construct a chart to show the musical likes and dislikes of your group.

Good Advice

WRITE AN ADVICE COLUMN Imagine that you write an advice column for a newspaper. Make up a letter that a character from this story might send you. Then write your answer to the letter. Point out what the character may be able to learn from his or her experience. If possible, use a word processing program to publish your column.

80

SCHOOL–HOME CONNECTION

Suggest that students work with family members to complete the activities on the copying master on page R17. You may want to assign some or all the activities as homework during the week.

TEST TUTOR   Family members can help students prepare for standardized or state tests on *The Learning Site* at **www.harcourtschool.com**

Copying Master, page R17 ▶

Activities

What Does It Mean?

MAKE A PHRASE BOOK You probably use slang words and phrases that don't mean what the dictionary says they mean. For example, the dictionary says *cool* means "slightly cold," but sometimes people say something is *cool* when they mean they like it. Create a phrase book to help new speakers of English understand some of these expressions. Include both the dictionary meanings and the slang meanings.

Musical Research

DRAW A DIAGRAM Choose a musical instrument mentioned in the story or another one that interests you. Use books or a computer to research how the instrument is constructed. Then make a drawing or diagram of the musical instrument, and label its parts.

81

Assessment

SELECTION COMPREHENSION TEST
To evaluate comprehension, see pages 7–9.

INFORMAL ASSESSMENT
PERFORMANCE ASSESSMENT Student work for the Good Advice activity may be used for performance assessment of story comprehension.

PORTFOLIO OPPORTUNITY
Students may want to add to their portfolios their phrase books from the What Does It Mean? activity.

REACHING ALL LEARNERS

INTERVENTION STRATEGIES

WRITING FOR ADVICE For the Good Advice activity, some students may need help identifying topics for their letters. Remind students that people write to an advice column for help in solving a problem. Provide page numbers where students can read about the problems some characters have:

Holly doesn't care about the Junior Chamber Orchestra.	page 69
Mrs. Yang says "Yes!" and upsets the Hansons.	page 76
Holly and Mrs. Hanson upset Mary by giggling.	page 77

Building Literacy Skills

REREADING FOR FLUENCY

Readers Theatre

Have groups of students read parts of "Yang the Third and Her Impossible Family" as a Readers Theatre. Divide the story into sections and assign each group a different section. Suggest that students choose two members of each group to take Mary's role: one to read Mary's narration and the other to read Mary's dialogue. Invite students to sit in chairs arranged in a semicircle in front of the class and to read their parts with expression.

LISTENING/READING

WRITING

New Ending

Have students write a new ending for the story, in which both Holly and Mary have an opportunity to try out for the Junior Chamber Orchestra. Explain that although students can develop their endings any way they choose, the endings should make sense and should not have the characters doing or saying things that do not suit their personalities. WRITING

ORAL LANGUAGE

Take the Hot Seat

Have students work in groups and take turns portraying different story characters, such as Mary, Holly, and Mrs. Hanson. While on the "hot seat," a student portrays a character and answers questions from other group members. Have students refer to the speaking and listening tips on Activity Card 5, page R12, to help them speak clearly and effectively. LISTENING/SPEAKING

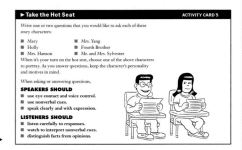

Activity Card 5 ▶

VIEWING

Special Lettering

Call attention to the sentences that are highlighted and called out with special lettering on pages 70, 72, and 77. Use the callout on page 72 and the musical staff on the top of page 68 to point out how the flow of the letters in the highlighted sentences mimics the movement of the notes on the staff. Have students select one or two sentences from the selection to write in a similar design or in a design of their own that conveys the music element of the story.

VIEWING/REPRESENTING

REACHING ALL LEARNERS

Intervention Strategies for Below-Level Readers

RETURN TO THE STRATEGY

Reinforce Comprehension

FOCUS STRATEGY **Apply the Self-Question strategy.** Talk with students about how using strategies while reading can help improve their comprehension of what they read. Remind students that the focus strategy for reading "Yang the Third and Her Impossible Family" is Self-Question. Discuss the strategy by asking questions such as these:

- **How does asking yourself questions increase your understanding of what you read?**
- **What kinds of questions should you ask yourself as you read?**

Have students practice using this strategy as they reread a section of "Yang the Third and Her Impossible Family." As students silently reread pages 72–78, have them note questions they ask themselves and the page numbers where the answers can be found. Suggest that they use a chart to record their use of the strategy.

Questions	Page Number	Answers
Why does Holly look uncomfortable when she starts to play?	page 74	She plays without feeling, and soon everyone will know it.
Why do Holly and her mother leave so abruptly?	page 76	They think the Yangs want Holly to fail her audition.
Why does Mrs. Hanson start singing the song "Yes! We Have No Bananas"?	pages 76–77	The word yes is used in the song the same way it is used by the Yang family.

LANGUAGE EXPLORATION

Cultural Foods

Discuss words that name foods of different cultures. In the story, Mary observes her mother carrying a stir-fried dish to the table (page 72). Explain that stir-fried dishes are considered part of the Chinese heritage. Most cultures have particular foods that they enjoy. Many of these have become a part of the mainstream American culture. Therefore the words for these foods are part of our everyday vocabularies.

Have students of various cultural backgrounds name favorite foods of their heritages. Have volunteers write this information in a chart or list, and help the class pronounce the names of the various foods. Lead students to notice that many of these words are probably familiar to them.

Chinese	stir-fry; bean sprouts; egg rolls; rice
African American	black-eyed peas; greens; gumbo
Japanese	tempura; sukiyaki
Hispanic	burritos; paella; tacos; salsa
Italian	pizza; spaghetti; meatballs
Jewish	potato latkes; blintzes; chicken soup
English	fish and chips; beef stew

OBJECTIVE:

To use context clues to understand the meaning of words

CHALLENGE

Students can create riddles using multiple-meaning words, such as *You won't be wrong if you don't go left. Who am I?* (right) They can then exchange riddles and solve them.

ESL

Have students complete these sentences. *Andy gave his piano teacher a birthday* present. *The concert could not begin until the band was* present. Then have students draw a picture to go with each sentence.

RETEACH See page R4 for a lesson in multiple modalities.

TECHNOLOGY

The *Mission: Comprehension™ Skills Practice* CD-ROM provides more practice with reading comprehension.

FOCUS SKILL Vocabulary in Context

AFTER READING

Return to the Concept

Extend the thinking.

Ask students how they used context clues to figure out unfamiliar words in the selection.

Model the thinking.

Have students read page 82. Then write the sentences below on the board. Have students name a context clue they can use to figure out the meanings of the underlined words.

Holly did not long to attend music camp, but there was nothing that Mary desired more.	(Synonym—desired)
Mary thought it was peculiar that Holly would rather raise dogs than go to music camp. She couldn't understand Holly's oddly different feelings.	(Definition—oddly different)

You may wish to use this model for the first sentence.

MODEL **I know the word *long* has more than one meaning. It can be an adjective that describes length or a verb that means "to want badly." When I look at the context, I see the word *desired*. I know that *desire* also means "to want very badly." It is a synonym for *long*. I can use it to figure out that here, *long* means "to want very badly."**

Summarize.

Ask students how using context to figure out the meanings of words helped them understand the selection.

Guided Practice

Discuss context rules.

Have students read page 83. Help them identify context clues they can use to figure out the meaning of each underlined word.

Test Prep

These tips can help students understand and answer test items on vocabulary in context:

• Look for synonyms or antonyms of the unfamiliar word.
• Look for groups of words that define, describe, explain, or give examples of the unfamiliar word.

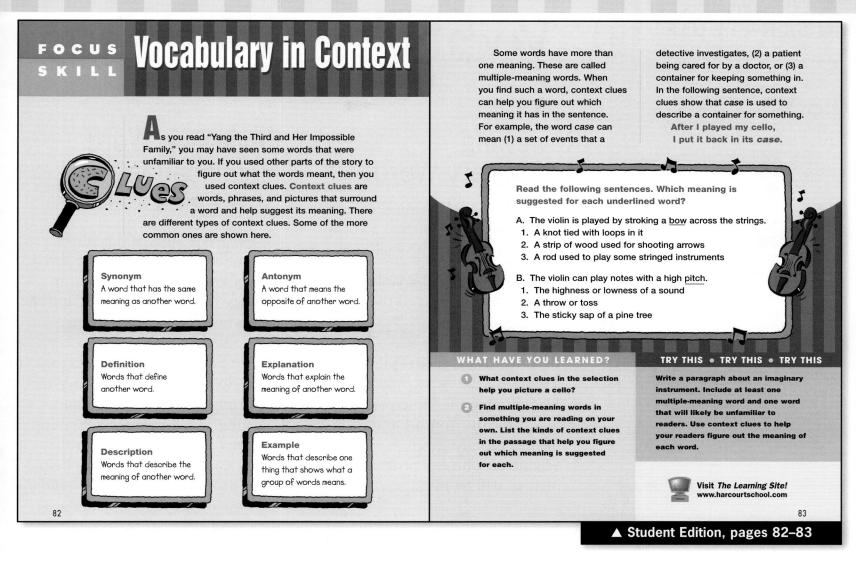

FOCUS SKILL **Vocabulary in Context**

Clues

As you read "Yang the Third and Her Impossible Family," you may have seen some words that were unfamiliar to you. If you used other parts of the story to figure out what the words meant, then you used context clues. Context clues are words, phrases, and pictures that surround a word and help suggest its meaning. There are different types of context clues. Some of the more common ones are shown here.

Synonym
A word that has the same meaning as another word.

Antonym
A word that means the opposite of another word.

Definition
Words that define another word.

Explanation
Words that explain the meaning of another word.

Description
Words that describe the meaning of another word.

Example
Words that describe one thing that shows what a group of words means.

82

Some words have more than one meaning. These are called multiple-meaning words. When you find such a word, context clues can help you figure out which meaning it has in the sentence. For example, the word *case* can mean (1) a set of events that a detective investigates, (2) a patient being cared for by a doctor, or (3) a container for keeping something in. In the following sentence, context clues show that *case* is used to describe a container for something.

> After I played my cello,
> I put it back in its *case*.

Read the following sentences. Which meaning is suggested for each underlined word?

A. The violin is played by stroking a <u>bow</u> across the strings.
  1. A knot tied with loops in it
  2. A strip of wood used for shooting arrows
  3. A rod used to play some stringed instruments

B. The violin can play notes with a high <u>pitch</u>.
  1. The highness or lowness of a sound
  2. A throw or toss
  3. The sticky sap of a pine tree

WHAT HAVE YOU LEARNED?

1 What context clues in the selection help you picture a cello?

2 Find multiple-meaning words in something you are reading on your own. List the kinds of context clues in the passage that help you figure out which meaning is suggested for each.

TRY THIS • TRY THIS • TRY THIS

Write a paragraph about an imaginary instrument. Include at least one multiple-meaning word and one word that will likely be unfamiliar to readers. Use context clues to help your readers figure out the meaning of each word.

Visit *The Learning Site!*
www.harcourtschool.com

83

▲ **Student Edition, pages 82–83**

Practice/Apply

Have students apply the skill. Have students answer the questions and complete the activity on page 83.

WHAT HAVE YOU LEARNED?

1 **Possible response:** Clues like *half-size*, *took up a lot of room*, and *I had a struggle fitting it in the car* reveal that the cello is large.

2 **Possible response:** Answers will vary. Students should list one or more of the following types of context clues: synonym, antonym, definition, explanation, description, and example.

 Students can use the Vocabulary in Context activities on *The Learning Site* at **www.harcourtschool.com**

TRY THIS

To help students develop ideas for their paragraphs, give examples of musical terms that have multiple meanings, such as *bow*, *note*, *string*. Suggest that students include a diagram or sketch of their instrument.

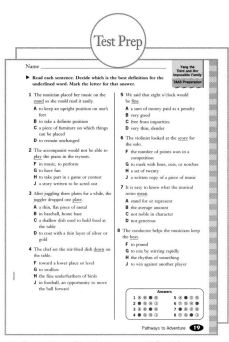

Test Prep

Name _____

▶ Read each sentence. Decide which is the best definition for the underlined word. Mark the letter for that answer.

Yang the Third and Her Impossible Family
TAAS Preparation

1 The musician placed her music on the <u>stand</u> so she could read it easily.
  A to keep an upright position on one's feet
  B to take a definite position
  C a piece of furniture on which things can be placed
  D to remain unchanged

2 The accompanist would not be able to <u>play</u> the piano in the tryouts.
  F in music, to perform
  G to have fun
  H to take part in a game or contest
  J a story written to be acted out

3 After juggling three plates for a while, the juggler dropped one <u>plate</u>.
  A a thin, flat piece of metal
  B in baseball, home base
  C a shallow dish used to hold food at the table
  D to coat with a thin layer of silver or gold

4 The chef set the stir-fried dish <u>down</u> on the table.
  F toward a lower place or level
  G to swallow
  H the fine underfeathers of birds
  J in football, an opportunity to move the ball forward

5 We said that eight o'clock would be <u>fine</u>.
  A a sum of money paid as a penalty
  B very good
  C free from impurities
  D very thin; slender

6 The violinist looked at the <u>score</u> for the solo.
  F the number of points won in a competition
  G to mark with lines, cuts, or notches
  H a set of twenty
  J a written copy of a piece of music

7 It is easy to know what the musical notes <u>mean</u>.
  A stand for or represent
  B the average amount
  C not noble in character
  D not generous

8 The conductor helps the musicians keep the <u>beat</u>.
  F to pound
  G to mix by stirring rapidly
  H the rhythm of something
  J to win against another player

Answers
1 Ⓐ Ⓑ ● Ⓓ   5 Ⓐ ● Ⓒ Ⓓ
2 ● Ⓖ Ⓗ Ⓙ   6 Ⓕ Ⓖ Ⓗ ●
3 Ⓐ Ⓑ ● Ⓓ   7 ● Ⓑ Ⓒ Ⓓ
4 ● Ⓖ Ⓗ Ⓙ   8 Ⓕ Ⓖ ● Ⓙ

Pathways to Adventure **19**

▲ **Practice Book, pages 18–19**

Yang the Third and Her Impossible Family **T131**

Vocabulary Workshop

Kwan's Big Performance

by Kimberly Jackson
illustrated by Carolina Arentsen

Have students read the
TAKE-HOME BOOK
Kwan's Big Performance
to reinforce vocabulary
words. See also *Guided
Reading Manual for Take-
Home Books*, page 4.

Reviewing Vocabulary Words

Read aloud the following sentence frames. Have a student use a vocabulary word to complete each one.

1. The boy playing the violin _____ when he played the wrong note. (*grimaced*)
2. He chose to play a _____ by Brahms for his recital piece. (*sonata*)
3. He will play the same piece at his _____ for the Youth Orchestra next month. (*audition*)
4. His sister, who is a professional pianist, will be his _____. (*accompanist*)
5. She played the _____ for him at his last tryout. (*accompaniment*)
6. The two musicians play this part of the piece _____. (*simultaneously*)

accompanist

simultaneously

audition

accompaniment

grimaced

sonata

Reviewing Word Identification Strategies

Decode using structural analysis.
Ask students to examine the word *uncomfortable* on page 74 and to identify its prefix, its suffix, and the base word. (prefix: *un-* meaning "not"; suffix: *-able* meaning "able to be"; base: *comfort*) Suggest that students look in their glossaries or a dictionary to confirm the pronunciation and meaning of *uncomfortable*. Remind students that recognizing prefixes, suffixes, and base words can help them pronounce and understand the new words they encounter as they read.

Have students analyze the following words, dividing them into prefixes, suffixes, and base words:

disagreeable
invalid
invisible
refreshment
unsuccessful

Cross-Curricular Words Ask students to analyze science words found in their science textbooks or in other science-related sources. (Possible responses: *hemisphere, reflex, antibiotic*) Have volunteers read and analyze their words aloud, identifying prefixes, suffixes, and base words.

Extending Vocabulary

Related Words

In "Yang the Third and Her Impossible Family," Mary asks her mother to accompany Holly. Point out the relationship between the words *accompany* and *company*. Begin a word web for words that are structurally related to *company*.

Place words in the web. Ask students to brainstorm words related to the word *company*. (Possible related words: *accompaniment, accompany, accompanist, unaccompanied, companion, companionship*) If necessary, help students think of words that are structurally related to *company* by providing prompts such as these: **If I were a pianist who played the music along with the main part, you could call me an _____.** (accompanist) Place the words in the web as students generate them. When you have completed the web, ask students to demonstrate their understanding of the words by using them in sentences.

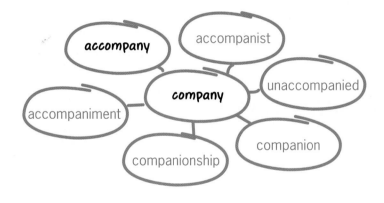

Reference Sources/Definitions

Ask students to skim the story and make a list of all the words related to music and music performance. (Possible responses: *rehearsal, orchestra, auditorium, accompanist, accompaniment, piece, musical, cello, viola, bow, pianist, sonata, violin, transposed*) Suggest that students alphabetize their lists and then use the parts of a dictionary entry to find and write the part of speech and a brief definition of each word on their lists.

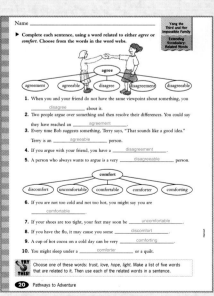

ESL

REACHING ALL LEARNERS

Help students recognize the structural relationship of the words in the word web by having them print the word *company* at the top of a column. As they list related words under *company*, tell them to line up the letters that are the same in each word.

▲ Practice Book, page 20

Yang the Third and Her Impossible Family

T133

Expressive Writing

REALISTIC STORY

Connect Writing to Reading

Point out that "Yang the Third and Her Impossible Family" is told from the first-person point of view. Ask why an author might choose the first-person point of view for a fictional story. (Possible response: It makes the narrator's experience seem real or true.) Ask why a writer might choose the third-person point of view. (Possible response: It would be easier to describe all the events in the story, no matter which characters were involved.)

Teach/Model

Display Transparency 16, and discuss the model of a story. Explain that the main purpose of most stories is to entertain or to get the reader to think.

STUDENT MODEL: STORY

A fictional story has four basic elements: characters, setting, conflict (or problem), and a plot (the actual events of the story). The plot has a clear beginning, middle, and ending. Here is a story about a prospector traveling in the Yukon during the winter. It was written by a student for a social studies assignment.

Title	*Adventure in the Yukon*
Beginning introduces character(s) and setting	*The prospector knew the temperature could get down to 50° below freezing in this part of Alaska, but he didn't care. "I'm young and strong," he scoffed. "I can survive any challenge. My friends were foolish not to come with me." As he trudged through the snow, the wind cut like a blade through his jacket. Soon the man's nose and toes were numb.*
introduces a conflict or problem	
Middle develops the conflict/problem	*The man was so cold that he decided to stop and light a fire. He gathered some twigs and branches, shaking the trees as he did. His fingers were so cold that he could hardly strike a match. With his last match he got a fire lit. Suddenly a pile of snow fell from the branches and put out the fire. "I'm doomed," he thought.*
Ending resolves the conflict/problem	*In the distance, he heard a faint whirring sound. Gradually the noise became louder, until finally it was directly above him. His friends had sent a rescue helicopter! The man was saved.*

▲ **Teaching Transparency 16**

ANALYZE THE MODEL

- Audience—other students
- Purpose—to entertain and to get reader to think
- Writer's task—to tell an entertaining story with a beginning, a middle, and an ending; to include details about the events and present them in time order

FOCUS ON ORGANIZATION

- Beginning introduces the characters, setting, and problem.
- Middle develops the plot and problem.
- Ending explains how the problem is resolved.

FOCUS ON ELABORATION

- The story contains interesting details. (*50° below freezing; wind cut like a blade through his jacket; man's nose and toes were numb; whirring sound*)
- Writer uses dialogue and quotations to tell the exact words the character speaks or thinks.

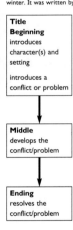

TECHNOLOGY
Students can use a word processing program such as *ClarisWorks for Kids*® to plan and write their stories.

Writing Prompts

Choose one of the following:

A Assign a prompt, for example:
Write a realistic story about a character who faced difficulties but changed for the better as a result of the experience. Include dialogue and interesting details to describe the experience.

B Have students write a story about a topic of their own choosing. Students should include details and dialogue in their story.

Prewrite and Draft

Have students brainstorm story ideas and choose one to write about. A graphic organizer such as the one on Transparency 17 can help students record their ideas about the characters, setting, and plot. A one-sentence summary of their story idea can provide focus.

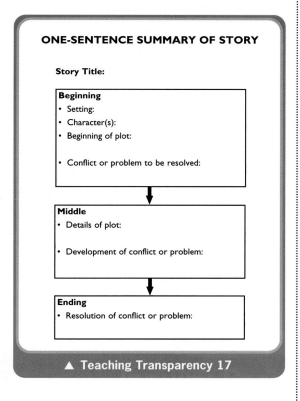

ONE-SENTENCE SUMMARY OF STORY

Story Title:

Beginning
• Setting:
• Character(s):
• Beginning of plot:

• Conflict or problem to be resolved:

Middle
• Details of plot:

• Development of conflict or problem:

Ending
• Resolution of conflict or problem:

▲ **Teaching Transparency 17**

Revise

Have students share their stories with a partner or small group. The following questions can help students work together constructively:

• **Are the characters, setting, and conflict introduced at the beginning of the story?**
• **Does the middle of the story develop the plot and conflict?**
• **Are dialogue and descriptive details included in the story?**
• **Does the ending clearly resolve the problem or conflict?**

After students have discussed each other's writing, have them revise their own stories.

Assessment

STUDENT SELF- AND PEER ASSESSMENT
Give students copies of the scoring rubric, page A9, to evaluate their own or each other's stories. They may add other points to the rubric.

PORTFOLIO OPPORTUNITY
Students may keep their revised stories in their work portfolios and complete them at a later date.

Test Prep

Remind students that when they write for a test, they should

• introduce the characters, setting, and conflict at the beginning of the story.
• present events in chronological order.
• include details.
• show how the problem or conflict is resolved.

EXPRESSIVE WRITING
Additional lessons:
  Personal Narrative, T50
  Descriptive Paragraph, T94
Complete Writing Process:
  T178
Tested or Timed Writing: T218

Language Handbook, pages 38–39

SCORING RUBRIC FOR SUGGESTED PROMPT

4 Advanced The story has a title that is intriguing and appropriate. Events are presented in time order. In the beginning, the writer introduces the characters, setting, and conflict. The middle develops the plot; the ending resolves the conflict in a logical and entertaining way. The writer uses dialogue and descriptive details.

3 Proficient The story has a title that fits the plot. Events are in chronological order. The beginning introduces the characters, setting, and conflict but may include unrelated details. The middle develops the plot, but events are not linked with time-order words. Dialogue and details are used. The ending resolves the plot logically.

2 Basic The story lacks a title or has one that does not fit the plot. The writer tries to state what the story is about but fails to introduce all the elements. The setting might not be identified, characters might not be introduced at the appropriate time, or the conflict might not be clear. The story lacks detail and dialogue.

1 Below Basic The story lacks a title and a coherent beginning, middle, or ending. Characters are not well developed. Events are not presented in a logical order or linked with time-order words. There are few details to flesh out events. The writer does not have a clear sense of purpose.

Complete and Simple Subjects

**Language Handbook,
pages 98–101**

REACHING ALL LEARNERS   **ESL**

Have students insert subjects into the following sentence frames. Prompt them by asking the question in parentheses.

_____ plays the piano. (Who?)

_____ like music. (Who?)

_____ made a lot of noise. (Who or what?)

_____ are going to the show. (Who?)

_____ is my favorite instrument. (What?)

DAY 1   Teach/Model

DAILY LANGUAGE PRACTICE

1. **What beautiful music I heard tonite?** (tonight!)
2. **The violinist played. With a powerful, smooth style.** (played with)

INTRODUCE THE CONCEPT   Use sentences 1–3 and the information on Transparency 18 as you discuss the following points:

- Every sentence is made up of two parts, a subject and a predicate. The **subject** tells who or what the sentence is about. The **predicate** tells what the subject is or does.
- The **complete subject** includes all the words that tell who or what the sentence is about.
- The **simple subject** is the main word in the complete subject.

Have students name the complete and simple subjects in items 1–3.

COMPLETE AND SIMPLE SUBJECTS

1. Mary put her cello case in the back seat. (Mary; Mary)
2. Holly's mother drove the car. (Holly's mother; mother)
3. The best players were selected for the orchestra.
   (The best players; players)

Subject	+	Predicate	=	Sentence
(Who or what?)		(Is or does what?)		

Complete Subject — all the words naming the person or thing
Simple Subject — main word or words in the complete subject

4. The accompanist had gotten sick.
   (The accompanist; accompanist)
5. Mary's mother had played a lot of chamber music. (Mary's mother; mother)
6. Holly didn't really care about the audition. (Holly; Holly)
   (For 7 and 8, responses will vary.)
7. Stacks were piled all over the room. (Possible response: Stacks of sheet music were piled all over the room.)
8. The notebook is mine. (Possible response: The red notebook with the bicycle stickers on it is mine.)

▲ **Teaching Transparency 18**

DAY 2   Extend the Concept

DAILY LANGUAGE PRACTICE

1. **Breath evenly when you sing** (Breathe; sing.)
2. **Dayly practice will improve any musician's skill!** (Daily; skill.)

DEVELOP THE CONCEPT   Display Transparency 18, and have students read sentences 4–6. Remind them that

- Sometimes the simple subject and the complete subject are the same.

Have students identify the complete subject and the simple subject in sentences 4–6 as you mark them in the sentences on the transparency.

Have students read sentences 7 and 8. Ask whether the sentences give much information. Have students rewrite the sentences, adding words to make a longer complete subject.

Name _____

Complete and Simple Subjects

Skill Reminder

- Every sentence is made up of two parts, a subject and a predicate. The subject names the person or thing the sentence is about. The predicate tells what the subject is or does.
- The complete subject includes all the words that name the person or thing the sentence is about. The simple subject is the main word or words in the complete subject.

▶ Draw a line between the complete subject and the predicate in each of the following sentences.

1. Fourth Brother talked with Mary about the cat named Rita.
2. The children worried about Rita's safety.
3. Mary remembered the juggling act in China.
4. Three plates spun at the ends of three chopsticks.
5. The Yangs' piano had not been tuned for some time.

▶ In each of the following sentences, underline the complete subject. Then write the simple subject on the line.

6. Piles of sheet music lay on the sofa and on the floor.   Piles
7. A clatter of falling music stands interrupted Mrs. Hanson.   clatter
8. Mother played a fast scale across the keyboard.   Mother
9. The look on Holly's face was uncomfortable.   look
10. Holly's technique was fairly good.   technique

▶ Choose two sentences from 6 through 10 above. Rewrite them, substituting a new complete subject for the original one in each sentence. Responses will vary.

11. _____

12. _____

Complete and Simple Subjects   GRAMMAR PRACTICE BOOK   **13**

▲ **Grammar Practice Book, page 13**

DAILY LANGUAGE PRACTICE

1. **Holly beleeves that dogs are more important than music** (believes; music.)
2. **Meanwile, Mary thinks just the opposite,** (Meanwhile; opposite.)

SUBJECT VS. PREDICATE Organize the class into three teams, and give index cards to the members of each team. Then say a sentence such as *Mary's cello filled the back seat of the car.* Team A must write down the complete subject of the sentence. Team B must write the simple subject, and Team C the predicate. Continue with four more sentences. Then ask students for their answers. Each correct answer scores a point. Continue alternating team tasks.

 DAY 4 Apply to Writing

DAILY LANGUAGE PRACTICE

1. **Mary choze to help holly with her audition.** (chose; Holly)
2. **Holly, wanted to proov that she could play the violin.** (Holly wanted; prove)

A LETTER Have pairs of students develop a letter that Holly might write to a friend about her visit to Mary's house. Tell them to use details to make some complete subjects more than two words.

Test Prep

These pointers about subjects can help students on language tests:

- To determine the complete subject, find the simple subject first. Then find the words or phrases that describe it.
- Words that describe the simple subject usually come before it. Descriptive phrases follow the subject.

The youngest violinist in the orchestra was eleven years old.

DAY 5 Cumulative Review

DAILY LANGUAGE PRACTICE

1. **The two families. Drov to the auditions.** (families drove)
2. **Mary's mother, believes that music is good for the sol.** (mother believes; soul.)

SENTENCE CATEGORY Write the following sentences on the board. Have students copy them on a sheet of paper and label each one as *declarative, interrogative, imperative,* or *exclamatory.* Then have students write each simple subject.

1. Many students in my class take music lessons.
2. Play it again.
3. Your class gave a great performance!
4. Will we have the same music teacher next year?

(1. declarative, *students*; 2. imperative, *you* [understood]; 3. exclamatory, *class*; 4. interrogative, *we*)

▲ **Grammar Practice Book, page 14**

▲ **Practice Book, page 21**

▲ **Grammar Practice Book, page 15**

SPELLING

Words with Long *o* and Long *u*

1. soul
2. smoke
3. move
4. clue
5. fruits
6. lose
7. chose
8. stole
9. prove
10. produce
11. juice
12. drove

BONUS WORDS

13. Tuesday*
14. rescue
15. continue
16. issue

*Word appearing in "Yang the Third and Her Impossible Family." Additional story words following the generalizations are *slowly, know, bow, tomorrow, low,* and *used.*

STUDENT-CHOSEN WORDS

17. _____
18. _____
19. _____
20. _____

CHALLENGE

REACHING ALL LEARNERS

Ask more-proficient spellers to find Student-Chosen Words with long *o* and long *u* by scanning newspaper or magazine articles.

DAY 1 — Pretest/Self-Check

ADMINISTER THE PRETEST. Say each word, and then use it in a Dictation Sentence. (See Day 5.) Help students self-check their pretests using the list at the top of Transparency 19.

OPEN SORT Have students look for ways to sort the Spelling Words. For example, they might sort them according to whether or not the words begin with a consonant blend. Ask volunteers to share their categories and sorted lists.

WORDS WITH LONG *o* AND LONG *u*

Spelling Words

1. soul	5. fruits	9. prove
2. smoke	6. lose	10. produce
3. move	7. chose	11. juice
4. clue	8. stole	12. drove

Long *o*	Long *u*
soul	move
smoke	clue
chose	fruits
stole	lose
drove	prove
	produce
	juice

• The long *o* sound can be spelled *o, ou,* or *o-e.*
• The long *u* sound can be spelled *o-e, ue, u-e, ui,* or *ui-e.*

▲ Teaching Transparency 19

DAY 2 — Teach/Model

CLOSED SORT Display the Spelling Words and chart headings on Transparency 19, or write the information on the board. Ask students to copy the chart and to write each Spelling Word where it belongs.

Have students look at the words in their first column and identify the ways the long *o* sound is spelled. Then ask them to identify the ways long *u* is spelled in the words in the second column. Uncover the generalizations, and have students read them to confirm their conclusions.

Handwriting Tip

Advise students to keep the joining stroke high when joining other letters to *o*. Otherwise, the letter *o* could look like an *a*.

os ol

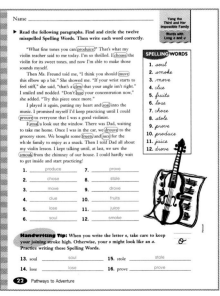

▲ Practice Book, page 22

DAY 3 — Spelling Strategies

COMPARING SPELLINGS Write the following word and its misspelling on the board:

hole　　　houl

Pronounce each word and ask how the long *o* sound should be spelled. Repeat the procedure with the words *blue* and *bloo*. Discuss with students the strategy of comparing spellings by writing a word two ways and seeing which one looks right. Remind students to look carefully at words when they are proofreading to see if the words look right.

✏ Apply to Writing

Tell students to carefully check words for vowel sounds as they proofread their own writing. Have them look for words with *ou*, *o-e*, *ue*, *u-e*, and *ui* to see if they are spelled correctly.

DAY 4 — Spelling Activities

SEE AND SPELL Have one person who is "It" write on a slip of paper the name of an object visible in the classroom. He or she gives the paper to another student, who confirms the spelling in a dictionary. The other students take turns trying to guess the name of the object by spelling it. They start by guessing the first letter, then the second, and so on. The student who is "It" writes the correct letters on the board as they are guessed. The student who completes the word becomes "It."

WRITING HAIKU Students can use the Spelling and Bonus Words to write haiku and other kinds of poems. Have students share their completed poems with the class.

DAY 5 — Posttest

Assess students' progress, using the Dictation Sentences.

DICTATION SENTENCES

1. **soul** Don't tell another **soul** about this.
2. **smoke** **Smoke** from the fireplace filled the room.
3. **move** We will **move** to our new house soon.
4. **clue** One small **clue** can help solve a mystery.
5. **fruits** Vegetables and **fruits** are good for you.
6. **lose** We hope we don't **lose** the final game.
7. **chose** She **chose** a mystery to read.
8. **stole** Someone **stole** my wallet!
9. **prove** Can you **prove** that your answer is right?
10. **produce** The fifth-grade students will **produce** a play.
11. **juice** My favorite kind of **juice** is orange.
12. **drove** Mother **drove** slowly on the wet road.

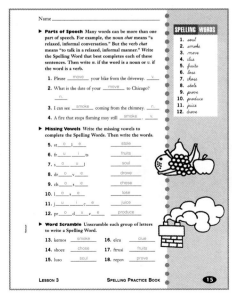

▲ Spelling Practice Book, page 14

▲ Spelling Practice Book, page 15

Yang the Third and Her Impossible Family **T139**

Cross-Curricular Connections

REACHING ALL LEARNERS

CHALLENGE

Students working on the Summer Camp Directory activity can write or make phone calls to the camps they identify on the Internet to learn of scholarship programs available for camp applicants.

ESL

Students can help translate information for a bilingual section of the Summer Camp Directory.

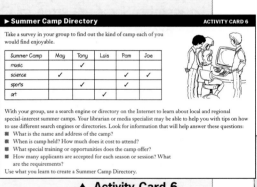

▲ Activity Card 6

Music Camp

SOCIAL STUDIES

Summer Camp Directory

MATERIALS
- a computer with Internet access
- paper
- pencils

RESEARCH SPECIALTY CAMPS In "Yang the Third and Her Impossible Family," Mary tried not to be envious of Holly's audition for the Junior Chamber Orchestra and the chance to go to a summer music camp. Have students use the Internet to find out what types of summer camps are available in their region and the opportunities these camps provide.

Activity Card 6, page R12, will help students focus their research and create their directories. Have students work in small groups to discuss their special interests. Ask groups to search the Internet to find summer camps related to these special interests. Groups can combine what they learn to create a Summer Camp Directory. READING ELECTRONIC TEXTS/VIEWING/ INQUIRY/ PRESENTING

Presenting the Classics

MATERIALS
- paper
- pencil
- cassette or CD player

ORAL PRESENTATION In "Yang the Third and Her Impossible Family," Holly plays a sonata by Johannes Brahms, one of the great classical composers of the 1800s. Provide students with a list of classical composers. The list may include the following: Bach (family), Ludwig van Beethoven, Johannes Brahms, Frédéric Chopin, Joseph Haydn, Franz Liszt, Wolfgang Amadeus Mozart, Giuseppe Verdi. Ask each student to choose a composer and use encyclopedia articles to research the composer for an oral presentation. Encourage them to use musical recordings of works written by the composer in their presentations.

Remind students that

- topics in an encyclopedia are arranged alphabetically in each volume.
- guide words at the top of each page indicate the topics on a page or facing pages.

FOCUS SKILL After students complete their presentations, have them discuss how they used context to figure out the meanings of any new or multiple-meaning words they encountered as they did their research. SPEAKING/READING

Inquiry Projects

"Yang the Third and Her Impossible Family" can be a springboard for inquiry into various topics and ideas. Brainstorm with students topics they would like to learn more about, and record these in a web. Students can use some resources shown here to begin their projects.

chamber music — youth orchestras — **Yang the Third and Her Impossible Family** — learning to play an instrument — Chinese customs

RESOURCES

Music by Carolyn Grimshaw. World Book, 1996. CHALLENGING

The Statue of Liberty by Jim Haskins. Lerner, 1986. AVERAGE

The Violin Man by Maureen Brett Hooper. Boyds Mills Press, 1991. EASY

Immigrant Girl: Becky of Eldridge Street by Brett Harvey. Holiday House, 1987. AVERAGE

"Dear Mrs. Parks" pp. 84–97

THEME
Look Inside

GENRE
Letters

- The **audience** is the person to whom the letter is written.
- The **purpose** is to express thoughts and feelings.

CROSS-CURRICULAR CONNECTIONS

- **SOCIAL STUDIES:** Rosa Parks
- **SCIENCE/ART:** Women in Science or Art

FOCUS STRATEGY — REREAD

- **Before Reading:** Strategy Reminder on page T151
- **During Reading:** Apply the Strategy on pages T154, T156, T162
- **After Reading:** Return to the Strategy on page T173

FOCUS SKILL — MAKE JUDGMENTS

- **Before Reading:** Introduce the Skill on pages T150–T151
- **During Reading:** Apply the Skill on pages T154, T156, T162
- **After Reading:** Practice the Skill on pages T174–T175

COMPANION SELECTION

- "The Crow and the Pitcher," "The Travelers and the Bear"
  Genre: Fable

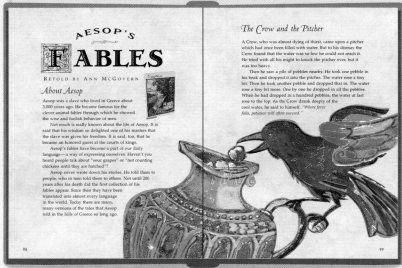

▲ **Student Edition, pages 98–101**

As students read "Dear Mrs. Parks," they will meet an inspiring individual and share in her advice to other young people about coping with their problems.

Selection Summary

The outstanding role that Rosa Parks has played in modern history has inspired many young people to seek her advice and guidance. This selection consists of letters written to Rosa Parks by students, along with her replies on subjects ranging from getting along in school to the changes she has seen in her lifetime.

Author Profile

Rosa Parks was born and grew up in rural Alabama. As a young woman, she became active in the fight against segregation and joined her husband Raymond in encouraging black citizens to register and vote. She was the central figure in the boycott of segregated buses in Montgomery, Alabama, in the 1950s, which brought Dr. Martin Luther King, Jr., to prominence. Rosa Parks has won numerous awards and honorary degrees for her contributions to society. In 1999 she received the Congressional Gold Medal, the highest honor awarded to a private citizen by the United States Congress.

REACHING ALL LEARNERS

BELOW-LEVEL READERS

EASY READER
"Lessons from Barbara Jordan," pp. 30–37. Reinforces selection vocabulary and these additional words from "Dear Mrs. Parks":

technology   peers   humanity

See *Timeless Tales Intervention Reader Teacher's Guide*, pp. 20–25.

CASSETTE
"Dear Mrs. Parks" and the accompanying fables are available on *Literature Cassette 2*.

CHALLENGE

READER'S CHOICE LIBRARY
Dear Benjamin Banneker by Andrea Davis Pinkney.
CHALLENGING

INQUIRY PROJECTS
See page T185. Students can suggest topics to research, such as women in politics and the computer age.

**DEAR
MRS. PARKS**

Skills and Strategies

Reading

Listening

Speaking

Viewing

Vocabulary

correspondence
ridiculed
potential
dignity
inspire
counsel
mentor

PRETEACHING AND READING

DAY 1

BUILDING BACKGROUND AND CONCEPTS
T148

INTRODUCING VOCABULARY T149
Transparency 20
Practice Book p. 23

PRETEACHING SKILLS
Before Reading
FOCUS SKILL Make Judgments (Introduce)
T150–T151
Transparency 21
FOCUS STRATEGY Reread T151

PREREADING STRATEGIES T152

READING THE SELECTION T152–T165
Literature Cassette 2
 Author Information T165

ALTERNATIVE SELECTION
Easy Reader: "Lessons from
Barbara Jordan"

**NOTE: Students may begin reading the selection
on Day 2.**

READING AND RESPONDING

DAY 2

LITERARY RESPONSE T164
Return to the Predictions/Purpose
Appreciating the Literature

THINK ABOUT IT T164

RETELL AND SUMMARIZE T165
Practice Book p. 25

VOCABULARY
✔ Vocabulary in Context (Review) T157
Practice Book p. 24

REREADING FOR FLUENCY
Role-Play T172

LITERATURE RESPONSE
Create a Flyer T172
Computer Station
T146
Activity Card 7, R13

**INTERVENTION STRATEGIES
FOR BELOW-LEVEL READERS** T173
FOCUS STRATEGY Return to the Strategy
Language Exploration

	DAY 1	DAY 2
Writing	**Expressive Writing: Personal Narrative** Connect Writing to Reading T178	Teach/Model T178 Analyze the Model *Transparency 23* *Language Handbook p. 54*
Grammar	**Complete and Simple Predicates** Teach/Model T180 *Transparency 25* *Language Handbook pp. 102–103*	Extend the Concept T180 *Grammar Practice Book p. 16*
Daily Language Practice	**1. Many children right to Mrs Parks.** (write; Mrs.) **2. What woud you ask her.** (would; her?)	**1. You, can chose to make a difference.** (You can choose) **2. The froots of hard work. are progress and strength.** (fruits; work are)
Spelling	**Vowels Before _r_** parts history warning declare despair shirt learning backward border prepared harsh research Pretest/Self-Check T182 *Transparency 26*	Teach/Model T182 *Practice Book p. 28* Handwriting Tip

---

KEY

✔ **Tested Skills**

■ **Management Option:** See Managing the Classroom,
page T146, for ongoing independent activities.

 Reaching All Learners: Support for "Lessons from
Barbara Jordan," an alternative selection, appears on
Timeless Tales Intervention Reader Teacher's Guide
pp. 20–25.

COMPANION SELECTION
"Aesop's Fables" T166–T169

RESPONSE ACTIVITIES
Write a Letter T170
Present a Radio Broadcast T170
■ Recording Station
Write a Story T170
Write a Fable T170
■ Publishing Station

Selection Comprehension Test

DECODING/PHONICS
✔ Prefixes and Suffixes (Review) T163

ORAL LANGUAGE
Present an Award T172

VIEWING
Placing Text T172

INDEPENDENT READING
Reader's Choice Library:
Dear Benjamin Banneker
T147

**Reader's Choice
Library Book** ▶

Writing Prompts T178
Prewrite and Draft T179
Transparency 24
 Imagination Express™, Destination:
Neighborhood

Oral Review/Practice T181
Grammar Practice Book p. 17

1. **Can you moove a mountain one rock at
   a time** (move; time?)
2. **she can prove that she is wright.**
   (She; right.)

Spelling Strategies T183
Apply to Writing
Spelling Practice Book p. 16

COMPREHENSION
After Reading
FOCUS SKILL Make Judgments (Introduce)
T174–T175
Transparency 22
Practice Book p. 26

GRAMMAR
Complete and Simple Subjects
(Review) T159

VOCABULARY T176–T177
Reviewing Vocabulary Words
Extending Vocabulary

TAKE-HOME BOOK
Dear Grandma T176

CROSS-CURRICULAR CONNECTIONS
Social Studies: Rosa Parks T184

Take-Home Book ▶

Edit T179
Publish T179

Apply to Writing T181
Practice Book p. 27

1. **Rosa Parks played an important role. In our
   historee.** (role in; history.)
2. **She protested. The unfare treatment of
   many Americans.** (protested the unfair)

Spelling Activities T183
Spelling Practice Book p. 17

CROSS-CURRICULAR CONNECTIONS
Science/Art: Women in Science or Art T185
Activity Card 8, R13
FOCUS SKILL Apply Make Judgments

INQUIRY PROJECTS T185
Research

SELF-SELECTED READING T147
• *If a Bus Could Talk: The Story of
  Rosa Parks*
• *Martin Luther King, Jr.: Free at Last*
• *More Than Anything Else*

Assessment T179
Student Self- and Peer Assessment
Scoring Rubric

Cumulative Review T181
Grammar Practice Book p. 18

1. **Our class is lirning about Rosa Parks**
   (learning; Parks.)
2. **My favorite partes of the book Are
   Rosa's answers.** (parts; book are)

Posttest T183

Managing the Classroom

While you provide direct instruction to individuals or small groups, other students can work on ongoing activities like the ones below.

Recording Station

OBJECTIVE

To practice and record a radio broadcast

MATERIALS

- tape recorder
- cassettes

After students have planned their radio broadcasts for the News Radio activity on page T170, they can record their rehearsals. They can then listen to the tapes to decide how they might improve their broadcasts.

Publishing Station

OBJECTIVE

To create a class book of fables

MATERIALS

- paper
- simple bookbinding materials

Students can combine their illustrated fables for the Making Connections activity on page T170 to create a class book of fables for your classroom library.

Computer Station

OBJECTIVE

To use software to create a flyer

MATERIALS

- computer
- desktop publishing software

Students can use desktop publishing software for the Create a Flyer activity on page T172. Ask students with desktop publishing experience to help other students create interesting and attractive flyers.

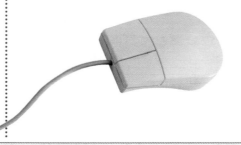

Current Events Station

OBJECTIVE

To learn about community involvement

MATERIALS

- community newsletters
- local newspapers

Rosa Parks encourages community involvement. Provide newsletters and news stories that tell how people are getting involved and helping others. Students can present brief oral reports on community projects that they find especially interesting.

Note: For more options, see pages T170–T171, T172–T173, and T184–T185.

EASY

If a Bus Could Talk: The Story of Rosa Parks by Faith Ringgold. Simon & Schuster, 1999. HISTORICAL FICTION: ROSA PARKS

More Than Anything Else by Marie Bradby. Orchard, 1995. HISTORICAL FICTION: WRITING

TAKE-HOME BOOK
Dear Grandma
REALISTIC FICTION: LETTER WRITING

EASY READER: TIMELESS TALES
"Lessons from Barbara Jordan," pp. 30–37. LETTERS: COMMUNICATION

AVERAGE

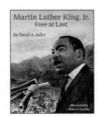

Martin Luther King, Jr.: Free at Last by David A. Adler. Holiday House, 1986. BIOGRAPHY: CIVIL RIGHTS LEADERS

I Am Rosa Parks by Rosa Parks with Jim Haskins. Dial, 1997. AUTOBIOGRAPHY: CIVIL RIGHTS LEADERS

READER'S CHOICE LIBRARY
And Then What Happened, Paul Revere? by Jean Fritz. NONFICTION: AMERICAN HISTORY

See the ***Reader's Choice Library* lesson plan** on pages T1414–T1415.

CHALLENGING

Live Writing by Ralph Fletcher. Avon, 1999. NONFICTION: WRITING

Regarding the Fountain by Kate Klise. Avon Camelot, 1998. REALISTIC FICTION: LETTER WRITING

Dare to Dream: Coretta Scott King and the Civil Rights Movement by Angela Shelf Medearis. Lodestar, 1994. BIOGRAPHY: CIVIL RIGHTS LEADERS

READER'S CHOICE LIBRARY
Dear Benjamin Banneker by Andrea Davis Pinkney. BIOGRAPHY: AMERICAN HISTORY/LETTERS

ESL

See *ESL Manual* pages 20–25. You may wish to introduce these additional words and phrases:

geniuses (page 87)
miles per hour (page 87)
taken for granted (page 89)
the old days (page 92)
walks of life (page 95)

OTHER BACKGROUND-BUILDING IDEAS

INTERNET Bonus Words and additional background ideas can be found on *The Learning Site* at **www.harcourtschool.com**

Building Background and Concepts

Access Prior Knowledge

Discuss role models.

Ask students what kinds of adults make good role models for young people. (Possible responses: those who have done good things in their lives; those who help others; those who are honest and caring)

Develop Concepts

Build a web using vocabulary words.

Have students begin a web about good role models. Ask questions to encourage them to add vocabulary to the web: **What should a role model *inspire* you to do? What qualities might a good role model have? If you could carry on *correspondence* with a role model, what would you ask him or her?** Highlight indicates vocabulary.

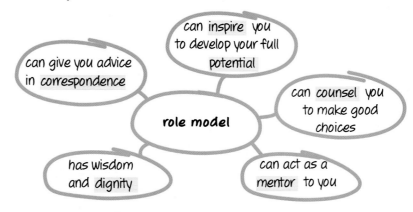

Tell students that Mrs. Parks, who wrote the letters in "Dear Mrs. Parks," has been a role model for many people.

BONUS WORDS

Introduce unfamiliar words. You may want to introduce the following words found in "Dear Mrs. Parks": *technology, aerobics, cyberspace.*

aerobics

Introducing Vocabulary

Build Word Identification Strategies

Decode familiar patterns.

Display Transparency 20, and have volunteers read the interview aloud. Remind students that recognizing familiar spelling patterns can sometimes help them figure out a word. Model decoding the word *ridiculed*:

> **MODEL** **The first syllable looks like the familiar word *rid*. The letters *ule* are familiar to me from words like *rule* and *mule*. I also see that the ending *-ed* has been added. I can use these familiar patterns to try pronouncing the word to see if it sounds like a word I know.**

As students decode the other vocabulary words, encourage them to confirm the meanings by asking questions like **Does it sound right? Does it make sense?**

CHECK UNDERSTANDING

Practice other vocabulary strategies. Have students answer questions with sentences that show what the vocabulary words mean. MEANINGFUL SENTENCES

- **Which vocabulary word comes from an ancient Greek legend about a man named Mentor, who was given the responsibility of educating a friend's young son?** WORD ORIGIN
- **What are the advantages and disadvantages of carrying on a correspondence, compared to using the telephone?** EXPLANATION
- **Which word has a meaning similar to *insulted*?** SYNONYM
- **How would you describe someone who acts with dignity?** DESCRIPTION
- **Who might counsel students about their problems?** EXAMPLE
- **Which word is the opposite of *discourage*?** ANTONYM
- **Which word is related to the word *potent*, which means "powerful" or "effective"?** RELATED WORDS

QUICKWRITE

READING NOTEBOOK Tell students that programs exist in some places to match young people with appropriate *mentors* in the community. Have students write a paragraph telling whether they think such programs are a good idea and why or why not.

VOCABULARY DEFINED

correspondence letter writing, or letters written

ridiculed made fun of

potential qualities that make the development of a talent, power, or skill possible or likely

dignity proud, calm, and controlled behavior

inspire to make someone want to do something and feel excited about doing it

counsel to give advice and support

mentor a wise, caring adviser

AN INTERVIEW WITH MR. GREEN

Interviewer: Mr. Green, what have you learned in your 90 years that you would like to share with our viewers?

Mr. Green: One thing I've learned is to have faith in yourself, even when you are **ridiculed** by others. Keep your **dignity**, even when those around you behave badly.

Interviewer: That's good advice. I know that you often visit schools to **counsel** students. What do you tell them?

Mr. Green: I tell them not to let anything stand in the way of reaching their **potential**. I try to **inspire** them to stay in school and always to do their very best.

Interviewer: I understand you also keep up an active **correspondence** with people all over the world, including many in your own age group. What advice do you have for people of your own generation?

Mr. Green: That's an easy one. Stay active. Put your experience to good use by acting as a **mentor** to a young person. Give the world the benefit of what you've learned.

Interviewer: Thank you for being here today, Mr. Green, and for sharing your wisdom with us all.

▲ **Teaching Transparency 20**

> Read the boldfaced Vocabulary Words and their definitions. Then read each set of words that follows. Decide which word is most closely related to the words in each set. Write that word on the line.

correspondence: An ongoing conversation carried on through letter-writing
ridiculed: criticized or made fun of someone in an embarrassing way
potential: an ability that has not yet been developed
dignity: self-esteem; self-worth
inspire: to motivate someone to accomplish or feel something
counsel: to give advice
mentor: a wise, devoted adviser

1. messages	stationery	pen pal	e-mail	correspondence
2. taunted	jeered	mocked	derided	ridiculed
3. spur	motivate	hearten	encourage	inspire
4. advise	direct	guide	instruct	counsel
5. teacher	coach	trainer	tutor	mentor
6. possibility	likelihood	capability	ability	potential
7. nobility	honor	self-respect	distinction	dignity

> Write a Vocabulary Word to complete each sentence.

8. Ben used blue stationery in his _____correspondence_____ to his friends.
9. When Carmen _____ridiculed_____ Claire's shirt, Claire was embarrassed.
10. Gary had great _____potential_____, but he still had to work hard to get results.

TRY THIS! Suppose you were a mentor to a younger person. Write a piece of advice that he or she could read for encouragement. Use all the Vocabulary Words in your note.

Pathways to Adventure **23**

▲ **Practice Book, page 23**

Dear Mrs. Parks **T149**

SKILL TRACE	
INTRODUCE	
• Before Reading:	T150–T151
• During Reading:	T154, T156, T162
• After Reading:	T174–T175
Reteach	R5
Review	T271

OBJECTIVE:

To make valid judgments about fiction and nonfiction

Preteach
FOCUS SKILL

Make Judgments

BEFORE READING

Preview the Literature

Preview the selection and discuss the genre.

Invite students to read the title and introduction on *Student Edition* pages 84–85 and to look at the illustrations. Ask why they think the selection is subtitled "A Dialogue with Today's Youth." (It is made up of letters between Rosa Parks and young people who have asked her for advice) Then have students read the letter from Jimmy on page 86. Ask students: **Why do you think Jimmy wrote this letter?** Remind them that letters often express thoughts and feelings and that the audience is the person who is to receive the letter.

Introduce the Skill

Discuss making judgments.

Tell students that when they determined Jimmy's reason for writing the letter, they were **making a judgment**. Display Transparency 21. Have volunteers read aloud the introduction and the labels and items in the Venn diagram. Discuss how students might make judgments about each item.

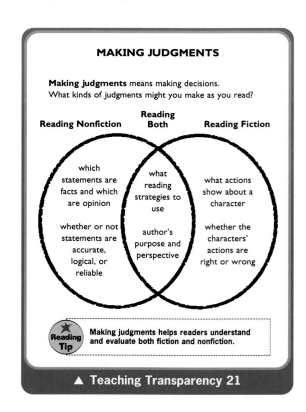

MAKING JUDGMENTS

Making judgments means making decisions. What kinds of judgments might you make as you read?

Reading Nonfiction | Reading Both | Reading Fiction

which statements are facts and which are opinion

whether or not statements are accurate, logical, or reliable

what reading strategies to use

author's purpose and perspective

what actions show about a character

whether the characters' actions are right or wrong

★ **Reading Tip** — Making judgments helps readers understand and evaluate both fiction and nonfiction.

▲ **Teaching Transparency 21**

Model the Thinking

Model making judgments.

Read aloud and discuss with students the Reading Tip on Transparency 21. Then use Jimmy's letter on page 86 of the *Student Edition* to model making judgments.

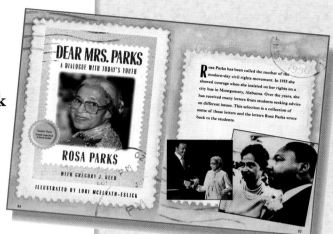

MODEL Jimmy's letter says that he wants to ask questions but has trouble doing so. From that information, I decide that Jimmy is curious but possibly somewhat shy or lacking in self-confidence. I have made a judgment about Jimmy based on what he says in the letter.

DURING/AFTER READING

- Apply the Skill, pages T154, T156, T162
- Practice the Skill, pages T174–T175

PRETEACH THE STRATEGY

FOCUS STRATEGY Reread ⭐

Encourage students to monitor their comprehension.

Remind students that they can reread to help themselves understand what they are reading. Explain that when an author refers to something that was mentioned earlier that you either don't remember or didn't fully understand, you can go back and reread to help you understand it.

- Apply the Strategy, pages T154, T156, T162
- Return to the Strategy, page T173

 See the Strategy Builder copying masters, pages A40–A45.

STRATEGIES GOOD READERS USE

- Use Prior Knowledge
- Make and Confirm Predictions
- Adjust Reading Rate
- Self-Question
- Create Mental Images
- Use Context to Confirm Meaning
- Use Text Structure and Format
- Use Graphic Aids
- Use Reference Sources
- Read Ahead
- **Reread** FOCUS STRATEGY
- Summarize and Paraphrase

Prereading Strategies

PREVIEW AND PREDICT

If students have not yet previewed the selection, have them look at the illustrations and read the title and introduction on pages 84–85 and the first letter to Mrs. Parks on page 86. Ask students to make predictions about what they may learn from Mrs. Parks's letters. Then have them begin a chart to record the problems or questions about which young people wrote to Mrs. Parks and her advice to them. Students can add information to their charts as they read. See *Practice Book* page 25.

Problem/Advice Chart

Letter Writer	Problem or Question	Mrs. Parks's Advice
Jimmy	Has trouble asking questions in school	

SET PURPOSE

Read to Solve Problems   Have students set a purpose for reading "Dear Mrs. Parks." Remind them that one purpose for reading is to solve problems. If students have difficulty setting a purpose, offer this suggestion:

MODEL **I understand from my preview that Mrs. Parks gives advice to young people. I am interested in finding out how she tries to solve their problems. I wonder whether her advice might also help my friends or me.**

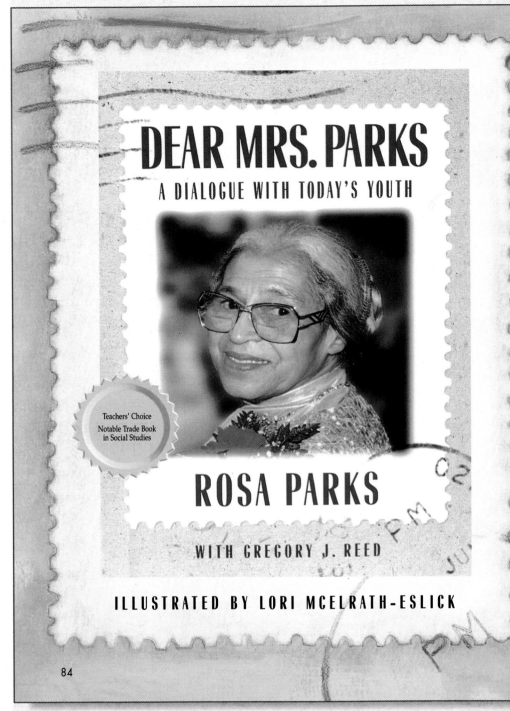

DEAR MRS. PARKS
A DIALOGUE WITH TODAY'S YOUTH

Teachers' Choice
Notable Trade Book
in Social Studies

ROSA PARKS

WITH GREGORY J. REED

ILLUSTRATED BY LORI MCELRATH-ESLICK

84

Options for Reading

DIRECTED READING
Use the **Monitor Comprehension** questions to check students' understanding. The **Guided Reading** strategies on pages T154, T156, T158, and T162 give additional support to students reading on or below level. WHOLE CLASS/SMALL GROUP

COOPERATIVE READING   Have students who read on or above level use *Comprehension Card 5* (p. R8) to focus on **author's purpose** and **perspective**.
INDEPENDENT/SMALL GROUP

INDEPENDENT READING Students reading on or above level may read independently. Encourage them to pause after reading each page to confer with partners and work together to fill in their problem/advice charts.
INDIVIDUAL/WHOLE CLASS

Rosa Parks has been called the mother of the modern-day civil rights movement. In 1955 she showed courage when she insisted on her rights on a city bus in Montgomery, Alabama. Over the years, she has received many letters from students seeking advice on different issues. This selection is a collection of some of those letters and the letters Rosa Parks wrote back to the students.

85

SKILLS IN CONTEXT

Informal Assessment

INTERVENTION STRATEGIES

MODIFIED INSTRUCTION Have students read the title, "Dear Mrs. Parks," and the introduction on page 85. Invite them to tell what they see on the first two pages. Discuss these selection words:

fascinated   values   grateful

Tell students to read through page 89 to find out what kinds of things some young people asked Mrs. Parks in their letters.

EASY READER
Students may read "Lessons from Barbara Jordan," found on pages 30–37 in **Timeless Tales.** See **Timeless Tales Intervention Reader Teacher's Guide** pages 20–25.

"Dear Mrs. Parks" and the accompanying fables are available on *Literature Cassette 2.*

Monitor Comprehension

❶ Do you think Mrs. Parks gives Jimmy good advice? Why or why not? (Possible response: yes; because she encourages him to ask questions and gives him good reasons for doing so)

FOCUS SKILL CRITICAL: MAKE JUDGMENTS

❷ What can you tell about the kind of person Mrs. Parks is from her replies on pages 86–87? (Possible response: She is curious, open-minded, and active; she enjoys life and is willing to try new things.) INFERENTIAL: DETERMINE CHARACTERS' TRAITS

Guided Reading

STRATEGIES GOOD READERS USE

FOCUS STRATEGY **Reread** If students have difficulty telling what kind of person Mrs. Parks is, they may need to reread her replies. With a small group of students, model rereading to find relevant information.

⟨MODEL⟩ **When I reread Mrs. Parks's reply on page 86, I recall that she is learning how to use the computer and how to swim and that she asks a lot of questions. On page 87, she says that she is still learning about life. These facts show me that she is an active, curious, open-minded person who enjoys trying new things.**

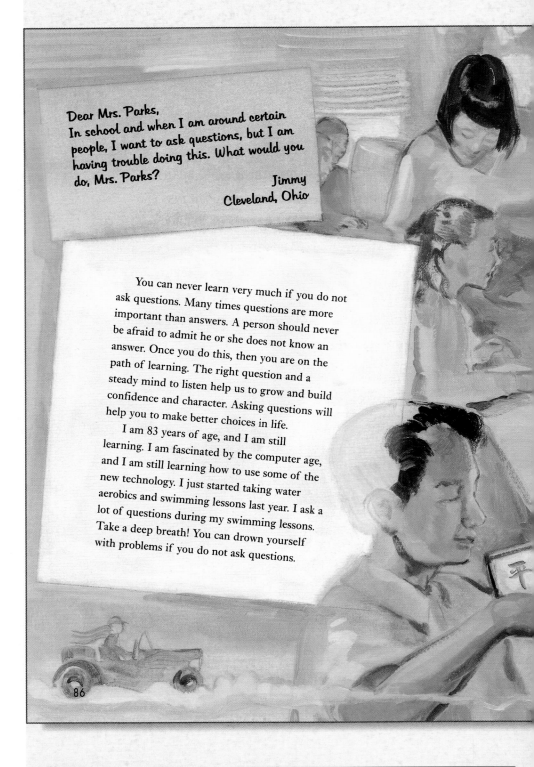

Dear Mrs. Parks,
In school and when I am around certain people, I want to ask questions, but I am having trouble doing this. What would you do, Mrs. Parks?

Jimmy
Cleveland, Ohio

You can never learn very much if you do not ask questions. Many times questions are more important than answers. A person should never be afraid to admit he or she does not know an answer. Once you do this, then you are on the path of learning. The right question and a steady mind to listen help us to grow and build confidence and character. Asking questions will help you to make better choices in life.

I am 83 years of age, and I am still learning. I am fascinated by the computer age, and I am still learning how to use some of the new technology. I just started taking water aerobics and swimming lessons last year. I ask a lot of questions during my swimming lessons. Take a deep breath! You can drown yourself with problems if you do not ask questions.

86

SCIENCE

EARLY CARS Explain that as far back as the 1400s, Robert Valturio had an idea for a cart with windmills attached to its wheels to provide power. The first successful automobiles were powered by steam, which was generated by burning kerosene to boil water that was held in a tank in the car. In 1896 the first gasoline-powered automobiles went into production, and steam cars soon fell out of favor.

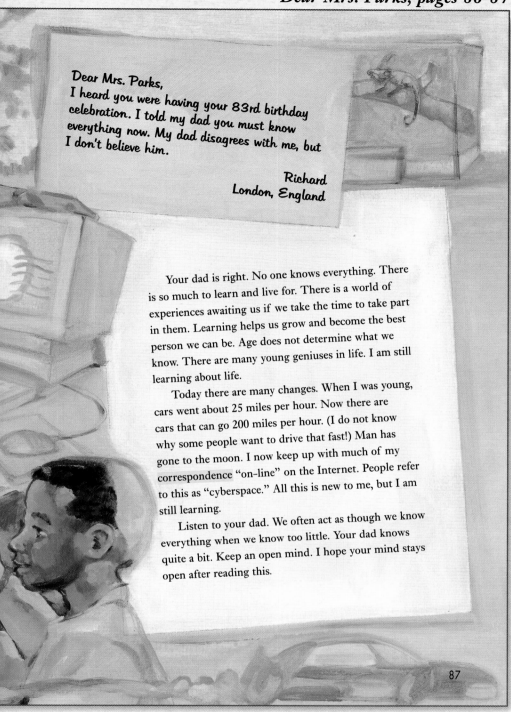

Dear Mrs. Parks,
I heard you were having your 83rd birthday celebration. I told my dad you must know everything now. My dad disagrees with me, but I don't believe him.

Richard
London, England

Your dad is right. No one knows everything. There is so much to learn and live for. There is a world of experiences awaiting us if we take the time to take part in them. Learning helps us grow and become the best person we can be. Age does not determine what we know. There are many young geniuses in life. I am still learning about life.

Today there are many changes. When I was young, cars went about 25 miles per hour. Now there are cars that can go 200 miles per hour. (I do not know why some people want to drive that fast!) Man has gone to the moon. I now keep up with much of my correspondence "on-line" on the Internet. People refer to this as "cyberspace." All this is new to me, but I am still learning.

Listen to your dad. We often act as though we know everything when we know too little. Your dad knows quite a bit. Keep an open mind. I hope your mind stays open after reading this.

87

REACHING ALL LEARNERS

ESL

COMMON EXPRESSIONS   Explain to students that *keep an open mind* is an expression that means "be willing to listen to new ideas." Demonstrate opening a door to let someone come in. Then compare opening the door with opening one's mind to let ideas come in.

"I have a new idea!"

Monitor Comprehension

❶ Do you think Mrs. Parks's reply will help Shata deal with her problem? Explain why you do or do not think so. (Possible response: Yes; because when people tease her, she can think about what Mrs. Parks said and try not to let the teasing bother her.)

FOCUS SKILL CRITICAL/METACOGNITIVE: MAKE JUDGMENTS

❷ What earlier statement that Mrs. Parks makes on page 89 has a meaning similar to *We are all leaders of something in life*?

(Possible response: *Each person in life has certain gifts or talents to give back to life*.)

INFERENTIAL: IMPORTANT DETAILS/PARAPHRASE

Guided Reading

STRATEGIES GOOD READERS USE

FOCUS STRATEGY **Reread** If students have difficulty identifying Mrs. Parks's earlier statement, discuss how rereading can help. Use these prompts:

- **Think about the meaning of the statement *We are all leaders of something in life*.**
- **State the meaning in your own words.**
- **Then reread Mrs. Parks's reply to find a statement with a similar meaning.**

Dear Mrs. Parks,
I like going to school. But I'm worrying about getting straight A's. My peers make fun of me when I get an A. I am trying to fit in.

Shata
Detroit, Michigan

11 MAY 1996

88

WORD STUDY

INTERESTING ORIGINS Point out that Mrs. Parks says everyone has talents. Tell students that the word *talent* comes from a Latin word, *talentum*, which was a unit of weight or money. The Latin word came from a Greek word, *talanton*, which was the name for the pan of a scale. Ask students to speculate on how the word's origins relate to its present meaning.

talanton

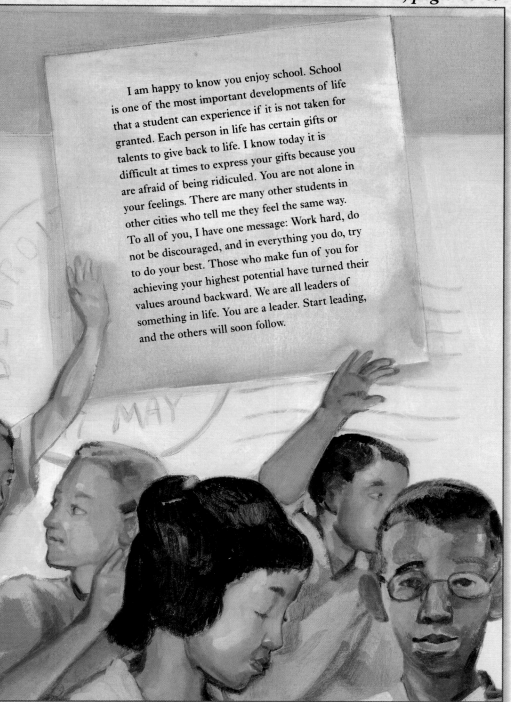

I am happy to know you enjoy school. School is one of the most important developments of life that a student can experience if it is not taken for granted. Each person in life has certain gifts or talents to give back to life. I know today it is difficult at times to express your gifts because you are afraid of being ridiculed. You are not alone in your feelings. There are many other students in other cities who tell me they feel the same way. To all of you, I have one message: Work hard, do not be discouraged, and in everything you do, try to do your best. Those who make fun of you for achieving your highest potential have turned their values around backward. We are all leaders of something in life. You are a leader. Start leading, and the others will soon follow.

REACHING ALL LEARNERS

INTERVENTION STRATEGIES

MODIFIED INSTRUCTION   Help students summarize Mrs. Parks's advice to this point.

- Mrs. Parks says that you should not be afraid to ask questions, because asking questions is how you learn.
- Mrs. Parks is <u>fascinated</u> by new things and is still learning at age 83.
- Mrs. Parks tells students to work hard and do their best, even if others make fun of them. She says that people who ridicule others have their <u>values</u> turned around.

Help students set a purpose for reading through page 93. (to find out what else Mrs. Parks thinks and feels)

SKILLS IN CONTEXT

VOCABULARY
TESTED SKILL

Vocabulary in Context

SKILL TRACE	
Introduce	T110, T130
Reteach	R4
Review 1	T157
Review 2	T199
Test	Theme 1
Maintain	T423

TEACH/MODEL

Call attention to the sentence in Shata's letter that begins *My peers . . . .* Remind students that they can sometimes use context to figure out the meaning of a word. Model using context to determine the meaning of *peers*:

> **MODEL** **I know that *peers* may mean "looks closely," but that meaning doesn't make sense in this sentence. Since the writer is talking about events that take place in school and about someone making fun of her, I can figure out that *peers* in this sentence means "equals" and refers to other students.**

PRACTICE/APPLY

Have students explain how to use context to determine the meanings of these multiple-meaning words on pages 88–89: *straight, express.*

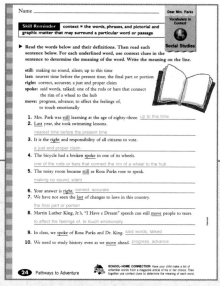

▲ **Practice Book, page 24**

Monitor Comprehension

1 **Do you think Rosa Parks may have appreciated school more than many children do? Explain.** (Possible response: Yes, because she had to stay at home when other children her age were in school; she did not take going to school for granted.) INFERENTIAL: DRAW CONCLUSIONS

2 **How do you know how Rosa Parks felt about her grandmother?** (Possible response: She talks about what her grandmother taught her, including very important qualities such as personal dignity and treating people with respect. She also says that she later took care of her grandmother based on the way her grandmother cared for others. I can tell that Rosa Parks loved and respected her grandmother deeply.) METACOGNITIVE: DETERMINE CHARACTERS' EMOTIONS

Guided Reading

STRATEGIES GOOD READERS USE

Use Prior Knowledge If students have difficulty explaining why Rosa Parks appreciated going to school, ask the following questions to help them call on prior knowledge:

- **How do children feel when they are not allowed to do what other children their age are doing?**
- **Do you generally appreciate something more or less when you have been waiting and wishing for it for a long time?**

> Dear Mrs. Parks,
> I am 12 years old, and my favorite subject is math. I want to work with computers when I grow up. Did you like school when you were young?
>
> Anthony
> Las Vegas, Nevada

90

SOCIAL STUDIES

FAMILY HISTORY Point out that Rosa Parks's grandmother taught her the history of their family. Tell students that many people are interested in finding out about the history of their families. Have students suggest and discuss ways that family members can discover facts about their family history. (Possible responses: talking to older relatives; old letters, diaries, photographs; records of births, deaths, marriages; immigration records; old newspapers; genealogy and family history Web sites)

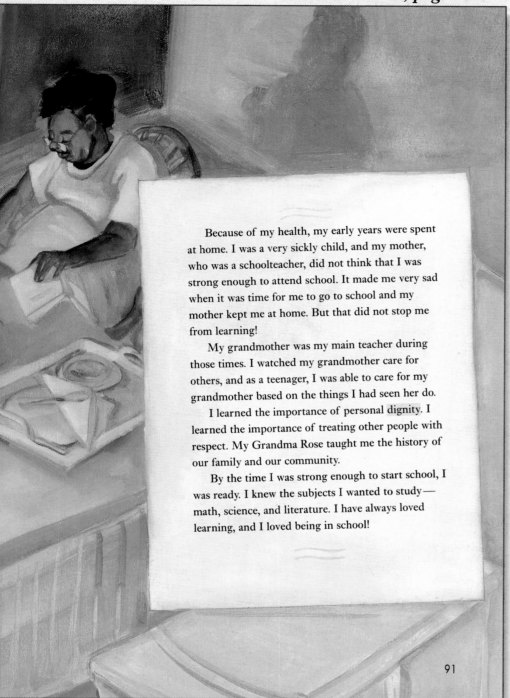

Because of my health, my early years were spent at home. I was a very sickly child, and my mother, who was a schoolteacher, did not think that I was strong enough to attend school. It made me very sad when it was time for me to go to school and my mother kept me at home. But that did not stop me from learning!

My grandmother was my main teacher during those times. I watched my grandmother care for others, and as a teenager, I was able to care for my grandmother based on the things I had seen her do.

I learned the importance of personal dignity. I learned the importance of treating other people with respect. My Grandma Rose taught me the history of our family and our community.

By the time I was strong enough to start school, I was ready. I knew the subjects I wanted to study—math, science, and literature. I have always loved learning, and I loved being in school!

91

CHALLENGE

REACHING ALL LEARNERS

THINKING ABOUT HISTORY Ask students why Rosa Parks's grandmother might have thought it was important to teach her granddaughter the history of their family and their community. Have students analyze and discuss reasons for teaching children about the past.

(Possible responses: to give them a sense of pride and understanding of their culture and heritage; to help them learn lessons that they may be able to apply in the future)

SKILLS IN CONTEXT

GRAMMAR

SKILL TRACE	
Introduce	T136–T137
Review	T159

Complete and Simple Subjects

TEACH/MODEL

Have students reread the first sentence on page 91. Remind them that the subject of a sentence tells who or what the sentence is about, and the predicate tells what the subject is or does. Explain that the **complete subject** includes all the words in the subject. The **simple subject** is the word or words that name the person, place, or thing that the sentence is about. Model identifying the complete subject and simple subject of the first sentence on page 91.

> MODEL The complete subject of this sentence is *my early years*, because it includes all the words in the subject. The simple subject is *years*, because that word names the thing the sentence is about.

PRACTICE/APPLY

Have students underline the complete subject and circle the simple subject in each of the following sentences:

My favorite subject is math.

Rosa's main teacher was her grandmother.

Caring for others is important to her.

The letters written by young people show their concerns.

Rosa Parks has strong beliefs and opinions.

Monitor Comprehension

1 **When you read Adrienne's letter, were you able to predict what Mrs. Parks's reply might be? Explain.** (Possible response: Yes, because she said in her reply to Anthony on page 91 that her grandmother had taught her the history of their family and community. Knowing this helped me predict that Mrs. Parks would tell Adrienne that learning about the past is important.) INFERENTIAL: MAKE AND CONFIRM PREDICTIONS

2 **Why does Mrs. Parks believe that listening to stories about the past prepares young people to take their place in the world of tomorrow?** (Possible responses: because the way people act does not change; because lessons that were learned in the past apply to the present and the future; because past events paved the way for the present) CRITICAL: INTERPRET AUTHOR'S VIEWPOINT

Dear Mrs. Parks,
My teacher told us that you just celebrated your 83rd birthday. My great-grandmother is 85 years old. She talks about the old days all the time. Sometimes I wonder what the old days have to do with me.

Adrienn
Vienna, Virgin

92

MATH

THE OLD DAYS Rosa Parks's grandmother often spoke of the times when she was a little girl. Challenge students to figure out the approximate time period when Rosa Parks's grandmother would have been the same age that they are now. Then have students compare their estimates and explain how they arrived at them.

1875

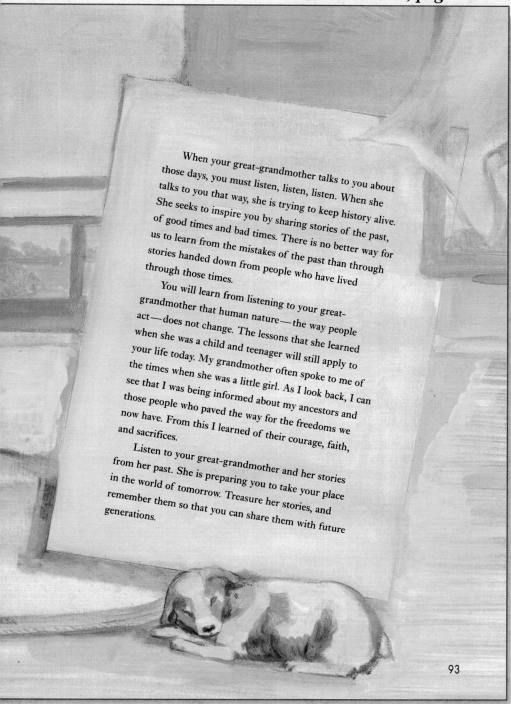

When your great-grandmother talks to you about those days, you must listen, listen, listen. When she talks to you that way, she is trying to keep history alive. She seeks to inspire you by sharing stories of the past, of good times and bad times. There is no better way for us to learn from the mistakes of the past than through stories handed down from people who have lived through those times.

You will learn from listening to your great-grandmother that human nature—the way people act—does not change. The lessons that she learned when she was a child and teenager will still apply to your life today. My grandmother often spoke to me of the times when she was a little girl. As I look back, I can see that I was being informed about my ancestors and those people who paved the way for the freedoms we now have. From this I learned of their courage, faith, and sacrifices.

Listen to your great-grandmother and her stories from her past. She is preparing you to take your place in the world of tomorrow. Treasure her stories, and remember them so that you can share them with future generations.

93

Informal Assessment

FOCUS SKILL **MAKE JUDGMENTS**

To assess students' ability to make judgments, ask the following questions:

1. **How can you tell when Mrs. Parks is stating an opinion?**

2. **How can you decide whether or not her opinion is reasonable?**

Further instruction on making judgments can be found on pages T174–T175.

REACHING ALL LEARNERS

INTERVENTION STRATEGIES

MODIFIED INSTRUCTION   Help students summarize the main ideas of the selection so far. You may wish to model summarizing:

MODEL **Mrs. Parks tells the young people who write to her that learning is important. When she was young, her grandmother taught her many things and talked to her about the past. Mrs. Parks believes that learning about what happened in the past can help us understand the present.**

Help students set a purpose for reading through page 95. (to find out more about what Mrs. Parks tells young people)

Monitor Comprehension

❶ Do you think Mrs. Parks gives good reasons for believing that this is a wonderful country? Explain. (Possible response: Yes. She gives examples of good things about our country, such as slavery being abolished, child labor laws, and women having the right to vote.) **FOCUS SKILL** CRITICAL: MAKE JUDGMENTS

❷ What do you think the word *herstory* means? What clues help you understand its meaning? (Possible response: history of women's accomplishments; it is used in the same sentence as *history*, and the previous sentence tells about women's accomplishments) INFERENTIAL: DRAW CONCLUSIONS

Guided Reading

STRATEGIES GOOD READERS USE

FOCUS STRATEGY **Reread** If students have difficulty explaining the meaning of *herstory*, model rereading to figure it out.

◁MODEL▷ **When I reread the sentence, I notice that the word *herstory* looks like the word *history*, except that it begins with *her* instead of *his*. The sentence before this one is about women taking their places in many areas of life. From this I can figure out that the word *herstory* means "her story," or the history of women.**

Dear Mrs. Parks,
I am 13 years old. Did you ever think that you would live to be 83 years old? What changes have you seen in the last 50 years?

Michael
Gary, Indiana

94

SOCIAL STUDIES

IMPORTANT DATES IN HISTORY Point out the important events in American history mentioned by Mrs. Parks on page 95. Explain that President Abraham Lincoln abolished slavery when he issued the Emancipation Proclamation on January 1, 1863. Women gained the right to vote when the 19th Amendment to the Constitution was ratified on August 18, 1920. Many states had passed child labor laws by the early 1900s, but federal laws were struck down by the Supreme Court and not upheld until 1941.

1863	1920	1941
Slavery ends	Women vote	Child labor laws upheld

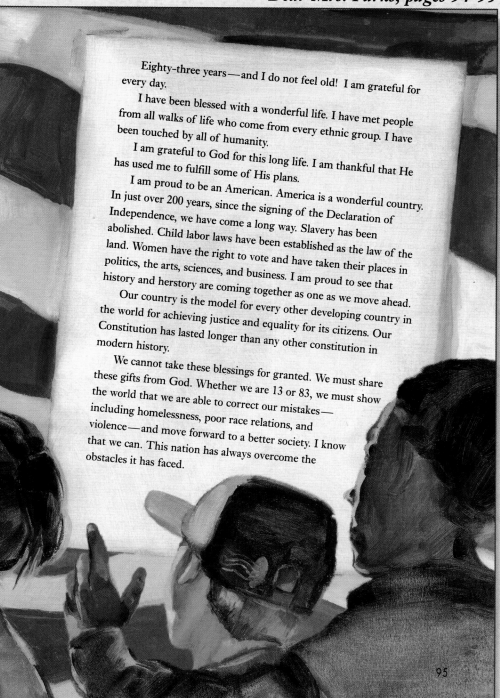

Eighty-three years—and I do not feel old! I am grateful for every day.

I have been blessed with a wonderful life. I have met people from all walks of life who come from every ethnic group. I have been touched by all of humanity.

I am grateful to God for this long life. I am thankful that He has used me to fulfill some of His plans.

I am proud to be an American. America is a wonderful country. In just over 200 years, since the signing of the Declaration of Independence, we have come a long way. Slavery has been abolished. Child labor laws have been established as the law of the land. Women have the right to vote and have taken their places in politics, the arts, sciences, and business. I am proud to see that history and herstory are coming together as one as we move ahead.

Our country is the model for every other developing country in the world for achieving justice and equality for its citizens. Our Constitution has lasted longer than any other constitution in modern history.

We cannot take these blessings for granted. We must share these gifts from God. Whether we are 13 or 83, we must show the world that we are able to correct our mistakes— including homelessness, poor race relations, and violence—and move forward to a better society. I know that we can. This nation has always overcome the obstacles it has faced.

95

INTERVENTION STRATEGIES

MODIFIED INSTRUCTION After students have read to the end of the selection on page 96, help them summarize the advice given by Mrs. Parks in this selection.

- It is good to ask questions.
- There is always more to learn about life.
- Students should always do their best, even if others make fun of them.
- Learning about the past is important.
- We should be <u>grateful</u> to live in a great country, but we must work to make it even better.
- We can all make a difference in the world by helping other people.

SKILLS IN CONTEXT

DECODING/PHONICS
TESTED SKILL

SKILL TRACE	
Introduce	T20, T46
Reteach	R2
Review 1	T81
Review 2	T163
Test	Theme 1
Maintain	T273

Prefixes and Suffixes

TEACH/MODEL

Have students locate the following words on page 95 and write them on the board: *wonderful, humanity, thankful, equality, homelessness.* Have students identify the suffixes and tell their meanings. (*-ful*: "filled with"; *-ity*: "condition or quality"; *-less*: "lacking or without"; *-ness*: "state of being") Discuss the meanings of the words with the suffixes added. Then write the following words from page 95 on the board: *touched, developing, justice, violence.* Model adding the prefix *un-* to the word *touched*:

> ⬭MODEL⬭ **The prefix *un-* means "not." Adding this prefix to the word *touched* forms the word *untouched*, which means "not touched."**

Similarly, have students add the prefix *re-* to *developing, in-* to *justice,* and *non-* to *violence,* and have them explain the meanings of the prefixes and of the new words that are formed.

PRACTICE/APPLY

Have students begin a chart like the one shown here. They can look back at previous pages in the selection to find words to add to the chart.

Word	Prefix or Suffix and Meaning	Meaning of Word
celebration	-tion (act of)	act of celebrating
disagrees	dis- (not)	does not agree
correspondence	-ence (act of)	act of corresponding

Literary Response

RETURN TO THE PREDICTIONS/PURPOSE

Were your predictions about what you might learn from Mrs. Parks's letters confirmed? Discuss with students whether their purpose for reading was met.

APPRECIATING THE LITERATURE

Did anything that Mrs. Parks wrote bring new questions to your mind? Explain. (Responses will vary.)

Think About It

1 **From what you have learned about Mrs. Parks, why do you think she took the time from her busy life to reply to these letters from young people?** (Possible responses: because she wants to share her ideas; because she believes young people can make a difference in the world) INFERENTIAL: SUMMARIZE/THEME CONNECTION

2 **Which question and reply did you find most interesting? Explain your answer.** (Responses will vary.) CRITICAL: PERSONAL RESPONSE

3 **Do you think this selection would have been as interesting if Mrs. Parks had written an article about her ideas and opinions without including the letters? Explain your answer.** (Responses will vary.) CRITICAL: LITERARY ANALYSIS

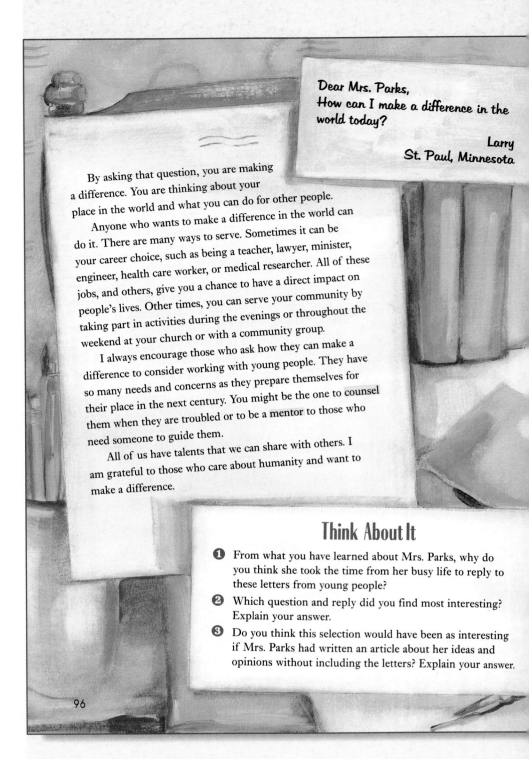

Dear Mrs. Parks,
How can I make a difference in the world today?

Larry
St. Paul, Minnesota

By asking that question, you are making a difference. You are thinking about your place in the world and what you can do for other people.

Anyone who wants to make a difference in the world can do it. There are many ways to serve. Sometimes it can be your career choice, such as being a teacher, lawyer, minister, engineer, health care worker, or medical researcher. All of these jobs, and others, give you a chance to have a direct impact on people's lives. Other times, you can serve your community by taking part in activities during the evenings or throughout the weekend at your church or with a community group.

I always encourage those who ask how they can make a difference to consider working with young people. They have so many needs and concerns as they prepare themselves for their place in the next century. You might be the one to counsel them when they are troubled or to be a mentor to those who need someone to guide them.

All of us have talents that we can share with others. I am grateful to those who care about humanity and want to make a difference.

96

Think About It

1 From what you have learned about Mrs. Parks, why do you think she took the time from her busy life to reply to these letters from young people?

2 Which question and reply did you find most interesting? Explain your answer.

3 Do you think this selection would have been as interesting if Mrs. Parks had written an article about her ideas and opinions without including the letters? Explain your answer.

Meet the Author
Rosa Parks

ROSA PARKS has strongly supported the peaceful pursuit of human rights, especially young people's rights, for over 40 years. She receives hundreds to thousands of letters each year. She says, "I have been truly blessed to receive so many letters from young people. I am grateful for each day God has given me to allow me to answer the letters I receive." She believes adults should set a good example for the younger generations. She says, "I am blessed to see changes in the world. But there is one thing that I hope never changes: that young people continue to seek answers to their questions. I am inspired by the energy of young minds."

97

Informal Assessment

RETELL

Have each student retell the selection to a partner. Monitor whether the student

☐ creates a focused and coherent structure and stays on topic.

☐ relates text to relevant experiences.

☐ evaluates the author's perspective, intent, or craft in creating the text.

☐ provides a summarizing statement.

SUMMARIZE

Ask students to summarize the selection by recalling the advice that Mrs. Parks gives. Students can refer to the problem/advice chart they completed while reading. See also *Practice Book* page 25.

ONE-SENTENCE SUMMARY Have students write one sentence that summarizes the selection.

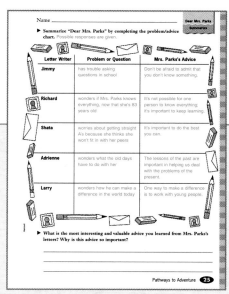

▲ **Practice Book, page 25**

ABOUT THE AUTHOR

In 1987, **ROSA PARKS** founded the Rosa and Raymond Parks Institute for Self-Development. She worked for many years in the office of U.S. Representative John Conyers, Jr., in Detroit, Michigan, where a street and an art center have been named after her. Despite health problems in recent years, she continues to speak out on the need to promote freedom. Discuss with students what Rosa Parks means when she speaks of "the energy of young minds." (Possible response: refers to the fact that young people are curious, ask many questions, and have active minds)

 INTERNET Additional author information can be found on *The Learning Site* at **www.harcourtschool.com**

Companion Selection

INTRODUCE THE FABLES

Have students preview the introduction and the two fables on pages 98–101. Ask them to tell what a fable is. (Possible response: a brief story that has a moral and often has animal characters that act like people)

Vocabulary   If students are unfamiliar with these words, share the definitions.

- **dismay:** a feeling of alarm, uneasiness, and confusion
- **lumbered:** moved along clumsily
- **deserts:** leaves a person, place, or thing, especially if one has a duty to stay

Create Mental Images   Have students set a purpose for reading the fables. (to find out what morals they illustrate) Remind students to create mental images as they read. Ask a volunteer to explain. (Creating mental images means visualizing in your mind what the author is describing.) Then tell students to read pages 98–101.

▼ FABLE

AESOP'S
FABLES

RETOLD BY ANN MCGOVERN

About Aesop

Aesop was a slave who lived in Greece about 3,000 years ago. He became famous for the clever animal fables through which he showed the wise and foolish behavior of men.

Not much is really known about the life of Aesop. It is said that his wisdom so delighted one of his masters that the slave was given his freedom. It is said, too, that he became an honored guest at the courts of kings.

Aesop's fables have become a part of our daily language—a way of expressing ourselves. Haven't you heard people talk about "sour grapes" or "not counting chickens until they are hatched"?

Aesop never wrote down his stories. He told them to people, who in turn told them to others. Not until 200 years after his death did the first collection of his fables appear. Since then they have been translated into almost every language in the world. Today there are many, many versions of the tales that Aesop told in the hills of Greece so long ago.

98

COMPARING TEXTS

Have students complete a Venn diagram to compare Aesop's fables to the letters of Rosa Parks. Prompt students with these questions: **What is the genre of each selection? What is the author's purpose for writing each selection? How else are the selections alike or different?**

Rosa Parks's letters	Both	Aesop's fables
give advice directly	purpose is to influence people to act in a better way	give advice in the form of a story
written in our own time		first told orally
		told in ancient times

The Crow and the Pitcher

A Crow, who was almost dying of thirst, came upon a pitcher which had once been filled with water. But to his dismay the Crow found that the water was so low he could not reach it. He tried with all his might to knock the pitcher over, but it was too heavy.

Then he saw a pile of pebbles nearby. He took one pebble in his beak and dropped it into the pitcher. The water rose a tiny bit. Then he took another pebble and dropped that in. The water rose a tiny bit more. One by one he dropped in all the pebbles. When he had dropped in a hundred pebbles, the water at last rose to the top. As the Crow drank deeply of the cool water, he said to himself, *"Where force fails, patience will often succeed."*

99

My Notes

Monitor Comprehension

SUMMARIZE

Ask students to tell how the fables showed wise and foolish behavior. (Possible response: The crow showed wise behavior by being patient and solving his problem in a clever way. The man who deserted his friend showed foolish behavior.)

Think About It

How are the two fables you read similar to each other? (Possible responses: very brief stories; feature animal characters; end with a statement of the moral or lesson that the fable teaches)

CRITICAL: SUMMARIZE/THEME CONNECTION

The Travelers and the Bear

Two men were traveling together when a Bear suddenly came out of the forest and stood in their path, growling. One of the men quickly climbed the nearest tree and concealed himself in the branches. The other man, seeing that there was no time to hide, fell flat on the ground. He pretended to be dead, for he had heard it said that a Bear will not touch a dead man.

The Bear came near, sniffed the man's head and body, and then lumbered away, back into the forest.

When the Bear was out of sight, the man in the tree slid down and said to his friend, "I saw the Bear whispering to you. What did he have to say?"

The other man replied, "The Bear told me never to travel with a friend who deserts me at the first sign of danger." He looked his companion straight in the eye. "The Bear said that, *in time of trouble, one learns who his true friends are.*"

Think About It

How are the two fables you read similar to each other?

100

101

Activity Choices

GOOD ADVICE

Write a Letter   Provide a sample of the correct form for a friendly letter that students can use as a model when writing their own letters.   CRITICAL: CONNECT TO PERSONAL EXPERIENCES

NEWS RADIO

Present a Radio Broadcast   Have students use what they have learned about Rosa Parks's beliefs and opinions to make up their own questions and replies, rather than echoing those in the selection.   CREATIVE: DRAMA

STORY TIME

Write a Story   After students have completed their stories, they might like to illustrate them and then create an oral history display for your classroom or another appropriate area in your school.   CREATIVE: WRITING

MAKING CONNECTIONS

Write a Fable   Students can collect their fables to create a book. See Managing the Classroom, page T146.   CRITICAL/CREATIVE: CONNECT IDEAS ACROSS TEXTS/WRITING

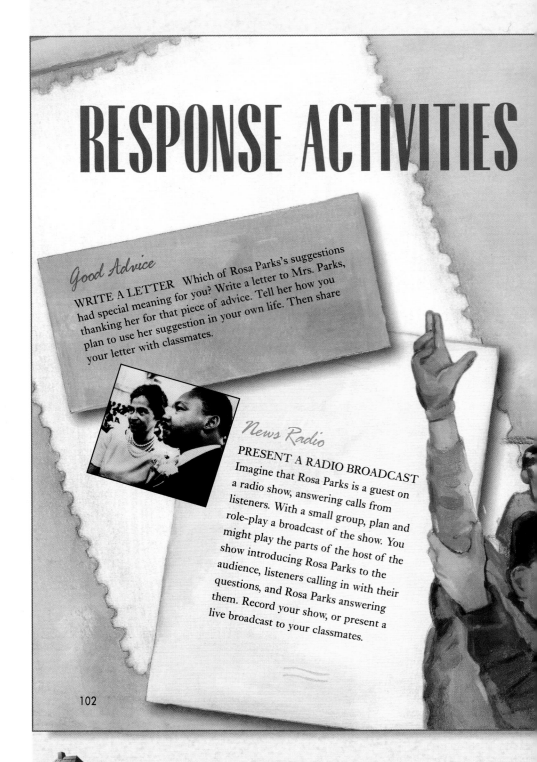

RESPONSE ACTIVITIES

Good Advice

WRITE A LETTER   Which of Rosa Parks's suggestions had special meaning for you? Write a letter to Mrs. Parks, thanking her for that piece of advice. Tell her how you plan to use her suggestion in your own life. Then share your letter with classmates.

News Radio

PRESENT A RADIO BROADCAST
Imagine that Rosa Parks is a guest on a radio show, answering calls from listeners. With a small group, plan and role-play a broadcast of the show. You might play the parts of the host of the show introducing Rosa Parks to the audience, listeners calling in with their questions, and Rosa Parks answering them. Record your show, or present a live broadcast to your classmates.

102

SCHOOL-HOME CONNECTION

The activities on the copying master on page R18 may be completed by students and family members. Some or all of the activities may be assigned as homework during the week.

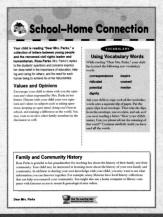

Copying Master, page R18 ▶

Story Time

WRITE A STORY Rosa Parks reminds us that it is important to listen to stories about the past. Think about a story you have heard from an older family member or friend. Who told this story to you and why? Will you retell this same story when you are older? Write the story that you were told, or make up a story that an older person might tell about the past.

Making Connections

WRITE A FABLE Rosa Parks gives advice in her letters. Aesop's fables also give advice through their morals or lessons. Rewrite one of Rosa Parks's letters in the form of a fable. Choose animals as characters for your fable, and end with a moral.

Assessment

SELECTION COMPREHENSION TEST

To evaluate comprehension, see pages 10–12.

INFORMAL ASSESSMENT

PERFORMANCE ASSESSMENT Student work for the Good Advice activity may be used for performance assessment of selection comprehension.

PORTFOLIO OPPORTUNITY

Students may want to add their stories for the Story Time activity to their portfolios.

INTERVENTION STRATEGIES

RECORD A FABLE Students who have difficulty doing an extended piece of writing can be offered the alternative of telling their fables orally. Have students tape-record and illustrate their fables. Encourage them to do some writing, such as writing captions for the illustrations and stating the moral of the fable in writing.

Building Literacy Skills

REREADING FOR FLUENCY

Role-Play

Have students play the roles of the young people writing to Mrs. Parks. Several students can share the role of Mrs. Parks, each reading aloud a letter or taking turns reading aloud longer paragraphs or groups of shorter paragraphs. Ask students to think about how Mrs. Parks might speak, based on what they know about her from her letters.

LISTENING/SPEAKING/READING

WRITING

Create a Flyer

Students can create flyers to advertise an appearance by Rosa Parks. You may want to make space on a bulletin board or elsewhere in your classroom to display the completed flyers. Students will find suggestions for writing the text and creating their flyers on Activity Card 7 on page R13. WRITING

▶ Create a Flyer   ACTIVITY CARD 7

Imagine that Rosa Parks is making a personal appearance to speak to young people in your city or town. Your job is to create a flyer that can be posted in schools, youth centers, and libraries to advertise this event.

TIPS FOR CREATING A FLYER

Text should
■ include all the information people need to know about the event.
■ tell who the speaker is and what she will be speaking about.
■ be brief and to the point.

Graphics should
■ make the flyer look attractive.
■ catch people's attention.
■ be appropriate for the subject of the flyer.

Activity Card 7 ▶

ORAL LANGUAGE

Present an Award

Ask students to imagine that your school has established a Rosa Parks Award for students whose behavior displays the same ideals and values that Mrs. Parks believes in and has shown in her life. Have students prepare a brief speech that they would give when presenting the first annual Rosa Parks Award to a student in your school. LISTENING/SPEAKING

Tips for Speakers
• Identify audience and purpose.
• Signal important ideas.

Tips for Listeners
• Note details.
• Compare your ideas with the speaker's.

VIEWING

Placing Text

Point out that the illustrations for this selection fill the pages, with the text placed so that it covers part of the illustration on each page. Encourage students to notice how the illustrator planned the illustrations and placed the text so viewers can visualize the parts that are hidden. Have students use the same technique to illustrate a poem or other brief text. VIEWING/REPRESENTING

City Streets

REACHING ALL LEARNERS

Intervention Strategies for Below-Level Readers

Reinforce Comprehension

FOCUS STRATEGY **Apply the Reread strategy.** Talk with students about how using reading strategies helps them better understand what they read. Remind students that the focus strategy for reading "Dear Mrs. Parks" is Reread. Discuss the strategy by asking questions such as these:

- **How can rereading help you understand a selection?**
- **When might you use this strategy?**

Have students practice and apply using the strategy by silently rereading the second paragraph of Mrs. Parks's letter on page 93. Ask them to recall what else they know about Mrs. Parks's grandmother.

Then have them reread the second and third paragraphs on page 91. Ask students to record their use of the strategy by completing a chart like this one.

New Selection Information	+	What I Recall When I Reread	=	A Better Understanding
Mrs. Parks's grandmother spoke about the times when she was younger. (page 93)		When Mrs. Parks was sick, her grandmother taught her at home. (page 91)		Mrs. Parks's grandmother was an important influence on Mrs. Parks.

Abstract Nouns

Discuss nouns that name ideas or qualities. Have a volunteer reread this sentence on page 91: *I learned the importance of treating other people with respect.* Remind students that a noun names a person, place, or thing. Ask whether they think the word *respect* is used as a noun in this sentence. Discuss the idea that nouns such as *paper, sky,* or *noise* name things that we can touch, see, or hear, but nouns such as *respect* name things that are ideas or qualities. Help students identify other nouns from "Dear Mrs. Parks" that name ideas or qualities, and list

them in the chart. Possible responses are shown.

Nouns (Ideas or Qualities)	Page Number
confidence	p. 86
values	p. 89
health	p. 91
dignity	p. 91
freedoms	p. 93
courage	p. 93
faith	p. 93
justice	p. 95
equality	p. 95

SKILL TRACE

INTRODUCE	
• Before Reading:	T150–T151
• During Reading:	T154, T156, T162
• After Reading:	T174–T175
Reteach	R5
Review	T271

OBJECTIVE:

To make valid judgments

CHALLENGE

Provide several informational books that include information about the author either on the book jacket or in the book. Have students work in pairs or small groups to discuss and evaluate each author's background and credentials and to decide whether they think the author is a reliable source of information on the subject.

INTERVENTION

Have students practice making judgments based on simple scenarios like the following: Bob saw that Andy had dropped his sandwich on the ground. Bob gave Andy half of his sandwich.

RETEACH See page R5 for a lesson in multiple modalities.

FOCUS SKILL Make Judgments

AFTER READING

Return to the Concept

Extend the thinking.

Ask students to recall and discuss some of the judgments they made while reading "Dear Mrs. Parks." Tell students that authors use a variety of techniques to persuade readers to agree with their point of view. Discuss and list some of these techniques. Then talk about why it is important for readers to make judgments about an author's opinions and about which techniques the author uses to try to influence or persuade readers.

Persuasive Techniques

giving good reasons to support opinion

giving facts to support opinion

quoting experts or people whose judgment you respect

stating opinion as if it is fact

appealing to emotion

Model the thinking.

Explain that a judgment is valid if there is evidence to support it. Model making a valid judgment about Rosa Parks's attitude toward young people:

> MODEL **I think Rosa Parks believes that young people are important and that they deserve respect and attention. I think my judgment is valid because she suggests working with young people as a way to make a difference in the world. The fact that she took the time to answer letters from young people and share her views with them is also evidence that supports my judgment.**

Guided Practice

Have students make judgments.

Tell students that analyzing how an author attempts to persuade readers will help them make valid judgments about whether the author's argument or conclusion is accurate or reliable. Display Transparency 22, or write the paragraphs on the board.

Have volunteers read aloud the directions and the two paragraphs. Then have other students read aloud and answer the questions. As you discuss the paragraphs with students, you may want to emphasize that they may have their own reasons for agreeing or disagreeing with each opinion. The point of this exercise is to recognize that the first paragraph expresses unsupported opinions, while the second paragraph presents a supporting fact and quotes someone who is probably a reliable source of information on this subject.

Summarize.

Ask students to tell how making judgments helped them read the selection more effectively.

Practice/Apply

YOU BE THE JUDGE

PERFORMANCE ASSESSMENT Provide an editorial or a letter to the editor on a suitable subject from a school or local newspaper or community newsletter. Have students work in pairs to identify the opinions expressed in the editorial or letter and to judge how effectively the writer supports those opinions. Then students can meet in groups to compare and discuss the judgments they have made. LISTENING/SPEAKING/READING/WRITING

PRESENT THE EVIDENCE

Tell students to choose a subject on which they have a strong opinion. Then have them write a paragraph expressing this opinion and using the best possible evidence to support it. Have students exchange paragraphs and make judgments about the evidence classmates have used.
LISTENING/SPEAKING/WRITING

MAKING VALID JUDGMENTS

Read each paragraph.
1. Playing team sports is a valuable experience for all students. It is a fact that students who play team sports learn to play fair and to get along well with others. Another important fact is that students who play sports enjoy themselves. Team sports are fun. This is why I think everyone should play team sports.

2. The peer counseling program in our school really seems to be working. Since the program began last year, the number of referrals for discipline has been cut almost in half. Our principal, Mrs. Barrett, says, "I think the program is making a real difference in the way our students relate to each other and settle their problems."

• What techniques does each writer use to try to persuade you?
• Does the writer give you good reasons to agree with his or her point of view? Explain your answer.

▲ **Teaching Transparency 22**

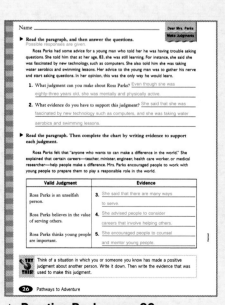

▲ **Practice Book, page 26**

Vocabulary Workshop

Dear Grandma

by Elizabeth Carter
illustrated by Charles Shaw

Have students read the
TAKE-HOME BOOK *Dear
Grandma* to reinforce vocabulary
words. See also *Guided Reading
Manual for Take-Home Books,*
page 5.

Reviewing Vocabulary Words

Tell students that four of the vocabulary words for this selection are nouns and three are verbs. Have students sort the words into these two categories and match them with their meanings.

Vocabulary Words	Meanings
Nouns	
correspondence	letter writing, or letters written
potential	qualities that make the development of a talent, power, or skill possible or likely
dignity	proud, calm, and controlled behavior
mentor	a wise, caring adviser
Verbs	
ridiculed	made fun of
inspire	to make someone want to do something and feel excited about doing
counsel	to give advice and support

Reviewing Word Identification Strategies

Decode familiar patterns. Have students locate the word *cyberspace* on page 87. Ask how they might use familiar patterns to help them read this word. (*cy* as in *cycle*; *ber* as in *number*; the familiar word *space*) Remind students that looking for familiar patterns can help them decode unfamiliar words.

Have students identify familiar patterns they see in these words.

cyclone	unicycle
tangerine	triathlon
fiberglass	cumbersome

Everyday Reading Sources Have students use everyday reading sources, such as signs, labels, recipes, how-to directions, and newspapers, to find and list examples of words with familiar patterns that can help them read the words.

Extending Vocabulary

Coined Words   Call students' attention to the word *herstory* on page 95. Tell students that this is an example of a **coined word**, or a word that has been invented fairly recently to fit a special need. Explain that *herstory* was created in 1971 by blending *her* and *history* to mean "history considered or presented from the point of view of women." Tell students that Mrs. Parks uses other coined words in her letters as well, including *aerobics*, *online*, *Internet*, and *cyberspace*. Then begin a chart like the one shown here, calling on volunteers to provide the definitions in the second column.

Coined Word	Meaning	When Invented
herstory	history from women's point of view; a blend of <u>her</u> and (his)tory	1971
aerobics	a system of physical exercise designed to increase respiration and heart rate	1967
online	connected to or available through a computer system	1950
Internet	international computer network	late 20th century
cyberspace	the imagined environment over which communication between computers takes place	after the word <u>cybernetics</u>, which was coined in 1948

Add to the chart. Work with students to add coined words to the chart. Students might suggest words related to computers or space travel, for example, and then look them up in a print or online dictionary that includes word origins. Examples of additional words might include *cybernetics*, *modem*, and *cyborg*.

Reference Sources/Word History or Word Origin References
In addition to using dictionaries, students can use references devoted to word histories or word origins, either in print or online, to find recently coined words. Have students work independently or in pairs.

CHALLENGE

Ask students to identify special needs that they think could be met by coining new words. Students should suggest coined words and tell why the words would be useful. Students' suggestions may be humorous or playful.

Expressive Writing

PERSONAL NARRATIVE

Connect Writing to Reading

Point out that the letters from Rosa Parks in "Dear Mrs. Parks" describe events that happened in the narrator's life. Remind students that a personal narrative also tells about events in the writer's life. It is written from the first-person point of view. A personal narrative should have a clear beginning, middle, and ending, with events related in chronological order.

Teach/Model

Display Transparency 23 and explain that it shows a model of a personal narrative. Tell students that they will review the qualities of a good personal narrative. They will then write and publish personal narratives of their own.

WRITING MODEL: PERSONAL NARRATIVE

Here is a personal narrative that a woman wrote to describe to her daughter an average day in her childhood.

title	*My Life in the 1960s*
beginning	*When I was a child, my normal day was very different from yours. On school mornings I ate a bowl of steaming oatmeal and then put on a crisp cotton school dress, socks, and dress shoes. I walked three blocks to school. At noon I walked home for a*
middle	*hot lunch, which my mother made. After school I sometimes roller-skated or played marbles with my friends in the neighborhood. In the fall we picked tiny potatoes the size of a baby's fist from the fields behind our house. In the winter we ice-skated on the pond and made snowmen. After dinner I helped wash the dishes and*
ending	*did my homework. I was so tired! I got tucked into bed by 8:00.*

▲ **Teaching Transparency 23**

ANALYZE THE MODEL

- Audience—writer's daughter
- Writer's task—write about a typical day in her childhood

FOCUS ON ORGANIZATION

- The first sentence tells what the personal narrative is about.
- The personal narrative has a clear beginning, middle, and ending.
- Events are related in chronological order, from the beginning to the end of the day.

FOCUS ON ELABORATION

- Writer includes interesting details. (*steaming oatmeal; crisp cotton school dress; hot lunch, which my mother made; tiny potatoes the size of a baby's fist*)
- Writer includes words and phrases to link ideas and show time order. (*mornings, then, At noon, After school, In the fall, In the winter, After dinner, by 8:00*)

 ## Writing Prompts

Choose one of the following:

A Assign a prompt, for example:
Write a personal narrative about how you spend a typical day. Imagine that you are writing for students who will be in the fifth grade 30 years from now. Describe what happens in time order, and provide details.

B Have students write a personal narrative about a topic of their own choosing for an audience of their choice.

TECHNOLOGY

Students may write and illustrate their narratives using *Imagination Express™, Destination: Neighborhood.*

Prewrite and Draft

Before students write their drafts, guide them in writing a topic sentence that tells what their narrative is about. For the suggested prompt, students may use the outline shown on Transparency 24 to record their topic sentence, events of the narrative, and specific details they wish to include.

PERSONAL NARRATIVE

Topic sentence:

Morning
Events:
Details:

Afternoon
Events:
Details:

Evening
Events:
Details:

▲ Teaching Transparency 24

Edit

Revise   Students can work in pairs or small groups to discuss their personal narratives, or they may review their own work individually. Then have them revise their own personal narratives.

Proofread   You may want to provide these questions as students proofread their personal narratives:

- **Did I use capital letters correctly?**
- **Did I use end marks correctly?**
- **Did I use an appropriate variety of sentence types?**
- **Did I spell all words correctly, especially confusing word pairs?**

Publish

Students may publish their personal narratives by
- using them as the basis for a tape-recorded oral history.
- printing them on a computer and binding them in a class book.

Assessment

STUDENT SELF- AND PEER ASSESSMENT
Give students copies of the scoring rubric, page A9. They may use it to evaluate their own or each other's personal narratives.

PORTFOLIO OPPORTUNITY
Students may keep their completed pieces in their show portfolios to be shared with others or reviewed by themselves at a later time.

Test Prep

Remind students that as they write personal narratives for a test, they should

- keep their purpose and audience clearly in mind.
- include specific details about the events they describe.
- use time-order words and phrases to link events and ideas.

EXPRESSIVE WRITING: NARRATIVE

Additional lessons:
Personal Narrative T50
Descriptive Paragraphs T94
Realistic Story T134
Tested or Timed Writing: T218

Language Handbook, page 54

SCORING RUBRIC FOR SUGGESTED PROMPT

4 Advanced
The personal narrative has an appropriate title, and the first sentence states the focus of the narrative. The events are linked by time-order words. The narrative is written from the first-person point of view and clearly reflects the writer's thoughts and feelings. The writer includes specific details and descriptive words.

3 Proficient
The title is appropriate, and the topic sentence accurately describes the narrative's contents. Time-order words help show the order of events. The writer maintains the first-person point of view consistently. Some details are provided. The language is appropriate to the audience.

2 Basic
The title is vague or uninteresting. The topic sentence adequately describes the contents. Chronological order is used, but events are not clearly linked by time-order words. The first-person point of view is not maintained. There are not enough details to give the reader a clear picture of the day's events.

1 Below Basic
The title is missing or does not accurately reflect the contents. There is no topic sentence, and events are not presented in chronological order. There is little detail, and the personal narrative is not told from the first-person point of view. The language would not be interesting to the audience.

Complete and Simple Predicates

Language Handbook, pages 102–103

ESL

Have students name the complete and simple predicates in the following sentences. Then have them say and write similar sentences:

People wrote.

People wrote letters.

People wrote letters to Mrs. Parks.

DAY 1 — Teach/Model

DAILY LANGUAGE PRACTICE

1. **Many children right to Mrs Parks.**
   (write; Mrs.)
2. **What woud you ask her.** (would; her?)

INTRODUCE THE CONCEPT Use Transparency 25 as you discuss the following points:

- The **complete predicate** includes all the words that tell what the subject of the sentence is or does.
- The **simple predicate** is the main word or words in the complete predicate.

Have students identify the complete and simple predicates in sentences 1–3. Ask them to rewrite sentences 4 and 5, making each simple predicate a longer complete predicate.

COMPLETE AND SIMPLE PREDICATES

1. Rosa Parks asks a lot of questions.
   (asks a lot of questions; asks)
2. Asking questions builds confidence and learning.
   (builds confidence and learning; builds)
3. Mrs. Parks's life changes.
   (changes; changes)
4. Mrs. Parks wrote.
   (Responses will vary.)
5. We listened.
   (Responses will vary.)

Complete Predicate = All the words that tell what the subject is or does

Simple Predicate = Main word or words in the complete predicate; the verb

6. Who wrote to Mrs. Parks?
   (wrote to Mrs. Parks; wrote)
7. Mrs. Parks uses the Internet for her correspondence.
   (uses the Internet for her correspondence; uses)
8. Everyone has special gifts or talents.
   (has special gifts or talents; has)

▲ Teaching Transparency 25

DAY 2 — Extend the Concept

DAILY LANGUAGE PRACTICE

1. **You, can chose to make a difference.**
   (You can choose)
2. **The froots of hard work. are progress and strength.** (fruits; work are)

DEVELOP THE CONCEPT Display Transparency 25, and have students read sentences 6–8 silently. Have volunteers tell you the complete predicate and the simple predicate, or verb, in each of sentences 6–8 as you mark the predicates on the transparency.

Then ask students to give examples of sentences in which the simple predicate and the complete predicate are the same.

Name _____

Complete and Simple Predicates

Skill Reminder

- The **complete predicate** includes all the words that tell what the subject of the sentence is or does.
- The **simple predicate** is the main word or words in the complete predicate.

▶ Underline the complete predicate in each sentence below. Then write the simple predicate on the line.

1. Rosa Lee Parks lived in Alabama. lived
2. She became famous in 1955. became
3. She rode on a bus one day in the city of Montgomery. rode
4. Mrs. Parks fought for her rights. fought
5. She claimed her seat on the bus. claimed
6. Mrs. Parks showed a great deal of courage. showed

▶ Rewrite each sentence, adding a simple predicate to replace the blank.
Possible responses are given.

7. Many people _____ to Mrs. Parks for advice.
   Many people write to Mrs. Parks for advice.
8. She _____ every letter.
   She answers every letter.
9. Mrs. Parks _____ a very wise person.
   Mrs. Parks is a very wise person.
10. Children _____ Mrs. Parks about many things.
    Children ask Mrs. Parks about many things.
11. Mrs. Parks _____ learning about life.
    Mrs. Parks enjoys learning about life.

16 GRAMMAR PRACTICE BOOK   Complete and Simple Predicates

▲ Grammar Practice Book, page 16

DAY 3 Oral Review/Practice

DAILY LANGUAGE PRACTICE

1. **Can you moove a mountain one rock at a time** (move; time?)
2. **she can prove that she is wright.** (She; right.)

NAME AND TELL List on the board the names of these young people who wrote a letter to Mrs. Parks—Jimmy, Richard, Shata, Anthony, Adrienne, Michael, and Larry. Invite students to say aloud sentences about each one, using the person's name as the subject of the sentence. Write examples of simple predicates from students' sentences beside each name.

Name _____

Complete and Simple Predicates

▶ A student wrote these notes for a book report about *Dear Mrs. Parks.* Use the notes to write complete sentences. In your sentences, underline each simple predicate. Responses will vary; possible responses are given.

1. Rosa Parks—book, *Dear Mrs. Parks*
   Rosa Parks wrote a book called *Dear Mrs. Parks*.
2. Gregory J. Reed—helped
   Gregory J. Reed helped her.
3. Book—short sections
   The book has short sections.
4. Section—letter to Mrs. Parks
   Each section begins with a letter to Mrs. Parks.
5. her reply to the letter
   Her reply to the letter follows.
6. Mrs. Parks—very wise person
   Mrs. Parks is a very wise person.
7. letters—her beliefs
   Her letters show her strong beliefs.
8. encourages—be special
   She encourages everyone to be special.

Complete and Simple Predicates   GRAMMAR PRACTICE BOOK **17**

▲ **Grammar Practice Book, page 17**

DAY 4 Apply to Writing

DAILY LANGUAGE PRACTICE

1. **Rosa Parks played an important role. In our historee.** (role in; history.)
2. **She protested. The unfare treatment of many Americans.** (protested the unfair)

TALENT SCOUTS Have students each write five separate sentences. Each sentence should tell in what way someone they know is talented. Have students trade papers with a partner and underline the complete predicate and circle the simple predicate in each sentence.

> ### Test Prep
> These tips about identifying predicates may help students on language tests:
> - Look for all the words that describe what the subject is or does. This is the complete predicate.
> - Look for the main verb and any helping verbs in the predicate. These words form the simple predicate.

Name _____

Dear Mrs. Parks
Grammar: Complete and Simple Predicates

▶ Underline the complete predicate in each of the following sentences. Write the simple predicate on the line.

1. Adrienne's teacher told the class about Rosa Parks.   told
2. Mrs. Parks is eighty-three years old.   is
3. Adrienne's great-grandmother celebrated her eighty-fifth birthday.   celebrated
4. She talks often about the old days.   talks

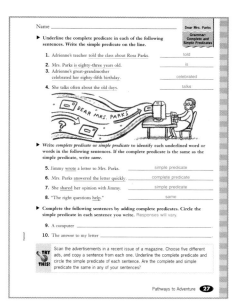

▶ Write *complete predicate* or *simple predicate* to identify each underlined word or words in the following sentences. If the complete predicate is the same as the simple predicate, write *same.*

5. Jimmy wrote a letter to Mrs. Parks.   simple predicate
6. Mrs. Parks answered the letter quickly.   complete predicate
7. She shared her opinion with Jimmy.   simple predicate
8. "The right questions help."   same

▶ Complete the following sentences by adding complete predicates. Circle the simple predicate in each sentence you write. Responses will vary.

9. A computer _____
10. The answer to my letter _____

Scan the advertisements in a recent issue of a magazine. Choose five different ads, and copy a sentence from each one. Underline the complete predicate and circle the simple predicate of each sentence. Are the complete and simple predicate the same in any of your sentences?

Pathways to Adventure **27**

▲ **Practice Book, page 27**

DAY 5 Cumulative Review

DAILY LANGUAGE PRACTICE

1. **Our class is lirning about Rosa Parks** (learning; Parks.)
2. **My favorite partes of the book Are Rosa's answers.** (parts; book are)

SENTENCE FRAMES Write the following paragraph and list on the board. Have students copy them and fill in the blanks with the sentence parts named in the list.

Rosa Parks __(1)__ a sickly child. __(2)__ was her main teacher. Grandma Rose __(3)__. " __(4)__ learned the importance of personal dignity," Mrs. Parks said.

(1) *simple predicate*
(2) *complete subject*
(3) *complete predicate*
(4) *simple subject*

(Possible responses: 1. was; 2. Her Grandma Rose; 3. taught the family history; 4. I)

Name _____

Cumulative Review

▶ Draw a line between the complete subject and the complete predicate in each of the following sentences.

1. Everyone in Tina's class interviewed an older person.
2. Tina talked with her father's aunt.
3. Her great-aunt Sophia is seventy-three years old.
4. She came to the United States from Greece as a young girl.

▶ Rewrite the following sentences, correcting errors in capitalization and punctuation. Then write whether each sentence is declarative, interrogative, imperative, or exclamatory.

5. look at this picture of Athens   Look at this picture of Athens. imperative
6. have you been to Greece   Have you been to Greece? interrogative
7. how tall those columns are   How tall those columns are! exclamatory
8. that building is the Parthenon   That building is the Parthenon. declarative
9. Greece has many olive trees   Greece has many olive trees. declarative
10. would you like to visit Greece   Would you like to visit Greece? interrogative

▶ In each of the following sentences, underline the complete predicate. Write the simple predicate on the line.

11. Her stories about Greece in the old days were interesting.   were
12. Sophia went to school in a small fishing village.   went
13. Most people in the village were very poor.   were
14. Sophia's parents brought her to the United States in 1946 after World War II.   brought

18 GRAMMAR PRACTICE BOOK

Four Kinds of Sentences
Complete and Simple Subjects
Complete and Simple Predicates

▲ **Grammar Practice Book, page 18**

SPELLING

Vowels Before *r*

SPELLING WORDS

1. parts
2. history*
3. warning
4. declare
5. despair
6. shirt
7. learning*
8. backward
9. border
10. prepared
11. harsh*
12. research

BONUS WORDS

13. carnival
14. particular
15. squirrel
16. harmful

*Words appearing in "Dear Mrs. Parks." Additional story words following the generalizations are *learn*, *important*, *character*, and *heard*.

STUDENT-CHOSEN WORDS

17. _____
18. _____
19. _____
20. _____

INTERVENTION

Encourage less-proficient spellers to add easier Student-Chosen Words that follow the generalizations—such as *cart*, *warm*, and *sir*—to their weekly spelling lists. Ask them to use the words in their daily activities.

DAY 1 — Pretest/Self-Check

ADMINISTER THE PRETEST. Say each word, and then use it in a Dictation Sentence. (See Day 5.) Help students self-check their pretests using the list at the top of Transparency 26.

OPEN SORT Ask students to think of ways to sort the Spelling Words, such as by number of syllables or whether or not the word has a suffix.

VOWELS BEFORE *r*

Spelling Words

1. parts	5. despair	9. border
2. history	6. shirt	10. prepared
3. warning	7. learning	11. harsh
4. declare	8. backward	12. research

car	fort	fair	dirt	outward
parts	warning	declare	shirt	history
harsh	border	despair	learning	backward
		prepared	research	

- The vowel sound in *car* is usually spelled *ar*.
- The vowel sound in *fort* can be spelled *or* or *ar*.
- The vowel sound in *fair* can be spelled *are* or *air*.
- The vowel sound in *dirt* can be spelled *ir* or *ear*.
- The second vowel sound in *outward* can be spelled *or* or *ar*.

▲ Teaching Transparency 26

DAY 2 — Teach/Model

CLOSED SORT Display Transparency 26. Ask students to copy the chart and to write each Spelling Word where it belongs.

Have students name the way to spell the vowel sound in *car* and the two ways to spell the vowel sounds in *fort*, *fair*, and *dirt*. Explain that the *r*-controlled vowel sound in an unaccented syllable, such as the second syllable in *backward*, is often spelled with an *a* or an *o*.

Handwriting Tip

Remind students to close the letter *d* and not to loop it, or the *d* could look like *cl*.

d dad

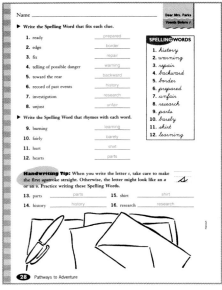

▲ Practice Book, page 28

GUESSING AND CHECKING Write the following words on the board: *carpet* and *carpit*. Ask students which is spelled correctly. *(carpet)* Discuss with students what they could do if they were uncertain about the spelling of a particular word. (Possible response: They could guess and then check in a dictionary to see if they are right.)

Apply to Writing

Have students correct misspelled words in a piece of writing that has been returned to them. Suggest that they guess how the word should be spelled and then check in a dictionary to see if they are right.

SPELLING PASSWORD "Spelling Password" is played with five students, two on each team and the fifth as a quizmaster. The quizmaster has a set of twelve cards, with a Spelling Word on each card. The quizmaster gives a card to a player on one team. That player gives the teammate a clue to the word, without using the word itself. If the teammate guesses the word and spells it correctly, that team gets a point. If the wrong word is guessed, a player from the other team gives his or her teammate a different clue for the same word. Teams take turns starting each new word.

NEWSPAPER HEADLINES Students can use Spelling Words, Bonus Words, and other words that follow the generalizations to create newspaper headlines. Encourage them to be creative.

Assess students' progress, using the Dictation Sentences.

DICTATION SENTENCES

1. **parts** This game has many small **parts**.
2. **history** Our class studied the **history** of Rome.
3. **warning** The train signal sounded a **warning**.
4. **declare** Only Congress may **declare** war.
5. **despair** He felt **despair** when his new model boat sank in the pond.
6. **shirt** I wore my new **shirt** to the party.
7. **learning** We are **learning** how to speak French.
8. **backward** She walked **backward** on the balance beam.
9. **border** Let's paint the **border** a different color.
10. **prepared** The reporter **prepared** his questions carefully.
11. **harsh** The coach's decision seemed **harsh**.
12. **research** Medical **research** helps find cures for diseases.

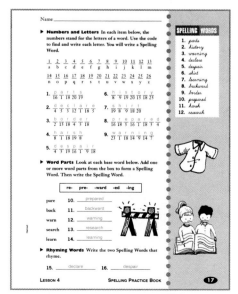

▲ Spelling Practice Book, page 16

▲ Spelling Practice Book, page 17

Cross-Curricular Connections

REACHING ALL LEARNERS

CHALLENGE

Ask students for creative suggestions to enhance scenes for the Rosa Parks activity. For example, students might add simple scenery or music, or they might write a poem to be included in the skit.

INTERVENTION

You may want to guide students doing research for the Women in Science or Art activity by helping them choose a subject on whom information can be found from sources that are easily accessible.

SOCIAL STUDIES

Rosa Parks

MATERIALS
- computer with Internet access
- encyclopedia in print, on CD-ROM, or online
- paper
- pencils

RESEARCH CIVIL RIGHTS Rosa Parks has been called the mother of civil rights. Have pairs or small groups of students use print or online encyclopedias or the Internet to research the civil rights movement in the United States and Rosa Parks's role in it. Students can share their information by writing and dramatizing scenes to perform for classmates.

If students do research on the Internet, remind them to try different search engines and to write down Web sites where they find useful information. Use the copying masters on pages A37–A39 to reinforce key Internet terms and to review Internet safety rules.

READING ELECTRONIC TEXTS/READING REFERENCE SOURCES/LISTENING/SPEAKING/WRITING

Harcourt

Back Forward Home Reload Search Mail Print Folder

The Mother of Civil Rights

Rosa Parks

SCIENCE/ART

Women in Science or Art

MATERIALS
- computer with Internet access
- encyclopedia in print, on CD-ROM, or online
- paper
- pencils

CREATE A POSTER In her reply to Michael, Mrs. Parks expresses satisfaction that women have taken their places in the arts and sciences, as well as in other areas of life. Students can research an outstanding woman in the field of either science or art in the past 100 years. They can then make posters for a class exhibition on Famous Women in Science and Art.

Activity Card 8 on page R13 gives students suggestions for carrying out this project.

FOCUS SKILL After students have completed their research, discuss how their ability to make judgments helped them find good information from reliable sources. READING ELECTRONIC TEXTS/READING REFERENCE SOURCES/REPRESENTING/INQUIRY

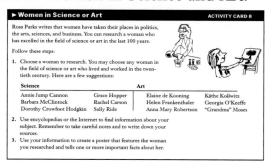

▶ Women in Science or Art   ACTIVITY CARD 8

Rosa Parks writes that women have taken their places in politics, the arts, sciences, and business. You can research a woman who has excelled in the field of science or art in the last 100 years.

Follow these steps:

1. Choose a woman to research. You may choose any woman in the field of science or art who lived and worked in the twentieth century. Here are a few suggestions:

Science	Art
Annie Jump Cannon	Elaine de Kooning
Barbara McClintock	Helen Frankenthaler
Dorothy Crowfoot Hodgkin	Anna Mary Robertson
Grace Hopper	Käthe Kollwitz
Rachel Carson	Georgia O'Keeffe
Sally Ride	"Grandma" Moses

2. Use encyclopedias or the Internet to find information about your subject. Remember to take careful notes and to write down your sources.
3. Use your information to create a poster that features the woman you researched and tells one or more important facts about her.

▲ Activity Card 8

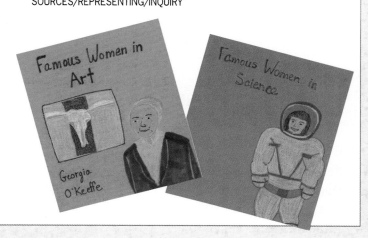

RESEARCH

Inquiry Projects

Students may develop many ideas and topics for inquiry based on "Dear Mrs. Parks." Have students brainstorm and create a web of possible research topics. The resources shown here can help students begin their own inquiry projects.

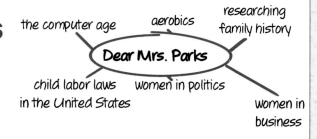

the computer age — aerobics — researching family history
Dear Mrs. Parks
child labor laws in the United States — women in politics — women in business

RESOURCES

I Am Rosa Parks
by Rosa Parks with Jim Haskins. Dial, 1997.
AVERAGE

A Picture Book of Thurgood Marshall
by David A. Adler. Holiday House, 1997.
EASY

READER'S CHOICE LIBRARY
Dear Benjamin Banneker
by Andrea Davis Pinkney.
AVERAGE

The Year They Walked
by Beatrice Siegel. Macmillan, 1992.
CHALLENGING

"Mick Harte Was Here"

GENRE

Realistic Fiction

- The **setting** could be a real place, usually contemporary.
- The **characters** and **events** are like people and events in real life.

CROSS-CURRICULAR CONNECTIONS

- **SOCIAL STUDIES:** Bike-Safety Program
- **MATH:** Conducting a Survey of Bike-Helmet Use

FOCUS STRATEGY **SUMMARIZE AND PARAPHRASE**

- **Before Reading:** Strategy Reminder on page T195
- **During Reading:** Apply the Strategy on pages T198, T204
- **After Reading:** Return to the Strategy on page T213

FOCUS SKILL **MAKE INFERENCES**

- **Before Reading:** Introduce the Skill on pages T194–T195
- **During Reading:** Apply the Skill on pages T198, T200, T206
- **After Reading:** Practice the Skill on pages T214–T215

a novel by BARBARA PARK

Young Adults' Choice

MICK HARTE WAS HERE

As students read "Mick Harte Was Here," they will see how coping with a serious situation can help people discover their inner strengths and appreciate what is most important to them.

Selection Summary

When twelve-year-old Mick Harte is killed in a bicycle accident, his sister, Phoebe, tries to cope with her feelings of guilt and anger about the incident. Phoebe feels responsible for Mick's death because on the day Mick died, he asked her to ride his bike home, but she couldn't. Reluctantly, Phoebe agrees to speak at a school bicycle-safety assembly. She stuns the audience into silence when she displays Mick's brand-new and never-worn helmet. Phoebe later realizes that her parents are also struggling with feelings of guilt.

Author Profile

Author **Barbara Park** feared that people wouldn't want to read "Mick Harte Was Here" because of its sad subject: the death of a child. She worked very hard, she said, trying "to achieve a balance between the humor and the sadness." After the book was published, Barbara Park went from city to city to publicize her book and to spread the book's message. She says, "I intended from the very beginning to get kids to do one specific thing: to wear a bicycle helmet, even if they don't think it's cool."

BELOW-LEVEL READERS

EASY READER
"That Day Last Week," pp. 38–45. Reinforces selection vocabulary and these additional words from "Mick Harte Was Here":

judgment   routine   memories

See *Timeless Tales Intervention Reader Teacher's Guide*, pages 26–31.

CASSETTE
"Mick Harte Was Here" is available on *Literature Cassette 2*.

CHALLENGE

Skinnybones by Barbara Park. Knopf, 1982. CHALLENGING

INQUIRY PROJECTS

See page T225. Have students pose selection-related questions. They can then do research to answer their questions.

MICK HARTE WAS HERE

Skills and Strategies

Reading

Listening

Speaking

Viewing

Vocabulary

sponsor
impact
reaction
podium
anticipation
perspective

BUILDING BACKGROUND AND CONCEPTS T192

INTRODUCING VOCABULARY T193
Transparency 27
Practice Book p. 29

PRETEACHING SKILLS
Before Reading
FOCUS SKILL Make Inferences (Introduce) T194–T195
Transparency 28
FOCUS STRATEGY Summarize and Paraphrase T195

PREREADING STRATEGIES T196

READING THE SELECTION T196–T209
 Literature Cassette 2
Author Information T209

ALTERNATIVE SELECTION
Easy Reader: "That Day Last Week"

NOTE: Students may begin reading the selection on Day 2.

LITERARY RESPONSE T208
Return to the Predictions/Purpose
Appreciating the Literature

THINK ABOUT IT T208

RETELL AND SUMMARIZE T209
Practice Book p. 30

REREADING FOR FLUENCY
Dramatic Reading T212
■ Recording Station

LITERATURE RESPONSE
A Letter from Phoebe T212

INTERVENTION STRATEGIES FOR BELOW-LEVEL READERS T213
FOCUS STRATEGY Return to the Strategy
Language Exploration

	DAY 1	DAY 2
Writing	**Expressive Writing: Tested or Timed** Discuss Tests of Writing T218	Teach/Model T218 Analyze the Prompt *Transparency 30*
Grammar	**Compound Subjects and Predicates** Teach/Model T220 *Transparency 32* *Language Handbook* pp. 104–105	Extend the Concept T220 *Grammar Practice Book* p. 19
Daily Language Practice	1. **We were. Not prepaired for the sudden accident.** (were not prepared) 2. **Did you see? The warnning sign?** (see the warning)	1. **My friend and I. Can skate backword.** (I can; backward.) 2. **We knows it is dangerous to skate without a helmet** (know; helmet.)
Spelling	**Words with /s/, /z/, and /sh/** percent silence years refused ancient pressure machine notice scene mention social special Pretest/Self-Check T222 *Transparency 33*	Teach/Model T222 *Practice Book* p. 34 Handwriting Tip

 KEY

✔ **Tested Skills**

■ **Management Option:** See Managing the Classroom, page T190, for ongoing independent activities.

Reaching All Learners: Support for "That Day Last Week," an alternative selection, appears on *Timeless Tales Intervention Reader Teacher's Guide* pp. 26–31.

READING AND RESPONDING

DAY 3

EXTENDING SKILLS & STRATEGIES

DAY 4

EXTENDING SKILLS & STRATEGIES

DAY 5

RESPONSE ACTIVITIES
Write a Journal Entry T210
Have a Discussion T210
Plan an Ad Campaign T210
Research a Discovery T210
Selection Comprehension Test

VOCABULARY
✔ Vocabulary in Context (Review) T199

ORAL LANGUAGE
Present a Health or Safety Message T212
Activity Card 9, R14

VIEWING
Puzzle Pieces and Snapshots T212

INDEPENDENT READING
Reader's Choice Library:
Zora Hurston and the Chinaberry Tree T191

Reader's Choice
Library Book ▶

COMPREHENSION
After Reading
FOCUS SKILL Make Inferences (Introduce)
T214–T215
Transparency 29
Practice Book p. 31

LITERARY CONCEPTS
✔ Character Development
(Review) T203

VOCABULARY T216–T217
Reviewing Vocabulary Words
Extending Vocabulary
Practice Book p. 32

TAKE-HOME BOOK
Taking Chances T216

CROSS-CURRICULAR CONNECTIONS
Social Studies: Bike-Safety
Program T224
Activity Card 10, R14
■ Art Station

Taking
Chances

Take-Home Book ▶

GRAMMAR
Complete and Simple Predicates
(Review) T207

CROSS-CURRICULAR CONNECTIONS
Math: Conducting a Survey of Bike-Helmet Use T225
FOCUS SKILL Apply Make Inferences

INQUIRY PROJECTS T225
Research

SELF-SELECTED READING T191
• *The Kid in the Red Jacket*
• *Don't Make Me Smile*
• *Skinnybones*

Practice Test T218
Prewrite and Draft T219
Transparency 31
🖥 *ClarisWorks for Kids®*

Edit and Evaluate T219

Assessment T219
Student Self- and Peer Assessment
Self-Assessment Checklist

Oral Review/Practice T221
Grammar Practice Book p. 20

Apply to Writing T221
Practice Book p. 33

Cumulative Review T221
Grammar Practice Book p. 21

---

1. We did reserch about safety rules and sines. (research; signs.)
2. Every safety sign. And signal has its on purpose. (sign and; own)

1. My brother Mick refussed to wear an helmet. (refused; a)
2. I talked to my classmates, and showed them Micks gifts. (classmates and; Mick's)

1. The audience's silense sounded. Louder than clapping. (silence sounded louder)
2. Finally, the students, and teachers applauded the spechial speaker. (students and; special)

Spelling Strategies T223
Apply to Writing
Spelling Practice Book p. 18

Spelling Activities T223
Spelling Practice Book p. 19

Posttest T223

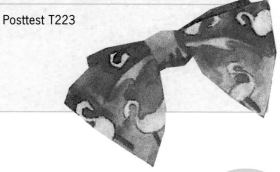

Visit *The Learning Site!*
www.harcourtschool.com

Managing the Classroom

While you provide direct instruction to individuals or small groups,
other students can work on ongoing activities like the ones below.

Recording Station

OBJECTIVE

To record and listen to dramatic readings

MATERIALS

- tape recorder
- cassettes

See page T212 for the Dramatic Reading activity. Have students tape-record their performances. They can then listen to their role-playing and discuss how their dramatic readings enhanced or detracted from the original text.

Art Station

OBJECTIVE

To create a Bike-Safety Program poster

MATERIALS

- poster board
- markers

After completing the Bike-Safety Program activity on page T224, students can design and create posters to advertise the event.

Computer Station

OBJECTIVE

To use the Internet to learn more about current bike-helmet laws in the United States

MATERIALS

- computer with Internet access

Ask students to research the Internet to find out which states have bike-helmet laws and how extensive those laws are. Invite students to share what they learn with the class.

Visit The Learning Site!
www.harcourtschool.com

Research Station

OBJECTIVE

To research bike helmets

MATERIALS

- brochures from bike-helmet manufacturers
- magazine and newspaper articles on bike helmets
- advertisements from sporting goods stores

After reading the story, students can research the latest and safest bike helmets and their approximate costs. Remind students to include independent sources. Lead them to conclude that advertisements are biased and that they need to consider this when making decisions as consumers.

Note: For more options, see pages T210–T211, T212–T213, and T224–T225.

GUIDED READING

Multi-Level Books

EASY

Crinkleroot's Guide to Walking in Wild Places by Jim Arnosky. Bradbury, 1990. NONFICTION: SAFETY

EASY READER: TIMELESS TALES *"That Day Last Week,"* pp. 38–45. REALISTIC FICTION: SAFETY

TAKE-HOME BOOK *Taking Chances* REALISTIC FICTION: ACCIDENTS

READER'S CHOICE LIBRARY *Zora Hurston and the Chinaberry Tree* by William Miller. BIOGRAPHY: FAMILY RELATIONSHIPS

See the *Reader's Choice Library* **lesson plan** on pages T230–T231.

AVERAGE

The Kid in the Red Jacket by Barbara Park. Knopf, 1987. REALISTIC FICTION: SELECTION AUTHOR

Don't Make Me Smile by Barbara Park. Random House, 1990. REALISTIC FICTION: SELECTION AUTHOR

READER'S CHOICE LIBRARY *A Cloak for a Dreamer* by Aileen Friedman. FOLKTALE: FAMILY RELATIONSHIPS

See the *Reader's Choice Library* **lesson plan** on pages T1173–T1174.

CHALLENGING

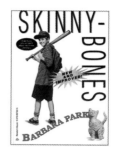

Skinnybones by Barbara Park. Knopf, 1982. REALISTIC FICTION: SELECTION AUTHOR

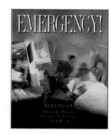

Emergency! by Joy Masoff. Scholastic, 1999. NONFICTION: SAFETY

The Cabin Faced West by Jean Fritz. Coward-McCann, 1958. HISTORICAL FICTION: FAMILY RELATIONSHIPS

LEVELED LIBRARY BOOK *Stone Wall Secrets* by Kristine and Robert Thorson. REALISTIC FICTION: FAMILY RELATIONSHIPS

Building Background and Concepts

Access Prior Knowledge

Discuss what it means to use good judgment. Ask students to explain what using good judgment means. (Possible response: making safe, sensible choices that are based on facts) Then ask students for examples of situations in which people their age are called upon to use good judgment.

Develop Concepts

Build a web using vocabulary words. Have students begin a web about the consequences of not using good judgment. Ask questions to encourage them to add vocabulary to the web: **Not using good judgment can result in serious injury or loss of life. What kind of *reaction* might there be after a child is injured in an accident? Who is affected? What might people do to help avoid future accidents?** Highlight indicates vocabulary.

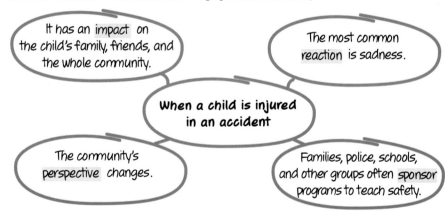

It has an impact on the child's family, friends, and the whole community.

The most common reaction is sadness.

When a child is injured in an accident

The community's perspective changes.

Families, police, schools, and other groups often sponsor programs to teach safety.

Then explain that "Mick Harte Was Here" is about a girl who struggles with a variety of emotions after her brother dies because he neglected to use good judgment when riding his bike.

OTHER BACKGROUND-BUILDING IDEAS

INTERNET Bonus Words and additional background ideas can be found on *The Learning Site* at **www.harcourtschool.com**

BONUS WORDS

Introduce slang expressions. If necessary, introduce the following slang expressions found in "Mick Harte Was Here": *ditching* (skipping school), *blurt out*, *squeal* (tell on someone).

ditching

blurt out

squeal

Introducing Vocabulary

Build Word Identification Strategies

Decode familiar patterns.

Display Transparency 27, and have volunteers read the paragraphs aloud. Remind students that they can sometimes figure out new words by looking for familiar patterns. Model decoding the word *anticipation*:

> **MODEL** **This word ends with the group of letters -*ation*, which I have seen in other words, like *imagination*. I also see that the consonant *c* is followed by an *i*, which means that *c* probably has the /s/ sound. I can use what I know about these sounds to decode this word.**

As students decode the other vocabulary, encourage them to confirm their pronunciation by asking questions like **Does the word sound right? Does it make sense?**

CHECK UNDERSTANDING

Practice other vocabulary strategies. Have students answer questions with sentences that show what the vocabulary words mean. MEANINGFUL SENTENCES

- **What word has the same ending as *participation*?** RELATED WORDS
- **What reaction might someone have to good news?** EXAMPLE
- **What word means the same as *perspective*?** SYNONYM
- **Where would you expect to see a podium?** PRIOR KNOWLEDGE
- **How would someone sponsor a food drive?** EXPLANATION
- **What kinds of events might have an impact on people?**

DESCRIPTION

QUICKWRITE

READING NOTEBOOK Point out that during the course of the day people make many decisions. Some decisions have more of an *impact* than others. Ask students to write about one decision they made that caused an important change or result.

VOCABULARY DEFINED

sponsor to pay for or plan and carry out a project or an activity

impact a force that produces a change or result or has an effect

reaction an action in response to something

podium a stand used by a speaker on a stage

anticipation a state of waiting for and expecting something to happen

perspective a way of looking at something that is influenced by your beliefs and experiences

---

VOCABULARY

Students and teachers filed into the auditorium. After everyone was seated, the principal walked onto the stage and over to the **podium**. Mr. Murray looked sad. "I have some difficult news to share with you," he said. "What I have to say will have a great **impact** on all of you."

You could feel the **anticipation** in the air as we all waited for Mr. Murray to go on.

"The city has decided to close this school for two years to make needed repairs. At the end of this semester, all students from our school will be sent to several other schools in the area." He cleared his throat and went on. "Next month the school will **sponsor** a program to help you and your families become familiar with your new schools."

As we left the auditorium, I heard angry voices. Students who didn't even seem to like school were complaining that the closing was unfair. I understood their **reaction**. I was angry, too. It's amazing how news like that can change your **perspective** about what's important.

▲ **Teaching Transparency 27**

▲ **Practice Book, page 29**

Mick Harte Was Here **T193**

Make Inferences

BEFORE READING

SKILL TRACE

INTRODUCE

• Before Reading:	T194–T195
• During Reading:	T198, T200, T206
• After Reading:	T214–T215
Reteach	R6
Review	T501

OBJECTIVE:

To understand how to make inferences

Preview the Literature

Preview the selection and discuss the genre.

Invite students to read the title and look at the illustrations to tell who and what the story might be about. (a person named Mick Harte; riding a bicycle) Then have them silently read the introductory paragraph on page 105.

Ask: **Does the story seem to be about characters and events from real life?** Have students discuss the characteristics of *realistic fiction*. (The characters and events are like those in real life. The setting could be a real place.)

Introduce the Skill

Discuss making inferences.

Explain to students that knowing how to make inferences can help them supply information the author has left out. It can also help them understand ideas that are unclear. Display Transparency 28 or write it on the board, and have a volunteer read the definition of an **inference** and the explanation of how to make an inference. Then help students apply that process to their reading of the paragraph.

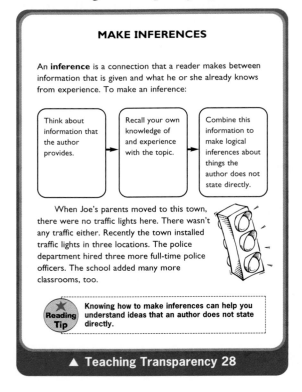

MAKE INFERENCES

An **inference** is a connection that a reader makes between information that is given and what he or she already knows from experience. To make an inference:

Think about information that the author provides.	→	Recall your own knowledge of and experience with the topic.	→	Combine this information to make logical inferences about things the author does not state directly.

When Joe's parents moved to this town, there were no traffic lights here. There wasn't any traffic either. Recently the town installed traffic lights in three locations. The police department hired three more full-time police officers. The school added many more classrooms, too.

★ Reading Tip Knowing how to make inferences can help you understand ideas that an author does not state directly.

▲ Teaching Transparency 28

Model the Thinking

Model making inferences.

Read aloud and discuss with students the Reading Tip on Transparency 28. Then use the first four paragraphs on *Student Edition* page 106 to model for students how to make inferences:

⬭MODEL As I read, I learn that the person telling the story lives near an intersection that used to be dangerous. She says that several accidents happened there and that the city finally installed a traffic signal. I can use all this information on the page and my personal experience with streets and traffic to infer that the intersection is very busy.

DURING/AFTER READING

- Apply the Skill, pages T198, T200, T206
- Practice the Skill, pages T214–T215

PRETEACH THE STRATEGY

 Summarize and Paraphrase

Encourage students to monitor their comprehension.

Explain to students that they can monitor their comprehension as they read by stopping occasionally to summarize and then paraphrase what they have read. Point out that summarizing can help readers restate the main ideas of a selection. Paraphrasing can ensure that readers have understood those main ideas by putting them into their own words.

- Apply the Strategy, pages T198, T204
- Return to the Strategy, pages T213

 See the Strategy Builder copying masters, pages A40–A45.

STRATEGIES GOOD READERS USE

- Use Prior Knowledge
- Make and Confirm Predictions
- Adjust Reading Rate
- Self-Question
- Create Mental Images
- Use Context to Confirm Meaning
- Use Text Structure and Format
- Use Graphic Aids
- Use Reference Sources
- Read Ahead
- Reread
- **Summarize and Paraphrase**
  FOCUS STRATEGY

Prereading Strategies

PREVIEW AND PREDICT

If students have not yet previewed the selection, have them look at the illustrations and read pages 104 and 105. Ask them to make predictions about the story. Remind students that a realistic fiction story has characters and events that are like people and events in real life. Then have them begin a story events chart for "Mick Harte Was Here." See *Practice Book* page 30.

Story Events Chart	
Event	Effect on Phoebe

SET PURPOSE

Read to Understand Have students set a purpose for reading "Mick Harte Was Here." Remind them that one purpose for reading is to understand. If students have difficulty setting a purpose, offer this suggestion:

MODEL **As I previewed this story, I saw that it is about a girl who must find a way to deal with the death of her brother, Mick. I think that when I read I will get a better understanding of the emotions someone might feel after a member of the family dies unexpectedly.**

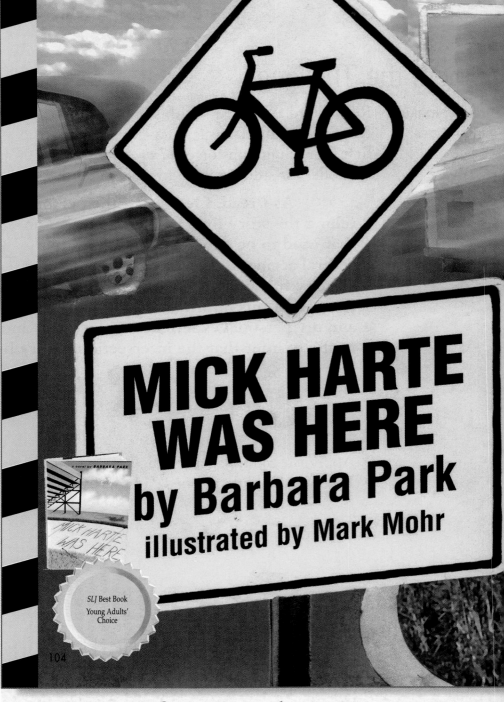

MICK HARTE
WAS HERE
by Barbara Park
illustrated by Mark Mohr

SLJ Best Book
Young Adults'
Choice

104

Options for Reading

DIRECTED READING	COOPERATIVE	INDEPENDENT
Use the **Monitor Comprehension** questions to check students' comprehension. The **Guided Reading** strategies on pages T198, T200, T202, T204, and T206 provide support for students reading below or on level. WHOLE CLASS/SMALL GROUP	**READING** Have students reading on or above level use *Comprehension Card 5* (p. R8) to focus on the **author's purpose.** INDEPENDENT/SMALL GROUP 	**READING** After students finish reading the story, have them discuss the questions at the end of the selection with another student who has read independently. PAIRS/ WHOLE CLASS

M ick Harte is a playful, amusing boy who likes to tease his family. But when Mick dies in a bicycle accident, his family is shattered. Every member is left to deal with the accident in his or her own way. His sister, Phoebe, must deal with her anger — toward Mick, toward other people, and toward herself.

INTERVENTION STRATEGIES

MODIFIED INSTRUCTION Have students read the title, "Mick Harte Was Here," and describe what they see on the first two pages. Introduce these story words:

forgive relaxed judgment memory helmet confession safety totally

Then have students read to page 109.

EASY READER Students may read "That Day Last Week," found on pages 38–45 in *Timeless Tales*. See *Timeless Tales* **Intervention Reader Teacher's Guide**, pages 26–31.

 "Mick Harte Was Here" is available on *Literature Cassette 2*.

Monitor Comprehension

1 **Why do you think the author tells the story about the dangerous intersection?** (Possible responses: to show that even smart people sometimes use bad judgment and that accidents can happen to anyone; to remind readers that busy roads are dangerous) **FOCUS SKILL** INFERENTIAL: MAKE INFERENCES/ DETERMINE AUTHOR'S PURPOSE

2 **What can you tell about Phoebe's dad from what she says about him on pages 106 and 107?** (Possible responses: He is an intelligent man who thinks about issues and usually uses good judgment.) **FOCUS SKILL** INFERENTIAL: MAKE INFERENCES/DETERMINE CHARACTERS' TRAITS

Guided Reading

STRATEGIES GOOD READERS USE

FOCUS STRATEGY **Summarize and Paraphrase** If students have difficulty making inferences, they may need help recognizing important ideas. Work in a small group discussing how summarizing and paraphrasing help a reader monitor comprehension. Aks these questions:

- **What happens as Phoebe's dad is lecturing her about people who don't use good judgment?**
- **What lesson does she say she learned that day?**

THREE BLOCKS FROM MY HOUSE, there used to be a dangerous intersection. It was one of those intersections where it was impossible for cars to pull out onto the main street without horns honking and brakes screeching and stuff.

My father griped about it every time we drove through there.

"The city's not going to put a light in here until someone gets hurt," he'd say. "You wait and see. It's going to take an accident before anything gets done."

Last year there were four accidents in seven months and they finally installed a traffic signal.

The first time we drove through it, some guy ran a red light and Pop had to swerve out of the way to keep from hitting him.

It scared us both to death. Pop swore at the guy and then started right in on this lecture about "how you can lead a horse to water, but you can't make him drink."

"It's a sad lesson, Phoebe," he said. "But no matter how many traffic lights they put in, they'll never be able to make people use common sense and good judgment."

106

SOCIAL STUDIES

MAPS: DANGEROUS INTERSECTIONS Many neighborhoods have a dangerous intersection like the one Phoebe describes, where accidents tend to occur. Display a road map of the area surrounding your school. Have students find and identify intersections that have heavy traffic. If possible, invite a representative from the police department to come to explain precautions the city or town has taken to make those intersections safer for drivers, bike riders, and pedestrians.

As he was talking, he turned around to make sure I was paying attention. While his head was turned, our car drifted into the next lane and two cars blasted their horns at us.

He made a quick recovery. It was close, though.

It was also the end of his talk on good judgment and common sense. And the lesson I ended up learning that day was that even smart guys with chemistry degrees do stupid stuff once in a while.

It's just that usually when you do stupid stuff, you luck out and get away with it. And if you luck out enough times, it's pretty easy to start believing that you're always going to luck out. *Forever*, I mean.

Like I can't even count how many soccer games I played in without shin guards before I finally got kicked in the leg and started wearing them. Over thirty, though, I bet.

And my mother had never had a major sunburn her whole entire life till she and Pop went to the beach for their anniversary last year. You can still see the blotchy places where her skin peeled from all the blisters, by the way.

107

REACHING ALL LEARNERS

ESL

FAMILIAR SAYINGS Point out Phoebe's mention of the saying "You can lead a horse to water, but you can't make him drink," and explain that this is a familiar saying that means "You can point out to people what is good or safe for them to do, but you can't force them to do it." Invite students to share similar sayings from their first language and explain what these sayings mean.

You can lead a horse to water, but you can't make him drink ▶

SKILLS IN CONTEXT

VOCABULARY
TESTED SKILL

Vocabulary in Context

SKILL TRACE	
Introduce	T110, T130
Reteach	R4
Review 1	T157
Review 2	T199
Test	Theme 1
Maintain	T423

TEACH/MODEL

Ask students what they think the word *griped* means in the sentence *My father griped about it every time we drove through there* on page 106. (complained) Then have them identify the surrounding words and phrases that they used to determine its meaning. If necessary, model how to figure out the meaning of a word by using context.

MODEL In the sentences that come before the word *griped*, I read that the intersection is a dangerous place. In the sentences that come after, I read what Phoebe's dad actually says. These words sound as if he's complaining. *Griped* must mean "complained."

PRACTICE/APPLY

Work with students to use context to determine the meaning of *swerve* and *lecture* on page 106 and *recovery* on page 107. Suggest that students record the words, their meanings, and the clues they used in a chart like the one shown below. Remind students that they can always use a dictionary or glossary to check the meaning of a word.

Word	Meaning	Context
swerve	to turn quickly in another direction	summary statement— Pop swerved out of they way to keep from hitting the other car.
lecture	speech given to teach a lesson	restatement—"It's a sad lesson, Phoebe." synonym—talk
recovery	the regaining of control	inference—Since they didn't get hurt, he must have regained control of the car.

Monitor Comprehension

1 **How do you know that Phoebe has been deeply affected by her brother's death?** (Possible responses: She can't forget the fact that Mick did not wear his helmet or forgive him for it. She has been missing school.) METACOGNITIVE: DETERMINE CHARACTERS' EMOTIONS

2 **How does Phoebe feel toward the woman from the PTA? How can you tell?** (Possible responses: She is upset with her. She dismisses what the woman says with the words *yadda, yadda, yadda*. She says she stared at the woman in disbelief. She wonders where the woman got the nerve to ask her to speak.) **FOCUS SKILL** INFERENTIAL: MAKE INFERENCES

Guided Reading

STRATEGIES GOOD READERS USE
Use Context to Confirm Meaning Ask students to read the seventh paragraph on page 108. If they misread a word, use prompts like these to help them:

- **You said ____. Would it make sense for the woman to say that here?** SEMANTIC CUES
- **You said ____. Does that sound right?** SYNTACTIC CUES

And then there was Mick. Who went twelve years and five months without ever falling off his bike.

So he refused to wear a helmet.

And it's the one thing about him that I've tried to forget. And to forgive him for.

And I'm sorry, but I can't seem to do either one.

IT WAS OVER A WEEK before Mrs. Berryhill called me down to her office again. I was kind of nervous when I got her note. Even though I knew my parents had explained to her about me ditching school that day, part of me was still expecting detention.

That's why I was relieved to see another woman sitting in her office when I walked in. Mrs. Berryhill introduced us. Her name was Mrs. Somebody-or-other from the PTA.

She shook my hand and said how "sincerely sorry" she was about what happened to my brother. Then she started right in on how the PTA wanted to make sure that nothing like that ever happened again, so they were going to sponsor this big assembly on bike safety. It was already in the works, she said. There were going to be police officers, and instructional videos, and demonstrations of the latest safety gear, and yadda, yadda, yadda . . .

"We'd like to invite you to sit onstage with the other speakers," she told me. Then she took my hand again and asked if I thought maybe I could say a few words to my classmates about bike safety. Because a few words from me would have "a tremendous impact," she thought.

And through all of this, I just sort of sat there, you know? Staring at her in disbelief. Because I swear I could not figure out what planet this woman had come from.

I mean where in the world had she ever gotten the nerve to ask me something like that? Had it never even dawned on her that the timing of a bicycle-safety assembly was just a little off for

108

SOCIAL STUDIES

THE PTA — OVER 100 YEARS OF CARING Parent-Teacher Associations (PTAs) are volunteer groups in which parents and teachers work together. PTAs meet to discuss such things as school needs, community health and safety issues, field trips, and additional educational programs. PTAs are associated with the National Congress of Parents and Teachers, which was founded in 1897. In the United States there are about 27,000 local PTAs with about 7 million members.

My Notes

me? That maybe I would have liked to see a safety assembly *before* my brother was killed?

I didn't make a scene. I just stood up and took my hand away.

"I can't," I said.

When I turned to go, Mrs. Somebody-or-other fell all over herself telling me how much she understood.

Which really killed me, by the way.

Because the woman didn't have a clue.

I DON'T KNOW when I changed my mind about speaking at the assembly.

I think it was just one of those flipflops you do sometimes. You know, like at first you have this gut reaction to something and you're positive that you're totally right. Only after a while, it creeps into your mind that the other guy may actually have a point. Then the next thing you know, his point's making more sense than your point. Which is totally annoying. But still, it happens.

It used to happen with me and Mick all the time. Like a couple of months ago, we were arguing about whether the Three Stooges were funny or not. I kept saying they were hilarious, and Mick kept saying they were just morons.

Then we started kind of wrestling around a little bit, and the next thing I know, Mick jumps up and starts slapping the top of his head with his hand and fluttering it up and down in front of my face. After that, he grabs my nose with his fist, twists it hard, and finally slaps it away with his other hand. He ended his performance with the classic Three Stooges laugh—Nyuk, nyuk, nyuk—and a quick move to boink my eyes out with his fingers.

109

REACHING ALL LEARNERS

INTERVENTION STRATEGIES

MODIFIED INSTRUCTION Help students summarize the story so far. Phoebe can't <u>forgive</u> Mick for not using good <u>judgment</u> by refusing to wear a bike <u>helmet</u>. It makes her both angry and sad that he died because of it. One day, a woman from the PTA asks Phoebe to speak at a bike-<u>safety</u> program. Although Phoebe doesn't say so, she thinks that it's <u>totally</u> thoughtless and insensitive of the group to ask her to speak at such an event. She refuses, but then she changes her mind and agrees to speak.

Help students set a purpose for reading through page 113. (to find out what Phoebe says and does at the bike-safety assembly)

Monitor Comprehension

1 **How and why do Phoebe's feelings about the Three Stooges change as a result of Mick's routine?** (Possible response: She finds them less funny because, rather than just observing, she has now had personal experience with this type of humor.)

INFERENTIAL: CAUSE-EFFECT

2 **What do you think Phoebe might do next? Why do you think so?** (Possible response: She might say something about bike helmets, using the same method Mick had used; to get people to think about the serious issue of bike safety; to show them that it isn't funny not to wear a bike helmet.)

INFERENTIAL: MAKE PREDICTIONS

Guided Reading

STRATEGIES GOOD READERS USE

Reread If students have difficulty understanding why Mick does an imitation of the Three Stooges, have them reread from the last two paragraphs on page 109 to the end of the section on page 110. Model thinking about how Mick behaved.

◯MODEL⟩ **When I reread, I find that Mick first expresses his opinion. Then he performs the routine, which is supposed to be funny. He ends the routine suddenly and asks in a serious way, with no expression, if Phoebe thinks it was funny.**

Fortunately, I was able to block it with my hand.

Mick stopped the routine as fast as he had started it. Then, without saying a word, he stood up real dignified-like and dusted himself off.

He looked at me without the trace of a smile. "Hilarious, wasn't I?" he said dryly.

"Yes," I lied. "You were."

But deep down I had already started to feel different about the Stooges.

THERE WERE eight hundred people in the gym when I walked to the microphone that morning. I wasn't nervous, though, which really surprised me. But I swear I felt almost relaxed when I set down my bag of stuff next to the podium.

"I'm Mick Harte's sister," I said. Then I bent down and reached into my plastic bag.

"When Mick was in third grade, this is what my grandmother from Florida sent him for Christmas."

I held it up. "It's a glow-in-the-dark bow tie with pink flamingos on it."

A couple of kids chuckled a little.

"Don't worry," I said. "He never wore it. He said it made him look like a dork."

There was more laughing then. And I reached into my bag again.

"When Mick was in fourth grade, my Aunt Marge sent him this from Michigan."

I held up a hat in the shape of a trout.

"Mick said this one went beyond dork, all the way to doofus," I said.

This time everybody really cracked up. Some of the kids in the first row even stood up and started craning their necks to see what I would pull out next.

110

SOCIAL STUDIES

HUMOR: THE THREE STOOGES Although many students will know who the Three Stooges were, you may wish to explain that they were an extremely popular stage and film comedy team that formed in 1922 and performed through the 1950s. Their routines were, and still are, often criticized for the abusive nature of their humor. Invite students to draw on their knowledge of the Three Stooges and Mick's imitation of them to tell whether they agree with Phoebe or with Mick.

They watched as I turned the bag upside down and a cardboard box fell onto the stage.

Carefully, I set it on the podium and waited for everything to get totally quiet.

"When Mick turned ten, my parents gave him this for his birthday."

I took my time opening the lid. I mean you could really feel the anticipation and all.

But when I finally pulled Mick's gift out of the box—still brand-new—there was just this gasp.

And no one laughed at all.

111

CHALLENGE

REACHING ALL LEARNERS

IT'S "COOL" TO SAVE LIVES Phoebe agrees to give the bicycle-safety speech to help save lives. She includes the slang terms *dork* and *doofus* to tell about how Mick thought he looked. Ask students to find words that meant "cool" to other generations. Suggest that they ask parents, aunts, uncles, and grandparents for ideas. Invite students to share what they learn with the class.

groovy

SKILLS IN CONTEXT

LITERARY CONCEPTS
TESTED SKILL

Character Development

SKILL TRACE	
Introduce	T66, T90
Reteach	R3
Review 1	T115
Review 2	T203
Test	Theme 1
Maintain	T307

TEACH/MODEL

Ask students how they would describe what Mick was like. (Possible responses: He was funny. He didn't like to look silly. He had a sophisticated sense of humor.) Then ask students how they formed their opinions of Mick. Remind students that story characters are developed through

- the author's description of the character.
- the character's own actions, words, and thoughts.
- other characters' actions, words, and thoughts.

If necessary, model how to recognize character development.

MODEL **One way that I learn what Mick was like is through Phoebe's memory of the time they were arguing about the Three Stooges, and he demonstrated how silly their classic routines were. This makes me think that Mick had a more sophisticated sense of humor that required people to use their intelligence to understand what was funny.**

PRACTICE/APPLY

Have students use a chart to keep track of character development in the selection. Students can fill in the chart as they read.

Character	What I learned about him or her	How I learned it
Phoebe		
Mick		
Mr. Harte		

Monitor Comprehension

1 **What methods does Phoebe use to get and keep the attention of her audience? How are these methods effective?** (Possible response: She uses humor and the element of surprise. These are effective because her listeners laugh at first but then gasp when they see the bike helmet.) INFERENTIAL: DRAW CONCLUSIONS

2 **Did you predict what Phoebe would do? What information did you use to make your prediction?** (Responses will vary.) INFERENTIAL: CONFIRM PREDICTIONS

3 **Phoebe wonders if what she said will make a difference. Do you think it will? Why?** (Possible response: Yes, because she was speaking from personal experience about the importance of bike helmets.) CRITICAL: SPECULATE

Guided Reading

STRATEGIES GOOD READERS USE

FOCUS STRATEGY **Summarize and Paraphrase** If students have difficulty determining whether Phoebe's speech will make a difference or not, help them summarize and paraphrase parts of the story. Use these prompts:

- **Paraphrase Mr. Harte's lecture on page 106.**
- **Summarize Phoebe's speech and her audience's reaction to it.**

No one even moved.

"This was my brother's bike helmet," I said.

My voice broke, but somehow I forced myself to finish.

"He said it made him look like a dork."

I DON'T KNOW if what I said at that assembly will make a difference. I don't know if it will help anyone use better judgment than my brother did. I hope so, though. . . . Because Mick died from a massive head injury. And yet the doctors said that just an inch of Styrofoam would have made the difference between his living and dying.

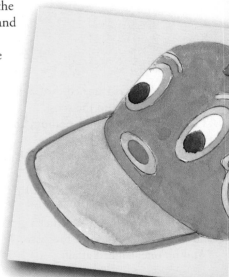

It's been a month since the accident now. Things have gotten a little better at home. Nana from Florida went back to Orlando. And my mother gets dressed in the mornings, usually. She's gone back to work, too—just two days a week, but it's a start.

We sit down to dinner every night at our new places. Eating

112

AUTHOR'S CRAFT

HAPPY TIMES AND SAD TIMES Explaining how she tried to keep young readers interested in a book about such a sad subject, author Barbara Park said, "I decided to include happy, funny remembrances of Mick. But I still needed to address all that his sister and parents were going through. I knew I couldn't soft-pedal the painful, real parts." Ask students if they think the author successfully achieved a balance between the happy times and the sad times in this story. Ask them to explain their answers.

still isn't a big deal with us, though. Like last night we had grilled cheese sandwiches and mashed potatoes. And on Sunday all the forks were in the dishwasher so we ate potato salad with soup spoons. My mother's eased up on stuff like that. Death sort of gives you a new outlook on the importance of proper silverware.

It's called *perspective*. It means your father doesn't iron a crease in his pants every morning. And the hamburgers come in all shapes and sizes.

I've started to laugh more often. But I still feel guilty when I'm having too good a time. Which is totally ridiculous. Because if I want to feel guilty, there're lots better reasons than that. Like I'm just now starting to deal with how Mick asked me to ride his bike home that day and all.

I kept that whole memory tucked away in the back of my mind after the accident happened. But bad memories must grow in the dark, I think, because it kept on creeping into my thoughts, till it was with me almost all the time, it seemed.

113

Informal Assessment

FOCUS SKILL **MAKE INFERENCES**
To assess whether students are making inferences as they read, ask these questions:

1. **Why does the audience gasp when Phoebe pulls Mick's brand-new helmet out of the box?**

2. **How do you think Mick and Phoebe's mother has changed her usual routine since Mick's death?**

Further instruction on making inferences can be found on pages T214–T215.

REACHING ALL LEARNERS

INTERVENTION STRATEGIES

MODIFIED INSTRUCTION Provide a model for summarizing what happened at the bike-safety assembly.

MODEL Phoebe feels almost <u>relaxed</u> when she gives her speech at the assembly. First, she makes the audience laugh when she shows the bow tie and the trout hat, both of which Mick never wore because they made him look silly. Then Phoebe shows the audience a bike helmet. The people gasp because they know how Mick died.

Help students set a purpose for reading through page 115. (to see if Phoebe and her family learn to deal with Mick's death)

Monitor Comprehension

❶ How has Mick's death changed his family's outlook on life?
(Possible response: Things that used to be important, like creased pants, hamburger shapes and sizes, and eating with proper silverware, don't have the same importance.) LITERAL: NOTE DETAILS

❷ What do you think Phoebe's dad is going to say to her? Why?
(Possible response: that she shouldn't blame herself because it was something she couldn't control) **FOCUS SKILL** INFERENTIAL: MAKE INFERENCES/MAKE PREDICTIONS

Guided Reading

STRATEGIES GOOD READERS USE

Self-Question If students have difficulty inferring from the evidence in the text and predicting Mr. Harte's reaction to Phoebe, they may need to ask themselves questions like the following:

- **What does Mr. Harte do as Phoebe is telling him she feels responsible for Mick's death?**
- **What would most caring people say in this situation?**

Then last Saturday, when my father and I were riding home from a soccer game, my stomach started churning like it always does right before I'm about to blurt out an unplanned confession.

It's one of the sickest feelings there is, by the way. To realize you're about to squeal on yourself like that.

The only thing sicker is keeping it inside.

So it all came busting out. All about how Mick asked me to ride his bike that day. And how I had soccer practice so I told him I couldn't do it.

"See, Pop? Don't you get it? I could have kept the accident from ever happening. If only I had ridden his bike home, Mick would still be here right now."

I was crying a little bit now. But except for handing me the travel tissues from the dashboard, my father hardly seemed to

114

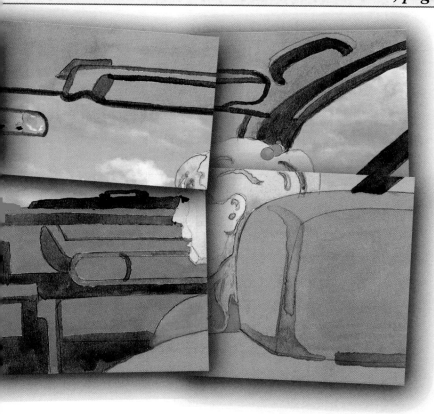

notice. Instead, he just kept staring out the window at the road in front of us.

Then slowly, he began shaking his head from side to side.

"I'm sorry, Pop. I'm sorry. I'm sorry," I said over and over again.

My face was buried in my hands when I finally felt him touch my shoulder.

"I'm going to make a list, Phoebe," he said. "And I want you to keep a count." His voice was real low and steady as he began.

"*If only* you had ridden Mick's bike home, Mick would still be here.

"*If only* the truck had been going a little faster or a little slower, Mick would still be here.

115

INTERVENTION STRATEGIES

MODIFIED INSTRUCTION   Discuss how Mick's death has affected Phoebe.

- First, Phoebe is really angry about Mick's death.
- Then, Phoebe puts her sadness and her anger aside to speak at a bike-safety assembly.
- Phoebe tries to get on with her life but one troubling memory creeps into her mind.
- Phoebe makes a confession to her father because she feels responsible for Mick's death.

SKILLS IN CONTEXT

GRAMMAR

SKILL TRACE	
Introduce	T180–T181
Review	T207

Complete and Simple Predicates

TEACH/MODEL

Ask students to identify the complete predicate and the simple predicate in the first sentence in the last paragraph on page 113. (complete predicate: *sit down to dinner every night at our new places*; simple predicate: *sit*) Model identifying complete and simple predicates.

MODEL I know that the complete predicate includes all the words of a sentence that tell what the subject of the sentence is or does. In this sentence, the subject is *We*. All the words that tell what the subject does are *sit down to dinner every night at our new places*. I know that the simple predicate is the main verb and any helping verbs. In this sentence, *sit* is the simple predicate.

PRACTICE/APPLY

Write the following sentences on the board, and have volunteers underline the complete predicate and circle the simple predicate in each sentence. Remind students that words in the complete predicate can come anywhere in a sentence.

Last night we had grilled cheese sandwiches and mashed potatoes.

I could have kept the accident from ever happening.

I did not make a scene.

He made a quick recovery.

Literary Response

RETURN TO THE PREDICTIONS/PURPOSE

Were your predictions about the story confirmed? If you changed your predictions, at what point in the story did you revise them? Discuss with students whether their purpose for reading was met.

APPRECIATING THE LITERATURE

What part of the story had the greatest impact on you? (Responses will vary.)

Think About It

1 **What does Phoebe learn as a result of Mick's accident?** (Possible responses: to use good judgment; that some things may not be as important as they seem; that you shouldn't blame yourself for things that aren't your fault)
INFERENTIAL: SUMMARIZE/THEME CONNECTION

2 **If you were a friend of Phoebe's, what might you say or do to help her get through this difficult time?** (Responses will vary.) CRITICAL: PERSONAL RESPONSE

3 **Why do you think this story is written as if Phoebe is telling it herself?** (Possible response: to make the reader feel closer to Phoebe and to the story) CRITICAL: LITERARY ANALYSIS

"*If only* his meeting had been scheduled one day earlier or one day later, Mick would still be here.

"*If only* it had been raining that day, I'd have driven him to school and Mick would still be here.

"*If only* one of his friends had kept him talking a second longer at his locker that afternoon . . .

"*If only* the house he was riding to had been in the other direction . . .

"*If only* that rock hadn't been on the sidewalk at the exact spot . . ."

He stopped then. And I was pretty sure he was finished. But all at once, he heaved this . . . awful sigh and whispered, "If only I had made him wear his helmet."

My heart broke for my father at that moment, and I reached my hand out to him.

He held on to it tight. Then he smiled the saddest smile you've ever seen.

"What number are we on, little girl?" He sounded so old. I scooted closer to him.

"I think we're done, Pop," I said softly.

He pressed my hand to his cheek.

The two of us drove home in silence.

1 What does Phoebe learn as a result of Mick's accident?

2 If you were a friend of Phoebe's, what might you say or do to help her get through this difficult time?

3 Why do you think this story is written as if Phoebe is telling it herself?

116

MEET THE AUTHOR
BARBARA PARK

Head injury is the main cause of death in fatal bicycle crashes.

Researchers tell us that if all bicyclists wore helmets, as many as one death *every day* and one head injury every *four* minutes could be prevented.*

I urge all of you who do not wear bike helmets to please reconsider your decision. Today.

Please.

It's your *life.*

*From the Division of Injury Control, National Center for Environmental Health and Injury Control, and the Division of Field Epidemiology.

This study was published in the *Journal of the American Medical Association,* December 4, 1991, Volume 266.

117

ABOUT THE AUTHOR

BARBARA PARK made the decision to be a children's novelist when she was around thirty. Although "Mick Harte Was Here" was the most difficult book Park has ever written, it is her favorite. "I would have loved to have known both Mick and his sister, Phoebe. And of course, the bike-helmet issue is extraordinarily important to me," she said.

Discuss why the author included the message to readers at the end of the story. (She wants people to understand how important it is to wear bike helmets.)

 INTERNET Additional author information can be found on *The Learning Site* at **www.harcourtschool.com**

Informal Assessment

RETELL
Have each student retell the story in his or her own words. Check to make sure that the student

☐ relates the main idea and relevant details in sequence.

☐ uses phrases, language, or vocabulary from the text.

☐ evaluates the author's perspective and intent in creating the story.

☐ relates text to relevant experiences.

SUMMARIZE
Have students summarize the story by recalling key story elements. Students can refer to the story events chart they completed while reading. See also *Practice Book* page 30.

ONE-SENTENCE SUMMARY Have students use their completed story events chart to summarize the selection in one sentence.

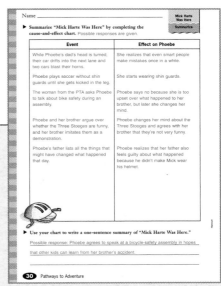

▲ **Practice Book, page 30**

Activity Choices

LISTEN TO PHOEBE

Write a Journal Entry   Ask students to explain in their journal entries exactly what Phoebe says and does to change or reinforce their feelings and opinions about wearing bike helmets.   CREATIVE: WRITING

STYLE OR SAFETY?

Have a Discussion   Suggest that students choose a discussion leader who will encourage each member of the group to express an opinion. They may also choose another group member to record the summary ideas. After the discussion, have groups compare their summaries.   CRITICAL: RESPOND APPROPRIATELY

USING YOUR HEAD

Plan an Ad Campaign   Work as a class to brainstorm a variety of ideas for campaign slogans to use in print advertisements and TV commercials. You might also provide examples of public service print advertisements for students to examine.   CREATIVE: WRITING/ILLUSTRATING

IF ONLY . . .

Research a Discovery   Direct students to use print resources and/or technology resources to research the history of important scientific discoveries.   CRITICAL: USE MULTIPLE SOURCES/MAKE OBSERVATIONS

RESPONSE ACTIVITIES

Listen to Phoebe

WRITE A JOURNAL ENTRY Imagine that you were in the audience the day Phoebe spoke at the assembly. How might her speech have changed your feelings or opinions about bike helmets? Write an entry in your journal describing your reaction to Phoebe's speech.

Style or Safety?

HAVE A DISCUSSION Mick thought wearing a bike helmet made him look silly. Meet with a small group of classmates. Discuss whether it makes sense for young people to worry about how they look when it comes to their safety. Work together to write a brief summary of your discussion.

118

SCHOOL-HOME CONNECTION

Students and family members can work together to complete the activities on the copying master on page R19. You may wish to assign some or all of the activities as homework during the week.

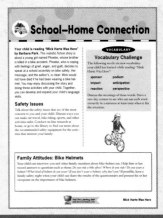

Copying Master, p. R19 ▶

Using Your Head

PLAN AN AD CAMPAIGN How can young people be persuaded to wear bike helmets? Plan a national ad campaign for bike helmets. Include a sketch for a print advertisement and a script for a TV commercial. List magazines and TV shows you would use for your ad, and explain why you chose each one.

If Only . . .

RESEARCH A DISCOVERY Use your science textbook or other sources to research a great scientific discovery. What other events, large or small, had to happen before this discovery could take place? For example, the microscope had to be invented before bacteria, the cause of many illnesses, could be discovered. Share with classmates what you find out.

119

Assessment

SELECTION COMPREHENSION TEST

To evaluate comprehension, see pages 13–15.

INFORMAL ASSESSMENT

PERFORMANCE ASSESSMENT Student work for the Listen to Phoebe activity may be used for performance assessment of story comprehension.

PORTFOLIO OPPORTUNITY

Students may want to add their Using Your Head activity ideas to their portfolios.

REACHING ALL LEARNERS

INTERVENTION STRATEGIES

WRITING A JOURNAL ENTRY In the Listen to Phoebe activity, some students may wish to take brief notes about Phoebe's speech. Students can use their notes to write their journal entries.

1. Phoebe introduces herself.
2. She shows Mick's glow-in-the-dark bow tie.
3. She shows Mick's trout hat.
4. She shows his brand-new helmet.

Building Literacy Skills

REREADING FOR FLUENCY

Dramatic Reading

Have students retell the story by role-playing the main story events. Students should reread the story and base their role-plays on lines in the story, but they should be allowed to expand on a scene if they wish. Provide students with an opportunity to rehearse their scenes before presenting them to the class. LISTENING/SPEAKING/READING

WRITING

A Letter from Phoebe

Have students write a letter that Phoebe might write to Mick to tell him how she feels about what happened. Suggest that students reread all or parts of the selection to identify the different emotions that Phoebe experiences in the story. Have students try to incorporate all those feelings in their letters. WRITING

ORAL LANGUAGE

Present a Health or Safety Message

Author Barbara Park makes an urgent plea for students to wear bike helmets. Have students write a brief message about a health or safety issue, such as a balanced diet, and present the message to the class. Point out that the author uses facts and statistics to make her message stronger and that students should, too. Have students refer to Activity Card 9, page R14, to help them deliver a clear, meaningful message. LISTENING/ SPEAKING

▶ Present a Health or Safety Message   ACTIVITY CARD 9

Write a message to people your age about a health or safety issue that is important to you. Be sure that your message
■ explains the issue clearly and directly.
■ states reasons the issue is important.
■ is supported with facts and statistics.

When the messages are presented,
SPEAKERS SHOULD
■ identify their audience and purpose.
■ signal important ideas.
■ use nonverbal cues.
■ speak clearly.
LISTENERS SHOULD
■ distinguish facts from opinions.
■ determine the speaker's purpose and viewpoint.
■ interpret nonverbal cues.
■ evaluate expressed points of view.

Exercise Is Important

Activity Card 9 ▶

VIEWING

Puzzle Pieces and Snapshots

Snapshots, or photographs, in an album are like pieces of a puzzle. Each snapshot shows a part of the story of a person's life. Point out the illustrations that are like puzzle pieces (pages 106–107, 109, 110–111, 114–115) and the snapshots (pages 105, 112–113). Ask students how these pictures help tell the story "Mick Harte Was Here." Then have students create puzzle-piece drawings or snapshot-like drawings that tell a story. VIEWING/ REPRESENTING

REACHING ALL LEARNERS

Intervention Strategies for Below-Level Readers

Reinforce Comprehension

FOCUS STRATEGY **Apply the Summarize and Paraphrase strategy.** Talk with students about how using strategies while reading can help them better understand and appreciate what they read. Remind students that the focus strategy for reading "Mick Harte Was Here" is Summarize and Paraphrase. Discuss the strategy by asking questions such as these:

• **What does it mean to summarize a selection?**
• **What is paraphrasing?**

Have students practice using this strategy as they reread a section of "Mick Harte Was Here." As students silently reread pages 108 to 116, suggest that they use a chart like the one shown to identify the main idea in each story part and then to summarize and paraphrase that part of the story.

Story Part	Summary/Paraphrase
Phoebe gets called to Mrs. Berryhill's office, pages 108–109.	Phoebe is invited to be a speaker at a bike-safety assembly. She thinks that there should have been such an assembly before Mick was killed, and so she refuses. Later, she changes her mind and agrees to speak.

Idioms

Discuss idioms. In "Mick Harte Was Here," the narrator uses the expression *luck out* (page 107) to explain that some people avoid problems by chance. Point out that *luck out* is an example of an idiom, a group of words that together mean something different from what the words by themselves mean. Draw on the board a chart like the following. Ask volunteers to help you write meanings for each of these idioms from the story.

Idiom	Meaning
luck out (p. 107)	get what you want by chance or because of good fortune
dawned on (p. 108)	occurred to, came to mind
fell all over herself (p. 109)	tried exceptionally hard to do something
didn't have a clue (p. 109)	had no understanding or idea about something

SKILL TRACE

INTRODUCE	
• Before Reading:	T194–T195
• During Reading:	T198, T200, T206
• After Reading:	T214–T215
Reteach	R6
Review	T501

OBJECTIVE:

To understand how to make inferences

INTERVENTION

Have each student draw a simple picture. Then have students exchange pictures and write a caption that includes information from the picture and something they know from their own experience.

CHALLENGE

Invite each student to write a paragraph from which classmates can make inferences. Students should keep in mind that classmates should be able to make inferences by using information provided in the paragraph as well as what they already know.

RETEACH See page R6 for a lesson in multiple modalities.

FOCUS SKILL

Make Inferences

AFTER READING

Return to the Concept

Extend the thinking.

Remind students that readers can make inferences by using information in the text and prior knowledge to understand relationships among ideas or to figure out the meaning of unclear text. Then discuss the process of making inferences, using this diagram.

> Find information that the author provides in the text.
> ↓
> Use your prior knowledge and past experience.
> ↓
> Make an inference about something that is not stated.

Have students use the diagram to explain some of the inferences they made as they read "Mick Harte Was Here."

Model thinking about making inferences.

Have students silently read page 107 and the top of page 108 in the *Student Edition*. Invite a volunteer to read aloud the sentences about Mick at the top of page 108. Ask students what they can infer about what happened to him. You may want to model the thinking.

MODEL **Phoebe says that Mick "went twelve years and five months without ever falling off his bike. So he refused to wear a helmet." She doesn't say so, but I can infer that he fell off his bike. I can also infer that since he refused to wear a helmet, he wasn't wearing one when he fell. On page 107 Phoebe talks about how people usually luck out when they do foolish things, but then one day their luck runs out. I can infer that Mick took a chance by not wearing his helmet and that this time his luck ran out.**

Guided Practice

Have students make inferences.

Explain that in realistic fiction like "Mick Harte Was Here," an author doesn't always state everything that happens. He or she expects readers to make inferences about characters and events. Display Transparency 29 or write the diagram on the board. Ask students to make additional inferences about a character or an event from the selection.

Summarize.

Ask students to tell how making inferences helped them better understand the meaning of the story.

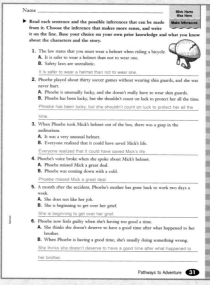

MAKE INFERENCES

Information from the Story +	What I Know from My Past Experience =	Inferences About Characters
Phoebe is called to Mrs. Berryhill's office. She has been there before for ditching school.	At our school, students have to go to the principal's office about absences without notes or permission.	Mrs. Berryhill must be the principal at Phoebe's school.
Phoebe says the shape of hamburgers, proper silverware, and creases in pants are no longer important after Mick's accident.	Sometimes it is difficult to pay attention to details when you have a concern or worry. You give more attention to the other matter.	Phoebe's family was careful about many details before Mick's accident.

▲ Teaching Transparency 29

Practice/Apply

WHAT DO YOU MEAN?

Organize students into small groups, and provide each group with the following statements.

- **Cynthia, who is my neighbor, flies home on weekends.**
- **They slipped away while we were talking over our plans.**
- **Mark took the last train to the city.**

Ask each group to write at least two inferences for each statement. Have interested students illustrate one or more of the statements, based on any one of the inferences they made. Then invite groups to share their inferences and discuss additional information they would need to make a correct inference for each statement. LISTENING/SPEAKING/WRITING

DIAGRAM IT

PERFORMANCE ASSESSMENT Invite students to find an article in a newspaper or magazine and use it to make inferences. Have them make a diagram to show how they used information from the text and their own prior knowledge and past experiences to make the inferences. READING/ORGANIZE INFORMATION

▲ Practice Book, page 31

Mick Harte Was Here T215

Vocabulary Workshop

Taking Chances

by Patricia Carmichael
illustrated by Erykah Saul

Have students read the
TAKE-HOME BOOK
Taking Chances to
reinforce vocabulary words. See
also *Guided Reading Manual for
Take-Home Books*, page 6.

Reviewing Vocabulary Words

Read aloud the following sentence frames. Have a student use a vocabulary word to complete each one.

1. There was great _____ among the students as we waited to hear who had won the poster contest. *(anticipation)*

2. Mr. Lee stood at the _____ on the stage and announced the winner. *(podium)*

3. When I didn't win, my first _____ was disappointment. *(reaction)*

4. Anna's bike-safety poster had the greatest _____ on the judges. *(impact)*

5. She said that being in a bike accident had changed her _____ on the importance of bike helmets. *(perspective)*

6. The police department plans to _____ a program on bicycle safety. *(sponsor)*

Reviewing Word Identification Strategies

Decode familiar patterns. Ask students to examine the word *indication* and identify its suffix. *(-ion)* Then ask them to explain what sound the letter *c* has in this word and how they know. (It has the /k/ sound because it's followed by the vowel *a*.) Remind students that knowing suffixes such as *-ion* and sounds for familiar letter patterns can help them pronounce new words they encounter in their reading, such as *indication*.

Give students this list of words and have them use an unabridged dictionary to show the base words or roots and the suffixes *-ion*, *-tion*, *-ation*, or *-sion*.

indicate + ion = indication

creation	celebration
admiration	combination
invitation	complication
participation	transportation
translation	confusion

Cross-Curricular Words Ask students to name words with the suffixes *-ion*, *-tion*, *-ation*, and *-sion* from other content areas. Suggest that they look through their textbooks or other sources to find words. Ask volunteers to read their words aloud and to identify the base words.

Extending Vocabulary

Synonyms

In "Mick Harte Was Here," Phoebe describes an argument she had with her brother, Mick, about whether the Three Stooges were funny. Phoebe thought they were hilarious. Help students develop a word line based on the concept *funny*. Have students brainstorm words that are synonyms of *funny* or have a similar meaning, and write their responses on the board. *(Possible responses: amusing, comical, hilarious, humorous, ridiculous, hysterical, foolish)*

Place words on the graphic. Work with students to think about the meaning of each word and to place it on the line according to the degree of humor it describes. Position words that describe something that is a little funny, such as *amusing*, on the far left. Place words that describe something that is very funny, such as *hilarious*, on the far right. Ask students to use the words in sentences to support their responses. (A possible word line is shown.)

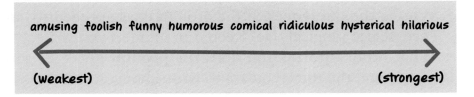

amusing foolish funny humorous comical ridiculous hysterical hilarious

(weakest) ←———————————————→ (strongest)

Reference Sources/Using Multiple Sources

Ask students to look up the word *Styrofoam* in a dictionary and an encyclopedia to learn why the word is capitalized. (It's a trademark that is often used to name any polystyrene plastic.) Then have students use multiple sources, including encyclopedias, dictionaries, and online references, to research other trademarked products whose names are often incorrectly used for other products with similar characteristics, for example, Kleenex for any brand of tissue, or Xerox for any copier or photocopy.

ESL

REACHING ALL LEARNERS

Help students grasp the concept of the different shades of meanings for synonyms by asking them to name someone (a person from real life or a television or movie character) they think is sort of funny and someone they think is hilarious. Invite them to describe the difference between the two people. Then ask them for synonyms in their first language that they would use to describe these two people.

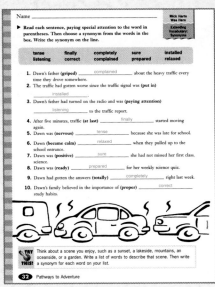

▲ Practice Book, page 32

Expressive Writing

TESTED OR TIMED

Discuss Tests of Writing

Remind students that a narrative is a story; a personal narrative is a story about an event in the writer's own life. Explain that they might sometimes be asked to write a narrative for a test. Ask students how this would be different from a regular assignment. (Possible responses: Everyone would probably have to write about the same topic and finish in the same amount of time; students would not be able to prepare notes ahead of time.)

Teach/Model

Display Transparency 30 and discuss it with students. Point out that students will be successful in writing a narrative for a test if they understand the instructions and use their time wisely.

ANALYZE THE PROMPT

Ask yourself these questions:
- **What is the writing form?** Look for details in the prompt. Focus on key words that tell you what kind of writing to do.
- **Who is the audience?** If the prompt does not identify an audience, select a logical one. Keep it in mind as you write.
- **What other information does the prompt give?** Be sure you understand the topic you are to write about.

BUDGET YOUR TIME

Decide how much time to spend on each step:
- **Prewrite** Brainstorm and list ideas. Use a graphic organizer to help you decide on a logical order for presenting your ideas.
- **Draft** Write your narrative. Refer to your graphic organizer for ideas. Add details and time-order words.
- **Revise/Proofread** Read your story. Make sure it has a clear beginning, middle, and ending. Cross out any details that do not directly address the point. Correct spelling errors, and check for the correct use of capital letters and end marks.

TESTED WRITING: NARRATIVE

In timed or tested writing, a writer responds to a prompt in a set amount of time. The prompt gives the writer the topic. It may also identify the audience.

Sample Prompt

Think about an important day in your life. Write a true story for a friend your age. Tell what made the day special for you. Describe the events in time order. (40 minutes)

STRATEGIES
Analyze the Prompt

1. What is the writing form?
   (a true story, or personal narrative)
2. Who is the audience?
   (a friend your age)
3. What will the story describe?
   (an important day in your life)

Budget the Time

prewrite	draft	revise and proofread
10 min.	25 min.	5 min.

40 minutes total

▲ **Teaching Transparency 30**

💻 **TECHNOLOGY**
Students may use a word processing program such as *ClarisWorks for Kids®* if they decide to publish their narratives.

✏️ Practice Test

Write this prompt on the board. Omit the time if it is not an issue.

Think about a time when you helped someone solve a problem. Write a story for your classmates describing the event. Make sure your story has a clear beginning, middle, and ending. (40 minutes)

Analyze the Prompt Help students identify the writing form, the audience, and the topic. Ask students whether this prompt calls for a personal narrative or a fictional story. (personal narrative)

Prewrite (10 MINUTES)

Have students brainstorm ideas, list them on a sheet of paper, and organize them on a graphic organizer like the one on Transparency 31.

Draft (25 MINUTES)

Tell students they will have 25 minutes to write a draft. Help students focus on organization and elaboration by reminding them to include the following:

- a clear beginning, middle, and ending
- time-order words that link ideas
- details that develop the story

Edit (5 MINUTES)

Tell students how much time they have to revise. You may want to ask questions such as these:

- **Are time-order words used to make the order of events clear?**
- **Is the personal narrative written in the first person?**
- **Is the narrative organized in paragraphs?**
- **Are all of the sentences complete? Are capital letters used correctly?**

Evaluate

After students have completed the practice test, ask volunteers to describe the features of a successful personal narrative. Read aloud the self-assessment checklist below, and have students use it to check their writing.

PERSONAL NARRATIVE

Title:
Topic:
Setting:
People involved:
Problem or conflict:

| What happens at the beginning? |
| Events: |
| Details: |

| What happens in the middle? |
| Events: |
| Details: |

| What happens at the end? |
| Resolution of problem or conflict: |

▲ Teaching Transparency 31

Assessment

STUDENT SELF- AND PEER ASSESSMENT
Instead of reading aloud the Self-Assessment Checklist, provide students with copies of the scoring rubric, page A9. Students may choose to add additional points to the rubric. They may use the rubric to evaluate their own or each other's narratives.

PORTFOLIO OPPORTUNITY
Students may keep their revised narratives in their work portfolios and compare them with later practice tests to assess their progress.

EXPRESSIVE WRITING: NARRATIVE
Additional lessons:
   Personal Narrative, T50
   Descriptive Paragraph, T94
   Realistic Story, T134
Complete Writing Process:
   T178

SELF-ASSESSMENT CHECKLIST

✔ My personal narrative describes a time when I helped someone solve a problem.
✔ My personal narrative is written in the first person.
✔ My personal narrative has a clear beginning, middle, and ending.

✔ I used time-order words to connect the events of my story.
✔ My story is appropriate for my classmates.
✔ I used capital letters and end marks correctly, and I proofread to correct any spelling errors.

Compound Subjects and Predicates

SKILL TRACE	
INTRODUCE	T220–T221
Review	T267

Language Handbook, pages 104–105

ESL

REACHING ALL LEARNERS

Have students insert the conjunctions *and, but,* or *or* into the following sentence frames:

Mick _____ Phoebe rode their bikes.

Mick got a helmet _____ didn't wear it.

A stop sign _____ a light is needed at this corner.

DAY 1 — Teach/Model

DAILY LANGUAGE PRACTICE

1. **We were. Not prepared for the sudden accident.** (were not prepared)
2. **Did you see? The warnning sign?** (see the warning)

INTRODUCE THE CONCEPT Use sentences 1 and 2 and the information on Transparency 32 as you discuss the following points:

- A **compound subject** is two or more subjects that have the same predicate. The subjects in a compound subject are usually joined by the **conjunction** *and* or *or*.
- A **compound predicate** is two or more predicates that have the same subject. The simple predicates in a compound predicate are usually joined by a conjunction such as *and*.

COMPOUND SUBJECTS AND PREDICATES

1. <u>Mom and Pop</u> went to the beach.
2. They <u>walked on the sand and swam in the water</u>.
3. The tie was in the plastic bag. The hat was in the plastic bag. **(and)** (The tie and the hat were in the plastic bag.)
4. No one laughed. No one moved. **(or)**
   (No one laughed or moved.)

Compound Subject
- **Two or more subjects with the same predicate**
- **Use *and* or *or* to separate two subjects.**
- **Use commas to separate three or more subjects.**

Compound Predicate
- **Two or more predicates with the same subject**
- **Use *and, but,* or *or* to separate predicates.**
- **Use commas to separate three or more predicates.**

5. The tie the hat and the bicycle helmet were gifts to Mick.
   (The tie, the hat, and the bicycle helmet were gifts to Mick.)
6. The kids gasped stared at the helmet and grew silent.
   (The kids gasped, stared at the helmet, and grew silent.)

▲ **Teaching Transparency 32**

DAY 2 — Extend the Concept

DAILY LANGUAGE PRACTICE

1. **My friend and I. Can skate backword.**
   (I can; backward.)
2. **We knows it is dangerous to skate without a helmet** (know; helmet.)

DEVELOP THE CONCEPT Display Transparency 32, and ask students to rewrite the sentence pairs in 3 and 4, combining each pair into one sentence. They should use the conjunction in parentheses to create a compound subject or predicate. Then explain that

- commas separate three or more subjects in a compound subject.
- commas separate three or more predicates in a compound predicate.

Have volunteers read aloud sentences 6 and 7 and tell where commas should be added. Correct the sentences on the transparency.

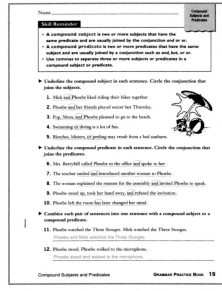

▲ **Grammar Practice Book, page 19**

DAY 3 — Oral Review/Practice

DAILY LANGUAGE PRACTICE

1. We did reseerch about safety rules and sines. (research; signs.)
2. Every safety sign. And signal has its on purpose. (sign and; own)

THREE OR MORE Ask students these or similar questions, and have them answer with at least three items in either a compound subject or a compound predicate:

- **What did you do at school today?** (compound predicate)
- **What do you do at home in the evenings?** (compound predicate)
- **Who are your favorite cartoon characters?** (compound subject)
- **What are your favorite foods?** (compound subject)

Point out the pauses that occur between the items in a series when they are said aloud. Ask students how the pauses are indicated in writing. (by commas)

▲ Grammar Practice Book, page 20

DAY 4 — Apply to Writing

DAILY LANGUAGE PRACTICE

1. My brother Mick refussed to wear an helmet. (refused; a)
2. I talked to my classmates, and showed them Micks gifts. (classmates and; Mick's)

SAFETY RULES Have students work in pairs. Each pair should write four sentences about bicycle or traffic safety. Have students use compound subjects in the first two sentences and compound predicates in the last two.

Test Prep

Share this tip about compound subjects and predicates as students prepare for writing tests:

- Look for sentence pairs that have the same predicate but different subjects, or the same subject but different predicates. These sentences can be rewritten as one sentence.

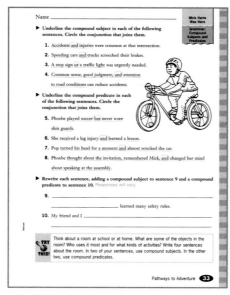

▲ Practice Book, page 33

DAY 5 — Cumulative Review

DAILY LANGUAGE PRACTICE

1. The audience's silense sounded. Louder than clapping. (silence sounded louder)
2. Finally, the students, and teachers applauded the spechial speaker. (students and; special)

COMBINING SENTENCES Have students combine each pair of sentences into a single sentence with a compound subject or compound predicate. Ask students to underline the compound subject or predicate in the new sentences.

1. Police officers attended the assembly. Safety experts also attended the assembly. (Police officers and safety experts attended the assembly.)
2. The students listened carefully. The students looked at the exhibits. (The students listened carefully and looked at the exhibits.)

▲ Grammar Practice Book, page 21

Words with /s/, /z/, and /sh/

SPELLING WORDS

1. percent
2. silence*
3. years*
4. refused*
5. ancient
6. pressure
7. machine
8. notice
9. scene
10. mention
11. social
12. special

BONUS WORDS

13. parachute
14. specialty
15. detention*
16. constitution

*Words appearing in "Mick Harte Was Here." Additional story words following the generalizations are *once, places, office, introduced, sincerely, those, sense, tissues, intersection, attention,* and *because.*

STUDENT-CHOSEN WORDS

17. _____
18. _____
19. _____
20. _____

REACHING ALL LEARNERS
CHALLENGE

Challenge more-proficient spellers to find additional words containing the /sh/ sound, such as *emotion* and *session.* Have them add these words to their Student-Chosen Words.

DAY 1 — Pretest/Self-Check

ADMINISTER THE PRETEST. Say each word, and then use it in a Dictation Sentence. (See Day 5.) Help students self-check their pretests using the list at the top of Transparency 33.

OPEN SORT Have students look for ways to sort the Spelling Words. For example, they might sort them according to number of syllables or put the words in alphabetical order.

WORDS WITH /s/, /z/, AND /sh/

Spelling Words

1. percent	5. ancient	9. scene
2. silence	6. pressure	10. mention
3. years	7. machine	11. social
4. refused	8. notice	12. special

Words with /s/	Words with /z/	Words with /sh/
percent	years	ancient
silence	refused	pressure
notice		machine
scene		mention
social		social
special		special

- The /s/ sound can be spelled *c, s, sc,* or *ce.*
- The /z/ sound can be spelled *s* or *se.*
- The /sh/ sound can be spelled *ci, ss, ch,* or *ti.*

▲ Teaching Transparency 33

DAY 2 — Teach/Model

CLOSED SORT Display the Spelling Words and chart headings on Transparency 33. Ask students to copy the chart and to write each Spelling Word where it belongs.

Have students identify the ways the /s/ sound is spelled in the words in their first column. Write the words on the transparency, and circle the letters as students name them. Repeat for the words with /z/ and /sh/. Uncover the generalizations, and have students read them to confirm their conclusions.

Handwriting Tip

Ask students to make their writing neat and legible, slanting all letters in the same direction. Remind students to keep their papers in the proper position and to hold their pencils or pens correctly.

▲ Practice Book, page 34

DAY 3	**Spelling Strategies**

READING BACKWARD Write the following sentence on the board:

A notise was on the board.

Ask students to read the sentence from left to right and then backward. Explain that reading backward when proofreading may help a reader spot a mistake. When you read forward, you think ahead, read quickly, and see what you expect to see. When you read backward, you are more likely to notice details and mistakes.

Apply to Writing

Suggest to students that they read a piece of their own writing backward to see if they can spot any mistakes. Have them correct any misspelled words they find.

▲ Spelling Practice Book, page 18

DAY 4	**Spelling Activities**

CROSSED WORDS Have students make up "Crossed Word" puzzles based on the spelling generalizations. First, students should list the words to be used in their puzzle and then select one word that the other words will cross. Have students write that word in a vertical column. Other words should be added horizontally to interlock with the first word, and students should write a definition clue for each horizontal word. Finally, have students transfer their puzzles to graph paper, leaving blank boxes where letters are to be filled in. Students can exchange papers with a partner and solve each other's puzzles.

WRITING CAPTIONS Ask students to write picture captions for their own photos or photos from magazines. They should use Spelling Words, Bonus Words, or other words that follow the generalizations.

▲ Spelling Practice Book, page 19

DAY 5	**Posttest**

Assess students' progress, using the Dictation Sentences.

DICTATION SENTENCES

1. **percent** He ate 25 **percent** of the pie.
2. **silence** There was **silence** as everyone watched the movie.
3. **years** We have lived in this town for many **years**.
4. **refused** The injured runner **refused** to give up the race.
5. **ancient** We study **ancient** civilizations in school.
6. **pressure** Put **pressure** on the wound to stop the bleeding.
7. **machine** Oil keeps a **machine** running smoothly.
8. **notice** A **notice** told us that the show was canceled.
9. **scene** The mountain **scene** was beautiful.
10. **mention** Did I **mention** the date of the party?
11. **social** The group got together for a **social** visit.
12. **special** Celebrations are **special** events.

Mick Harte Was Here T223

Cross-Curricular Connections

REACHING ALL LEARNERS

CHALLENGE

Students can contact the local police department to request information on bicycle safety and to invite a representative to speak about bike-safety programs at a school assembly for the Bike-Safety Program activity.

ESL

Students can help create flyers and public service announcements with bilingual information for the Bike-Safety Program activity.

MATERIALS
- a computer with Internet access
- paper
- pencils, markers

SOCIAL STUDIES

Bike-Safety Program

PLAN A COMMUNITY BIKE-SAFETY PROGRAM In "Mick Harte Was Here," Phoebe speaks at a school assembly on bike safety. Have students use the Internet to find out about bike safety and bike-safety programs.

Have students work in pairs or small groups to research bike-safety tips and bike-safety programs across the country. Groups can then work together to use the information that they found to plan a bike-safety program for their own community.

Activity Card 10, page R14, will help students learn how to do online research. READING ELECTRONIC TEXTS/VIEWING/INQUIRY

▶ **Bike-Safety Program**   ACTIVITY CARD 10

In "Mick Harte Was Here," Phoebe speaks at a school assembly on bike safety. With your group, use the Internet to research bike safety. Type the words *bike safety* in the search box. Then search the results. Look for information that will help answer these questions:

■ What are some important bike-safety tips?

■ What safety equipment should every bike have?

■ What safety gear should every bike rider wear?

When you do your Internet research, be sure to

■ use several online search engines to find information.

■ use specific search terms.

■ take good notes on the information you find.

■ bookmark or write down Web site addresses in case you need to return for more information later.

Then use what you have learned to plan your own bike-safety program.

▲ **Activity Card 10**

Conducting a Survey of Bike-Helmet Use

MATERIALS
- paper
- pencil

CHART SURVEY RESULTS At the end of "Mick Harte Was Here," author Barbara Park urges bicyclists everywhere who do not wear bike helmets to start wearing them. Work with students to develop a list of survey questions related to bike-helmet use. Then have students use the survey to interview five people at school about their helmet use, including classmates and teachers. After they have completed their surveys, have students tally their results and use the results to create a class chart.

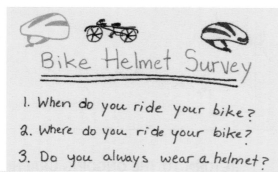

Here are some questions students might use in their surveys:

- **Do you have a bicycle?**
- **Do you own a helmet?**
- **Do you always, sometimes, or never wear a bike helmet when you ride your bike?**
- **If not, why don't you wear a helmet?**
- **Do your friends wear bike helmets?**
- **Do family members wear bike helmets?**
- **Do you believe that wearing a bike helmet can save your life?**

FOCUS SKILL After students complete their chart, have them make inferences about the information in it.

LISTENING/SPEAKING/WRITING/REPRESENTING

Inquiry Projects

"Mick Harte Was Here" can be a springboard for inquiry into a variety of topics and ideas. Brainstorm with students topics they would like to investigate, and record their ideas in a web. Students can use some of the resources shown here to help them begin their own inquiry projects.

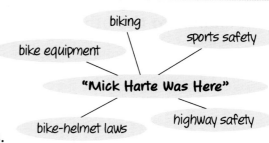

RESOURCES

Emergency! by Joy Masoff. Scholastic, 1999. CHALLENGING

Crinkleroot's Guide to Walking in Wild Places by Jim Arnosky. Bradbury, 1990. EASY

READER'S CHOICE LIBRARY
Zora Hurston and the Chinaberry Tree by William Miller. EASY

Mississippi Mud by Ann Turner. HarperCollins, 1997. AVERAGE

Theme Wrap-Up

What's the Problem?

FIND THE PROBLEM Think about the main characters of the stories in this theme. Each main character faces a problem. Make a two-column chart like the one shown below. In the first column, list each main character. In the second column, write the problem he or she faces.

Character	Problem
Derek and Rory	
Walnut	
Mary	
Phoebe	

Here's the Solution!

DESCRIBE THE RESOLUTION Choose two characters from the chart, and think about the problem each one has to solve. Write a paragraph comparing and contrasting the problems these characters face and what each one learns from his or her experience. Then describe how each character changes by the end of the story.

Talk Across the Cultures

DISCUSS CULTURES The characters in this theme represent many different cultures. Work in a small group, and review the selections in this theme. Each group member should choose a quote, a sentence, or a saying from one of the selections that reflects a particular culture. Each member should then read his or her example aloud. As a group, discuss how the example reflects that culture. Discuss how the culture is similar to or different from other cultures.

120

121

RETURN TO THE LITERATURE

1 **How is "Dear Mrs. Parks" different from the other selections in this theme? How is it similar to the other selections?** (Possible response: "Dear Mrs. Parks" is a series of letters to and from a real person. It is similar to the other selections because all of them deal with the subject of young people learning about themselves and how to get along in the world.) CRITICAL: CONNECT IDEAS AND THEME/COMPARE AND CONTRAST

2 **If Mrs. Parks could speak to one or more of the fictional characters in this theme, whom do you think she would choose, and what would she say?** (Responses will vary.) CRITICAL: SPECULATE

ASSIGN THEME WRAP-UP ACTIVITIES Organize students interested in the Discuss Cultures activity ("Talk Across the Cultures") into groups. The other Wrap-Up activities may be completed independently and shared among students later. CRITICAL: CONNECT AND COMPARE

RETURN TO THE ONGOING GRAPHIC ORGANIZER Ask students to review their graphic organizers and revise them to include new ideas based on the selections they have read and listened to.

Who Looked Inside	What the Character or Characters Learned
Rory and Derek	not to judge other people before getting to know them
Walnut	that each of us has different strengths and abilities
Mary	that everyone makes mistakes; that she should be proud of her family for its accomplishments
Mrs. Parks	that it is important to know about the past; that all people can do their best and contribute to society
Phoebe	not to blame yourself or others for accidents that can't be helped; that some good can come out of bad experiences

Theme Review

Vocabulary Review

accompaniment	exhausted	reaction
accompanist	grimaced	ridiculed
anticipation	impact	simultaneously
audition	incredible	sonata
authority	inspire	souvenir
commotion	mentor	sponsor
compose	moss	sternly
correspondence	perspective	tread
counsel	podium	vow
dignity	potential	
exaggerate	quiver	

Have students review vocabulary from the theme by playing a "Mystery Word" game. Write vocabulary words on index cards and place each card in an envelope. On the envelope, write clues such as these:

This word has (does not have) a prefix (suffix).

This word has ___ syllable(s). This word means "___ ."

Students take turns choosing an envelope and figuring out the vocabulary word from the rules.

Grammar Review

▲ Grammar Practice Book, pages 22–23

Comprehension Review

You may wish to use the Listening to Literature selection (pages T6–T9) to review the tested focus skills for this theme. Reread the selection, and ask questions like the following:

1 **How does knowing about prefixes help you understand what the author means when she says that Djeow Seow was *insignificant*?** (Possible response: The prefix *in-* means "not"; *insignificant* means "not significant" or "not important.") **FOCUS SKILL** PREFIXES AND SUFFIXES

2 **The word *strands* can have several different meanings. How can you use the context to figure out what *strands* means in this sentence?** *She twined a string of grass and vines, and wove in strands of her own long black hair.* (Possible response: Since she was using grass and vines to make a rope and weaving in strands of her hair, the word *strands* must mean long pieces of hair.) **FOCUS SKILL** VOCABULARY IN CONTEXT: MULTIPLE-MEANING WORDS

Spelling Review

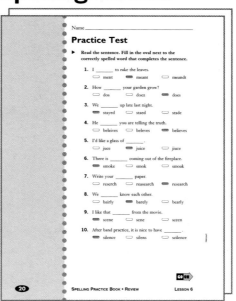

▲ Spelling Practice Book, pages 20–21

Look Inside **T227**

▲ *The Black Stallion* by Walter Farley

THEME: Look Inside
As students read *The Black Stallion*, they will see how a young boy's experiences help him discover the strength of his own spirit.

GENRE: FICTION
Summary: Young Alec Ramsay and a magnificent untamed black stallion are the only survivors of a shipwreck. Alone on a deserted island, the boy and the horse form a special bond that helps them both survive. When they are finally rescued, Alec takes the stallion home and trains him to race. Alec's fierce determination helps him overcome various obstacles to achieve a stunning success.

ABOUT THE AUTHOR
Walter Farley grew up loving horses and learning about them from his uncle, a professional horseman. Walter Farley began writing *The Black Stallion* when he was a high school student, and it was published while he was still in college. He went on to write more than thirty other books about horses, including many more Black Stallion stories.

Reader's Choice Library

Access Prior Knowledge

Show students the book cover, read the title aloud, and have a volunteer tell what a stallion is. Invite students to share what they know about raising and training horses.

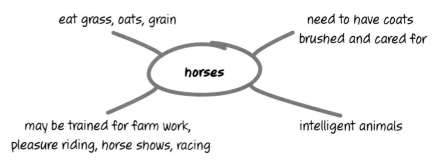

eat grass, oats, grain

need to have coats brushed and cared for

horses

may be trained for farm work, pleasure riding, horse shows, racing

intelligent animals

Set Purpose/Predict

Have students read "Homeward Bound," the first chapter of *The Black Stallion*. Ask them to identify the main character and the setting of the story. Then have them use their prior knowledge and their preview to predict what might happen in this story and to set a purpose for reading. (to be entertained)

DEVELOP VOCABULARY

As students read each chapter, have them list unfamiliar vocabulary words from that chapter in their Reading Notebooks. If students are unable to figure out the meanings of the unfamiliar words from context, they can look them up in a dictionary.

Options for Reading

DIRECTED READING

FOCUS STRATEGY **Strategy Reminder** Ask students how **using prior knowledge** can help them understand and draw conclusions about story characters and events. During reading, ask the reading questions at the far right and help students monitor their own comprehension of the events in this story. WHOLE CLASS/SMALL GROUP

COOPERATIVE READING

Have groups of three or four students use Comprehension Card 3 (Plot) to guide their discussion. INDEPENDENT/SMALL GROUP

INDEPENDENT READING

Students can write in their Reading Notebooks about whether their predictions were confirmed and whether they would recommend this book to a friend and why. After reading, have students complete the self-evaluation forms found on pages A25–A26 and add them to their reading portfolios. INDEPENDENT/WHOLE CLASS

TEACHER READ-ALOUD

Read aloud from the beginning of the story to the section break near the top of page 5 as students listen responsively. Remind students that asking themselves questions about what might happen next will help them read the story with greater interest. Students may then complete the book independently.
INDEPENDENT/WHOLE CLASS

Options for Responding

PERSONAL RESPONSE

Have students answer the responding questions at the lower right to demonstrate understanding and share their interpretations.

COMPARE SELECTIONS

Have students compare this book to "Sees Behind Trees" by completing the chart below. INDEPENDENT/WHOLE CLASS

Story	Main Character	Setting	Problem	Solution
Sees Behind Trees				
The Black Stallion				

DISCUSS PLOT

Point out that throughout the story, the author creates a series of problems that Alec needs to overcome in order to achieve his goals. Have students identify specific problems and discuss how these problems increase the reader's interest and suspense.
SMALL GROUP/WHOLE CLASS

WILD AND FREE

Have small groups of students create Black Stallion dances. Suggest that students close their eyes and imagine the Black Stallion in motion. Then they can translate their ideas into movements to share with the group. The various movements that students suggest can be combined to create the dances. SMALL GROUP

Reader's Choice Library

▲ *Zora Hurston and the Chinaberry Tree* **by William Miller**

THEME: Look Inside
As students read this biography, they will see how childhood experiences shaped Zora Hurston's understanding of who she was and how she chose to live her life.

GENRE: BIOGRAPHY
Summary: This biography focuses on the childhood of the writer Zora Neale Hurston. Her mother teaches her to climb a chinaberry tree and encourages Zora to follow her dreams, regardless of society's conventions and expectations. When her mother dies, Zora seeks solace in the branches of the tree and in her determination to continue pursuing her goals as her mother taught her.

ABOUT THE AUTHOR
William Miller is a teacher of African American literature and of creative writing at York College in York, Pennsylvania. Another book he has written for young readers is about the great American abolitionist and orator, Frederick Douglass.

Access Prior Knowledge

Display the book cover and read the title aloud. Explain that this book is a biography of a famous writer, Zora Hurston. Create a web by asking what students know about biographies.

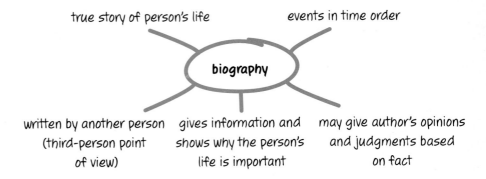

Set Purpose/Predict

Have students read the first two pages of text and look at the illustrations that accompany them. Ask students to predict what they might learn from reading this biography. Then have them use their prior knowledge and their preview to set a purpose for reading. (to find out about Zora Hurston's life)

DEVELOP VOCABULARY

As they read, have students list unfamiliar vocabulary in their Reading Notebooks. They can then organize the words in alphabetical order and use a dictionary to add definitions. Encourage students to create their own glossary of new words.

Options for Reading

DIRECTED READING

FOCUS STRATEGY **Strategy Reminder** As they read, remind students to use the **self-question** strategy to help them understand events the author tells about. During reading, ask the reading questions at the far right and help students monitor their own comprehension. WHOLE CLASS/SMALL GROUP

COOPERATIVE READING

Have groups of three or four students use Comprehension Card 4 (Theme and Mood) to guide their discussion. INDEPENDENT/SMALL GROUP

INDEPENDENT READING

Students can write in their Reading Notebooks about whether their predictions were confirmed and whether they would recommend this book to a friend and why. After reading, have students complete the self-evaluation forms found on pages A25–A26 and add them to their reading portfolios. INDEPENDENT/ WHOLE CLASS

TEACHER READ-ALOUD

Read aloud the first several pages of *Zora Hurston and the Chinaberry Tree*, and tell students to listen for the poetic quality of the language. Remind them to keep their purposes for listening in mind as they read. Students may then read the whole book independently. INDEPENDENT/ WHOLE CLASS

Options for Responding

PERSONAL RESPONSE

Have students answer the responding questions at the lower right to demonstrate understanding and share their interpretations. INDEPENDENT/WHOLE CLASS

COMPARE SELECTIONS

Have students compare this book to "Dear Mrs. Parks" by answering questions like those below. INDEPENDENT/WHOLE CLASS

- In what ways are the two selections alike?
- How are the two genres different, and how does that difference affect the way the information is presented?
- What similarities do you see between the lives of Rosa Parks and Zora Hurston?
- Do you think the two women would agree with each other's philosophy? Why or why not?

DISCUSS AUTHOR'S PURPOSE

Have students identify the author's main purpose in writing this book. (to inform) Then discuss whether the author may have had additional purposes, such as to inspire readers and to entertain through the use of poetic language. SMALL GROUP/WHOLE CLASS

BACKGROUND MUSIC

Provide a variety of instrumental music on tape. Encourage students to choose appropriate background music to accompany a reading of *Zora Hurston and the Chinaberry Tree*. Students may choose a passage to read aloud for classmates while playing the background music. INDEPENDENT/WHOLE CLASS

OPTIONS FOR READING

1 **What difficulties did Zora have to overcome as a young girl?** (society's beliefs about how girls should behave; her mother's death) INFERENTIAL: SUMMARIZE

2 **What did Zora's mother mean by telling Zora that the world belonged to her?** (that Zora could be or do anything she wanted or go anywhere; that she should not set or accept limits on herself) INFERENTIAL: UNDERSTAND FIGURATIVE LANGUAGE

3 **Why does this biography begin and end with Zora climbing the chinaberry tree?** (Her mother taught her to climb the tree. It is a symbol of everything her mother taught her about striving to achieve her goals.) CRITICAL: AUTHOR'S CRAFT/INTERPRET IMAGERY

OPTIONS FOR RESPONDING

1 **How might Zora Hurston's experiences have been different if she were growing up today?** (Responses will vary.) CRITICAL: COMPARE AND CONTRAST

2 **Do you agree or disagree with Zora's mother's ideas? Explain.** (Responses will vary.) METACOGNITIVE: EXPRESS PERSONAL OPINIONS

REACHING ALL LEARNERS **ESL**

Have students tell who the people are in each illustration, what they are doing, and what they might be saying.

Look Inside **T231**

NAME _____

Fill in the spaces to tell about the book you are reading.

MAIN CHARACTERS

TITLE

MINOR CHARACTERS

AUTHOR

The character is like me in these ways:

_____
_____
_____
_____

If I could meet a character in the story, I would like to meet _____,

because _____

_____
_____
_____

The character is different from me in these ways:

_____
_____
_____
_____

Choose an event or a conversation from the story. If you took this character's place in the story, what would you do or say differently? Write your ideas below.

_____
_____
_____
_____

PLOT

Name: _____

During Reading

1. What are the main things that have happened so far?

   _____

   _____

2. What is the main problem in the story? How do you think it will be solved?

   _____

   _____

3. What do you think will happen next? What do you think will happen at the end?

   _____

   _____

After Reading

4. Tell the main events that happened in the story.

   _____

   _____

5. What was the solution to the main story problem?

   _____

   _____

6. Did you guess the ending of the story? How else might the author have ended it?

   _____

   _____

7. What do you think was the best part of the story? Why?

   _____

   _____

SETTING

Name: _____

During Reading

1. Where does the story take place?

   _____
   _____

2. Describe the place.

   _____
   _____

3. Have you ever been to a place like this? If you have, how was it like the place in the story?

   _____
   _____

4. When does the story take place—long ago, in the future, or in the present? How do you know?

   _____
   _____

After Reading

5. How did the place affect what happened in the story?

   _____
   _____

6. How would the story be different if it were set in a different place?

   _____
   _____

7. How would the story be different if it were set in a different time?

   _____
   _____

8. If you could visit the place, would you go? Why or why not?

   _____
   _____

Harcourt

SAFETY RULES and SIGNS

Safety Rules for Walkers

1. Be careful in parking lots. Look and listen for cars that are pulling in and out.

2. Stay on the sidewalk if there is one. If there is not, stay away from the street and the curb.

3. Look both ways before you cross a street. If possible, cross where there is a stop sign or traffic light.

4. Walk, don't run, when you cross a street.

5. If you are at a busy intersection, wait until the walk signal says **WALK** or **GO.**

Signs

~ News From Maple Hill School ~
October

Field Trip Notes

The fifth-grade classes went on a field trip to the Historical Museum on September 25. They saw an exhibit on the resistance movement during World War II. They learned about the many brave resistance workers who helped save people who were in danger during the war.

Our Stars

Congratulations to Tracy Quill for winning the school writing contest on the topic of helping others. Tracy used humor and many interesting details to tell how she helped her parents with her baby brother. Tracy's essay is posted in the media center for all to read.

Congratulations to our champion speller, Brian Macon. He came in second in the county spelling bee on September 18.

Special Announcements

To the Rescue is a group that helps people who have lost their homes or belongings as a result of a disaster. You can help, too. Bring items from home such as pots and pans, dishes, and clothes to give to the group. There will be a box outside the school office during the month of October.

Book Corner

Want to read a good book about friends coming to the rescue? Try *Number the Stars* by Lois Lowry. This book is set during World War II. It is about a girl whose family hides a Jewish girl in a time of great danger.

Spotlight On
The Bicycle Safety Club

The Bicycle Safety Club will be sponsoring bicycle safety classes on October 10. Judy Nelson, from the Community Sidewalk and Street Patrol will also be available to answer questions about helmets, reflectors, and bicycles.

The Bicycle Safety Club sponsored over 30 safety classes last year.

Important Dates

October 10   Bicycle safety classes, 7 p.m.

October 16   P.T.A. meeting, 7 p.m., followed by open house

October 25   Dads' Club nature trail clean-up, 8 a.m.

Harcourt

 News from

 School Bus

Dear Family,
I'd like to take a
moment to talk about

Spotlight on

 SPECIAL ANNOUNCEMENTS

Something to Try at Home

From Your Child

We have been very busy lately!

BOOK CORNER

Student 1 _____   **Student 2** _____

Title of Book: _____   Author: _____

Pages Read: _____   Date: _____

Have a written conversation about the book you are reading. Take turns filling in the lines below.

Student 1 Personally, I think that _____

_____ .

A question I have about the book: _____

_____

Student 2 My answer to the question: _____

_____

My opinion: _____

My question: _____

Student 1 My answer to the question: _____

_____

Next, talk about your ideas together. On a separate sheet of paper, tell whether you would recommend this book to other students. Explain why or why not.

Harcourt

CRITIC'S CORNER

Complete the newspaper page to tell about your book.

WEATHER:
A good day
for reading

The Literary Ledger

"Turning pages
into ideas"

Date: _____

Today's
Top
Story
_____
(your name)
Reviews
_____
(book title)

Some of the most interesting things
about this book are listed below:

_____

_____

_____

_____

A SCENE FROM THE BOOK

Critic's
o
r I thought this book was
n
e _____
r
   because _____

   _____

   _____

THIS PICTURE SHOWS

_____

_____

_____

Assessment Strategies and Resources

Formal Assessment Tools

READING SKILLS ASSESSMENT
If you want to know more about a student's mastery of **selection vocabulary, prefixes** and **suffixes,** and **vocabulary in context, then** administer the multiple-choice diagnostic **Reading Skills Assessment.**

HOLISTIC READING ASSESSMENT
If you want to know more about a student's ability to read a passage and apply literal, inferential, and critical thinking skills in a global and holistic manner and to respond to multiple-choice and open-ended questions, **then** administer the **Holistic Reading Assessment.**

READING/WRITING PERFOR-MANCE ASSESSMENT **If** you want a comprehensive view of a student's reading and writing progress, **then** administer the **Reading/Writing Performance Assessment** in which a student reads "Sable," responds by answering open-ended questions, and demonstrates the ability to write a story about a personal experience.

INFORMAL ASSESSMENT TOOLS

Using Anecdotal Records

If you want information about an individual student's development in both independent and group situations, **then** keep **anecdotal records** for that student.

You will want to begin keeping anecdotal records early in the instructional program so you can continue tracking a student's progress in literacy development throughout the school year. The following are some recommended procedures:

- Use a spiral notebook, setting aside several pages for each student.
- During the school day, jot down your observations and impressions on index cards, self-stick notes, or adhesive labels. At the end of the day, transfer your notes to the spiral notebook.
- Choose one to three specific behaviors or understandings to focus on each week.
- Keep your notes brief and objective.
- Use anecdotal records in conferences with students, parents, or administrators.

Other Informal Assessment Options

If you want more information about a student's oral reading fluency, **then** use the guidelines in the Teacher's Edition of the **Placement and Individual Diagnostic Inventory** or the **Individual Reading Inventory** on pages A27–A35.

If you want more information about a student's ability to assess his or her own reading development, **then** use the **self-assessment forms** on pages A25–A26.

If you want to know more about an individual student's overall reading comprehension skills, **then** conduct **story retellings** with the student.

Look Inside

Resources

FOCUS SKILL # Prefixes and Suffixes

OBJECTIVE: *To use prefixes and suffixes for independent decoding of words*

Share the following information with students:

Prefixes and suffixes are special word parts. A prefix is a word part added to the beginning of a word. A suffix is a word part added to the end of a word. Adding a prefix or a suffix to a base word creates a new word with a different meaning. Using what you know about prefixes, suffixes, and base words can help you figure out the meaning of unfamiliar words.

Reteach the Skill

VISUAL MODEL Write the following prefixes and suffixes, with their meanings, on the board:

<u>un-</u> means "not" or "do the opposite of"
<u>dis-</u> means "not" or "do the opposite of"
<u>-ment</u> means "the condition of being"
<u>-able</u> means "able or likely to"

Then write the following sentence pairs on the board. Underline one word in the first sentence of each pair, as shown.

1. **First the workers had to <u>load</u> the boxes onto the truck. Later, they had to unload all the boxes.**
2. **The boxes were carefully <u>organized</u> in the back of the truck. During the long, bumpy trip, the boxes became disorganized.**
3. **The workers hoped to <u>amaze</u> their boss with the neat stacks of boxes. Imagine their own amazement when they saw the mess!**
4. **Did anything inside the boxes <u>break</u>? Fortunately, the contents were not breakable.**

Have students read the sentence pairs and identify the word in the second sentence that is made from the underlined word plus a prefix or suffix. (unload, disorganized, amazement, breakable) Have volunteers

use the meanings of the prefixes and suffixes to give informal definitions of those words. Then follow the suggestions in **Summarize/Assess.**

KINESTHETIC MODEL Prepare two large suffix cards by writing the suffix <u>-ful</u> on one and the suffix <u>-less</u> on the other. Place the cards on the chalk ledge. Next, prepare eight large base word cards with the following words: *thought, hope, care, joy, help, fear, purpose, law.* Ask pairs of students to choose one of the base word cards. Then have each pair of students go to the board and take turns forming a new word by placing their base word card next to a suffix card and acting out its meaning. Then follow the suggestions in **Summarize/Assess.**

AUDITORY MODEL Display and read aloud the list of prefixes, suffixes, and meanings from the Visual Model. Then read aloud each pair of sentences from that model. As students listen to each pair, have them identify the word in the second sentence that is formed from a word in the first sentence plus a prefix or suffix. (unload, disorganized, amazement, breakable) Write each word on the board, and help students discuss its meaning. Then follow the suggestions in **Summarize/Assess.**

Summarize/Assess

Ask students to summarize what they have learned. (A prefix is a word part that is added to the beginning of a base word. A suffix is a word part that is added to the end of a base word. Understanding prefixes and suffixes can help you read new words.) To check their understanding, have students identify and discuss the meanings of words with prefixes and suffixes in other reading selections.

Character Development

OBJECTIVE: *To understand how an author develops characters*

FOCUS

Share the following information with students:

There are three methods that authors use to develop characters. Authors may give information
- **directly.**
- **through a character's own thoughts, words, and actions.**
- **through other characters' thoughts, words, and actions.**

Ask yourself what the story information tells you about the character.

Reteach the Skill

VISUAL MODEL Draw the following chart on the board:

Thoughts
Walnut thought about his friend Frog and was sure Frog could win the contest.

+

Words
"Don't be nervous, Frog," said Walnut. "I know you can win."

+

Actions
Walnut gave a brief smile and then stood silently, watching his friend lift the bow.

↓

Conclusion
Walnut was a good, loyal friend.

Explain that the chart presents a situation that could have taken place between Walnut and Frog. The author has chosen to develop the character of Walnut through Walnut's own thoughts, words and actions. Guide students in discussing the chart. Next, have students work together to make similar charts, illustrating how the thoughts, words, and actions of Walnut's mother show the development of Walnut's self-confidence. Then follow the suggestions in **Summarize/Assess.**

KINESTHETIC MODEL On separate index cards, write words that identify various character traits, such as *loyalty, kindness, jealousy, wisdom, compassion, selfishness, shyness.* Have small groups of students select a card and then plan and present a brief skit showing a person with that trait. Remind students to demonstrate the character trait without using the word that identifies it. After each skit, ask the students who watched it to identify the trait and the method or methods used to reveal it. Then follow the suggestions in **Summarize/Assess.**

AUDITORY MODEL Read aloud the following paragraph, explaining that it presents a situation that could have taken place between Walnut and Frog.

> **As Walnut walked toward his friend Frog, he thought, "Frog's aim is getting better all the time. I'm sure he'll win this contest."**
>
> **When he reached Frog, Walnut said, "Don't be nervous, Frog. I know you can win." He smiled at his friend and then stepped away. Walnut watched proudly as Frog placed an arrow in his bow.**

Have students discuss what the thoughts, words, and actions of Walnut show about the character. Then follow the suggestions in **Summarize/Assess.**

Summarize/Assess

To check their comprehension, have students summarize what they have learned. (Authors use three methods to develop their characters.) **Ask** students to identify the story information that helped them understand character development in other stories they have read recently.

FOCUS SKILL · Vocabulary in Context

OBJECTIVE: *To use context clues to understand the meaning of words*

FOCUS

Share the following information with students:

When you read, you may come across an unfamiliar word or a word with more than one meaning or pronunciation. You can often use context clues to figure out the meaning of the word. Context clues can be other words or phrases in the same sentence or nearby sentences, or they can be pictures that accompany a selection.

Reteach the Skill

VISUAL MODEL Write the following paragraph on the board:

> **The <u>piccolo</u> looked small in Mr. Ortiz's hands. However, when he played the little instrument, everyone was pleased with the beautiful music it made. Afterward, Mr. Ortiz commented, "It does look like a pint-sized flute, doesn't it?"**

If possible, display a drawing or a photograph of a piccolo. After students have read the paragraph and looked at the picture, ask them to identify clues that can help them figure out the meaning of the word *piccolo*. (Possible responses: the words *little instrument*, *pint-sized flute*; the picture of a piccolo) Have students suggest informal definitions, based on the context clues. (a musical instrument that looks like a small flute) Then follow the suggestions in **Summarize/Assess.**

KINESTHETIC MODEL Distribute copies of the paragraph from the Visual Model. Have pairs of students read and discuss the sentences. Instruct them to underline the words and phrases that give clues to the meaning of the word *piccolo*. Ask partners to work together to write an informal definition of the word, based on the context clues in the sentences. Then follow the suggestions in **Summarize/Assess.**

AUDITORY MODEL Read aloud the paragraph from the Visual Model. Ask students to listen carefully for words and phrases that give clues to the meaning of the word *piccolo*. Then read the paragraph aloud again. This time, have students write down the words and phrases that are context clues. Ask volunteers to share the clues that they wrote down. Next, have students suggest informal definitions of the word, and record their ideas on the board. Then follow the suggestions in **Summarize/Assess.**

Summarize/Assess

Ask students to summarize what they have learned. (When you read, you can use context clues such as pictures and words and phrases to figure out what a new word means.) Remind students that they can use a dictionary to confirm a word's definition. Then have volunteers discuss their experiences using context clues to figure out the meanings of unfamiliar words they have encountered in their reading.

FOCUS SKILL Make Judgments

OBJECTIVES: *To make valid judgments about fiction and nonfiction*

FOCUS

Share the following information with students:

Whenever you read, you make judgments, or decisions, about the selection and the author. For example, you might make judgments about the author's purpose for writing a specific selection or about the author's qualifications for writing about a given topic. When you read nonfiction, you make judgments about the facts and opinions presented. When you read fiction, you make judgments about the decisions and actions of the characters.

Reteach the Skill

VISUAL MODEL   Write the following paragraph on the board, or distribute a copy to each student.

> **I encourage every student to stay in school and to graduate. Forty years ago, I had great plans for my life. I left high school and went to work, thinking that I could get an early start on moving up the career ladder. What I didn't realize was that without an education, I could never climb very high. The jobs I wanted all went to people with a good education. I hope you will take my advice—keep studying and get a good education.**

Have students read and discuss the paragraph. Ask them to make judgments about

- the main idea of the paragraph: **Is this good advice? Why or why not?**
- the person who wrote the paragraph: **Does this individual seem qualified to express this opinion?**
- the decision the writer made forty years ago: **Was that a good decision? Why or why not?**

Next, ask students how making these judgments focused their attention on the paragraph and

helped them understand it more fully. Then follow the suggestions in **Summarize/Assess.**

KINESTHETIC MODEL   Have students form small groups, and give each group a copy of the paragraph from the Visual Model. Ask one member of each group to read the paragraph aloud, playing the part of the person who wrote the paragraph. Have the other group members play students who listen to this brief speech and ask questions and make judgments. Students should discuss the advice given, the qualifications of the speaker to give that advice, and the decision the speaker made forty years ago. When students have completed the activity, help them identify the judgments they made. Then follow the suggestions in **Summarize/Assess.**

AUDITORY MODEL   Read aloud the paragraph from the Visual Model. Ask students what judgment questions they want to ask themselves about the paragraph. (For example: What is the author's opinion? How reliable is the author? Should I follow the author's advice?) Record students' suggestions on the board. Then read the paragraph aloud once more. Using the suggested questions as a guide, have students discuss their judgments about the paragraph and its author. Then follow the suggestions in **Summarize/ Assess.**

Summarize/Assess

Check comprehension by asking students to summarize what they have learned. (Making judgments about nonfiction usually involves making decisions about the author's purpose, opinions, and reliability. When you read fiction, you make judgments about the decisions and actions of story characters.) Then have students work in groups to select and read brief articles from a local newspaper. Direct group members to discuss the judgments they can make about the information in the article and about the writer.

FOCUS SKILL Make Inferences

OBJECTIVE: *To understand how to make inferences*

FOCUS

Share the following information with students:

When you read, you can make inferences about details that the author does not include in the selection. To make an inference, use the information provided by the author along with your own knowledge and experience. Making inferences can help you understand what the author means but has not directly stated.

Reteach the Skill

VISUAL MODEL Write the following paragraph on the board, or distribute copies of the paragraph to each student:

I walked slowly toward the podium. My knees were shaking, and I was afraid they might buckle. When I reached the podium I looked out at the audience and tried to smile. It was a struggle to make the corners of my mouth curve up. As I reached for my note cards, my hands were trembling.

After students have read the paragraph, guide them in discussing it. Ask: **Who is the narrator? What is that person doing? How does that person feel?** Have students give details from the paragraph and their personal experiences to support each of the inferences they make. Then follow the suggestions in **Summarize/Assess.**

KINESTHETIC MODEL Provide small groups with old magazines from which students can cut out photographs featuring one person. Have each student describe to the rest of the group what his or her pictured person is doing, what facial expression he or she has, and so on. Next, lead students to make inferences about the pictured individuals, using both what they see in the picture and their own experiences. Have students use the inferences they have made to act out what

the pictured individual might be doing and saying. Then follow the suggestions in **Summarize/ Assess.**

AUDITORY MODEL Ask two volunteers to read aloud the following script:

Character 1: **See you later!**
Character 2: **Bye. Have fun! Don't forget to put on your helmet.**
Character 1: **I can't take the time. Everyone's waiting for me.**
Character 2: **It will only take a few seconds to put on your helmet. It's important!**

Have students discuss the inferences they can make about the two characters in the dialogue. Ask: **Who are the characters? How do your own experiences help you identify them? What intentions do they have? How did you make those inferences?** After this discussion, have students work in pairs to improvise a dialogue the same two characters might have later in the day. Then follow the suggestions in **Summarize/Assess.**

Summarize/Assess

Ask students to summarize what they have learned. (Making inferences involves combining information that the author provides with your own knowledge and experience. Making inferences can help you understand a selection more completely.) **To check students' understanding, have them recall characters from previous selections. Ask them to tell what inferences they made about those characters and to describe the process by which they made them.**

AFTER READING

4. Choose one character. Why is this character important in the story?

5. What trait does the main character have that is important to the story outcome?

6. What word best describes the way the main character acts or feels?

-- FOLD --

▶Characters

DURING READING

1. Who are the main, or most important, characters?
   Who are the minor, or less important, characters?

2. Do the characters know each other? If so, are they relatives, friends, classmates, or neighbors?

3. What problems do the characters face?

Harcourt

► Author's Purpose and Perspective   COMPREHENSION CARD 5

AFTER READING

3. Did the author do a good job of informing, entertaining, explaining, or persuading? Tell why you think as you do.

4. What question would you ask the author about his or her purpose for writing this selection?

FOLD

► Author's Purpose and Perspective   COMPREHENSION CARD 5

DURING READING

1. Do you think the author wrote this selection

    ■ to inform?

    ■ to entertain?

    ■ to explain?

    ■ to persuade?

2. What clues from the story helped you figure out the author's purpose?

Harcourt

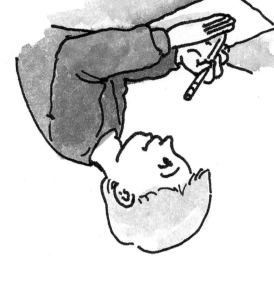

► **Author's Craft**　　　　　　　　**COMPREHENSION CARD 6**

AFTER READING

5. What is your favorite sentence or paragraph in the story? Why is it your favorite?

6. What did the author do best?
- tell the story
- write about the characters
- describe the setting

7. Would you like to read something else by this author? Why or why not?

--------------------------------FOLD--------------------------------

►Author's Craft

COMPREHENSION CARD 6

DURING READING

1. Have you noticed anything you think the author might bring up again later in the story? If so, what have you noticed?

2. Tell about any pictures the author has left in your mind.

3. What words has the author used so far to help you

   ■ see things in the story?

   ■ hear things in the story?

   ■ feel things in the story?

4. Does the way the characters talk sound like the way real people talk? Why or why not?

Harcourt

▶ Perspective in Art

Perspective is the art of drawing or painting objects on a flat surface in such a way that they appear to have depth and distance. You can learn about perspective by looking at the illustrations for "The Hot and Cold Summer." Then you can draw your own picture.

1. Look at the illustration on pages 22–23 of "The Hot and Cold Summer."
   - ■ The figure of Bolivia is much larger than the figures of the two boys. Her shadow towers over them.
   - ■ Larger objects appear to be closer. Smaller objects appear to be farther away.
   - ■ Why might the artist have chosen to draw the picture this way?

2. Look at the illustration on pages 32–33.
   - ■ Why is the parrot so much larger than the people on the ground?
   - ■ To see the scene from this angle, where would you have to be?

3. Now look at the illustration on pages 36–37.
   - ■ Compare the sizes of Derek (holding the radio) and the parrot.
   - ■ Notice the sizes of the firefighters and other elements.
   - ■ To see the scene from this angle, where would you have to be?

4. Compare the illustration on pages 38–39 with those on pages 32–33 and 36–37. How are the illustrations alike and different?

5. Now draw a picture of your own. Decide from what angle you want to show the scene. Use perspective to create a feeling of depth and distance.

▶ Parrot Facts

In "The Hot and Cold Summer," Derek is eager to learn about Bolivia's pet parrot. You can do research to find out more about these fascinating birds and then create a fact sheet.

- ■ If you use a **print encyclopedia**, remember to use **alphabetical order** and **guide words** to find the entry word *parrot*.

- ■ If you use a **CD-ROM** or **online encyclopedia**, type the **keyword** *parrot* in the **search box**.

- ■ Write down interesting facts that you find. Remember to write down your sources, too.

- ■ Create a fact sheet that lists six to ten interesting facts about parrots. Add illustrations if you want. Try to make your fact sheet attractive and entertaining as well as informative.

Harcourt

Try to listen the way Walnut listens. Then tell your classmates about the sounds you heard.

- Find a good time and place to listen. With your eyes closed, listen to the sounds around you.
- What do you hear? Who or what is making each sound? How can you describe each sound to others? What vivid adjectives and verbs can you use?
- Tell classmates what you heard. Be as descriptive as possible.

When you are speaking,
- change your voice to fit the sounds you are describing. You might speak more quickly or slowly, at a higher or lower pitch, or more loudly or softly.
- use gestures and facial expressions to help convey the quality of each sound.
- make eye contact with your audience.

When you are listening,
- identify and appreciate the vivid sound words used by others.
- try to imagine what your classmate experienced.

"Sees Behind Trees" is Walnut's new name, given to honor his special ability. Famous people in many fields have been known by names that tell something about their talents or accomplishments. Follow these steps to research a famous person and write a biographical sketch.

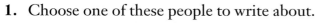

1. Choose one of these people to write about.

   Simón Bolívar (El Liberador, The Liberator)   *Richard I (the Lion-Hearted)*

   Florence Nightingale (Lady with the Lamp)   *William Cody (Buffalo Bill)*

   Harriet Tubman (Moses <u>or</u> the Moses of Her People)   *Andrew Jackson (Old Hickory)*

   Martha Jane Canary (Calamity Jane)   *Chris Evert (the Ice Maiden)*

2. Use print and online encyclopedias and other references to research the person by both the real name and the special name.

3. Answer these questions: **Why is this person famous? How did this person acquire his or her special name?**

4. Take notes on your research and write down your sources.

5. Use your information to write a biographical sketch. Include the person's real name and special name, why the person was given the special name, and other interesting facts about the person's life.

Write one or two questions that you would like to ask each of these
story characters:

- Mary
- Holly
- Mrs. Hanson
- Mrs. Yang
- Fourth Brother
- Mr. and Mrs. Sylvester

When it's your turn on the hot seat, choose one of the above characters
to portray. As you answer questions, keep the character's personality
and motives in mind.

When asking or answering questions,

SPEAKERS SHOULD
- use eye contact and voice control.
- use nonverbal cues.
- speak clearly and with expression.

LISTENERS SHOULD
- listen carefully to responses.
- watch to interpret nonverbal cues.
- distinguish facts from opinions.

► Summer Camp Directory   ACTIVITY CARD 6

Take a survey in your group to find out the kind of camp each of you
would find enjoyable.

Summer Camp	May	Tony	Luis	Pam	Joe
music		✓			
science	✓			✓	✓
sports		✓		✓	
art			✓		

With your group, use a search engine or directory on the Internet to learn about local and regional
special-interest summer camps. Your librarian or media specialist may be able to help you with tips on how
to use different search engines or directories. Look for information that will help answer these questions:
- What is the name and address of the camp?
- When is camp held? How much does it cost to attend?
- What special training or opportunities does the camp offer?
- How many applicants are accepted for each season or session? What
  are the requirements?

Use what you learn to create a Summer Camp Directory.

Imagine that Rosa Parks is making a personal appearance to speak to young people in your city or town. Your job is to create a flyer that can be posted in schools, youth centers, and libraries to advertise this event.

TIPS FOR CREATING A FLYER

Text should

- ■ include all the information people need to know about the event.
- ■ tell who the speaker is and what she will be speaking about.
- ■ be brief and to the point.

Graphics should

- ■ make the flyer look attractive.
- ■ catch people's attention.
- ■ be appropriate for the subject of the flyer.

► Women in Science or Art   **ACTIVITY CARD 8**

Rosa Parks writes that women have taken their places in politics, the arts, sciences, and business. You can research a woman who has excelled in the field of science or art in the last 100 years.

Follow these steps:

1. Choose a woman to research. You may choose any woman in the field of science or art who lived and worked in the twentieth century. Here are a few suggestions:

Science		Art	
Annie Jump Cannon	Grace Hopper	Elaine de Kooning	Käthe Kollwitz
Barbara McClintock	Rachel Carson	Helen Frankenthaler	Georgia O'Keeffe
Dorothy Crowfoot Hodgkin	Sally Ride	Anna Mary Robertson	"Grandma" Moses

2. Use encyclopedias or the Internet to find information about your subject. Remember to take careful notes and to write down your sources.
3. Use your information to create a poster that features the woman you researched and tells one or more important facts about her.

▶ Present a Health or Safety Message ACTIVITY CARD 9

Write a message to people your age about a health or safety issue that is important to you.
Be sure that your message

- ◼ explains the issue clearly and directly.
- ◼ states reasons the issue is important.
- ◼ is supported with facts and statistics.

When the messages are presented,

SPEAKERS SHOULD

- ◼ identify their audience and purpose.
- ◼ signal important ideas.
- ◼ use nonverbal cues.
- ◼ speak clearly.

LISTENERS SHOULD

- ◼ distinguish facts from opinions.
- ◼ determine the speaker's purpose and viewpoint.
- ◼ interpret nonverbal cues.
- ◼ evaluate expressed points of view.

▶ Bike-Safety Program ACTIVITY CARD 10

In "Mick Harte Was Here," Phoebe speaks at a school assembly on bike safety. With your group, use the Internet to research bike safety. Type the words *bike safety* in the search box. Then search the results. Look for information that will help answer these questions:

- ◼ What are some important bike-safety tips?
- ◼ What safety equipment should every bike have?
- ◼ What safety gear should every bike rider wear?

When you do your Internet research, be sure to

- ◼ use several online search engines to find information.
- ◼ use specific search terms.
- ◼ take good notes on the information you find.
- ◼ bookmark or write down Web site addresses in case you need to return for more information later.

Then use what you have learned to plan your own bike-safety program.

Harcourt

 # School–Home Connection

Your child is reading a realistic fiction story called "The Hot and Cold Summer" by Johanna Hurwitz. The story tells about two boys, Rory and Derek, and what happens when a girl named Bolivia comes to visit their neighbors for the summer. At first the boys go to great lengths to avoid her and another visitor named Lucette, who they think is Bolivia's baby sister. When Lucette turns out to be a talking parrot and flies out a window, causing great excitement in the neighborhood, Derek is so excited and curious that he forgets his vow not to speak to Bolivia.

Johanna Hurwitz

Johanna Hurwitz has written many books for young people. You and your child might enjoy visiting your local public library to borrow some of them. The following titles feature the same characters your child read about in "The Hot and Cold Summer."

■ *The Cold and Hot Winter* by Johanna Hurwitz, illustrated by Carolyn Ewing. William Morrow & Company, 1988.

■ *The Up and Down Spring* by Johanna Hurwitz, illustrated by Gail Owens. William Morrow & Company, 1993.

■ *The Down and Up Fall* by Johanna Hurwitz, illustrated by Gail Owens. William Morrow & Company, 1996.

VOCABULARY

Using Vocabulary Words

While reading "The Hot and Cold Summer," your child has learned the following new vocabulary words:

authority	**vow**
souvenir	**commotion**
incredible	**exhausted**

Ask your child to use each of these words in a sentence that also includes the word *parrot* or *parrots*. Then have your child tell you the meaning of each vocabulary word.

Mistaken Impressions

Ask your child to tell you how the characters Rory and Derek discovered that Lucette was not a baby but a parrot. With your child, recall other situations either in real life or in stories, including TV and movies, in which funny things happened because a character had a mistaken idea about who or what a person or animal was.

Harcourt

 **Visit *The Learning Site!*** www.harcourtschool.com

The Hot and Cold Summer

School–Home Connection

Your child is reading a story called "Sees Behind Trees" by Michael Dorris. In this story, a Native American boy named Walnut is unable to learn to shoot a bow because he has difficulty seeing. When it is time for boys his age to prove themselves in a test of shooting, Walnut is sure he will fail. This year, however, there is a new test to find a person with the special ability to hear what others cannot, one who "sees behind trees." Because Walnut has sharpened his sense of hearing to compensate for his poor eyesight, he passes the test and earns a new name, *Sees Behind Trees.*

Native Americans in Literature

If your child enjoyed reading "Sees Behind Trees," he or she might like to read other books by Michael Dorris, such as the following which you might find at your public library:

- *Guests*, Hyperion Press, 1994.
- *Morning Girl*, Hyperion Press, 1992 (winner of the Scott O'Dell Award for Historical Fiction).

Many other excellent books on Native American subjects, both fiction and nonfiction, are also available. Your librarian may be able to offer suggestions.

VOCABULARY

Living Vocabulary

While reading "Sees Behind Trees," your child has learned the following new vocabulary words:

tread	**compose**
moss	**exaggerate**
sternly	**quiver** (case for carrying arrows)

Check your child's understanding of these words by asking him or her to demonstrate their meanings. For instance, you might ask your child to show you how to walk with a light *tread*, how someone might *exaggerate* the size of a fish he or she caught, or how to take an arrow from a *quiver*.

New Names

Ask your child to tell you how the characters in "Sees Behind Trees" receive their grown-up names. Then you and your child can think of similar names that emphasize the good qualities or accomplishments of family members, friends, and neighbors.

Harcourt

Sees Behind Trees

Visit *The Learning Site!*
www.harcourtschool.com

 # School–Home Connection

Your child is reading "Yang the Third and Her Impossible Family" by Lensey Namioka.
This realistic fiction story is about a young Chinese girl whose musically talented family members keep embarrassing her with their traditional Chinese ways. Mary, as Yingmei chooses to be called, learns a valuable lesson about her family and herself when she tries to help her mother overcome social mistakes and help her new American friend, Holly Hanson, at the same time. You may enjoy discussing the story and doing these activities with your child. Together you can develop and explore your child's language skills.

A Sense of Belonging

Talk about the problems young people often have fitting in at a new school or in a new community. Discuss how much more difficult it is to fit in when the language and culture are different. You and your child might enjoy sharing other books related to this subject:

- ◼ *Immigrant Girl: Becky of Eldridge Street* by Brett Harvey. Holiday House, 1987.
- ◼ *Yang the Youngest and His Terrible Ear* by Lensey Namioka. Yearling, 1994.

VOCABULARY

Vocabulary and Music

The following words are new vocabulary your child has learned while reading "Yang the Third and Her Impossible Family":

accompanist	grimaced
accompaniment	audition
simultaneously	sonata

Discuss the meanings of these words. Encourage your child to use as many of these words as possible as you discuss the story.

Family Music: What's Your Preference?

Your child can interview you and other family members about music preferences. Discuss the answers to such questions as: What kind of music do you prefer? Do you listen to the same kind of music whether you're happy or sad? How does this music make you feel? Do you have a favorite composer or performer? If possible, have a family music night to play, listen to, and discuss the music preferred by individual family members.

Harcourt

 **Visit *The Learning Site!***
www.harcourtschool.com

Yang the Third and Her Impossible Family

School–Home Connection

Your child is reading "Dear Mrs. Parks," a collection of letters between young people and the renowned civil rights leader and humanitarian, Rosa Parks. Mrs. Parks's replies to the students' questions and concerns express her deep belief in the importance of education, helping and caring for others, and the need for each human being to achieve his or her full potential.

Values and Opinions

Encourage your child to share with you the opinions and values expressed by Mrs. Parks in her letters. Discuss with your child your own opinions and values on subjects such as asking questions, keeping an open mind, doing one's best in school, and making a difference in the world. You may want to involve other family members in the discussion as well.

VOCABULARY

Using Vocabulary Words

While reading "Dear Mrs. Parks," your child has learned the following new vocabulary words:

correspondence	inspire
ridiculed	counsel
potential	mentor
dignity	

Ask your child to copy each of the vocabulary words onto a separate slip of paper. Put the paper slips in an envelope. Then take the slips from the envelope, one at a time, and ask, as if you were reading a letter: "Dear (your child's name), Can you please tell me the meaning of this word?" Continue similarly until you have used all the words.

Family and Community History

Rosa Parks is grateful to her grandmother for teaching her about the history of their family and their community. Your child may be interested in learning more about the history of your own family and community. In addition to sharing your own knowledge with your child, you may want to see what information you can discover together. For example, many libraries have local history collections that can help you research your community. You might also use a home computer or library computer with Internet access to research genealogical sites online.

Harcourt

Dear Mrs. Parks

Visit *The Learning Site!* www.harcourtschool.com

School-Home Connection

Your child is reading "Mick Harte Was Here" by Barbara Park. This realistic fiction story is about a young girl named Phoebe, whose brother is killed in a bike accident. Phoebe, who is coping with feelings of grief, anger, and guilt, decides to speak at a school assembly on bike safety. Her message, and the author's, is clear: Mick would not have died if he had been wearing a bike helmet. You may enjoy discussing the story and doing these activities with your child. Together, you can develop and expand your child's language skills.

Safety Issues

Talk about the safety issues that are of the most concern to you and your child. Discuss ways you can make car travel, bike riding, sports, and other activities safer. Conduct online research at home, or go to the library to find out more about the recommended safety equipment for the activities that interest your family.

Vocabulary Challenge

The following words are new vocabulary your child has learned while reading "Mick Harte Was Here":

sponsor	podium
impact	anticipation
reaction	perspective

Discuss the meanings of these words. Have a one-day contest to see who can use each word correctly in a sentence at least once when it fits the situation.

Family Attitudes: Bike Helmets

Your child can interview you and other family members about bike-helmet use. Help him or her record answers to questions such as these: *Do you ride a bike often? Where do you ride? Do you wear a helmet? What kind of helmet do you wear? If you don't wear a helmet, why don't you?* If possible, have a family safety night when your child can share the results of the questionnaire and present his or her viewpoint on the importance of bike helmets.

Harcourt

Visit *The Learning Site!* www.harcourtschool.com

Mick Harte Was Here

Additional Reading

The following list is a compilation of the Multi-Level Books selected for the lesson plans.

Adler, David A.
Martin Luther King, Jr.: Free at Last
Holiday House, 1986. A biography of the Baptist minister who worked unceasingly for his dream of a world without hate, prejudice, or violence and was assassinated in the attempt to accomplish this. *Notable Social Studies Trade Book*

Adler, David A.
A Picture Book of Thurgood Marshall
Holiday House, 1997. A biography of the Civil Rights leader.

Arnosky, Jim
Crinkleroot's Guide to Walking in Wild Places
Bradbury, 1990. Crinkleroot the forest dweller provides tips for walking in wild places and avoiding such hazards as ticks, poisonous plants, and wild animals.

Dorris, Michael
Guests
Hyperion, 1994. Moss grapples with the difficulties of growing up when his father invites outsiders who dress in strange clothes to the village's harvest meal. *ALA Notable Book; Notable Children's Book in the Language Arts*

Dorris, Michael
Morning Girl
Hyperion, 1994. Morning Girl, who loves the day, and her younger brother Star Boy, who loves the night, take turns describing their life on an island in pre-Columbian America. *SLJ Best Book; Booklist Editors' Choice; Notable Children's Book in the Language Arts*

Fisher, Leonard Everett
Anasazi
Atheneum, 1997. Describes the day-to-day life of the Anasazi Indians.

Fletcher, Ralph
Live Writing
Avon, 1999. Based on the simple idea that every writer has a toolbox containing words, imagination, a love of books, a sense of story, and ideas for how to make the writing live and breathe.

Freedman, Russell
Buffalo Hunt
Holiday House, 1988. Examines the importance of the buffalo in the lore and day-to-day life of the Indian tribes of the Great Plains and describes hunting methods and the uses found for each part of the animal that could not be eaten. *ALA Notable Book; SLJ Best Book; Teachers' Choice*

Fritz, Jean
The Cabin Faced West
Coward-McCann, 1958. Ten-year-old Ann overcomes loneliness and learns to appreciate the importance of her role in settling the wilderness of western Pennsylvania.

Giff, Patricia Reilly
Lily's Crossing
Delacorte, 1997. During a summer spent at Rockaway Beach in 1944, Lily's friendship with a young Hungarian refugee causes her to see the war and her own world differently. *Newbery Honor; ALA Notable Book; Teachers' Choice*

Gilson, Jamie
Hobie Hansen, You're Weird
William Morrow, 1987. With his best friend away at computer camp, Hobie reluctantly shares adventures with a girl classmate the summer after fourth grade.

Grimshaw, Carolyn
Music
World Book, 1996. Brief text and illustrations introduce the history and instruments of music.

Harvey, Brett
Immigrant Girl: Becky of Eldridge Street
Holiday House, 1987. Becky, whose family has immigrated from Russia to avoid being persecuted as Jews, finds growing up in New York City in 1910 a vivid and exciting experience.

Haskins, Jim
The Statue of Liberty
Lerner, 1986. A history of America's most famous statue, discussing how it was built and why it was given to the United States.

Hooper, Maureen Brett
The Violin Man
Boyds Mills Press, 1991. Luigi, the Violin Man, travels throughout Italy searching for rare Stradivarius violins. Young Antonio helps Luigi uncover a lost Stradivarius in his small village.

Hurwitz, Johanna
The Adventures of Ali Baba Bernstein
William Morrow, 1985. Eight-year-old David is convinced that his life will be more adventurous when he changes his name to Ali Baba. *Children's Choice*

Hurwitz, Johanna
Aldo Peanut Butter
William Morrow, 1990. Peanut and Butter, the two dogs Aldo gets for his eleventh birthday, create chaos inside the house while his parents are out of town and then get accused of tearing up the neighbor's lawn.

Hurwitz, Johanna
The Cold and Hot Winter
William Morrow, 1988. Fifth grader Derek and his best friend Rory are delighted when their neighbors' niece, Bolivia, comes to town for another visit, until a lot of missing objects make Derek begin to doubt Rory's honesty.

Hurwitz, Johanna
A Llama in the Family
William Morrow, 1994. Because Adam hopes that the "big surprise" awaiting him at home has two wheels and pedals, he is unprepared for the unusual addition to his Vermont family.

Klise, Kate
Regarding the Fountain
Avon Camelot, 1998. When the principal asks a fifth-grader to write a letter regarding the purchase of a new drinking fountain for their school, he finds that all sorts of chaos results.

Lord, Bette Bao
In the Year of the Boar and Jackie Robinson
HarperCollins, 1987. In 1947, a Chinese child comes to Brooklyn where she becomes Americanized at school, in her apartment building, and by her love for baseball. *ALA Notable Book; SLJ Best Book; Children's Choice*

MacLachlan, Patricia
The Facts and Fictions of Minna Pratt
HarperCollins, 1998. An eleven-year-old cellist learns about life from her eccentric family, her first boyfriend, and Mozart. *ALA Notable Book; Teachers' Choice*

Masoff, Joy
Emergency!
Scholastic, 1999. Discusses all aspects of emergency medicine, including the medical personnel and equipment needed to successfully help the patient.

Medearis, Angela Shelf
Dare to Dream
Lodestar, 1994. A brief biography of the widow of Martin Luther King, Jr., telling about her involvement in the Civil Rights movement.

Namioka, Lensey
The Laziest Boy in the World
Holiday House, 1998. When Xiaolong devises a way to capture the thief who breaks into his family's home, all the people in the Chinese village change their minds about the "lazy" boy.

Namioka, Lensey
Yang the Second and Her Secret Admirers
Little, Brown, 1998. While her younger siblings have adopted many American customs since moving from China to Seattle, Yinglan Yang clings to her Chinese heritage, so her brother and sister hatch a plot to convert her to American culture.

Namioka, Lensey
Yang the Youngest and His Terrible Ear
Yearling, 1994. Recently arrived in Seattle from China, musically untalented Yingtao is faced with giving a violin performance to attract new students for his father when he would rather be working on friendships and playing baseball.

Park, Barbara
Don't Make Me Smile
Random House, 1990. A young boy has trouble adjusting to his parents' divorce.

Park, Barbara
The Kid in the Red Jacket
Knopf, 1987. When ten-year-old Howard has to move with his family to a distant state, he is forced to live on a street named Chester Pewe, adjust to a new school, and get used to being shadowed by a little girl from a nearby house. *Children's Choice; SLJ Best Book*

Park, Barbara
Skinnybones
Knopf, 1982. Alex's active sense of humor helps him get along with the school braggart, make the most of his athletic talents, and simply get by in a hectic world. *Texas Bluebonnet*

Parks, Rosa, with Jim Haskins
I Am Rosa Parks
Dial, 1997. The black woman whose acts of civil disobedience led to the 1956 Supreme Court order to desegregate buses in Montgomery, Alabama, explains what she did and why. *ALA Notable Book; Notable Social Studies Trade Book*

Peters, Russell M.
Clambake: A Wampanoag Tradition
Lerner, 1992. Steven Esquibel, a twelve-year-old Wampanoag Indian in Massachusetts, learns from his grandfather how to prepare a clambake in the tradition of his people. *Teachers' Choice; Notable Social Studies Trade Book*

Ringgold, Faith
If a Bus Could Talk: The Story of Rosa Parks
Simon & Schuster, 1999. A brief biography of the black woman in Montgomery, Alabama, whose experiences with segregation led to her role in the early days of the Civil Rights movement, as told to a young girl who climbs on a talking bus.

Robinson, Barbara
My Brother Louis Measures Worms and Other Louis Stories
HarperCollins, 1990. Young Mary Elizabeth relates the humorous misadventures of her brother Louis and the other wacky members of her unpredictable, very odd family.

Rodowsky, Colby
Dog Days
Farrar, Straus & Giroux, 1990. When a famous author and her dog move in right next door, 9-year-old Rosie thinks maybe her summer won't be quite so bad after all.

Sherrow, Victoria
American Indian Children of the Past
Millbrook Press, 1997. Describes what life was like for Indian children growing up in various regions—Northeast Woodlands, Southeast, Southwest, Plains, and Northwest Coast—during the eighteenth, nineteenth, and early twentieth centuries.

Siegel, Beatrice
The Year They Walked
Macmillan, 1992. Examines the life of Rosa Parks, focusing on her role in the Montgomery bus boycott. *Notable Social Studies Trade Book*

Smith, Doris Buchanan
A Taste of Blackberries
HarperCollins, 1993. A young boy recounts his efforts to adjust to the accidental death of his best friend.

Turner, Ann
Mississippi Mud
HarperCollins, 1997. Poems reflecting the points of view of three pioneer children describe their family's journey from Kentucky to Oregon. *Notable Social Studies Trade Book; Notable Children's Book in the Language Arts*

Westridge Young Writers Workshop
Kids Explore the Gifts of Children with Special Needs
John Muir, 1994. Students write about 10 young people with disabilities ranging from dyslexia, attention deficit disorder, and Down syndrome to hemophilia, brittle bone disease, and dwarfism.

Whelan, Gloria
The Indian School
HarperCollins, 1996. When ten-year-old Lucy comes to live with her aunt and uncle at their mission school, she becomes troubled by their harsh treatment of the Indian children at the school, a situation brought to a head when a young girl named Raven runs away.

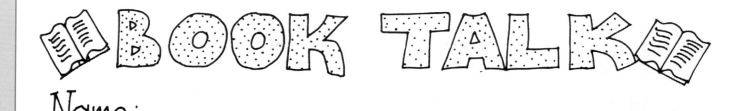

Name: _____

You have many ideas about the books you read. It's fun to talk about those ideas with other readers. Here are some steps you can follow in your Book Talk.

1. First, work by yourself. Write your answers to these questions.

   What was your book about? _____

   _____

   What did you like or dislike about the book? _____

   _____

   Do you think other readers would like the book? Why? _____

   _____

2. Write questions you'd like to ask the other readers in your group.

   _____

   _____

3. Now meet with your group. Discuss your ideas.

GRAPH-A-BOOK

Dear Family Members,

As a book is read at home, have the student graph his or her response. The student should write the title of the book and the author's name on the numbered line and then color the corresponding boxes on the graph, up to the level of the rating. Ask the student to give a reason for his or her rating.

Book Titles and Authors' Names

1. _____

2. _____

3. _____

4. _____

5. _____

6. _____

Bar Graph

Book 1				
Book 2				
Book 3				
Book 4				
Book 5				
Book 6				

Would Not Recommend	OK	Good	GREAT!

Please return the graph to school when completed. Thank you.

Signature _____

Harcourt

Additional Resources

Introducing the Glossary

Explain to students that a glossary often is included in a book so that readers can find the meanings of words used in the book. Read aloud the introductory pages. Then model looking up one or more words, pointing out how you rely on alphabetical order and the guide words at the top of the Glossary pages to help you locate the entry word. You may also want to demonstrate how to use the pronunciation key to confirm the correct pronunciation.

As students look over the Glossary, point out that illustrations accompany some definitions. Have students read a Word Origins note and a Fact Finder note, and discuss the type of information in each.

Encourage students to look up several words in the Glossary, identifying the correct page and the guide words. Then have them explain how using alphabetical order and the guide words at the top of each page helps them locate the words.

Tell students to use the Glossary to confirm the pronunciations of vocabulary words during reading and to help them better understand the meanings of unfamiliar words.

Using the Glossary

Like a dictionary, this glossary lists words in alphabetical order. To find a word, look it up by its first letter or letters.

To save time, use the **guide words** at the top of each page. These show you the first and last words on the page. Look at the guide words to see if your word falls between them alphabetically.

Here is an example of a glossary entry:

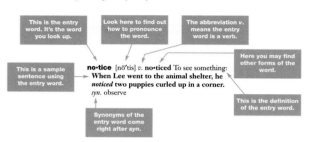

This is the entry word. It's the word you look up.

Look here to find out how to pronounce the word.

The abbreviation *v.* means the entry word is a verb.

Here you may find other forms of the word.

This is a sample sentence using the entry word.

no·tice [nō′tis] *v.* **no·ticed** To see something: **When Lee went to the animal shelter, he *noticed* two puppies curled up in a corner.** *syn.* observe

Synonyms of the entry word come right after *syn.*

This is the definition of the entry word.

Word Origins

Throughout the glossary, you will find notes about word origins, or how words got started and changed. Words often have interesting backgrounds that can help you remember what they mean.

Here is an example of a word-origin note:

familiar At first, *familiar* meant "of the family," from the Latin word *familiaris*. Its meaning grew to include friends and to become "known from being around often." *Familiar* began to be used in English in the 1300s.

626

Pronunciation

The pronunciation in brackets is a respelling that shows how the word is pronounced.

The **pronunciation key** explains what the symbols in a respelling mean. A shortened pronunciation key appears on every other page of the glossary.

PRONUNCIATION KEY*

a	add, map	m	move, seem	u	up, done	
ā	ace, rate	n	nice, tin	û(r)	burn, term	
â(r)	care, air	ng	ring, song	yōō	fuse, few	
ä	palm, father	o	odd, hot	v	vain, eve	
b	bat, rub	ō	open, so	w	win, away	
ch	check, catch	ô	order, jaw	y	yet, yearn	
d	dog, rod	oi	oil, boy	z	zest, muse	
e	end, pet	ou	pout, now	zh	vision, pleasure	
ē	equal, tree	ŏŏ	took, full	ə	the schwa, an	
f	fit, half	ōō	pool, food		unstressed vowel	
g	go, log	p	pit, stop		representing the	
h	hope, hate	r	run, poor		sound spelled	
i	it, give	s	see, pass		*a* in *above*	
ī	ice, write	sh	sure, rush		*e* in *sicken*	
j	joy, ledge	t	talk, sit		*i* in *possible*	
k	cool, take	th	thin, both		*o* in *melon*	
l	look, rule	th	this, bathe		*u* in *circus*	

Other symbols
- • separates words into syllables
- ′ indicates heavier stress on a syllable
- ‚ indicates light stress on a syllable

Abbreviations: *adj.* adjective, *adv.* adverb, *conj.* conjunction, *interj.* interjection, *n.* noun, *prep.* preposition, *pron.* pronoun, *syn.* synonym, *v.* verb

* The Pronunciation Key, adapted entries, and the Short Key that appear on the following pages are reprinted from *HBJ School Dictionary*. Copyright © 1990 by Harcourt, Inc. Reprinted by permission of Harcourt, Inc.

627

A

ab·a·lo·ne [ab′ə·lō′nē] *n.* An edible water animal that lives in a shell: **The *abalone* shell has a pearl-like lining.**

abalone

ab·sorb [ab·zôrb′] *v.* **ab·sorbed** To be so interested in something as not to notice anything else: **Jan was so *absorbed* in her book that she didn't hear the doorbell.** *syn.* preoccupy

ac·com·pa·ni·ment [ə·kum′pə·nē·mənt] *n.* Music that is played along with another's performance: **The dancer needs a piano's *accompaniment*.**

ac·com·pa·nist [ə·kum′pə·nist] *n.* A person who plays music while another person performs: **The *accompanist* waited for the singer's signal.**

ac·cord [ə·kôrd′] *n.* 1. Harmony; agreement. 2. A choice made without being asked: **Cindy cleaned her room on her own *accord*.**

ace [ās] *adj.* Best: **She is the *ace* player on our team.** *syn.* star

aisle [īl] *n.* A passageway, such as between rows of seats: **Don't block the *aisle* when people are leaving the auditorium.** *syn.* walkway

al·tim·e·ter [al·tim′ə·tər] *n.* An instrument that measures height above ground: **The plane's *altimeter* read 5,000 feet when it flew over the field.**

an·them [an′thəm] *n.* A song in honor of a country, a school, or some other institution: **"The Star-Spangled Banner" is the national *anthem*.** *syn.* theme song

an·tic·i·pa·tion [an·tis′ə·pā′shən] *n.* The feeling of looking forward to something: **George felt *anticipation* before he started camp.** *syn.* expectation

ap·pren·tice [ə·pren′tis] *n.* A person who is in training in a craft or an art under the supervision of an expert: **The sculptor's *apprentice* polished the finished pieces.**

ar·ti·fi·cial [är′tə·fish′əl] *adj.* Manufactured by humans as a substitute for something natural: **Dentures are *artificial* teeth.** *syn.* synthetic

as·ton·ish [ə·stän′ish] *v.* **as·ton·ished** To amaze or shock: **Paul was *astonished* to learn he had won the contest.** *syn.* surprise

a·toll [a′tôl] *n.* A narrow, ring-shaped island: **The *atoll* was made of coral.**

au·di·tion [ô·dish′ən] *n.* A tryout for a performing role or a job: **We wished Ari luck before his *audition* for the play.** *syn.* test

— Word Origins —
audition At the root of the word *audition* is the Latin base *aud*, which has to do with hearing. Other related words are *audio*—the sound component of electronics; *auditorium*—a place where you go to hear a performance; and *audience*—the people who hear the performance.

au·thor·i·ty [ô·thär′ə·tē] *n.* A person who knows a lot about a particular subject and is considered to be an expert: **Ray is the class *authority* on baseball.** *syn.* master

B

bar·ren [bar′ən] *adj.* Without the conditions necessary to support life: **The *barren* desert had received no rain for years.** *syn.* desolate

beam [bēm] 1. *v.* **beam·ing** To smile in a warm way at someone: **Sally was *beaming* at her best friend.** *syn.* glow 2. *n.* A heavy crosspiece of a ship or building: **The main *beam* gave the ship its structure.** *syn.* crossbar

beam

bolt [bōlt] *v.* To move, go, or spring suddenly: **The horse will *bolt* if she is frightened.** *syn.* flee

boom [bōōm] *v.* **boom·ing** To increase or prosper suddenly: **Business was *booming*, so they opened a second store.** *syn.* expand

break·through [brāk′thrōō] *n.* An important advance in a field of knowledge: **The medical *breakthrough* saved many lives.** *syn.* discovery

brood [brōōd] *v.* **brood·ed** To mope and worry for a long time over something: **Lana *brooded* after she had argued with a friend.** *syn.* sulk

bulge [bulj] *n.* A swollen part or place: **The *bulge* in the tire means it needs replacement.** *syn.* protrusion

628

---

bulk [bulk] *n.* The largeness of something, including what it weighs or how much room it takes up: **The massive bear threw its *bulk* against the door.** *syn.* mass

bur·row [bar′ō] *v.* **bur·rowed** To dig into the ground for protection: **The mouse *burrowed* into a pile of leaves.** *syn.* tunnel

C

cam·paign [kam·pān′] *n.* The process of running for elected office: **The candidate made speeches during her *campaign*.**

— Word Origins —
campaign The word *campaign* traces its origins back to the French word *campagne*, meaning "countryside." The open country was the site of military maneuvers and battles. *Campaign* also means "the military operations involved in winning a battle." The idea of "winning a battle" carries over to politics.

can·o·py [kan′ə·pē] *n.* A rooflike covering: **The forest *canopy* is made up of the uppermost leaves and branches.** *syn.* awning

char·coal [chär′kōl] *n.* A black substance used as a drawing crayon: **Students did their sketches in *charcoal*.**

com·mo·tion [kə·mō′·shən] *n.* A disturbance; confusion: **A *commotion* occurred in the halls on the first day because students didn't know where their classes were meeting.** *syn.* uproar

com·pose [kəm·pōz′] *v.* To calm oneself: **Juan had to *compose* himself before the test.** *syn.* relax

con·coct [kən·käkt′] *v.* **con·coc·ted** To invent or develop something: **Pat *concocted* a delicious shake from five kinds of juice.** *syn.* devise

con·trap·tion [kən·trap′shən] *n.* A mechanical device, sometimes fanciful: **This *contraption* wakes you up and finds your socks in the morning.** *syn.* gadget

con·trol tow·er [kən·trōl′ tou′ər] *n.* The tower at an airport from which planes are guided to take off and land: **The pilot got clearance from the *control tower* to take off.**

cor·re·spon·dence [kôr′ə·spän′dəns] *n.* Communication by means of writing letters or electronic mail: **The pen pals kept up their *correspondence* for three years before they met in person.**

cos·mo·naut [käz′mə·nôt′] *n.* The Russian term for a person trained to make flights in space: **The *cosmonaut*, Yuri Gagarin, was the first human to go into space.** *syn.* astronaut

— Fact File —
cosmonaut The terms *cosmonaut* and *astronaut* have almost the same meanings. *Cosmonaut* is the Russian term and *astronaut* is the English term. Cosmonaut Yuri Gagarin (1934–1968) was the first person to orbit the Earth. He did so in April 1961, a few weeks before American astronaut Alan Shepard's flight. In 1975 American and Soviet scientists worked together in space as part of the Apollo-Soyuz project. American astronauts worked aboard the Russian space station, *Mir*. Russian cosmonauts and American astronauts will be stationed on the ISS, the International Space Station, now under construction.

coun·sel [koun′səl] *v.* To give advice: **My older brother likes to *counsel* me on how to handle my friends.** *syn.* advise

D

de·ci·pher [dē·sī′fər] *v.* To make out the meaning of something such as code or illegible handwriting: **My handwriting was hard to *decipher* at first.** *syn.* decode

ded·i·cate [ded′ə·kāt] *v.* **ded·i·cat·ed** To declare—often in writing—that an artwork or a project is in honor of a person: **John *dedicated* his first symphony to his father.** *syn.* inscribe

de·flect [di·flekt′] *v.* **de·flec·ted** To cause something to veer off course; to cause something to bounce off: **The armor *deflected* arrows well.** *syn.* avert

— Word Origins —
deflect The word *deflect* has in it the root *flect*, meaning "bend," and the prefix *de-*, meaning "off," or "away from." Some other words containing *flect* are *reflect*—"to bend back"—as light waves bend back from a mirror, and *genuflect*—"to bend the knee."

a	add	e	end	o	odd	ōō	pool	oi	oil	th	this	*a* in *above*
ā	ace	ē	equal	ō	open	u	up	ou	pout	zh	vision	*e* in *sicken*
â	care	i	it	ô	order	û	burn	ng	ring			*i* in *possible*
ä	palm	ī	ice	ŏŏ	took	yōō	fuse	th	thin			*o* in *melon*
												u in *circus*

ə =

629

de·ject·ed·ly [di·jek′tid·lē] *adv.* Having a depressed attitude: **The team members walked home *dejectedly* after they lost the game.** *syn.* sadly

de·scend [di·send′] *v.* **de·scen·ded** To come down from ancestors or to have a characteristic that comes down from them: **You are *descended* from a long line of painters.**

de·sig·nate [dez′ig·nāt] *v.* **de·sig·na·ted** To set something apart for a special honor: **This day has been *designated* Best Friends Day.** *syn.* appoint

de·spair [di·spâr′] *n.* A feeling of hopelessness: **Mark felt *despair* because he thought he would never understand the work.**

de·spise [di·spīz′] *v.* **de·spised** To dislike intensely: **I *despise* television programs that insult my intelligence.** *syns.* loathe, detest

de·vote [di·vōt′] *v.* To dedicate oneself to a person, a career, and so on: **Lana knew that she would *devote* herself to achieving her dream.** *syn.* commit

dig·ni·ty [dig′nə·tē] *n.* The state of having pride and self-worth: **Aunt Flo always carried herself with *dignity*.**

dis·charge [dis·chärj′] **dis·charged** *v.* To relieve of duty; to dismiss from a job: **Irene was *discharged* from being class president after the term ended.** *syn.* dismiss

disengage

dis·en·gage [dis·ən·gāj′] *v.* To unfasten or release: **The spacecraft can *disengage* itself from the space station.** *syn.* detach

dis·may [dis·mā′] *n.* Worry; discouragement; a feeling of alarm, uneasiness: **Gwen sighed in *dismay* when so few came to the meeting.**

dis·re·gard [dis·ri·gärd′] *v.* **dis·re·gard·ed** To pay no attention: **The loud student *disregarded* the whisper policy in the library.** *syn.* ignore

dis·tin·guished [dis·tin′gwisht] *adj.* Having high position and honor: **The mayor was one of the *distinguished* guests.** *syn.* famous

dis·tress [dis·tres′] **dis·tressed** *v.* To feel discomfort or sorrow: **Paul was *distressed* that he had missed the bus.** *syn.* upset

dis·trib·u·tor [dis·trib′yə·tər] *n.* A person or thing that provides a product or a service throughout a certain area: **Stripes Company is the *distributor* of school software in our county.** *syn.* dealer

do·mes·ti·cat·ed [də·mes′tə·kāt·əd] *adj.* Accustomed to people or trained to work with people: ***Domesticated* elephants can do heavy work, such as carrying large logs.** *syn.* tame

du·pli·cate [dōō′plə·kit] *n.* An exact copy: **This ring is a *duplicate* of one we saw in the museum.** *syn.* reproduction

dwin·dle [dwin′dəl] *v.* **dwin·dled** To shrink in size, value, or quantity: **Joseph's savings *dwindled* because he often bought snacks from vending machines.** *syn.* decrease

E

e·di·tion [i·dish′ən] *n.* A number of copies of something, such as a book, all printed in the same way and at about the same time: **The first *edition* of her book came out in May.**

ember

em·ber [em′bər] *n.* **em·bers** In a fire, a glowing piece of wood or coal: **We toasted marshmallows over the *embers*.** *syn.* coal

en·cour·age [in·kûr′ij] *v.* **en·cour·aged** To give confidence, praise, or emotional support to another person: **The teacher *encouraged* her students to succeed.** *syn.* inspire

en·dorse [in·dôrs′] *v.* To give support to something or someone, such as a product or a candidate for office: **The company asked famous sports stars to *endorse* its products.** *syn.* recommend

en·er·gy [en′ər·jē] *n.* Power that is used to do work: **Food gives your body *energy* to move and grow.**

en·gross [in·grōs′] *v.* **en·grossed** To be occupied completely: **Rita was so *engrossed* in her book that she did not notice the time.** *syn.* absorb

Word Origin
engross This word traces its origins to the Old French word *engrosser*, "to acquire in large quantity." One might buy up all of something, creating a monopoly (controlling all sales and prices). The word *engross* came to mean "to take all of something" or "to require all of something." The connection between the word's original meaning and its current meaning lies in the idea of taking up all of something, whether an object or one's attention.

en·roll [in·rōl′] *v.* **en·rolls** To sign up for a club, membership, or a school: **Kayla *enrolls* in college next year.** *syn.* register

er·rand [er′ənd] *n.* **er·rands** A short trip on which someone does something, often a trip for someone else: **Sally's job was to run *errands* for her father's grocery store.**

er·ror [er′ər] *n.* A mistake in thinking or in judgment; in baseball, a mistake in fielding the ball: **Noel was charged with an *error* when he dropped the ball and the runner made it to second base.** *syn.* blunder

e·vap·o·rate [i·vap′ə·rāt′] *v.* **e·vap·o·rat·ing** To vanish, in the same way water turns to vapor: **She spent her allowance so fast it seemed to *evaporate*.** *syn.* disappear

ex·ag·ger·ate [ig·zaj′ə·rāt′] *v.* To add to the facts in a way that distorts the meaning: **If you *exaggerate* the facts of the news story, then it is no longer good journalism.** *syn.* overstate

ex·haust [ig·zôst′] *v.* **ex·haust·ed** To make tired: **The mule was *exhausted* from carrying the heavy packs.** *syn.* fatigue

ex·o·dus [ek′sə·dəs] *n.* A large group of people going out from a place: **At first only a few refugees left, but soon an *exodus* began.** *syn.* migration

ex·quis·ite [eks·kwi′zit] *adj.* Beautiful and elegant: **The art lover filled his home with *exquisite* paintings and sculptures.** *syn.* charming

F

field [fēld] *v.* **field·ed** In baseball or softball, to catch a ball that is in play and throw it if necessary: **Emily *fielded* a ground ball and tossed it to home plate.** *syn.* retrieve

flex·i·bil·i·ty [flek′sə·bil′i·tē] *n.* The quality of being able to bend without breaking: **Some types of plastic have *flexibility*, but wood does not.** *syn.* malleability

for·lorn [fər·lôrn′] *adj.* Feeling miserable, lost, or abandoned: **Sarah wore a *forlorn* expression when no one played with her.** *syn.* sad

for·mu·la [fôr′myə·lə] *n.* **for·mu·las** In math, a set of symbols that stands for a fact or an exercise: **Luis memorized many *formulas* so he could easily use them.** *syn.* method

furl [fûrl] *v.* To wrap up tightly and then tie, such as a sail: **Dori had to *furl* the sail after tying the small sailboat to the dock.** *syn.* roll

G

gen·er·ate [jen′ə·rāt] *v.* **gen·er·at·ed** To cause something to happen because of a physical or a chemical change: **The light *generated* a lot of heat.** *syn.* produce

gey·ser [gī′zər] *n.* A spring of water heated by an underground source so that it boils at regular intervals, shooting water and steam into the air: **The tourists were misted with warm water when the geyser shot upward through the ground.**

Fact File
geyser The word *geyser* is the only Icelandic word commonly used in the English language. *Geysir* is the name of a certain geyser in southern Iceland. The word means "gusher." Geysir has quieted in the past 60 years, but other Icelandic geysers are quite active.

geyser

a add	e end	o odd	ōō pool	oi oil	th this	ə = a in *above*
ā ace	ē equal	ō open	u up	ou pout	zh vision	e in *sicken*
â care	i it	ô order	û burn	ng ring		i in *possible*
ä palm	ī ice	ŏŏ took	yōō fuse	th thin		o in *melon*
						u in *circus*

gorge [gôrj] *v.* **gorged** To overeat; to gobble food like an animal: **The hungry lions *gorged* themselves on their prey.** *syn.* stuff

grade [grād] *n.* The steepness of the land; the steepness of an angle: **The road's *grade* grew steeper as it approached the mountain.**

graf·fi·ti [grə·fē′tē] *n.* A kind of vandalism in which people write their names or draw pictures on others' property: **The students who wrote the *graffiti* had to stay after school and scrub it off.** *syn.* scrawl

grav·el·ly [grav′əl·lē] *adj.* Having a rough sound: **Her bad cold made her voice sound *gravelly*.** *syn.* raspy

grav·i·ta·tion·al [grav′ə·tā′shən·əl] *adj.* Having to do with the law in physics that states that two objects exert a pull on each other: **The Earth's *gravitational* pull is one reason objects have weight; the other is the mass of the objects themselves.**

gri·mace [grim′əs] *v.* **gri·maced** To twist one's face, as if in pain: **Cal *grimaced* as he heard the off-key music.**

guar·an·tee [gar′ən·tē′] *v.* To pledge that something will be done as promised: **We *guarantee* that you will like our product, or we will give you back your money.** *syn.* affirm

H

han·dler [han′dlər] *n.* **han·dlers** A person who trains or manages an animal in a race, a show, or a contest: **The show dogs looked to their *handlers* for instructions.** *syn.* manager

har·ness [här′nis] *n.* Leather straps or bands used to hitch an animal to something it will pull: **The *harness* fastened the horse to the carriage.**

head·quar·ters [hed′kwôr′tərz] *n.* The central office for controlling an operation, campaign, or business: **Lila sent a letter of complaint to company *headquarters* and got a reply.**

Word Origins
headquarters The head, because it houses the brain and contains four major sense organs, is the center of control for all of the body's functions. Some words in our language that expand on this idea are *headline*—the most important part of a news story; *headmaster*—the principal of a school; and *headspring*—the source of a spring of water.

heave [hēv] *v.* **heaved** To use much effort to lift and toss something: **The passenger *heaved* her knapsack onto the luggage rack.** *syn.* pitch

home·stead [hōm′sted] *v.* To develop a substantial piece of land, including building on it and farming it: **The Smith family decided to *homestead* rather than stay in the crowded city.**

hon·or [än′ər] *n.* **hon·ors** Recognition of or respect for someone's achievement: **She received a certificate of *honor* for her high grades.** *syns.* tribute, award

hud·dle [hud′əl] *v.* **hud·dled** To nestle close together, as for protection: **The pigeons *huddled* together under the awning.** *syn.* crowd

I

il·lus·trate [il′ə·strāt′] *v.* **il·lus·trat·ing** To make pictures that go along with written material, such as books: **Emily enjoys writing and *illustrating* her own books.** *syn.* draw

Word Origins
illustrate The word *illustrate* is derived from the Latin word *illustratus*, "to light up." One meaning of *illustrate* is "to make clear or explain" by using examples and comparisons. Illustrations "shed light on" the words of a book.

im·mo·bil·i·ty [i·mō·bil′ə·tē] *n.* The condition of not being able to move: **An engine problem caused the car's *immobility*.** *syn.* motionlessness

im·pact [im′pakt] *n.* The effect of an idea or an action on someone's feelings or behavior: **The movie about fire safety had an *impact* on the audience.** *syn.* influence

im·pul·sive·ly [im·pəl′siv·lē] *adv.* With suddenness; without hesitation: **Josh makes decisions *impulsively* and pays the consequences later.**

in·cred·i·ble [in·kred′ə·bəl] *adj.* Too unusual to be believed: **Eighty years ago, space travel seemed an *incredible* idea.** *syn.* unbelievable

in·cred·u·lous·ly [in·krej′ə·ləs·lē] *adv.* With disbelief: **The team listened *incredulously* as the coach explained why the soccer tournament had been canceled.** *syn.* skeptically

in·debt·ed [in·det′id] *adj.* Feeling that one owes something in return for a favor: **We are *indebted* to you for your help after the earthquake.** *syn.* obligated

in·ef·fi·cient [in′ə·fish′ənt] *adj.* Not able to do the job in the best way: **The old engine made *inefficient* use of its fuel.** *syn.* ineffective

in·let [in′let] *n.* A narrow strip of water; a small bay or creek: **We traveled the *inlet* in a small canoe.** *syn.* passageway

in·spire [in·spīr′] *v.* To motivate someone to accomplish or feel something: **A good teacher seeks to *inspire* the class.** *syn.* encourage

in·stall·ment [in·stôl′mənt] *n.* **in·stall·ments** One part of a total amount of money that is owed: **Jennie paid her mother back for the broken vase in three *installments*.** *syn.* payment

in·su·late [in′sə·lāt′] *v.* **in·su·lat·ed** To cover, as with a material that does not conduct electricity or a material that does not allow heat or cold to pass through: **The wires were not *insulated* well and so posed a fire hazard.** *syn.* wrap

in·ter·na·tion·al [in′tər·na′shə·nal] *adj.* Having to do with many nations: **Antarctica is the site of *international* scientific research.** *syn.* global

in·ter·pret·er [in·tür′prə·tər] *n.* A person who translates spoken words from one language into another: **Kim acted as *interpreter* between her sister and the salesclerk.** *syn.* translator

J

jaun·ty [jôn′tē] *adj.* Stylish; lively in appearance: **Jessica looked confident and *jaunty* as she walked to the podium to deliver her speech.**

L

la·goon [lə·gōōn′] *n.* An area of water that is surrounded by a circular thin strip of land called an atoll: **The water in the *lagoon* was very calm.**

lagoon

lair [lâr] *n.* The home of some kinds of animals: **The bear hibernated all winter in her *lair*.** *syn.* den

line·up [līn′up′] *n.* In baseball or softball, the batting order for a team: **Ken batted third in the *lineup*.** *syn.* order

lurk [lûrk] *v.* **lurked** To be ready to attack while hiding from view: **The leopard *lurked* in the jungle, quietly searching for food.** *syn.* skulk

M

me·an·der [mē·an′dər] *v.* To move back and forth in a snakelike fashion: **The cat likes to *meander* through the garden.** *syn.* wind

men·tor [men′tər] *n.* An advisor and tutor who works one-on-one with a young person: **With a *mentor's* help, Cyd became a music protégé.** *syn.* teacher

Fact File
mentor In Greek mythology, Mentor was a friend of Odysseus, the hero of Homer's epic poem *The Odyssey*. Mentor became the helper and teacher of Odysseus' son, Telemachus. Odysseus had been called away to battle, and he encountered many adventures and difficulties during his return journey. Throughout Odysseus' absence, Mentor often helped Telemachus choose the right course of action.

mi·grant [mī′grənt] *adj.* Moving regularly from place to place: ***Migrant* farmers must often move from place to place.** *syn.* nomadic

mi·grate [mī′grāt] *v.* **mi·grat·ed** To move with others of the same group to a place that is far away: **The birds *migrated* south in winter in search of food and warmth.** *syn.* relocate

mis·lead [mis·lēd′] *v.* **mis·lead·ing** To give a false idea to others: **The robber tried *misleading* the police when he was questioned.** *syn.* deceive

moss [môs] *n.* A class of small plants that grow in moist, shaded areas: ***Moss* grows on the north side of trees in the Northern Hemisphere.**

muf·fle [muf′əl] *v.* To lower the volume by covering or enclosing the source of the noise: **Dina used a pillow to *muffle* the ringing of the alarm clock.** *syn.* deaden

a add	e end	o odd	ōō pool	oi oil	th this	ə = a in *above*
ā ace	ē equal	ō open	u up	ou pout	zh vision	e in *sicken*
â care	i it	ô order	û burn	ng ring		i in *possible*
ä palm	ī ice	ŏŏ took	yōō fuse	th thin		o in *melon*
						u in *circus*

mur•mur [mûr′mər] *n.* A soft, constant, unclear sound: **The audience began to *murmur* when the movie ended.** *syn.* mumble

N

ne•go•ti•ate [ni•gō′shē•āt] *v.* **ne•go•ti•at•ing** To hold a discussion with the goal of making an agreement: **The student government is *negotiating* with the principal for the right to run a radio station.** *syn.* arbitrate

nu•mer•ous [n(y)ōō′mər•əs] *adj.* Consisting of a large group of things or events: **He tried *numerous* times to grow plants from seeds in his backyard.** *syn.* many

O

oath [ōth] *n.* An oral or written promise about a serious matter, such as honesty or faithfulness to an ideal: **At his inauguration, President Washington took the first *oath* of office.** *syn.* vow

oath

ob•nox•ious [əb•näk′shəs] *adj.* Extremely unpleasant or offensive: **The landfill gave off an *obnoxious* smell.** *syn.* intolerable

Word Origins
obnoxious The word *obnoxious* is from the Latin word *obnoxiosus*, meaning "exposed to danger." It is made up of the word parts *ob*, which means "to" or "toward," and *noxa*, which means "harm." The word is used today with a meaning that is closer to "annoying," such as "an obnoxious attitude." However, the original meaning was more danger-oriented. (See *ominous.*)

om•i•nous [äm′ə•nəs] *adj.* Threatening, dangerous: ***Ominous* storm clouds darkened the sky.** *syn.* menacing

over•come [ō′vər•kum′] *v.* To feel weak or helpless: **Elizabeth was *overcome* with fear because she had to compete.** *syn.* overwhelm

P

pace [pās] *n.* A rate of walking, running, or doing other activities: **The scouts hiked at a fast *pace*.** *syn.* tempo

par•ti•tion [pär•tish′ən] *n.* A divider; a wall: **A *partition* usually divides the big gym into two smaller ones.** *syn.* separation

pas•tel [pas•tel′] *n.* **pas•tels** A chalklike colored crayon, used for art: **The technique for using *pastels* often involves blending colors.**

pawn•shop [pôn′shäp′] *n.* A business in which a person is licensed to lend money in exchange for goods, which may be redeemed if the loan is repaid: **In the *pawnshop* were cases of watches and jewelry.**

perch [pûrch] *n.* A place to sit or stand, especially at a height: **Our parakeet thinks my shoulder is her *perch*.** *syn.* roost

per•spec•tive [pər•spek′tiv] *n.* A point of view that puts things in correct relation to each other: **Greg put the lost watch in *perspective* when he heard about the car accident.**

pitch [pich] *v.* **pitched** For a ship to plunge down and rise up again repeatedly: **The ship *pitched* violently on the rough waves.** *syn.* dip

po•di•um [pō′dē•əm] *n.* A small platform on a stage where a conductor or a speaker may stand: **The lecturer stepped up to the *podium* and began to speak.**

point•ed•ly [poin′tid•lē] *adv.* Clearly showing one's sharp feelings: **Katie *pointedly* asked Mona why she hadn't been invited.** *syn.* bitingly

pol•i•cy [päl′ə•sē] *n.* A set of rules of an organization that are in keeping with its philosophical point of view: **The restaurant has a good *policy* toward refunding money to unsatisfied customers.** *syn.* practice

po•li•o [pō′lē•ō] *n.* Short form of *poliomyelitis*, a virus that causes paralysis and deformity, especially in children: **Dr. Jonas Salk developed a vaccine that conquered *polio*.** *syn.* infantile paralysis

Fact File
polio Polio was a terrifying killer and a crippler of both children and adults. Franklin D. Roosevelt was paralyzed by polio in 1921. After he returned to public life, he was elected governor of New York State and President of the United States, the office he held from 1932 until his death in 1945. Dr. Jonas Salk's vaccine was introduced in 1955, followed by the Sabin vaccine. These vaccines have practically eradicated polio.

po•si•tion [pə•zish′ən] *n.* **po•si•tions** The places occupied by people or things: **The runners took their *positions* in their lanes before the race began.** *syn.* post

po•ten•tial [pō•ten′shəl] *n.* An ability that has not yet been used: **Zoe has the *potential* to be a great violinist.** *syn.* capacity

pro•duce [prō′dōōs] *n.* Something that has been grown, such as fruits and vegetables: **You'll find fresh corn in the *produce* department of the supermarket.** *syn.* harvest

pros•per [präs′pər] *v.* **pros•per•ing** To have success and wealth: **Todd's dog grooming business is *prospering*, and now he needs to hire an assistant.** *syn.* flourish

prowl [proul] *v.* **prowls** To search around like an animal hunting prey: **Our cat *prowls* around the backyard searching for mice.** *syn.* stalk

Q

qui•ver [kwiv′ər] *n.* A container for arrows: **Sean drew an arrow from the *quiver* and pulled back the bowstring.** *syn.* sheath

quiver

R

ra•tion [rash′ən] *n.* **ra•tions** A system of distributing goods that would be scarce if they were not controlled: ***Rations* were a way for both soldiers and civilians to get enough supplies during World War II.** *syn.* quota

Fact File
ration During World War II many countries, including the United States, practiced rationing. Basic supplies, like meat, eggs, footwear, gasoline, rubber tires, and butter, were rationed rather than freely available. Each family received a coupon book and then gave stores ration coupons along with money to buy items.

re•ac•tion [rē•ak′shən] *n.* A feeling one has or response one makes as a result of a situation: **His immediate *reaction* to the cry for help was to run toward it.** *syn.* response

reef [rēf] *n.* A ridge of rock or coral lying near or just above the surface of the water: **Anna and James used snorkels as they explored the coral *reef*.** *syn.* shoal

re•fin•er•y [ri•fīn′ə•rē] *n.* A place where a raw material is processed into a finished product, such as sugar or oil: **All impurities from the sugarcane were filtered out at the *refinery*.** *syn.* plant

re•peal [ri•pēl′] *v.* To cancel or withdraw something, such as a penalty: **The judge will *repeal* the parking fine.** *syn.* annul

rep•u•ta•tion [rep′yə•tā′shən] *n.* The opinion most people have about the character of someone or something: **Our school has a *reputation* for graduating many honor students.**

re•sem•ble [ri•zem′bəl] *v.* **re•sem•bled** To be similar in appearance or character to someone or something else: **This case *resembled* an earlier case the police had solved.** *syn.* parallel

res•i•dence [rez′i•dəns] *n.* The place where one lives: **Our *residence* was an apartment on the top floor of a three-story house.** *syn.* dwelling

re•tire [ri•tīr′] *v.* **re•tired** To take something out of use because of advancing age: **Andrew *retired* his baseball glove when it became too small for his hand.**

a add	e end	o odd	ōō pool	oi oil	th this		ə = a in *above*
ā ace	ē equal	ō open	u up	ou pout	zh vision		e in *sicken*
â care	i it	ô order	û burn	ng ring			i in *possible*
ä palm	ī ice	ŏŏ took	yōō fuse	th thin			o in *melon*
							u in *circus*

rid•i•cule [rid′ə•kyōōl] *v.* **rid•i•culed** To criticize or make fun of someone in a way that embarrasses him or her: **The boys *ridiculed* the new student for the way she dressed.** *syns.* mock, belittle

rig•ging [rig′ing] *n.* The lines and chains used with sails and masts on a sailing vessel: **Julian found that the hardest part of making a model ship was setting up the *rigging* correctly.**

rook•ie [rŏŏk′ē] *n.* A beginner in a given profession: **The basketball player was a *rookie*, but she surprised the crowd by racking up 20 points in her first game.** *syns.* apprentice, novice

S

sat•el•lite [sat′əl•īt′] *n.* A human-made object that has been sent into space to orbit Earth: **A *satellite* was launched that will send weather information back to Earth.**

satellite

schol•ar•ship [skäl′ər•ship] *n.* Money that is awarded to pay for a student's tuition: **Charles was admitted to college with a full *scholarship*.** *syns.* stipend, grant

sen•sor [sen′sər] *n.* **sen•sors** A device that measures or monitors physical events: ***Sensors* on a seismograph detect and record earth movement.**

se•ries [sir′ēz] *n.* A number of things coming one after another in time or place: **A *series* of concerts will be held at Town Hall this winter.** *syn.* sequence

set•tle•ment [set′əl•mənt] *n.* A place people develop so they can live there: **These ruins show that there was once a large *settlement* here.** *syn.* colony

shal•low [shal′ō] *adj.* Something, such as water, that is not deep: ***Shallow* puddles were all over the parking lot after the rainstorm.**

side•track [sīd′trak] *v.* To make something go off the proper course: **The rodeo clown's important job is to *sidetrack* a charging bull.** *syn.* distract

Fact File
sidetrack The word *sidetrack* has a more literal meaning than the one we commonly use. It means to switch a train from its main track to a siding—a short piece of track where the train can wait while it is being loaded or while another train passes.

si•mul•ta•ne•ous•ly [sī′mul•tā′nē•əs•lē] *adv.* At the same time: **The children explained the story *simultaneously*.** *syn.* concurrently

snort [snôrt] *v.* To make a noise by quickly forcing air through the nostrils: **Horses only breathe through their noses, so when they run, they *snort*.**

so•na•ta [sə•nät′ə] *n.* A musical piece written for one or two instruments, consisting of one or more movements, or sections: **Beethoven's "Moonlight *Sonata*" is a piano piece.**

sou•ve•nir [sōō′və•nir′] *n.* **sou•ve•nirs** An item that is a reminder of a person, place, or event: **The tourist bought a *souvenir* postcard in the gift shop.** *syn.* remembrance

Word Origins
souvenir The word *souvenir* is the French verb meaning "to remember." It contains the root word *venir*, "to come." On Quebec's license plates, the motto "*Je me souviens*" ("I remember") is imprinted.

spon•sor [spän′sər] *v.* **spon•sor•ing** To promote and pay for an event: **The PTA is *sponsoring* this year's bike safety campaign.** *syn.* support

sta•di•um [stā′dē•əm] *n.* A large structure where sports events are played on a field before an audience: **Tickets for the playoffs went on sale at Lions *Stadium* today.** *syn.* arena

Word Origins
stadium In ancient Greece and Rome, a stadium was a unit of measurement equal to about 607 feet. Some foot races were a stadium long. These races were held on a track, and alongside the track were tiers of seats for the cheering spectators.

stam•pede [stam•pēd′] *n.* **stam•pedes** An occurrence in which a herd of animals suddenly runs at top speed, usually in fear: **The roar of hooves was deafening during the cattle *stampede*.**

stampede

stern•ly [stûrn′lē] *adv.* In a severe, strict, or scolding manner: **The teacher talked to him *sternly* about listening in class.** *syn.* sharply

sto•lid•ly [stä′lid•lē] *adv.* With little or no emotion: **While the rest of her class was excited when the teacher announced they would be taking a field trip, Kim met the news *stolidly*.** *syn.* impassively

stump [stump] *v.* **stumps** To puzzle or baffle someone, as during a quiz: **The spelling word "xyster" *stumps* even our best contestants.** *syn.* confuse

sub•mit [sub•mit′] *v.* **sub•mit•ted** To display or show something so that others can judge it or comment upon it in some way: **Jan *submitted* her poem to the school magazine, and it was printed.** *syn.* present

suf•frage [suf′rij] *n.* The right to vote for candidates for political office: **Women's *suffrage* became a reality after World War I in the United States.**

sus•cep•ti•ble [sə•sep′tə•bəl] *adj.* Able to be affected by something: **In the winter people seem more *susceptible* to catching colds.** *syn.* vulnerable

sus•pend [sə•spend′] *v.* **sus•pen•ded** To hang up and leave dangling: **The fish was *suspended* from Libby's line.** *syn.* dangle

T

tan•gle [tang′əl] *n.* Something that is snarled or muddled: **There was a *tangle* in Melissa's hair that was so stubborn it had to be cut out.** *syn.* knot

thrive [thrīv] *v.* **thrived** To prosper under the effect of something: **The plant *thrived* when it got enough sun and water.** *syns.* flourish, succeed

tim•id [tim′id] *adj.* Lacking self-confidence; fearful; shy: **The *timid* child found it hard to make new friends.** *syn.* bashful

tin•der [tin′dər] *n.* Material that catches fire easily because it is very dry, brittle, and thin: **The camper added dry twigs as *tinder* to get the campfire started.** *syn.* kindling

tread [tred] *n.* Soft, careful steps: **My brother's quiet *tread* allowed him to surprise people all the time.** *syn.* footfall

treaty [trē′tē] *n.* An official agreement between peoples or countries, stating what each side will do about a certain issue: **The peace *treaty* ended the long war.** *syns.* arrangement, compact

U

un•de•ni•a•ble [un′di•nī′ə•bəl] *adj.* Something that one is sure of beyond question: **It is *undeniable* that Lewis is the best student in class.** *syn.* indisputable

un•du•late [un′dyə•lāt] *v.* **un•du•lat•ing** To move in waves or like a wave: **The snake was *undulating* its way across the desert road.**

V

vain [vān] *adj.* **vain•er** Being excessively proud of one's appearance and honor: **The actor had become *vainer* and demanded the largest dressing room.** *syn.* conceited

vast [vast] *adj.* Of very large size; enormous; huge: **The Atlantic Ocean is *vast* in size.** *syn.* great

veer [vēr] *v.* **veered** To turn sharply from one direction to another: **The driver *veered* sharply to the right.** *syn.* swerve

vow [vou] *n.* A promise about a serious matter: **Ted made a *vow* to help the new classmate in any way that he could.** *syn.* pledge

W

wrang•ler [rang′lər] *n.* **wrang•lers** A cowboy whose job it is to herd livestock, especially horses: **The *wranglers* are herding the horses into the corral.**

a add	e end	o odd	ōō pool	oi oil	th this		ə = a in *above*
ā ace	ē equal	ō open	u up	ou pout	zh vision		e in *sicken*
â care	i it	ô order	û burn	ng ring			i in *possible*
ä palm	ī ice	ŏŏ took	yōō fuse	th thin			o in *melon*
							u in *circus*

Introducing the Index of Titles and Authors

Explain to students that an index often is found at the back of a book and that it usually consists of an alphabetical listing of topics covered in that book. Tell students that books sometimes have special kinds of indexes, such as the Index of Titles and Authors at the back of their Student Editions.

As you look over the first page of the Index—page 638—with students, point out that all of the entries are in alphabetical order and that authors are listed with last names first. Ask students how they can tell at a glance which entries are selection titles and which are authors' names. Tell students that the page numbers in color print are author features. Then you may want to select several index entries and have students predict what they will find when they turn to the page or pages listed.

Index of Titles and Authors

Page numbers in color refer to biographical information.

638

639

Acknowledgments

Rubrics for Students

A rubric is a tool a teacher can use to score a student's work. A rubric lists the criteria for evaluating the work, and it describes different levels of success in meeting those criteria. Rubrics are useful assessment tools for teachers, but they can be just as useful for students. In fact, rubrics can be powerful teaching tools.

BEFORE WRITING

- When you **introduce** students to **a new kind of writing** through a writing model, discuss the criteria listed on the rubric, and ask students to decide how well the model meets each criterion. Have students add to the rubric other criteria they think are important.

- Before students attempt a new kind of writing, have them focus on the **criteria for excellence** listed on the rubric so that they have specific goals to aim for.

DURING WRITING AND EDITING

- As students are **prewriting** and **drafting,** have them refer to the rubric for important aspects of organization and elaboration that they need to include in their writing.

- When students are ready to **revise,** have them check their writing against the rubric to determine if there are any aspects of organization and elaboration that they can improve.

- As students **proofread,** the rubric will remind them to pay attention to grammar, usage, punctuation, and sentence variety. You may wish to have individual students add to their rubrics, depending on particular language problems they have demonstrated.

AFTER WRITING

- The rubric can be used by individuals to **score their own writing** or by pairs or small groups for peer assessment. Students can highlight the parts of the rubric that they believe apply to a piece of writing.

- Students can keep the marked rubric in their portfolios with the piece of writing it refers to. The marked rubrics will help students **see their progress** through the school year. In conferences with students and family members, you can refer to the rubrics to point out both strengths and weaknesses.

Score of 4

☆ ☆ ☆ ☆

The story fits the purpose for writing very well. The audience it was written for would enjoy it.

The story has a beginning that introduces the problem, a middle that tells events in a clear order, and an ending that gives the solution to the problem.

The story has description and rich details that help the reader visualize the events.

The story has interesting words and phrases, such as specific nouns, vivid verbs, sensory words, and comparisons.

The sentences are written in a variety of ways to make the writing interesting to read.

The story has very few errors in spelling, grammar, and punctuation.

Other:

Score of 3

☆ ☆ ☆

The story fits the purpose for writing. The audience it was written for would probably enjoy it.

The story has a beginning that introduces the problem. The order of the events in the middle is mostly clear. The ending tells how the problem was solved.

The story has some description and a few good details.

The story has some interesting words and phrases.

Some of the sentences show variety, but many are the same type.

There are a few errors in spelling, grammar, and punctuation.

Other:

Score of 2

☆ ☆

The purpose of the story is not very clear. It is hard to tell what audience it was written for.

The story does not have a clear beginning, middle, or ending. There is a problem, but the story does not give a good solution. Some events are missing or out of order.

The story has only a few details and just a little description.

The story has very few words or phrases that are colorful or interesting.

Almost all of the sentences are written in the same way.

There are many errors in spelling, grammar, and punctuation.

Other:

Score of 1

☆

The story does not have a clear purpose. There is no way to tell what audience it was written for.

The story does not have a beginning, a middle, and an ending. The events are hard to follow. There is no problem to solve.

The story has almost no description or details.

The story has no interesting words or phrases.

Most sentences are not written correctly.

There are so many errors that the writing is hard to understand.

Other:

Score of 4 ☆☆☆☆	Score of 3 ☆☆☆	Score of 2 ☆☆	Score of 1 ☆
The paper fits the purpose for writing very well. The audience it was written for would understand it.	The paper fits the purpose for writing. The audience it was written for would probably understand it.	The purpose of the paper is not very clear. It is hard to tell what audience it was written for.	The paper does not have a clear purpose. There is no way to tell what audience it was written for.
The paper has a clear beginning that introduces the topic, a middle that gives facts or directions about the topic in a logical order, and an ending that summarizes or draws a conclusion.	The paper has a beginning that introduces the topic. The facts or directions in the middle are mostly in logical order. The ending summarizes or draws a conclusion.	The paper does not clearly introduce the topic at the beginning. Some of the facts or directions in the middle are out of order or drift from the topic. The paper does not have a clear ending.	The paper does not have an introduction. It does not present facts or directions about one topic. The writing just stops, without giving a summary or a conclusion.
The paper has description and rich details that add information about the facts or directions.	The paper has some description and a few good details about the facts or directions.	The paper has only a few details and not enough description to help the reader understand the topic.	The paper has almost no description or details to explain the topic.
The paper has interesting words and phrases, especially specific nouns.	The paper has some interesting words and phrases, but most of the writing is not very specific.	The paper has very few words or phrases that are interesting or specific.	The paper has no interesting or specific words or phrases.
The sentences are written in a variety of ways to make the writing interesting to read.	Some of the sentences show variety, but many are the same type.	Almost all of the sentences are written in the same way.	Most sentences are not written correctly.
The paper has very few errors in spelling, grammar, and punctuation.	There are a few errors in spelling, grammar, and punctuation.	There are many errors in spelling, grammar, and punctuation.	There are so many errors that the writing is hard to understand.
Other:	Other:	Other:	Other:

Harcourt

Score of 4

☆ ☆ ☆

The paper fits the purpose for writing very well. It is designed to persuade a particular audience.

The paper has a clear statement of opinion at the beginning, a middle that gives logical reasons that support the opinion, and an ending that restates the opinion and calls for action.

The paper has details, description, and/or examples that give more information about the reasons.

The paper has interesting words and phrases, such as specific nouns, vivid verbs, emotional language, and comparisons.

The sentences are written in a variety of ways to make the writing interesting.

The paper has very few errors in spelling, grammar, and punctuation.

Other:

____

Score of 3

☆ ☆ ☆

The paper fits the purpose for writing. It might persuade the audience it was written for.

The paper has a statement of opinion at the beginning. Most of the reasons in the middle support the opinion. The ending restates the opinion but does not call for action.

The paper has some description, examples, and/or a few good details that give information about the reasons.

The paper has some interesting and/or emotional words and phrases, but most of the writing is not very vivid or colorful.

Some of the sentences show variety, but many are the same type.

There are a few errors in spelling, grammar, and punctuation.

Other:

Score of 2

☆ ☆

The purpose of the paper is not very clear. It is hard to tell what audience it was written for.

The paper states an opinion at the beginning, but the reasons offered to support the opinion are not logical or clear. The ending does not restate the opinion.

The paper has only a few details that add information about the reasons.

The paper has very few words or phrases that are interesting or emotional.

Almost all of the sentences are written in the same way.

There are many errors in spelling, grammar, and punctuation.

Other:

Score of 1

☆

The paper does not have a clear purpose. There is no way to tell what audience it was written for.

The paper states an opinion but does not support it. The ideas are poorly organized and drift from the topic.

The paper has no description or details.

The paper has no interesting or emotional words or phrases.

Most sentences are not written correctly.

There are so many errors that the writing is hard to understand.

Other:

Harcourt

Score of 4 ★★★★	Score of 3 ★★★	Score of 2 ★★	Score of 1 ★
The paper fits the purpose for writing very well. The audience it was written for would understand it.	The paper fits the purpose for writing. The audience it was written for would probably understand it.	The purpose of the paper is not very clear. It is hard to tell what audience it was written for.	The paper does not have a clear purpose. There is no way to tell what audience it was written for.
The paper has a clear beginning that introduces the topic, a middle that logically classifies information and ideas about the topic, and an ending that summarizes or draws a conclusion.	The paper has a beginning that introduces the topic. The middle classifies ideas about the topic, but they are not all in logical order. The ending summarizes or draws a conclusion.	The paper does not clearly introduce the topic. A few ideas drift from the topic or purpose. The paper does not have a clear ending.	The paper does not have an introduction. It does not classify ideas about one topic. The writing just stops, without giving a summary or a conclusion.
The paper has description and rich details that add information about the topic.	The paper has some description and a few good details about the topic.	The paper has only a few details and not enough description to help the reader to understand the topic.	The paper has almost no description or details about the topic.
The paper has signal words and phrases that help the reader understand how the ideas are related.	The paper has some signal words and phrases, but they do not always help the reader understand how the ideas are related.	The paper has very few signal words or phrases that help the reader understand how the ideas are related.	The paper has no signal words or phrases.
The sentences are written in a variety of ways to make the writing interesting to read.	Some of the sentences show variety, but most are the same type.	Almost all of the sentences are written in the same way.	Most sentences are not written correctly.
The paper has very few errors in spelling, grammar, and punctuation.	There are a few errors in spelling, grammar, and punctuation.	There are many errors in spelling, grammar, and punctuation.	There are so many errors that the writing is hard to understand.
Other:	Other:	Other:	Other:

Harcourt

Score of 4

☆ ☆ ☆ ☆

The research report fits the purpose for writing very well. The audience it was written for would understand it.

The report has a clear beginning that introduces the topic. The middle sections give logically organized information and ideas about the topic. The ending summarizes or draws a conclusion.

The report presents ideas and information from a variety of sources.

The report has description, rich details, and/or narrative parts that add information about the topic.

The report has signal words and phrases that help the reader understand how the ideas are related.

The sentences are written in a variety of ways to make the writing interesting to read.

The report has very few errors in spelling, grammar, and punctuation.

Other:

Score of 3

☆ ☆ ☆

The research report fits the purpose for writing. The audience it was written for would probably understand it.

The report has a beginning that introduces the topic. The ideas and information about the topic in the middle are mostly in logical order. The ending summarizes or draws a conclusion.

The report presents information from at least two sources.

The report has some description and several good details about the topic. A few details drift from the topic or purpose.

The report has some signal words and phrases, but they do not always help the reader understand how the ideas are related.

Some of the sentences show variety, but many are the same type.

There are a few errors in spelling, grammar, and punctuation.

Other:

Score of 2

☆ ☆

The purpose of the research report is not very clear. It is hard to tell what audience it was written for.

The report introduces the topic at the beginning. The information and ideas in the middle are not clearly organized. The report does not have a clear ending.

The report presents information from only one source.

The report doesn't have many details or much description. Some of the details are not about the topic.

The report has very few signal words or phrases that help the reader understand how the ideas are related.

Almost all of the sentences are written in the same way.

There are many errors in spelling, grammar, and punctuation.

Other:

Score of 1

☆

The research report does not have a clear purpose. There is no way to tell what audience it was written for.

The report does not have an introduction. It does not organize ideas about one topic. The writing just stops, without giving a summary or a conclusion.

The report does not present information from any sources.

The report has almost no description or details about a topic.

The report has no signal words or phrases.

Most sentences are not written correctly.

There are so many errors that the writing is hard to understand.

Other:

Harcourt

Handwriting
Manuscript Alphabet

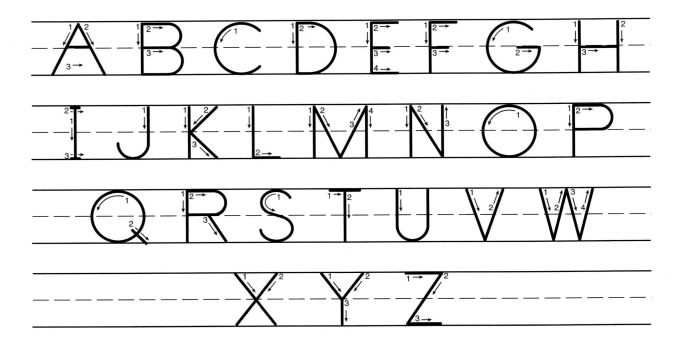

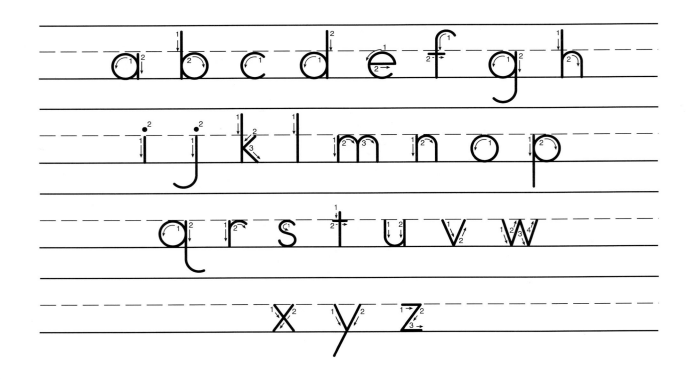

HANDWRITING MODEL

Harcourt

Handwriting
Cursive Alphabet

$\mathcal{A}$ $\mathcal{B}$ $\mathcal{C}$ $\mathcal{D}$ $\mathcal{E}$ $\mathcal{F}$ $\mathcal{G}$ $\mathcal{H}$

$\mathcal{I}$ $\mathcal{J}$ $\mathcal{K}$ $\mathcal{L}$ $\mathcal{M}$ $\mathcal{N}$ $\mathcal{O}$ $\mathcal{P}$

$\mathcal{Q}$ $\mathcal{R}$ $\mathcal{S}$ $\mathcal{T}$ $\mathcal{U}$ $\mathcal{V}$ $\mathcal{W}$

$\mathcal{X}$ $\mathcal{Y}$ $\mathcal{Z}$

a b c d e f g h

i j k l m n o p

q r s t u v w

x y z

HANDWRITING MODEL

Pathways to Adventure A15

D'Nealian
Handwriting
Manuscript Alphabet

A B C D E F G H
I J K L M N O P
Q R S T U V W
X Y Z

a b c d e f g h
i j k l m n o p
q r s t u v w
x y z

Harcourt

HANDWRITING MODEL

D'Nealian
Handwriting
Cursive Alphabet

A B C D E F G H
I J K L M N O P
2 R S T U V W
X Y Z

a b c d e f g h
i j k l m n o p
q r s t u v w
x y z

Benchmarks and Checklists

Views on assessment (the process of gathering information) and evaluation (the process of judging that information) have evolved in recent years. We now recognize that one strategy or tool is not sufficient due to the complex nature of literacy and its acquisition. A single measure is likely to be misleading or erroneous. Instructional decisions are too important to make on the basis of a single measure or assessment tool.

Collections supports this view by providing a variety of formal assessment tools and a variety of informal assessment tools and strategies, such as the Benchmarks and Checklists on the following pages, to ensure that students develop the literacy skills they need to be successful learners.

The Benchmarks present a framework across grade levels of content goals or standards—what students should know about language and should be able to do with language to be successful readers, writers, and communicators. This framework of general indicators reflects literacy development of oral language and communication skills, progress toward becoming independent readers and writers, and mastery of previously learned skills in increasingly complex presentations, reading selections, and written compositions.

The Benchmarks provide guidance for the behaviors teachers should be observing. The accompanying Checklists provide a form for recording and documenting these observable behaviors. Together the Benchmarks and Checklists identify the learning goals and indicate instructional emphasis. Benchmarks do not dictate the means of achieving the goals or prescribe the instructional methods; the teacher needs to translate the information gained into classroom practice.

Benchmarks

These benchmark statements represent a continuum of learning. The highlighted column describes observable behaviors most of your students should exhibit by the end of the school year.

LISTENING

Determines purpose for listening
Listens attentively and responds to a variety of literature and texts
Responds appropriately in discussions to questions, directions, spoken messages
Notes language of literature

Participates effectively in small groups, in cooperative groups
Monitors ability to listen, understand, recall main idea, details, facts
Evaluates speaker's message; compares own perception with others' perceptions
Listens to others' opinions and points of view

Understands and summarizes the major ideas and supporting evidence in spoken message and presentations
Uses visualization to "see" a story being read

Recognizes that use of words, tone, and emotion may persuade an audience

---

Determines purpose for listening
Listens attentively and responds to a variety of literature and texts
Responds appropriately in discussions to questions, directions, spoken messages
Describes how the language of literature affects the listener
Participates effectively in small groups, in cooperative groups
Monitors ability to listen, understand, recall main idea, details, facts
Evaluates speaker's message; compares own perception with others' perceptions
Listens to and evaluates others' opinions and points of view; pros and cons
Analyzes spoken message for the major ideas and supporting evidence

Visualizes speaker's examples and/or analogies
Recognizes persuasion/bias/prejudice/propaganda/emotional appeals

---

Determines purpose for listening
Listens attentively and responds to a variety of literature and texts
Responds appropriately in discussions to questions, directions, spoken messages
Describes how the language of literature affects the listener
Participates effectively in small groups, in cooperative groups
Monitors ability to listen, understand, recall main idea, details, facts
Evaluates speaker's message; compares own perception with others' perceptions
Listens to and evaluates others' opinions and points of view; pros and cons
Analyzes spoken messages for the major ideas and supporting evidence

Visualizes speaker's examples and/or analogies
Recognizes persuasion/bias/prejudice/propaganda/emotional appeals

SPEAKING

Discusses, reenacts, retells, dramatizes stories, or story parts
Communicates/shares experiences, ideas, opinions with others; clarifies, supports ideas with evidence
Uses appropriate/new vocabulary to describe feelings, experiences, ideas clearly
Speaks confidently in a variety of situations, including oral reports
Adapts spoken language to the audience, purpose, occasion
Controls grammar and usage when speaking
Uses verbal and nonverbal communication in effective ways
Reads aloud with accuracy, fluency, comprehension, and expression
Poses possible answers to *how, why, what if* questions; asks relevant questions
Gives precise oral directions or instructions
Identifies how language reflects regions/cultures

Discusses, reenacts, retells, dramatizes stories, or story parts
Communicates/shares experiences, ideas, opinions with others; clarifies, supports ideas with evidence
Uses appropriate/new vocabulary to describe feelings, experiences, ideas clearly
Speaks confidently in a variety of situations, including oral reports
Adapts spoken language to the audience, purpose, occasion
Controls grammar and usage when speaking
Uses verbal and nonverbal communication in effective ways
Reads aloud with accuracy, fluency, comprehension, and expression
Asks relevant questions; poses possible answers to *how, why, what if* questions
Gives precise oral directions or instructions
Identifies how language reflects regions/cultures

Discusses, reenacts, retells, dramatizes stories, or story parts
Communicates/shares experiences, ideas, opinions with others; clarifies, supports ideas with evidence
Uses appropriate/new vocabulary to describe feelings, experiences, ideas clearly
Speaks confidently in a variety of situations, including oral reports
Adapts spoken language to the audience, purpose, occasion
Controls grammar and usage when speaking
Uses verbal and nonverbal communication in effective ways
Reads aloud with accuracy, fluency, comprehension, and expression
Asks relevant questions; poses possible answers to *how, why, what if* questions
Gives precise oral directions or instructions
Identifies how language reflects regions/cultures

VIEWING

Discusses a variety of illustrations and media
Analyzes the purpose and effects of illustrations, visuals, media
Interprets information from maps, charts, tables, diagrams, graphs, timelines
Analyzes the ways visual images/graphics contribute to, effect, and support meaning
Selects, organizes, produces visuals to complement and extend meaning
Uses technology/media to communicate, to compare ideas, points of view
Compares/contrasts print, visuals, media

Critiques a variety of illustrations and media
Analyzes the purpose and effects of illustrations, visuals, media
Interprets information from maps, charts, tables, diagrams, graphs, timelines
Analyzes the ways visual images/graphics contribute to, effect, and support meaning
Selects, organizes, produces visuals to complement and extend meaning
Uses technology/media to communicate, to compare ideas, points of view
Compares/contrasts print, visuals, media

Critiques a variety of illustrations and media
Analyzes the purpose and effects of illustrations, visuals, media
Interprets information from maps, charts, tables, diagrams, graphs, timelines
Analyzes the ways visual images/graphics contribute to, effect, and support meaning
Selects, organizes, produces visuals to complement and extend meaning
Uses technology/media to communicate, to compare ideas, points of view
Compares/contrasts print, visuals, media

Listening, Speaking, and Viewing Checklist

Student _____ Teacher _____ Grade _____

	Date____	Date____	Date____	Date____	Date____	Date____
LISTENING						
Determines purpose for listening						
Listens attentively and responds appropriately to a variety of literature and texts, discussions, questions, directions, and spoken messages						
Participates effectively in groups; contributes and listens to others						
Monitors ability to listen, understand, recall main idea, details, and facts						
Summarizes important events and ideas; evaluates speaker's message						
Summarizes the major ideas and supporting evidence of spoken messages and presentations						
Recognizes similarities and differences between two types of media						
SPEAKING						
Discusses a variety of texts						
Reenacts, retells, dramatizes stories, role-plays characters						
Communicates/shares experiences, ideas, opinions with others						
Speaks confidently in a variety of situations, including oral reports						
Adapts spoken language to the audience, purpose, occasion; uses new vocabulary						
Controls grammar and usage when speaking						
Uses verbal and nonverbal communication in effective ways						
Reads aloud with accuracy, fluency, comprehension, and expression						
Gives precise oral directions or instructions						
VIEWING						
Discusses a variety of illustrations and media						
Interprets and evaluates information from graphics, visuals, and media						
Analyzes the ways visual images and graphics represent, contribute to, effect, and support meaning of text						
Selects, organizes, and produces visuals to complement and extend meaning						
Uses available technology/appropriate media to communicate information and ideas; to compare ideas, points of view						
Compares and contrasts print, visuals, and electronic media						

Comments: _____

Key:

N = Not Observed

O = Observed Occasionally

R = Observed Regularly

Harcourt

Benchmarks

These benchmark statements represent a continuum of learning. The highlighted column describes observable behaviors most of your students should exhibit by the end of the school year.

READING: DECODING AND VOCABULARY

Applies structural cues to decode and recognize single and multisyllable words: compounds, base words, inflections, contractions, prefixes, suffixes, letter and spelling patterns, syllable patterns

Uses word order, language structure, context to support word identification or to confirm word meaning

Expands vocabulary through listening, reading, writing

Recognizes word relationships: synonyms, antonyms, multiple-meaning words, homophones, homographs

Consults dictionary, reference sources to build or confirm meaning

---

Applies structural cues to decode and recognize single and multisyllable words: compounds, base words, inflections, contractions, prefixes, suffixes, letter and spelling patterns, syllable patterns

Uses word order, language structure, context clues, and prior knowledge to support word identification or to confirm word meaning

Expands vocabulary through listening, reading, writing

Identifies word relationships: synonyms, antonyms, multiple-meaning words, homophones, homographs

Consults dictionary or other reference materials for pronunciation or meaning

---

Applies structural cues to decode and recognize single and multisyllable words: compounds, base words, inflections, contractions, prefixes, suffixes, letter and spelling patterns, syllable patterns

Uses word order, language structure, context clues, and prior knowledge to support word identification or to confirm word meaning

Expands vocabulary through listening, reading, writing

Identifies word relationships: synonyms, antonyms, multiple-meaning words, homophones, homographs

Consults dictionary or other reference materials for pronunciation or meaning

READING: COMPREHENSION

Discusses and retells selections and articles

Uses title, illustrations, prior knowledge to hypothesize and predict content; reads to confirm

Identifies and recalls main idea, characters, events, setting, plot, sequence of events

Analyzes characters' traits, feelings, relationships, conflicts, points of view

Produces artwork and writing to reflect understanding of and to extend meaning of text

Uses punctuation as clues to meaning

Produces summaries of text selections

Monitors own reading and self-corrects using strategies: rereading, searching for clues, asking for help, self-questioning, reading aloud, using references/resources

Establishes and adjusts purpose for reading

Connects, compares, contrasts across texts: characters, topics, themes, scope, organization, treatment

Distinguishes between reality-fantasy; fact-opinion; fiction-nonfiction

Represents text in a variety of ways

Follows written directions

Self-selects and reads a variety of texts voluntarily

Draws and explains inferences from text: important ideas, causes-effects, predictions, conclusions, generalizations

Identifies use of literary devices; determines point of view

Uses alphabetical order to locate information

Identifies and discusses author's purpose/intent, and viewpoint

---

Discusses and retells selections and articles

Uses title, illustrations, prior knowledge to hypothesize and predict content; reads to confirm

Identifies and recalls main idea, characters, events, plot, solution, sequence of events

Analyzes and compares characters' traits, feelings, relationships, conflicts, motives and points of view

Produces artwork and writing to reflect understanding of and to extend meaning of text

Uses punctuation as clues to meaning

Summarizes, paraphrases, and discusses text selections; compares texts

Monitors own reading and self-corrects using strategies: adjusting reading rate, rereading, searching for clues, creating visual images, asking for help, self-questioning, reading aloud, and using references/resources

Establishes and adjusts purpose for reading

Connects, compares, contrasts across texts: characters, topics, themes, scope, organization, treatment

Distinguishes between reality-fantasy; fact-opinion; fiction-nonfiction

Creates and completes graphic organizers (outlines, timelines, graphs, charts) to represent text

Follows written directions

Self-selects and reads a variety of texts voluntarily

Draws and explains inferences from text: important ideas, causes-effects, predictions, conclusions, generalizations

Identifies use of literary devices; determines point of view

Uses alphabetical order to locate information

Discusses author's purpose/intent/viewpoint/techniques; recognizes persuasive techniques

Recognizes evidence that supports an opinion/argument; justifies answers

---

Discusses and retells selections and articles

Uses title, illustrations, prior knowledge to hypothesize and predict content; reads to confirm

Identifies and recalls main idea, characters, events, plot, solution, sequence of events

Analyzes and compares characters' traits, feelings, relationships, conflicts, motives, and points of view

Produces artwork and writing to reflect understanding of and to extend meaning of text

Uses punctuation as clues to meaning

Summarizes, paraphrases, and discusses text selections; compares texts

Monitors own reading and self-corrects using strategies: adjusting reading rate, rereading, searching for clues, creating visual images, asking for help, self-questioning, reading aloud, and using references/resources

Establishes and adjusts purpose for reading

Connects, compares, contrasts across texts: characters, topics, themes, scope, organization, treatment

Distinguishes between reality-fantasy; fact-opinion; fiction-nonfiction

Creates and completes graphic organizers (outlines, timelines, graphs, charts) to represent text

Follows written directions

Self-selects and reads a variety of texts voluntarily

Draws and explains inferences from text: important ideas, causes-effects, predictions, conclusions, generalizations

Identifies use of literary devices; determines point of view

Uses alphabetical order to locate information

Discusses author's purpose/intent/viewpoint/techniques; recognizes persuasive techniques

Recognizes evidence that supports an opinion/argument; justifies answers

Reading Checklist

Student _____ Teacher _____ Grade _____

	Date____	Date____	Date____	Date____	Date____	Date____
DECODING AND VOCABULARY						
Applies structural cues to decode and recognize single and multisyllable words						
Uses word order, language structure, context to support word identification or to confirm word meaning						
Expands vocabulary through listening, reading, writing						
Recognizes word relationships: synonyms, antonyms, multiple-meaning words, homophones, homographs						
Consults dictionary, reference sources to build or confirm meaning						
COMPREHENSION						
Establishes and adjusts purpose for reading						
Reads a variety of self-selected texts for interest and own purpose						
Uses book parts and prior knowledge to hypothesize and predict content						
Monitors own reading and self-corrects using strategies: use prior knowledge, predict content, reread, search for clues, use punctuation as clues to meaning, ask for help, self-question, read aloud, read to confirm; uses references/resources						
Identifies and recalls main idea, characters, events, setting, plot, sequence of events						
Analyzes characters' traits, feelings, relationships, conflicts, points of view						
Summarizes, retells, and produces artwork to retell text						
Identifies use of literary devices; determines point of view						
Identifies and discusses author's purpose, intent, and viewpoint						
Connects, compares, contrasts across texts						
Distinguishes between reality-fantasy; fact-opinion; fiction-nonfiction						
Draws and explains inferences from text: important ideas, causes-effects, predictions, conclusions, generalizations						
Follows written directions						

Comments:

Key:

N = Not Observed

O = Observed Occasionally

R = Observed Regularly

Harcourt

Benchmarks

These benchmark statements represent a continuum of learning. The highlighted column describes observable behaviors most of your students should exhibit by the end of the school year.

WRITING: CONTENT AND ORGANIZATION

Writes for a variety of purposes and audiences	Employs a range of writing styles appropriate for purposes and audiences	Employs a range of writing styles appropriate for purposes and audiences
Writes paragraphs focused on a single topic; includes concepts of order and time	Writes paragraphs focused on a single topic; includes concepts of order and time	Writes paragraphs focused on a single topic; includes concepts of order and time
Includes introduction, development, and closing in writing	Includes introduction, development, and closing in writing	Includes introduction, development, and closing in writing
Writes stories that draw on personal experience	Writes a variety of stories that draw on personal experience, imaginative ideas, or reading experiences	Writes a variety of stories that draw on personal experience, imaginative ideas, or reading experiences
Uses supporting ideas to develop topic and specific details to support ideas	Uses supporting ideas to develop topic and specific details to support ideas	Uses supporting ideas to develop topic and specific details to support ideas
Joins related sentences into paragraphs to organize information and ideas	Joins related sentences and related paragraphs to organize information and ideas	Joins related sentences and related paragraphs to organize information and ideas
Generates ideas before writing on assigned, self-selected tasks	Generates ideas individually or in a group before writing on assigned, self-selected tasks	Generates ideas individually or in a group before writing on assigned, self-selected tasks
Routinely revises, edits, and proofreads own work, and describes editing decisions; evaluates own writing to determine if achieved purpose	Routinely revises, edits, and proofreads own work, and describes editing decisions; evaluates own writing to determine if achieved purpose	Routinely revises, edits, and proofreads own work, and describes editing decisions; evaluates own writing to determine if achieved purpose
Responds constructively to others' writing	Responds constructively to others' writing	Responds constructively to others' writing
Uses available technology to compose, edit, publish	Uses available technology to compose, edit, publish	Uses available technology to compose, edit, publish
Writes using a range of vocabulary appropriate to purpose and audience, precise and vivid words, specialized words related to the topic or setting, descriptive language, transitional words and phrasing	Writes using a range of vocabulary appropriate to purpose and audience, precise and vivid words, specialized words related to the topic or setting, descriptive language, transitional words and phrasing	Writes using a range of vocabulary appropriate to purpose and audience, precise and vivid words, specialized words related to the topic or setting, descriptive language, transitional words and phrasing
Makes own decisions about which pieces to work and publish	Makes own decisions and offers suggestions to others about which pieces to work and publish	Makes own decisions and offers suggestions to others about which pieces to work and publish

WRITING: CONVENTIONS AND MECHANICS

Recognizes and produces simple, compound, and complex sentences and paragraphs	Recognizes and produces simple, compound, and complex sentences and paragraphs	Recognizes and produces simple, compound, and complex sentences and paragraphs
Uses punctuation and capitalization correctly	Uses punctuation and capitalization correctly; consults reference resources	Uses punctuation and capitalization correctly; consults reference resources
Makes few errors in usage	Employs standard English usage, makes few errors	Employs standard English usage, makes few errors

WRITING: SPELLING

Applies spelling generalizations; uses conventional spelling	Uses conventional spelling; uses resources to find correct spelling, synonyms, and replacement words	Uses conventional spelling; uses resources to find correct spelling, synonyms, and replacement words

Writing Checklist

Student _____ **Teacher** _____ **Grade** _____

	Date____	Date____	Date____	Date____	Date____	Date____
CONTENT AND ORGANIZATION						
Generates ideas before writing on assigned, or self-selected tasks						
Writes for a variety of purposes and audiences						
Writes paragraphs focused on a single topic; includes concepts of order and time						
Includes introduction, development, and closing in writing						
Writes stories that draw on personal experience						
Organizes information and ideas into paragraphs						
Uses supporting ideas to develop topic and specific details to support ideas						
Writes using a range of vocabulary appropriate to purpose and audience, precise and vivid words, specialized words related to the topic or setting, descriptive language, transitional words and phrasing						
Revises, edits, and proofreads own work and describes editing decisions; evaluates own writing to determine if achieved purpose						
Makes own decisions about which pieces to work and publish						
Responds constructively to others' writing						
Uses available technology to compose, edit, publish						
CONVENTIONS AND MECHANICS						
Recognizes and produces simple, compound, and complex sentences and paragraphs						
Uses punctuation and capitalization correctly						
Makes few errors in usage						
SPELLING						
Applies spelling generalizations						
Uses conventional spelling						

Comments:

Key:

N = Not Observed

O = Observed Occasionally

R = Observed Regularly

Harcourt

Thinking About My Reading

Student:_____ Date:_____ Grade:_____

Teacher:_____ School:_____

I think about why I am reading something.	**Always**	**Sometimes**	**Need to work on this**
I think about what I already know about the topic.	**Always**	**Sometimes**	**Need to work on this**
I think about what might happen in the story.	**Always**	**Sometimes**	**Need to work on this**
I picture in my mind what I am reading.	**Always**	**Sometimes**	**Need to work on this**
I ask myself if what I'm reading makes sense.	**Always**	**Sometimes**	**Need to work on this**
I think about what kind of story it might be.	**Always**	**Sometimes**	**Need to work on this**

When I come to an unfamiliar word I might:

☐ Reread to see how the word is used.

☐ Look for meaning clues.

☐ Look for patterns or word parts.

☐ If the word does not seem important to the meaning, skip it and continue reading.

☐ Use a dictionary or ask for help.

I   do/do not   like to read because _____

_____.

I know that a book is too hard or too easy for me when _____

_____.

I am becoming a better reader because _____

_____.

Harcourt

My Reading Log

Student: _____   Date: _____ Grade: _____

Teacher: _____   School: _____

Book Title: _____   Book Author: _____

Total number of pages: _____

Date I started the book: _____   Date I finished the book: _____

I read: (date) _____ (pages) _____   (date) _____ (pages) _____

        (date) _____ (pages) _____   (date) _____ (pages) _____

        (date) _____ (pages) _____   (date) _____ (pages) _____

I am spending   more time/less time   reading because _____

_____.

I chose this book to read because _____

_____.

My favorite part of the book was _____

_____.

This book was   easy/difficult   to read because:

   ☐ I could figure out _____ of the words.   (all, most, some, a few)

   ☐ I   understood/didn't understand   the topic.

   ☐ I   liked/disliked   the author.

   Other: _____

I   would/would not   choose another book like this because _____

_____.

I   would/would not   recommend this book to a friend because _____

_____.

# Individual Reading Inventory

What Is an Individual Reading Inventory?

An Individual Reading Inventory (IRI) is an assessment tool for gaining insights into and knowledge about a student's use of strategies while reading, the student's reading fluency comprehension, and to confirm the student's instructional reading level. An IRI provides qualitative information for tracking a student's individual strengths and weaknesses to help you plan instruction.

An IRI has two primary parts: oral reading passages for conducting a miscue analysis (Running Record) and literal and inferential questions. The student orally reads a passage while the teacher records errors and patterns on a duplicated copy of the passage. After the reading, the student answers comprehension questions. The IRI passage can also be used to gain information about a student's reading fluency by timing the reading and noting the number of correct words read per minute.

For conducting an IRI on a periodic basis, one passage for oral reading has been identified in each theme of instruction in *Pathways to Adventure*. Each passage appears on a form for recording miscues and errors. Another form has been provided for summarizing the information gained.

Administering the IRI

1. Explain the task—the student will read a passage aloud and answer four questions.

2. As the student is reading, unobtrusively record oral miscues on the IRI Recording Form. Use the Marking Oral Reading Miscues chart for recording student errors and self-corrections. As an alternative, tape-record the student reading and record and analyze the student's miscues and self-corrections at a later time.

3. Optional. For a fluency score, use a stopwatch to time words read per minute. Use the IRI Recording Form to mark off the words read in one-minute intervals.

4. After the reading, ask the student the four questions at the bottom of the IRI Recording Form. Mark correct (+) and incorrect (-) responses.

Scoring and Interpreting the IRI

Complete the IRI Recording Form and the IRI Summary Form. Save both forms to track reading growth and for sharing with parents and guardians.

Miscue Analysis (Running Record)

Total the number of miscues and self-corrections and compute the Error Rate. Look for an Error Rate of 10% or less to confirm instructional reading level; 5% or less for independent reading level.

Computing the Error Rate

1. Total the number of miscues.

2. Subtract the total number of self-corrections from the total number of miscues for a subtotal.

3. Divide this subtotal by the word count of the passage.

Analyzing Reading Miscues

1. How many miscues did the student make?

The number of miscues provides an indication of the student's ability to process material at this level of difficulty. *Note*: Do not count self-corrections, dialect variations, hesitations, and repetitions. Self-corrections indicate that the student is monitoring his or her reading and is attempting to construct meaning. Consistent mispronunciation of a word (especially proper nouns) should be counted only once. If the student omits an entire line, count it as one miscue.

2. What type of miscues did the student make?

Look for patterns in the types of miscues that the student makes. Types of miscues are more important than the number. Some miscues represent attempts to maintain or preserve the author's meaning; other miscues represent decoding or word recognition weaknesses. If many of the student's miscues are meaningful and do not alter the author's intended meaning, a higher error rate can be tolerated.

- **If** most miscues are meaning-based, **then** the student knows reading should make sense.

- **If** most miscues are graphics/sound based, **then** the student is not automatically applying decoding skills and requires practice.

3. Does the student self-correct miscues?

Note the number of student self-corrections. Self-correction is an indication that the student is monitoring his or her reading and constructing meaning. However, not all self-corrections are reflective of a concern for meaning. In examining the student's self-corrections, make distinctions between self-corrections for meaning, those that are unnecessary, and those that are focused on decoding or word recognition.

- **If** the student rarely self-corrects, even when miscues disrupt meaning, **then** the student may be focused on decoding, not on meaning.

- **If** the student always self-corrects, even when meaning is not disrupted, **then** the student may think accuracy is more important than meaning.

Reading Fluency

Oral reading fluency combines two factors: rate and accuracy. Count the number of words read correctly in one minute. Count repetitions of correctly read words and self-corrections as correctly read words. Look for a range of 110–130 correctly read words per minute for this grade level.

When judging oral reading fluency, consider qualitative features such as phrasing (Did the student group words as phrases or read them as individual elements?), intonation (Did the student read with expression?), and punctuation (Did the student use punctuation to guide the reading?). Summarize your analysis of oral reading fluency on the IRI Summary Form.

Comprehension

Total the number of correct responses to the questions about the passage on the IRI Recording Form. Look for a score of 75% or higher to confirm instructional reading level. Because questions 1 and 2 are literal questions, and questions 3 and 4 require inferential thinking, use the student's responses to determine whether the student needs instruction and practice with specific types of questions. A score below 75% may also indicate that the student is focusing on decoding at the expense of meaning and needs to recognize that reading should make sense.

Note: See the **Collections** *Placement and Individual Inventory Teacher's Guide* for additional information about an IRI.

MARKING ORAL READING MISCUES		
READING MISCUE	**MARKING**	**SAMPLE**
1. omissions	Circle the word, word part, or phrase omitted.	I will let you ⟨go⟩ in.
2. insertions	Insert a (^), and write in the inserted word or phrase.	We bought a ^big parrot.
3. substitutions	Write the word the student replaces in the text.	Dad fixed ~~my~~ the bike.
4. mispronunciations	Write the phonetic mispronunciation over the word.	Have you ~~fed~~ feed the dog?
5. self-corrections	Write the letters SC next to the miscue that is self-corrected.	We took our ~~spot~~ SC space.
6. repetitions	Draw a line under any part of the text that is repeated.	It is your <u>garden</u> now.
7. punctuation	Circle punctuation missed. Write in any punctuation inserted.	Take them home⊙Then come back, and you and I will go to town.
8. hesitations	Place vertical lines at places where the student hesitates excessively.	Pretend ǀ this is mine.

IRI Recording Form

Student:_____   Date:_____

Selection Title: "Yang the Third and   Page: 72
                 Her Impossible Family"

Passage: Grade 5, Theme 1   Word Count: 104

I had too many things to worry about. Rita kept escaping from the

basement. Having Mother accompany Holly might ruin my friendship

with her. And my family kept disgracing themselves in public.

Once I saw a juggling act in China. A girl balanced three plates

simultaneously by spinning them at the ends of three chopsticks. I felt

like that juggler. At any minute, one of the plates might fall and smash

into bits.

Mrs. Hanson called Tuesday night when we were having dinner. I

answered the phone. "Mary," she said, "do you still think your mother

could play the accompaniment tomorrow for Holly's audition?"

Indicate correct (+) or incorrect (−) response for each question.

1. ☐ **Who is the narrator and main character of this passage?** *(This passage is about a girl named Mary.)*

2. ☐ **What is Mary's problem?** *(Mary is worried.)*

3. ☐ **Why does Mary compare herself to a juggling act?** *(Mary is worried about three things and is reminded of a girl she saw in China juggling three plates on chopsticks.)*

4. ☐ **What does Mrs. Hanson want? Why is it a problem for Mary?** *(Mrs. Hanson wants Mary's mother to play the piano for her daughter's audition. Mary is afraid it will ruin her friendship with Holly.)*

IRI Recording Form

Student:_____   Date:_____

Selection Title: "We'll Never Forget You, Roberto Clemente"   Page: 129

Passage: Grade 5, Theme 2   Word Count: 112

The Pirates were playing the New York Mets. Tom Seaver was pitching. If Seaver could win this game, it would be another twenty-game season for the Met's ace pitcher.

The crowd cheered loudly as Roberto walked up to the plate in the first inning.

One of Seaver's fastballs whizzed over the plate. Roberto swung hard but did not get much wood on the ball. It bounced over Seaver's glove. The second baseman ran in to grab it. The ball bounced off his glove. Roberto pulled up at first base.

Was the play a hit or an error? If the scorekeeper said it was an error, Roberto would not get his 3,000th hit.

Indicate correct (+) or incorrect (−) response for each question.

1. ☐ **What game is Roberto playing? What clues tell you?** *(Roberto is playing baseball because there is a pitcher, innings, plate, base, hit, error, they use gloves. Also, the Pirates and the New York Mets are baseball teams. Answers may vary.)*

2. ☐ **Why is winning this game important to Tom Seaver?** *(Winning this game would mean that Tom Seaver pitched twenty winning games this season.)*

3. ☐ **Do you think Roberto Clemente was a popular player? Why?** *(Yes, he was popular because the crowd cheered loudly when he walked up to the plate.)*

4. ☐ **What does the author mean: Roberto "did not get too much wood on the ball"?** *(It means that he did not hit the ball with the bat very hard or on center.)*

IRI Recording Form

Student:_____   Date:_____

Selection Title: "Earthquake Terror"   Pages: 220–223

Passage: Grade 5, Theme 3   Word Count: 105

Thunder? He looked up. The sky was bright and cloudless. The noise came closer; it was too sharp to be thunder. It was more like several rifles being fired at the same time.

Hunters! he thought. There are hunters in the woods and they heard us move and they've mistaken us for deer or pheasant. Moose must have seen them or heard them or possibly smelled them.

"Don't shoot!" he cried.

As he yelled, Jonathan felt a jolt. He stumbled forward thrusting an arm out to brace himself against a tree. Another loud noise exploded as Jonathan lurched sideways.

He dropped the leash.

Abby screamed.

Indicate correct (+) or incorrect (–) response for each question.

1. ☐ **What is the setting of this passage?** *(The setting is in the woods.)*

2. ☐ **What is the problem?** *(Something is making a loud, sharp noise and is frightening Jonathan and Abby.)*

3. ☐ **Why does Jonathan yell "don't shoot!"?** *(He thinks the noise is coming from hunters who may also be in the woods.)*

4. ☐ **How do you know the noise isn't thunder?** *(Jonathan looked up at the sky and it was bright and cloudless. There wasn't any rain falling and he felt a jolt.)*

Harcourt

IRI Recording Form

Student:_____   Date:_____

Selection Title: "Hattie's Birthday Box"   Page: 311

Passage: Grade 5, Theme 4   Word Count: 101

All the decorations are up, and now that Momma's sure everything is all set, she tells me to stay with Grandaddy and keep him calm while she runs home to get the cake and soda.

But there is no way to keep Grandaddy calm. "What'd you do that was so bad, Grandaddy? What was it?"

I watch Grandaddy wringing his hands and tapping his slippered feet nervously. He keeps glancing out the window to the road outside, like he's waiting for some old lynch mob to come riding over the hills. This is the story I finally got out of him.

Indicate correct (+) or incorrect (–) response for each question.

1. ☐ **How is Grandaddy feeling? How do you know?** *(Grandaddy is nervous. He is wringing his hands, tapping his feet, and glancing out the window.)*

2. ☐ **Why is the narrator alone with Grandaddy?** *(Her mother tells her to stay with Grandaddy to keep him calm.)*

3. ☐ **What do you think everything is set for? How do you know?** *(It is set for a party or celebration because decorations are up and mother went for cake and soda.)*

4. ☐ **What is the narrator's problem?** *(She doesn't know what is making Grandaddy so nervous, and she has to keep him calm.)*

Harcourt

IRI Recording Form

Student:_____   Date:_____

Selection Title: "Dear Mr. Henshaw"   Page: 471

Passage: Grade 5, Theme 5   Word Count: 101

"Who cares?" said Mrs. Badger with a wave of her hand. She's the kind of person who wears rings on her forefingers. "What do you expect? The ability to write stories comes later, when you have lived longer and have more understanding. *A Day on Dad's Rig* was splendid work for a boy your age. You wrote like you, and you did not try to imitate someone else. This is one mark of a good writer. Keep it up."

I noticed a couple of girls who had been saying they wanted to write books exactly like Angela Badger exchange embarrassed looks.

Indicate correct (+) or incorrect (–) response for each question.

1. ☐ **What words let you know Mrs. Badger thought "A Day on Dad's Rig" was good?** *(Mrs. Badger said it was splendid work.)*

2. ☐ **What does Mrs. Badger say is one mark of a good writer?** *(She says the mark of a good writer is to write like oneself, not to imitate another writer.)*

3. ☐ **How do you know Mrs. Badger is a writer?** *(A couple of girls said they wanted to write books exactly like Angela Badger.)*

4. ☐ **Why did the girls exchange embarrassed looks?** *(They heard the author tell the boy that he wrote like himself and did not try to imitate another writer, as they wanted to do.)*

Harcourt

IRI Recording Form

Student:_____   Date:_____

Selection Title: "Black Frontiers"   Page: 576

Passage: Grade 5, Theme 6   Word Count: 116

Farmers in Nicodemus owned only three horses. One man plowed with a milk cow, and others broke ground with shovels and spades. White farmers saw how hard their new neighbors worked and lent the new settlers a team of oxen and a plow. Black farmers planted their first crops and in time they prospered. By the turn of the century there were about eight thousand black homesteaders in Nicodemus and Dunlap.

Some black settlers moved farther west to Nebraska and Oklahoma where they built three new black communities—Taft, Langston, and Boley. George Washington Bush went all the way to Oregon Territory where he introduced the first mower and reaper into the area around Puget Sound.

Indicate correct (+) or incorrect (−) response for each question.

1. ☐ **What is another word for *homesteader*?** (*Accept* farmer *or* settler.)

2. ☐ **How did the white farmers help the new settlers?** (*They saw how hard it was for the black farmers to break the ground, so they lent them a team of oxen and a plow.*)

3. ☐ **Eight hundred homesteaders started Nicodemus and Dunlap. How do you know they prospered?** (*By the turn of the century, there were eight thousand homesteaders in Nicodemus and Dunlap.*)

4. ☐ **What is George Washington Bush known for?** (*George Washington Bush introduced the first mower and reaper to Puget Sound.*)

Harcourt

IRI Summary Form

Student: _____ Grade: _____ Date: _____

Teacher: _____

Passage Administered: _____ Word Count: _____

1. Miscues

Total number of miscues _____

    Meaning-based miscues   _____

    Graphic/sound-based miscues   _____

Comments and patterns observed:_____

_____

Total number of self-corrections   _____

Comments and patterns observed:_____

_____

Error Rate

- Subtract number of self-corrections from total number of miscues for a subtotal.
- Divide the subtotal by the word count of the passage.

$$\underset{\text{(Subtotal)}}{\underline{\hspace{3cm}}} \div \underset{\text{(Word count)}}{\underline{\hspace{3cm}}} = \underset{\text{Error Rate}}{\underline{\hspace{3cm}}}$$

2. Fluency

Number of words read per minute _____

$$\underset{\substack{\text{(Number of}\\\text{correct words}\\\text{read per minute)}}}{\underline{\hspace{3cm}}} \div \underset{\text{(Word count)}}{\underline{\hspace{3cm}}} = \underset{\text{Fluency Rate}}{\underline{\hspace{3cm}}}$$

Comments and patterns observed:_____

_____

3. Comprehension

$$\underset{\text{(Total correct answers)}}{\underline{\hspace{4cm}}} \div 4 \times 100 = \underset{\text{Comprehension score}}{\underline{\hspace{3cm}}} \%$$

Comments and patterns observed:_____

_____

Summary Comments

Videocassette Distributors

The names, addresses, and telephone numbers of videocassette producers or distributors are listed here as a service to teachers using the program.

Agency for Instructional Technology

P.O. Box 1397
1800 N. Stonelake Drive
Bloomington, IN 47404
1-800-457-4509
www.ait.net

Chip Taylor Communications

15 Spollett Drive
Derry, NH 03038
1-800-876-2447
FAX 1-603-432-2723
www.chiptaylor.com

GPN

P.O. Box 80669
Lincoln, NE 68501-0669
1-800-228-4630
FAX 1-800-306-2330
http://gpn.unl.edu

Library Video Company

P.O. Box 580
Wynnewood, PA 19096
1-800-843-3620
www.libraryvideo.com

National Geographic Society

P.O. Box 10579
Des Moines, IA 50340-0579
1-800-368-2728
www.nationalgeographic.com

Phoenix Films & Video

2349 Chaffee Drive
St. Louis, MO 63146
1-800-221-1274
FAX 1-314-569-2834

Society for Visual Education

6677 North Northwest Highway
Chicago, IL 60631-1304
1-800-829-1900
www.svemedia.com

Integrated Technology Components

This page focuses on technology resources that are integrated components of *Collections*. These components, all available from Harcourt, are referenced at appropriate points of use within *Collections* teaching plans to enhance, extend, and enliven instruction.

MISSION: COMPREHENSION™ SKILLS PRACTICE CD-ROM is an interactive software program designed for independent practice in reading comprehension skills for grades 4, 5, and 6. Rex the Robot guides students through lively previews and appealing practice activities. Students apply each skill to passages related to selections in their *Collections* student editions. The software contains a Teacher Management System for scoring and tracking students' or groups' progress. (This software is also available in Spanish.)

INTERNET—*THE LEARNING SITE* features interactive activities, resources, and current-events updates for students, teachers, and parents. **www.harcourtschool.com**

IMAGINATION EXPRESS™, School Version, is a series of six CD-ROM programs that go a marvelous step beyond electronic books, enabling children to be not consumers, but creators of their own multimedia books and reports. The following destinations are cited in various themes: *Castle, Neighborhood, Rain Forest, Ocean,* and *Time Trip, USA.*

Just for Teachers

ASSESSMENT WORKSHOP: SCORING STUDENT WRITING is a software resource that instructs teachers in holistic scoring of children's writing. It is available in *Primary, Intermediate,* and *Middle School* levels.

Traveling on the Internet

There are so many things to see and do on the Internet that new users may wish they had a "tour guide" to help them see the most interesting sites and make sure they don't miss anything. There are many ways to become a savvy Web traveler—one is by learning the language. Here are some common terms.

BOOKMARK A function that lets you return to your favorite Web sites quickly.

BROWSER Application software that allows you to navigate the Internet and view a Web site.

BULLETIN BOARD/NEWSGROUP Places to leave an electronic message or to share news that anyone can read and respond to.

CHAT ROOM A place for people to converse online by typing messages to each other. Once you're in a chat room, others can contact you by e-mail. Some online services monitor their chat rooms and encourage participants to report offensive chatter. Some allow teachers and parents to deny children access to chat rooms altogether.

COOKIE When you visit a site, a notation known as a "cookie" may be fed to a file in your computer. If you revisit the site, the cookie file allows the Web site to identify you as a return guest—and offer you products tailored to your interests or tastes. You can set your online preferences to limit or let you know about cookies that a Web site places on your computer.

CYBERSPACE Another name for the Internet.

DOWNLOAD To move files or software from a remote computer to your computer.

E-MAIL Messages sent to one or more individuals via the Internet.

FILTER Software that lets you block access to Web sites and content that you may find unsuitable.

ISP (Internet Service Provider) A service that allows you to connect to the Internet.

JUNK E-MAIL Unsolicited commercial e-mail; also known as "spam."

KEYWORD A word you enter into a search engine to begin the search for specific information or Web sites.

LINKS Highlighted words on a Web site that allow you to connect to other parts of the same Web site or to other Web sites.

LISTSERV An online mailing list that allows individuals or organizations to send e-mail to groups of people at one time.

MODEM An internal or external device that connects your computer to a phone line that can link you to the Internet.

PASSWORD A personal code that you use to access your Internet account with your ISP.

PRIVACY POLICY A statement on a Web site describing what information about you is collected by the site and how this information is used.

SEARCH ENGINE A function that helps you find information and Web sites. Accessing a search engine is like using the catalog in a library.

URL (Uniform Resource Locator) The address that lets you locate a particular site. For example, **http://www.ed.gov** is the URL for the U.S. Department of Education. All government URLs end in **.gov**. Nonprofit organizations and trade associations end in **.org**. Commercial companies now end in **.com**, and non-commercial educational sites end in **.edu**. Countries other than the United States use different endings.

VIRUS A file maliciously planted in your computer that can damage files and disrupt your system. Antivirus software is available.

WEB SITE An Internet destination where you can look at and retrieve data. All the Web sites in the world, linked together, make up the World Wide Web or the "Web."

Visit *The Learning Site!*
www.harcourtschool.com

Harcourt

My Rules for Internet Safety

I agree that

- **I will never give out private information,** such as my last name, my address, my telephone number, or my parents' work addresses or telephone numbers on the Internet.

- **I will never give out the address or telephone number** of my school on the Internet without first asking an adult's permission.

- **I understand which sites I can visit** and which ones are off-limits.

- **I will tell an adult right away** if something comes up on the screen that makes me feel uncomfortable.

- **I will never agree to meet in person** with anyone I meet online.

- **I will never e-mail a person any pictures** of myself or my classmates without an adult's permission.

- **I will tell an adult** if I get an inappropriate e-mail message from anyone.

- **I will remember that going online** on the Internet is like going out in public, so all the safety rules I already know apply here as well.

- **I know the Internet is a useful tool,** and I will always use it responsibly.

- **I will follow these same rules when I am at home,** in school, at the library, or at a friend's.

X _____   _____
    (Student signs here)   (Parent/Guardian signs here)

Visit *The Learning Site!*
www.harcourtschool.com

Harcourt

▶ Use Prior Knowledge

Your own knowledge and experience can often help you better understand what you read. When you think about what you already know and relate it to what you read, you are using prior knowledge. This strategy can be helpful for reading both stories and informational books.

Ask yourself questions like these when you read.

- ■ Do I know anyone who is like this character?

- ■ Have I ever been to a place like this? What was it like?

- ■ Have I ever done anything like this? How did it make me feel?

- ■ What do I know about this topic? How does the information here support or add to what I already know?

- ■ What purpose does an author usually have for writing this kind of book?

▶ Make and Confirm Predictions

As you read a story, do you think about what might happen next? When you do this, you are making predictions. When you read on to see whether your predictions are correct, you are confirming predictions.

Making and confirming predictions will help you better understand and enjoy what you read. These suggestions will help you use this strategy.

- ■ Before reading, think about the title and look at the illustrations. What do you think the story will be about?
- ■ Read the first few paragraphs. Who do you think the main character or characters will be? What problem might the character(s) face?
- ■ Continue reading the first section or chapter. Are your predictions confirmed? If not, you may not have had all the information you needed.
- ■ Think about what you just read. Have you learned anything else about the story problem? What else do you know about the character(s)? Use what you have learned to make new predictions.
- ■ Read to see whether your predictions are correct. Then make new predictions based on the new information.

Harcourt

▶ Adjust Reading Rate

Have you noticed that you are able to read some things more quickly than others? For example, you can probably read a comic strip much faster than you can read your science textbook.

Think about the type of selection you are reading and your purpose for reading it. This will help you decide whether you can read quickly or whether you should read more slowly.

- Textbooks and other materials that include many facts and details should be read slowly. This is especially true if you are reading to learn or find information.

- Things that have small amounts of text like lists, menus, and signs can usually be read quickly.

- Stories with informal, chatty language can be read more quickly than those with formal language.

- Sometimes different reading speeds are appropriate for the same text. For example, you can quickly scan a source such as an encyclopedia or a newspaper until you find the information you are looking for. Then read more slowly the section that includes that information.

▶ Self-Question

Get in the habit of asking yourself questions as you read. This strategy helps you check your understanding of the selection. It also helps you focus on important ideas.

These are examples of the kinds of questions you can ask yourself as you read.

- Why did the character(s) do or say that? Does this make sense, based on what I know about the character(s) so far?

- How would I feel if I had been in a situation like this one?

- Why did the author include this information here?

- How does this information compare with what I already know about this topic?

▶ Create Mental Images

As you read, picture in your mind what is happening or being described. Creating pictures in your mind of characters and events makes them more real.

Paying attention to the author's descriptive details will help you

- picture what characters look like and how they act. Noting details such as a character's hair and eye color, height, clothing, and facial expressions can help you better "see" the character.

- picture the setting of a story. It will also help you picture the objects or other items that are described. Look for color words and adjectives that describe them. Is the house a dull gray? A bright green? These details will help you picture the setting and the objects in a story.

- understand the action in the story. Look for words that describe actions. For example, an author's description of the wobbly and awkward movements of a newborn calf will help you picture the animal taking its first steps.

▶ Use Context to Confirm Meaning

As you read, you may come across an unfamiliar word. When this happens, you can often use the words and sentences around the word to help you figure it out.

When you see an unfamiliar word, try to guess what the word might be. Then ask yourself whether it makes sense in the sentence and with what is happening in the selection.

These are some of the kinds of context clues you may see as you read.

- A **synonym** is a word that has the same meaning as another word. An **antonym** is a word that has the opposite meaning of another word. You may find a synonym or an antonym for an unfamiliar word in the text around it.

- Sometimes authors provide **definitions** in the text for words they think readers may be unfamiliar with.

- An **explanation** is a group of words that explains the meaning of another word. A **description** is a group of words that describes the meaning of another word. Explanations or descriptions may follow an unfamiliar word.

▶ Use Text Structure and Format

Authors organize their writing in some logical way. As you read, think about how the text is organized. Knowing how a selection is organized will help you locate and recall information. Here are some ways text can be organized and some words that can signal the organization:

- description or example
- general to specific
- main idea and supporting details
- time order (signal words: *first, next, then, before, finally*)
- cause-effect (signal words: *so, so that, because, as a result, since*)
- compare and contrast (signal words: *same as, different from, alike, unlike*)
- problem and solution (signal words: *the problem is, the problem is solved by*)

Pay attention to the format, or text features, of a selection as well. Informational articles, such as those in your textbooks, often use text features to help readers better understand the information. When you read, look for these text features:

- headings and subheadings
- captions
- text that is set off, for example, in margins
- graphic aids/pictures/illustrations

- boldface or italic type
- color highlighting
- numbering
- symbols

▶ Use Graphic Aids

Some selections provide graphic aids that show important information. Graphic aids include pictures, graphs, charts, diagrams, maps, and time lines. These can all make information easier to understand than text can. For example, showing how big one thing is compared with another or where one location is in relation to another can be shown more clearly by an image than in a written description.

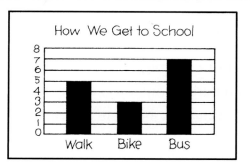

Keep the following tips in mind as you read selections that include graphic aids.

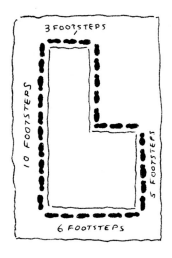

- Read all the captions. They usually describe what is being shown or explain how the image relates to the text.
- Be sure to look carefully at features such as distance scales and legends on maps.
- Ask yourself how the graphic aid is related to the text. Does it help you "see" an idea that is described in the selection? Does it add to information given in the text?
- If you don't understand something in the graphic aid, look back at the text. Information in the text will often explain what is shown in the image.

Harcourt

▶ Use Reference Sources

As you read, you may find unfamiliar words or ideas. First, read the surrounding text to see whether it explains what these unfamiliar words or ideas mean. If you cannot find the information in the selection, you may need to look in a reference source.

Here are some common reference sources that may help you find the information you are looking for.

- Dictionary/glossary/thesaurus: Use these sources to find the meanings and pronunciations of unfamiliar words.
- Encyclopedia: Use this source to find information on a topic.
- Almanac: Use this source to find information about the weather, sun, moon, and many other topics.

- Informational books: Use these sources to find more information on a topic.
- Atlas: Use this source to find maps of a place or region. Many atlases also include diagrams that show information about regions, such as their population, climate, and natural resources.

▶ Read Ahead

If something you read doesn't make sense, keep reading. The meaning may become clearer when you have more information. For example, the selection may include an explanation or more details about a topic. Or the reason a character said or did something may become clear once the plot is further developed.

Sometimes authors will not give you all the information you need right away. This helps to create suspense. For example, authors of mystery stories often hold back some information until later in the story. That way, you know how the characters feel as they try to figure out what is happening.

Harcourt

If something you are reading doesn't make sense, you may have missed an important point made earlier in the selection. Look back to parts of the selection you have already read. Reread these sections to see if you can find information that will help you.

It is usually not necessary to reread everything you have already read. Begin by skimming through the earlier parts. Look for information that relates to the part that confuses you. When you find the information, reread it carefully. It should help you make sense of what is puzzling you.

► **Summarize and Paraphrase**

STRATEGY BUILDER

As you read, it is helpful to pause from time to time and summarize or paraphrase what you have read so far. Think about the main points of the article or the events that have happened so far in the story. This strategy will help you understand and remember what you read.

Remember that a summary does not include all the details, just the important points or main events. When you paraphrase, you restate in your own words what you have read. Being able to summarize and paraphrase what you have read so far will help you make sense of the rest of the selection. It will help you connect new information to what you have read.

Harcourt

Program Reviewers

Arlene Adams
Teacher
Lewisville, Texas

Susan L. Artwohl
Teacher
Chicago, Illinois

Kelli Atkinson
Teacher
Webster, Texas

Sandy Bialick
Early Childhood Teacher
Somerset, New Jersey

Sara A. Bishop
Teacher
Rowlett, Texas

Tamera Bostic
Teacher
Houston, Texas

Kay Briski
Curriculum and Staff Development
Coordinator/Communication Arts
Janesville, Wisconsin

Felice Bryant
Teacher
Katy, Texas

Kris Calderon-Hamby
Teacher
Houston, Texas

Caroline P. Carnell
Teacher
Dothan, Alabama

Katherine Dianne Crowley
Teacher
Lubbock, Texas

Barbara Cummings
Teacher
Arlington, Texas

Cathie J. DeVito
Teacher
Fairmont, West Virginia

Toni Dillon
Teacher
Chicago, Illinois

Reah Force
Reading Specialist
Philadelphia, Pennsylvania

Lambie Fry
Teacher
Wayne, West Virginia

Barbara A. Galvin
Principal
Walden, New York

Louise Garmise
Reading Specialist
East Northport, New York

Susan Garrett
Teacher
Martinsburg, West Virginia

Mary Ellen Graham
Teacher
Schenectady, New York

Patricia Hadalski
Reading Specialist
Levittown, Pennsylvania

Dr. Shelley Jefferson Hamler
Assistant Superintendent, Princeton
City School District
Cincinnati, Ohio

Mildred Harris
Teacher
Gary, Indiana

Diane Y. Hedderick
Teacher
La Porte, Texas

Karol Hobbs
Teacher
Austin, Texas

Suzanne Holmes
Teacher
Richardson, Texas

Janne Hurrelbrink
Curriculum Specialist
Warren, Ohio

Dr. Annmarie B. Jay
K-12 Language Arts/Title 1
Coordinator
Folsom, Pennsylvania

Debbie O'Dell Johnson
Teacher
Fairmont, West Virginia

Kathleen E. Judge
Teacher
Rockaway Beach, New York

Anne Ruth Kaufman
Teacher
Brooklyn, New York

Mary Beth Kreml
Teacher
Spring, Texas

Vilma Laurel
Reading Resource Teacher
Pharr, Texas

Linda R. Mapes
Media Specialist
Chesterton, Indiana

Delores Marshall
Teacher
Houston, Texas

Frances Mary Martinez
Bilingual Teacher
El Paso, Texas

Betty McDowell
Teacher
Mesquite, Texas

Joanne K. Monroe
Language Arts/Social Studies
Supervisor
Flemington, New Jersey

Ada M. Newton
Teacher
Las Vegas, Nevada

Yukie Oishi
Teacher
Sierra Vista, Arizona

Kathleen A. Opihory
Basic Needs Teacher
Palisades Park, New Jersey

Shirley Ann Outlaw
Teacher
Evansville, Indiana

Deborah Ann Petruzzelli
Teacher
Tarrytown, New York

Sandra Pfeil
Teacher
Victoria, Texas

Vickie E. Roe
Teacher
Garland, Texas
Irving, Texas

Evelyn M. Rubel
Teacher
Salem, Oregon

Michele Salon
Early Childhood Reading Lab Teacher
Bronx, New York

Agnes Shtogren
Teacher
Sierra Vista, Arizona

Judith D. Smith
Teacher
Niels, Illinois

Mary Lou South
Teacher
Irving, Texas

Edmund Stevens
Teacher
Hillsboro, Oregon

Patricia A. Thompson
Reading Supervisor
Camden, New Jersey

Carol L. Todd
Library Media Specialist
Glassboro, New York

Bibs Toney
Teacher
Plano, Texas

Winsome Waite
Instructional Specialist
La Plata, Maryland

Kathryn A. Waltz
Teacher
Scranton, Pennsylvania

Marie Willis
Teacher
Kuna, Idaho

KINDERGARTEN REVIEWERS

Michele Beckley
Teacher
Cielo Vista Elementary School
El Paso, Texas

Iris Brown
Teacher
Steelton-Highspire Elementary School
Steelton, Pennsylvania

Marcia Figueroa-Stewart
Teacher
John R. Davis School
Phoenix, Arizona

Laura McCarthy
Teacher
Country Isles Elementary
Weston, Florida

Cathy Taylor
Teacher
Ardmore Elementary School
Ardmore, Alabama

Gloria Valdez
Teacher
Glenwood Elementary School
Amarillo, Texas

Julianna Wynn
Teacher
J. L. Everhart Primary School
Longview, Texas

STUDENTS

Brittney
North Hartford Middle School
Street, Maryland

Caleb
Irwin Elementary
Fort Wayne, Indiana

Candace
Eastwood Hills Elementary
Kansas City, Missouri

Chad
Maedgen Elementary
Lubbock, Texas

Cristina
Collins Intermediate School
The Woodlands, Texas

David
Dr. Eugene Skinner Magnet Center
Omaha, Nebraska

Jeanelle
Aikman Elementary
Hereford, Texas

Jill
Forest Lakes Elementary
Bel Air, Maryland

Julian
Franklin Elementary
East Chicago, Indiana

Megan
Mountainside Middle School
Scottsdale, Arizona

Micara
Gregory Middle School
Naperville, Illinois

Michelle
George Schneider Public School
Chicago, Illinois

Nicholas
Dickey Ave. Elementary
Warren, Ohio

Patricia
Sally K. Ride Elementary
The Woodlands, Texas

Randy
Alpha Elementary
Omaha, Nebraska

Robby
Mountain Shadows Elementary
Magna, Utah

Samantha
Mill Valley Elementary
Marysville, Ohio

Scope and Sequence

	GR K	GR 1	GR 2	GR 3	GR 4	GR 5	GR 6
Thinking							
Observing	░	░	░	░	░	░	░
Brainstorming	░	░	░	░	░	░	░
Classifying and Categorizing	░	░	░	░	░	░	░
Comparing and Contrasting	░	░	░	░	░	░	░
Evaluating/Making Judgments	░	░	░	░	░	░	░
Imaging	░	░	░	░	░	░	░
Making Inferences	░	░	░	░	░	░	░
Making Predictions	░	░	░	░	░	░	░
Problem Solving	░	░	░	░	░	░	░
Questioning	░	░	░	░	░	░	░
Analyzing		░	░	░	░	░	░
Synthesizing		░	░	░	░	░	░
Print Awareness							
Alphabet Knowledge							
Distinguish among numerals, symbols, and letters	░	░					
Recognize, name, match, produce all uppercase and lowercase letters	░ ●	░ ●					
Know the order of the alphabet	░	░ ●					
Alphabetic Principle/Word Awareness							
Recognize that print represents spoken language and conveys meaning	░	░					
Understand that spoken words are represented in written language by specific sequences of letters	░	░					
Recognize own name, others' names, environmental print	░	░					
Know left–to–right and top–to–bottom directionality	░	░					
Know print concepts such as letters, words, sentences, questions, paragraphs, capitalization, punctuation marks; Track print	░	░					
Phonological Awareness							
Segment spoken sentences into individual words	░	░					
Identify and produce rhyming words (onset—rime knowledge)	░ ●	░					
Demonstrate understanding that spoken words consist of a sequence of phonemes	░ ●	░					
Identify and isolate the initial and final sounds of a spoken word	░ ●	░ ●					
Blend sounds (phonemes) to make spoken words	░ ●	░					
Identify, segment, blend phonemes and syllables within and to make spoken words	░	░					
Decoding							
Phonics							
Initial, Medial, Final Consonants	░ ●	░ ●	░				
Phonograms, Letter Patterns, Word Patterns		░	░				
Short Vowels, Long Vowels		░ ●	░				
Consonant Blends, Consonant Digraphs		░ ●	░				
R-Controlled Vowels		░	░ ●				
Vowel Diphthongs, Vowel Digraphs, Variant Vowels		░ ●	░ ●				
Spelling Patterns, Syllable Patterns, Schwa		░	░				
Structural Analysis							
Inflected Nouns and Verbs (With and Without Spelling Changes)		░ ●	░				
Possessives, Comparatives, Superlatives		░	░				

Shaded Area Explicit Instruction/Modeling/Application • Tested
Testing options include Skills Assessment, Holistic Reading Assessment, Reading and Writing Performance Assessment.

	GR K	GR 1	GR 2	GR 3	GR 4	GR 5	GR 6
Contractions		•					
Compound Words							
Syllables, Syllabication							
Prefixes, Suffixes, Derivations			•	•	•	•	•
Greek and Latin Roots							•
Word Identification							
Graphophonic Cues (Phonic Analysis), Context Cues, Semantic Cues, Syntactic Cues, Combination of Cueing Systems							
Analogy/Rhyming Words							
Letter, Spelling, Syllable Patterns							
Syllabication: Accent, Stress							
Picture Cues							
Word Origins/Etymology							
Related Words							
Vocabulary							
High-Frequency Words		•					
Selection Vocabulary		•	•	•	•	•	•
Specialized Vocabulary: Content—Area Words, British Words, Spanish Words, Native American Words, Topic—Related Words, Current Events Words							
Synonyms/Antonyms			•	•			
Multiple–Meaning Words				•	•	•	•
Homophones/Homographs							
Context Clues			•	•	•	•	•
Connotation/Denotation							
Glossary/Dictionary (for Word Meaning)							
Word or Phrase Origins (Acronyms, Brand names, Clipped and Coined Words, Regionalisms, Etymology, Jargon and Slang)							
Analogies							
Comprehension							
Author's Purpose					•	•	•
Author's Perspective					•	•	•
Cause–Effect			•	•	•	•	•
Classify–Categorize							
Compare–Contrast					•	•	•
Details: Descriptive, Important, Supporting		•	•	•	•	•	•
Draw Conclusions					•	•	•
Fact–Opinion				•	•	•	•
Generalize							•
Main Idea		•	•	•	•	•	•
Paraphrase					•	•	•
Predict Outcomes		•	•	•	•	•	•
Problem Solve							
Reality—Fantasy, Fact—Fiction			•				
Referents							
Relate Pictures to Text							
Sequence		•	•	•	•	•	•
Summarize			•	•	•	•	•
Strategic-Metacognitive Reading							
Adjust Reading Rate							
Make and Confirm Predictions							
Create Mental Images							
Preview							

Shaded Area Explicit Instruction/Modeling/Application • Tested

Testing options include Skills Assessment, Holistic Reading Assessment, Reading and Writing Performance Assessment.

	GR K	GR 1	GR 2	GR 3	GR 4	GR 5	GR 6
Apply Prior Knowledge							
Set/Adjust Purpose							
Reread or Read Ahead							
Self–Questioning							
Summarize/Paraphrase							
Use Cueing Systems							
Use Graphic Aids							
Use Text Structure and Format							

Reading Fluency

	GR K	GR 1	GR 2	GR 3	GR 4	GR 5	GR 6
Read regularly in independent-level and instructional-level materials							
Read aloud with accuracy, expression, appropriate phrasing, attention to punctuation, comprehension							
Adjust reading rate based on purpose for reading and type of text							
Read and listen to a variety of texts to accomplish assigned and self-selected purposes							
Self-select reading materials for individual needs based on purpose; interest; knowledge of authors, illustrators; level of difficulty							

Literary Concepts

Literary Elements

	GR K	GR 1	GR 2	GR 3	GR 4	GR 5	GR 6
Narrative Text							
Plot (Problem—Solution, Internal/External Conflict, Conflict—Resolution, Flashback, Foreshadowing)				•	•	•	•
Setting			•	•	•	•	•
Character (Major–Minor, Traits, Feeling, Attitudes, Goals, Motives, Relationships)			•	•	•	•	•
Theme							
Mood/Tone (Humor, Suspense, Irony)							
Point of View							
Narration							
Dialogue							
Expository Text							
Structure and Organization (Description, Collection/List, General—Specific, Main Idea—Supporting Details, Compare—Contrast, Sequence)							
Text Adjuncts (Graphic Aids, Illustrations, Headings and Subheadings)							

Literary Forms

	GR K	GR 1	GR 2	GR 3	GR 4	GR 5	GR 6
Fiction: Realistic Fiction, Fantasy, Story, Riddle, Informational Story, Historical Fiction, Science Fiction, Story, Short Story, Mystery, Informational Narrative, Novel, Chapter Book							
Nonfiction: Magazine Article, How-to Article, Biography, Personal Narrative, News Story, Feature Story, Photo Essay, Letter, Autobiography, Journal/Diary, Essay, Interview, Speech, Personal Narrative, Letter, Editorial, Newspaper Article, Manual, Textbook							
Traditional: Folktale, Fairy Tale, Fable, Tall Tale, Porquoi Tale, Nursery Rhyme, Myth, Legend							
Poetry and Verse: Haiku, Concrete, Limerick, Song, Couplet, Tongue Twister, Lyric, Free Verse, Narrative, Stanza, Couplet, Ballad							
Drama: Radio/Stage/TV/Play							
Functional: Recipe, Menu, Poster, Directions, Calendar, Schedule, Sign, Chart, List, Forms, Application, Electronic Print							

Literary Devices/Author's Craft

	GR K	GR 1	GR 2	GR 3	GR 4	GR 5	GR 6
Character Development, Characterization (Author's Description, Character's Actions or Words, Other Characters' Actions or Words)					•	•	•
Figurative Language (Hyperbole, Metaphor, Simile, Personification, Puns, Euphemisms, Adages and Proverbs, Regionalisms)							

Shaded Area Explicit Instruction/Modeling/Application • Tested

Testing options include Skills Assessment, Holistic Reading Assessment, Reading and Writing Performance Assessment.

	GR K	GR 1	GR 2	GR 3	GR 4	GR 5	GR 6
Imagery							
Informal Language (Idiom, Slang, Jargon, Dialect)							
Narration							
Pattern and Repetition							
Sound Devices (Rhythm, Rhyme, Alliteration, Onomatopoeia)							
Dialogue							
Point of View (First-Person, Third-Person, Omniscient)							
Irony and Satire							

Literary Response

Connect, Compare, Contrast

	GR K	GR 1	GR 2	GR 3	GR 4	GR 5	GR 6
Characters, ideas, themes, purposes, style, organization, topics, treatment (in fiction and nonfiction)							
Text content with one's own experiences; across cultures, customs, regions							
Print with electronic versions, performance with electronic version, story variants							
Respond: In discussions, writing, art projects, journal writing; using available technology; through movement, music, dramatizations, demonstrations, projects, choral reading							

Research/Study Skills

Study Skills and Strategies

	GR K	GR 1	GR 2	GR 3	GR 4	GR 5	GR 6
Use study strategies to learn and recall important ideas from text (KWL, SQ3R, Note Taking, Reading Rate, Skim/Scan, Outline)							
Follow and give directions							

Research/Inquiry

	GR K	GR 1	GR 2	GR 3	GR 4	GR 5	GR 6
Find, identify, revise questions for inquiry							
Use pictures, print, people, media, multiple sources, alphabetical order to gather information and answer questions							
Library, Media Center, Card Catalog, Electronic Databases, Electronic Search Engines, Media							
Almanac, Atlas, Dictionary, Electronic Text, Encyclopedia, Globe, Telephone Directory, Thesaurus, Synonym Finder, *Books in Print*			•	•	•	•	•
Maps, Charts, Graphs, Diagrams, Time Lines, Tables, Schedules, Calendars			•	•	•	•	•
Book Parts and Text Organizers (Title Page, Table of Contents, Indices, Chapter Titles, Headings, Graphic Features, Guide Words, Entry Words, Bibliography, Glossary, Footnotes, Marginal Notes)			•	•	•	•	•
Summarize and organize information to present findings							
Outline, Map, Web, Cluster, Venn Diagram, Chart, Table, Time Line							
Displays, Murals, Dramatizations, Oral Reports, Written Reports, Projects, Posters, Speeches							

Cultural Awareness

	GR K	GR 1	GR 2	GR 3	GR 4	GR 5	GR 6
Connect information and events in texts to life and life to text experiences							
Connect experiences, information, and ideas with those of others							
Identify and compare language and oral traditions that reflect customs, regions, and cultures							
View concepts and issues from diverse perspectives							
Recognize the universality of literary themes across cultures and languages							

Listening and Speaking

	GR K	GR 1	GR 2	GR 3	GR 4	GR 5	GR 6
Listen for a purpose (respond to a variety of literature and texts, enjoyment, information, vocabulary development, directions, problem-solve, speaker's intent or message, specific details, main idea, answer questions, recognize persuasion techniques/bias, respond to questions, recall information)							

Shaded Area   Explicit Instruction/Modeling/Application • Tested
Testing options include Skills Assessment, Holistic Reading Assessment, Reading and Writing Performance Assessment.

	GR K	GR 1	GR 2	GR 3	GR 4	GR 5	GR 6
Identify rhyme, repetition, patterns, musical elements of language	■	■	■	■	■	■	■
Participate in conversations, discussions, small groups, cooperative groups	■	■	■	■	■	■	■
Listen critically to interpret and evaluate	■	■	■	■	■	■	■
Ask for repetition, restatement, or explanation to clarify meaning	■	■	■	■	■	■	■
Participate in reading or creating rhymes, patterned stories, shared reading, songs, storytelling, discussions, conversations, choral reading	■	■	■	■	■	■	■
Discuss and compare/contrast a variety of texts	■	■	■	■	■	■	■
Reenact, retell, dramatize, role-play literature read or heard	■	■	■	■	■	■	■
Communicate experiences, ideas, opinions with others; clarify or support ideas with evidence	■	■	■	■	■	■	■
Adapt spoken vocabulary to the purpose, audience, and occasion; to describe, inform, communicate, persuade	■	■	■	■	■	■	■
Read or retell stories orally with expression, phrasing, intonation, comprehension	■	■	■	■	■	■	■
Present oral reports or speeches, conduct interviews or surveys		■	■	■	■	■	■

Viewing

	GR K	GR 1	GR 2	GR 3	GR 4	GR 5	GR 6
Enjoy and discuss a variety of illustrations and illustrators	■	■	■	■	■	■	■
Analyze the purposes and effects of illustrations, visuals, media	■	■	■	■	■	■	■
Discuss illustrators' choices of techniques and media		■	■	■	■	■	■
Analyze the way visual images, graphics, and media represent, contribute to, and support meaning	■	■	■	■	■	■	■
Interpret information from maps, charts, tables, diagrams, graphs, time lines, media, illustrations	■	■	■	■	■	■	■
Select, organize, produce visuals to complement and extend meaning		■	■	■	■	■	■
Use available technology or appropriate media to communicate information and ideas; to compare ideas, information, viewpoints	■	■	■	■	■	■	■
Compare and contrast print and electronic media					■	■	■

Writing

Composition

	GR K	GR 1	GR 2	GR 3	GR 4	GR 5	GR 6
Writing Process (Prewriting, Drafting, Revising, Proofreading, Publishing)	■	■	■	■	■	■	■
Select and use reference materials and models for writing, revising, and editing	■	■	■	■	■	■	■
Use technology to create, revise, edit, and publish texts		■	■	■	■	■	■

Writer's Craft

	GR K	GR 1	GR 2	GR 3	GR 4	GR 5	GR 6
Capture Reader's Interest	■	■	■	■	■	■	■
Identify Audience and Purpose	■	■	■	■	■	■	■
Use Appropriate Language		■	■	■	■	■	■

Writing Approaches

	GR K	GR 1	GR 2	GR 3	GR 4	GR 5	GR 6
Collaborative Writing		■	■	■	■	■	■
Shared Writing	■						
Timed Writing		■	■	■	■	■	■
Writing to Prompts		■	■	■	■	■	■
Responding to Essay Questions			■	■	■	■	■

Forms of Writing

	GR K	GR 1	GR 2	GR 3	GR 4	GR 5	GR 6
Expository Writing (Compare/Contrast, Explanation, Directions, Speech, How-to Article, Friendly/Business Letters, News Story, Essay, Report)		■	■	■	■	■	■
Narrative Writing (Stories, Paragraphs, Personal Narrative, Personal Journal, Play, Poetry)	■	■	■	■	■	■	■
Descriptive Writing (Titles, Captions, Ads, Posters, Paragraphs, Stories, Poetry)	■	■	■	■	■	■	■
Persuasive Writing (Paragraphs, Essay, Letter)	■	■	■	■	■	■	■
Cross-Curricular Writing (Paragraph, Report)		■	■	■	■	■	■
Everyday Writing (Journals, Messages, Forms, Note-Taking, Summaries, Labels, Captions)	■	■	■	■	■	■	■

Shaded Area Explicit Instruction/Modeling/Application • Tested

Testing options include Skills Assessment, Holistic Reading Assessment, Reading and Writing Performance Assessment.

	GR K	GR 1	GR 2	GR 3	GR 4	GR 5	GR 6
Revision Skills							
Correct Sentence Fragments/Run-ons							
Combine Sentences							
Add/Delete/Rearrange Information							
Choose Words Effectively (Exact/Precise Words, Vivid Words, Trite/Overused Words, Clichés)							
Elaborate (Details, Examples, Dialogue, Quotations)							
Unity and Coherence							
Vary Sentence Structure, Word Order, and Sentence Length							
Grammar							
Sentences							
Types (Declarative, Interrogative, Exclamatory, Imperative)		•					
Structure (Simple, Compound, Complex)							
Parts (Subjects/Predicates: Complete, Simple, Compound; Clauses: Independent, Subordinate; Phrases)		•					
Complements (Direct/Indirect Objects; Predicate Nominative/Adjectives)							
Word Order		•					
Nouns (Singular, Plural, Common, Proper, Possessive, Collective, Abstract, Concrete, Abbreviations)		•					
Verbs (Action, Helping, Linking, Transitive, Intransitive, Regular, Irregular)		•					
Verb Tenses (Present, Past, Future; Present, Past, and Future Perfect); Participles; Infinitives							
Adjectives (Common, Proper; Articles; Comparison)		•					
Adverbs (Place, Time, Manner, Degree)							
Pronouns (Subject, Object, Possessive, Reflexive, Demonstrative)		•					
Prepositions; Prepositional Phrases							
Conjunctions							
Usage and Mechanics							
Nouns (Abbreviations, Plural Forms, Appositives)							
Verbs (Subject—Verb Agreement)							
Adjectives (Articles; Positive, Comparative, Superlative)							
Adverbs (Positive, Comparative, Superlative)							
Pronouns (Antecedents; Subject, Object, Possessive, and Reflexive Forms)		•					
Troublesome Words							
Capitalization (Sentence, Pronoun I, Proper Nouns and Adjectives, Titles, Direct Quotations and Dialogue, Greetings and Closings of Letters)		•					
Punctuation (Indention, Period, Question Mark, Exclamation Point, Comma, Underlining, Apostrophe, Quotation Marks, Colon, Hyphen, Semicolon, Parentheses, Dash)		•					
Handwriting							
Letter Forms (Manuscript, Cursive)							
Elements; Common Errors							
Spelling							
Sound-Letter Relationships (Consonants, Vowels, Schwa, Double Letters, Stress, and Accents)							
Word Structure (Plural Nouns/Inflected Verbs and Adjective With and Without Spelling Changes, Prefixes, Suffixes, Greek and Latin Roots, Abbreviations, Contractions, Possessives, Compound Words)							
Word Analysis (Syllable/Letter Patterns, Pronunciation and Stress, Phonograms, Rhyming Words, Related Words, Word Origins)							
Study Methods and Strategies (Rhyming Words, Pronunciation, Word Shapes, Placeholders, Dictionary, Related Words, Mnemonic Devices, Proofreading)							
Apply Spelling Generalizations and Spelling Strategies							

Shaded Area   Explicit Instruction/Modeling/Application • Tested

Testing options include Skills Assessment, Holistic Reading Assessment, Reading and Writing Performance Assessment.

Index

Index

T1063, T1113, T1151, T1217,
T1265, T1303, T1347, T1393
student self- and peer assessment
My Reading Log: T1416, A26
reading development: T232
rubrics for writing: A8–A13
Thinking About My Reading: A25
writing: T51, T95, T135, T179,
T219, T285, T327, T365, T403,
T445, T517, T561, T601, T643,
T691, T708, T751, T795, T833,
T877, T923, T1161, T1176,
T1357, T1403, T1416
See also **Portfolio Opportunities.**
performance assessment: T43, T87,
T91, T127, T171, T175, T211, T215,
T277, T319, T323, T395, T399,
T435, T439, T441, T509, T551,
T555, T557, T593, T633, T637,
T639, T683, T687, T743, T787,
T791, T825, T869, T873, T913,
T917, T919, T936, T975, T999,
T1017, T1063, T1069, T1113,
T1117, T1151, T1155, T1157,
T1217, T1265, T1269, T1303,
T1347, T1351, T1353, T1393,
T1397, T1399, T1416
Portfolio Assessment Teacher's Guide:
T1176
portfolio opportunities: T43, T51, T87,
T95, T127, T135, T171, T179, T211,
T219, T277, T285, T319, T327,
T357, T365, T395, T403, T435,
T445, T509, T517, T551, T561,
T593, T601, T633, T643, T683,
T691, T743, T751, T787, T795,
T825, T833, T869, T877, T913,
T923, T975, T983, T1017, T1025,
T1063, T1073, T1113, T1121,
T1151, T1161, T1217, T1225,
T1265, T1273, T1303, T1311,
T1347, T1357, T1393, T1403

Atlas.
See **Reference Sources; Study and
Research Skills, multiple resources.**

At-Risk Students.
See **Intervention Strategies for
Below-Level Readers.**

**Audiences, Communicate with a Variety
of.**
See **Writing, purposes, audiences.**

Audiovisual Materials.
See **Technology, videocassettes.**

Auditory Teaching Modality: R2–R6,
R26–R31, R50–R55, R74–R77,
R98–R103, R122–R128

Author and Illustrator Profiles
about the author: T13, T41, T59, T83,
T103, T125, T143, T165, T187,
T209, T293, T315, T335, T355,
T373, T393, T411, T431, T481,
T507, T525, T545, T569, T591,
T609, T651, T677, T721, T741,
T759, T781, T803, T823, T841,
T864, T885, T909, T949, T973,
T991, T1013, T1033, T1061, T1081,
T1109, T1129, T1147, T1149,
T1189, T1214, T1233, T1260,
T1281, T1301, T1319, T1340
about the illustrator: T253, T865,
T1215, T1365
about the poet: T85, T435, T681, T911,
T1015, T1111

Author's Craft: T74, T78, T264, T384,
T496, T536, T582, T814, T964, T1200
alliteration: T1344
describing words: T76
dialogue: T308, T860
happy times/sad times balance: T204
hints: T1106
humorous details: T1265
images: T540
indirect information: T1006
letters that represent sounds: T854
mood: T1052
similes: T72
unnamed characters: T1200
using a song to help understanding:
T122
using real-life experiences: T1056
word power: T1048
See also **Appreciating the Literature;
Literary Concepts.**

Authors of Program:
Abrahamson, Dr. Richard F.: iv
Ada, Dr. Alma Flor: iv
Beck, Dr. Isabel L.: iii
Cullinan, Dr. Bernice E.: iv
Farr, Dr. Roger C.: iii
McKeown, Dr. Margaret: iv
Roser, Dr. Nancy: iv
Smith, Patricia: iv
Strickland, Dr. Dorothy S.: iii
Wallis, Dr. Judy: iv
Yokota, Dr. Junko: v
Yopp, Dr. Hallie Kay: v

Author's Purpose and Perspective.
See **Comprehension.**

Autobiography:
selections: T812–T823, T1000–T1013
See also **Genre; Literary
Forms/Genre.**

Background and Concepts, Building:
T18, T64, T108, T148, T192, T258,
T298, T340, T378, T416, T486, T530,
T574, T614, T656, T726, T764, T808,
T846, T890, T954, T996, T1038, T1086,
T1134, T1194, T1238, T1286, T1324,
T1370

Base Words.
See **Decoding/Phonics, structural
analysis.**

Below-Level Readers.
See **Intervention Strategies for
Below-Level Readers.**

Benchmarks.
See **Assessment, informal.**

Biography
selections: T262–T275, T894–T909,
T1242–T1261
See also **Genre; Literary
Forms/Genre.**

Blends.
See **Decoding/Phonics.**

Book Parts
acknowledgments page: A7
glossary, using: A2–A5
index, using: A6–A7
maintain: T29
table of contents, using: xviii, xix–xxii
See also **Study and Research Skills,
book parts.**

Books on Tape: T13, T23, T59, T69,
T103, T113, T143, T153, T187, T197,
T253, T263, T293, T303, T335, T345,
T373, T383, T411, T421, T481, T491,
T525, T535, T569, T579, T609, T619,
T651, T661, T721, T731, T759, T769,
T803, T813, T841, T851, T885, T895,
T949, T959, T991, T1001, T1033,
T1043, T1081, T1091, T1129, T1139,
T1189, T1199, T1233, T1243, T1281,
T1291, T1319, T1329, T1365, T1375
See also **Literature Cassettes.**

KEY

✔ = Tested   Blue = Pages in this book

Index

Index

Index

Index

KEY

✔ = Tested   Blue = Pages in this book

Index

Index

Dramatic Interpretations, Present: T42, T44, T88, T212, T320, T358, T436, T510, T634, T701, T744, T788, T914, T976, T1064, T1218, T1338, T1394

✔**Draw Conclusions/Make Generalizations**
 See **Comprehension; Thinking,**
  inferential.

Easy Reader: T13, T17, T59, T63, T103, T107, T143, T147, T187, T191, T253, T257, T293, T297, T335, T339, T373, T377, T411, T415, T481, T485, T525, T529, T569, T573, T609, T613, T651, T655, T721, T725, T759, T763, T803, T807, T841, T845, T885, T889, T949, T953, T991, T995, T1033, T1037, T1081, T1085, T1129, T1133, T1189, T1193, T1233, T1237, T1281, T1285, T1319, T1323, T1365, T1369

Edit: T1120–T1121
 See also **Writing Processes, edit.**
Elements of Nonfiction.
 See **Literary Concepts, nonfiction.**
Encyclopedia.
 See **Study and Research Skills, multi-**
  ple sources.
Encyclopedia article: T866–T867
End Marks.
 See **Mechanics; Grammar, sentences.**
End-of-Year Reading Skills Assessment.
 See **Assessment, Formal.**
Environmental Print.
 See **Real-Life Reading.**
ESL.
 See **Reaching All Learners.**
Etymologies.
 See **Word Origins.**
Evaluation, Checklists for
 listening: A20
 reading: A22
 speaking: A20
 viewing: A20
 writing: A24
Everyday Reading, Reader's Purpose.
 See **Study and Research Skills,**
  reader's purpose.

Exaggeration.
 See **Literary Concepts.**
Examples from Text, Support
 Interpretations or Conclusions with:
 T28, T34, T72, T76, T78, T118, T158, T162, T200, T204, T304, T310, T390, T424, T494, T538, T588, T736, T852, T906, T962, T970, T1004, T1006, T1008, T1050, T1051, T1200, T1210, T1248, T1252, T1256, T1294, T1336, T1382, T1384
Exclamations.
 See **Grammar.**
Expressive Writing.
 See **Writing Forms.**
Extending Skills and Strategies.
 See **Extending Vocabulary;**
  Comprehension;
  Decoding/Phonics; Grammar;
  Spelling; Study and Research Skills;
  Vocabulary; Writing.
Extending Vocabulary
 acronyms: T689
 analogies: T401
 analyzing a word: T1271
 antonyms: T599
 borrowed words: T921
 character trait words: T283
 coined words: T177
 etymology: T49, T1159
 homophones: T1401
 hyphenated adjectives: T325
 idioms: T363
 metaphors: T93
 multiple-meaning words: T793
 ocean life words: T443
 puns: T1023
 related words: T133, T641, T1119
 semantic mapping: T1355
 shipping and commerce words: T1071
 similes: T749
 slang: T831
 Spanish words: T981
 specialized vocabulary: T1223
 synonyms: T217
 verbs that show emotion: T875
 vivid verbs: T559
 words and features: T1309
Extra Support.
 See **Intervention Strategies for**
  Below-Level Readers; Modified
  Instruction; Reaching All Learners.

Fable: T166–T167
✔**Fact and Opinion.**
 See **Comprehension.**
Family Involvement.
 See **School-Home Connection.**
Fiction.
 See **Classic Fiction; Historical Fiction;**
  Realistic Fiction; Genre; Literary
  Forms/Genre.
Fiction from Nonfiction Sources,
 Distinguish.
 See **Comprehension, fiction from**
  nonfiction, distinguish.
Figurative Language: T384, T386, T388
 See also **Literary Concepts, figurative**
  language.
Fix-Up Strategies.
 See **Guided Reading; Strategies Good**
  Readers Use.
Fluency.
 See **Comprehension, fluency.**
Focus Skills
 comprehension
 ✔author's purpose and perspective:
  T1040–T1041, T1044, T1048,
  T1054, T1055, T1066–T1067,
  T1078
 ✔cause and effect: T488–T489, T494,
  T500, T502, T512–T513, T523
 classify/categorize: T1326–T1327,
  T1330, T1334, T1336,
  T1350–T1351
 ✔compare and contrast: T300–T301,
  T306, T311, T312, T322–T323
 ✔draw conclusions/make generaliza-
  tions: T260–T261, T264, T266,
  T268, T269, T280–T281, T290
 ✔fact and opinion: T810–T811, T816,
  T817, T818, T828–T829, T838
 ✔main idea and supporting details:
  T1288–T1289, T1292, T1294,
  T1298, T1306–T1307
 make inferences: T194–T195, T198,
  T200, T205, T206, T214–T215,
  T225
 make judgments: T150–T151, T154,
  T156, T161, T162, T174–T175,
  T185

KEY	
✔ = Tested	Blue = Pages in this book

Index

Index

KEY	
✔ = Tested	Blue = Pages in this book

Index

Index

skill instruction: T90, T174, T214, T280, T322, T360, T398, T438, T596, T638, T686, T746, T828, T978, T1020, T1066, T1068, T1156, T1350, T1396

Irony: T1272

Jargon/Slang: T495, T831, T1071

Judgments, Make
See **Comprehension, make judgments.**

Kinesthetic Teaching Modality: T42–T43, T86–T87, T126–T127, T170–T171, T210–T211, T276–T277, T318–T319, T356–T357, T394–T395, T434–T435, T508–T509, T550–T551, T592–T593, T632–T633, T682–T683, T742–T743, T786–T787, T824–T825, T868–T869, T912–T913, T974–T975, T1016–T1017, T1062–T1063, T1112–T1113, T1150–T1151, T1216–T1217, T1264–T1265, T1302–T1303, T1346–T1347, T1392–T1393, R2–R6, R26–R31, R50–R55, R74–R79, R98–R103, R122–R128

Knowledge, Demonstrate in a Variety of Ways.
See **Inquiry and Research.**

K-W-L Strategy: T262, T534, T578, T606, T812, T1290, T1328

Language Exploration: T45, T89, T129, T173, T213, T279, T321, T359, T397, T437, T511, T553, T595, T635, T685, T745, T789, T827, T871, T915, T977, T1019, T1065, T1115, T1153, T1219, T1267, T1305, T1349, T1395

See also **Intervention Strategies for Below-Level Readers.**

Lesson Planners: T14–T15, T60–T61, T104–T105, T144–T145, T188–T189, T254–T255, T294–T295, T336–T337, T374–T375, T412–T413, T482–T483, T526–T527, T570–T571, T610–T611, T652–T653, T722–T723, T760–T761, T804–T805, T842–T843, T886–T887, T950–T951, T992–T993, T1034–T1035, T1082–T1083, T1130–T1131, T1190–T1191, T1234–T1235, T1282–T1283, T1320–T1321, T1366–T1367

Letters
selection: T152–T165
See also **Genre; Literary Forms/Genre.**

Letters, Writing: T170, T212, T320, T376, T742, T786, T844, T914, T976, T1016, T1064, T1310, T1311

Letter-Sound Correspondences, Using.
See **Decoding/Phonics.**

Library/Media Center.
See **Study and Research Skills.**

Listening.
See **Oral Language Development.**

Listening to Literature Lessons: T6–T9, T246–T249, T474–T477, T714–T717, T942–T945, T1182–T1185

Literacy Skills.
See **Building Literacy Skills.**

Literary Concepts
alliteration: T1331, T1344
author's craft/technique
appreciate language: T78, T264, T496, T536
interpret imagery: T74, T964
interpret mood: T1200
See also **Author's Craft.**
characters' feelings and actions
characters' emotions: T32, T34, T36, T78, T116, T158, T200, T304, T306, T310, T352, T422, T494, T620, T736, T770, T860, T900, T902, T1050, T1092, T1200, T1206, T1210
characters' motivations: T26, T74, T426, T492, T502, T734, T852, T902, T962, T966, T1002, T1010, T1054, T1098, T1100, T1140, T1202, T1204
characters' traits: T116, T154, T198, T350, T388, T422, T494, T504,

T734, T738, T772, T776, T854, T856, T898, T960, T970, T1006, T1044
✔character development: T72, T76
informal assessment: T77
introduce
before reading: T66–T67
after reading: T90–T91
maintain: T307
reteach: R3
review: T115, T203
exaggeration: T737, T1342, T1356
figurative language (hyperbole, metaphor, personification, simile): T70, T384, T386, T388, T1224–T1225, T1246
introduce
before reading: T380–T381
after reading: T398–T399
reteach: R29
review: T855
humor: T767, T1041, T1110, T1342, T1343
See also **Writing Forms.**
illustrator's craft/purpose: T34, T970, T1100, T1378
imagery: T74, T434, T964
irony: T1272
mood/tone: T770, T1094, T1200
informal assessment: T775
introduce
before reading: T766–T767
after reading: T790–T791
reteach: R75
review: T1009
✔narrative elements: plot, character, setting: T308, T732, T734, T736, T1096
informal assessment: T735
introduce
before reading: T728–T729
after reading: T746–T747
maintain: T1051
reteach: R74
review: T771, T853
nonfiction, literary forms: T1240, T1244, T1246
informal assessment: T1257
introduce
before reading: T1240–T1241
after reading: T1268–T1269
reteach: R123
review: T1333
photographer's craft: T352

KEY	
✔ = Tested	Blue = Pages in this book

Index

Index

KEY	
✔ = Tested	Blue = Pages in this book

Index

Index

Index

KEY

✔ = Tested   Blue = Pages in this book

Index

Index

T854, T856, T858, T860, T896,
T898, T900, T902, T904, T906,
T960, T962, T964, T966, T968,
T970, T1002, T1004, T1006, T1008,
T1010, T1044, T1046, T1048,
T1050, T1052, T1054, T1056,
T1058, T1092, T1094, T1096,
T1098, T1100, T1102, T1104,
T1106, T1140, T1142, T1144,
T1200, T1202, T1204, T1206,
T1208, T1210, T1244, T1246,
T1248, T1250, T1252, T1256,
T1292, T1294, T1296, T1298,
T1330, T1332, T1334, T1336,
T1344, T1376, T1378, T1380,
T1382, T1384, T1390

response activities: T42–T43, T86–T87,
T126–T127, T170–T171,
T210–T211, T276–T277,
T318–T319, T356–T357,
T394–T395, T434–T435,
T508–T509, T550–T551,
T592–T593, T632–T633,
T682–T683, T742–T743,
T786–T787, T824–T835,
T868–T869, T912–T913,
T974–T975, T1016–T1017,
T1062–T1063, T1112–T1113,
T1150–T1151, T1216–T1217,
T1264–T1265, T1302–T1303,
T1346–T1347, T1392–T1393

retell and summarize: T41, T83, T125,
T165, T209, T275, T315, T355,
T393, T431, T507, T545, T591,
T629, T677, T741, T781, T823,
T863, T909, T973, T1013, T1061,
T1109, T1147, T1213, T1259,
T1301, T1339, T1387

think about it questions: T40, T82,
T124, T164, T208, T274, T314,
T354, T392, T430, T506, T544,
T590, T628, T676, T740, T780,
T822, T864, T908, T972, T1012,
T1060, T1108, T1146, T1214,
T1260, T1300, T1340, T1386

Selection Comprehension Tests.
See **Assessment, formal.**
Selection Information: T12–T13,
T58–T59, T102–T103, T142–T143,
T186–T187, T252–T253, T292–T293,
T334–T335, T372–T373, T410–T411,
T480–T481, T524–T525, T568–T569,
T608–T609, T650–T651, T720–T721,
T758–T759, T802–T803, T840–T841,

T884–T885, T948–T949, T990–T991,
T1032–T1033, T1080–T1081,
T1128–T1129, T1188–T1189,
T1232–T1233, T1280–T1281,
T1318–T1319, T1364–T1365
See also **Technology, Internet/The
Learning Site, author information.**
Selection Summaries: T13, T59, T103,
T143, T187, T253, T293, T335, T373,
T411, T481, T525, T569, T609, T651,
T721, T759, T803, T841, T885, T949,
T991, T1033, T1081, T1129, T1189,
T1233, T1281, T1319, T1365

Selections in *Student Edition.*
"Across the Wide Dark Sea,"
T1198–T1215
"Black Frontiers," T1290–T1301
"Boonsville Bombers, The,"
T302–T315
"Case of the Shining Blue Planet,
The," T618–T629
"Cowboys of the Wild West,"
T1328–T1341
"Dear Mr. Henshaw," T1042–T1061
"Dear Mrs. Parks," T152–T165
"Earthquake Terror," T490–T507
"Empty Box, The," T768–T781
"Evelyn Cisneros: Prima Ballerina,"
T894–T909
"Frindle," T1138–T1147
"Hattie's Birthday Box," T730–T741
"Hot and Cold Summer, The,"
T22–T41
"Hundred Dresses, The,"
T1090–T1109
"Iditarod Dream," T344–T355
"Island of the Blue Dolphins,"
T420–T431
"Little by Little," T1000–T1013
"Mick Harte Was Here,"
T196–T209
"Name This American,"
T1374–T1387
"Oceans," T578–T591
"Off and Running," T958–T973
"Satchmo's Blues," T850–T865
"Seeing Earth from Space,"
T660–T677
"Sees Behind Trees," T68–T83
"Summer of Fire," T534–T545
"We'll Never Forget You, Roberto
Clemente," T262–T275
"What's the Big Idea, Ben
Franklin?," T1242–T1261

"Woodsong," T382–T393
"World of William Joyce Scrapbook,
The," T812–T823
"Yang the Third and Her Impossible
Family," T112–T125
Self-Question.
See **Strategies Good Readers Use.**
Self-Selected Reading.
See **Trade Books.**
Sentences.
See **Grammar; Writing.**
✔**Sequence.**
See **Comprehension.**
Set Purpose.
See **Prereading Strategies.**
Setting.
See **Literary Concepts, narrative
elements.**
Short Story: T730–T741
Signal Words and Phrases: T284, T326,
T397, T402, T750, T832, T833, T876
Simile: T398–T399, T749
See also **Literary Concepts, figurative
language.**
Skills.
See **Comprehension;
Decoding/Phonics; Literary
Concepts; Skills in Context; Study
and Research Skills; Vocabulary.**
Skills Assessment.
See **Assessment, formal.**
Skills in Context
action verbs and linking verbs: T1007
adjectives and articles: T821
adverbs: T1331
✔author's purpose and perspective:
T1101, T1145, T1249
blends and digraphs: T385
book parts: T29
case of pronouns: T737
✔cause and effect: T537, T581, T779
✔character development: T115, T203,
T307
clauses: T353
common and proper nouns: T427
✔compare and contrast: T347, T389,
T773
comparing with adjectives: T899
comparing with adverbs: T1377
complete and simple predicates: T207
complete and simple subjects: T159
complex sentences: T391
compound subjects and predicates;
conjunctions: T267

KEY

✔ = Tested   Blue = Pages in this book

Index

Index

words with suffixes: *-ant* and *ent*:
T646–T647
words with suffixes: *-eer, -ist, -ian,*
-or, and *-er*: T798–T799
words with suffixes: *-tion* and *-ness*:
T694–T695
spelling strategies: T55, T99, T139,
T183, T223, T289, T331, T369,
T407, T449, T521, T565, T605,
T647, T695, T755, T799, T837,
T881, T927, T987, T1029, T1077,
T1125, T1165, T1229, T1277,
T1315, T1361, T1407
syllable constructions: T289, T407,
T369, T1029
word sorts: T55, T98, T138, T182,
T222, T288, T330, T406, T441,
T520, T564, T604, T646, T694,
T754, T798, T836, T880, T926,
T986, T1028, T1076, T1124, T1164,
T1228, T1276, T1304, T1360, T1406

Standard Grammar and Usage.
See **Grammar.**
Statements.
See **Grammar.**
Stations
art: T106, T190, T296, T528, T572,
T724, T762, T806, T844, T952,
T994, T1084, T1132, T1192, T1368,
T1284
computer: T62, T146, T190, T256,
T338, T414, T572, T654, T762,
T844, T888, T952, T994, T1036,
T1084, T1236, T1284, T1322
current events: T146, T296, T484,
T888, T952, T1036
handwriting: T414, T484, T1284
learning log: T106, T414, T612, T888
listening: T16, T256, T528, T612,
T654, T888, T1036, T1322
map and stamp: T16, T296, T528,
T654, T762, T1192, T1236
post office: T376, T612, T806, T952,
T994, T1192
publishing: T16, T62, T106, T146,
T612, T724, T806, T994, T1084,
T1132
reading: T376, T484, T654, T806,
T1236, T1368
recording: T16, T146, T190, T296,
T376, T414, T762, T844, T1132,
T1192, T1284, T1322, T1368
research: T62, T190, T338, T572,
T1368

response journal: T256, T528, T724,
T1322
stamp: T1036
vocabulary: T62, T146, T190, T256,
T414, T572, T654, T762, T844,
T888, T952, T994, T1036, T1084,
T1236, T1284, T1322
word web: T338, T572
writing: T256, T338, T844
✔**Story Elements: Setting, Character,
and Plot.**
See **Literary Concepts, story
elements.**
Story Map: T112, T196, T302, T618,
T730, T1090, T1198
See also **Study and Research Skills,
organizing information graphically.**
Strategies Good Readers Use: xxiii–xxiv
adjust reading rate: T580, T586, T896,
T900, T904, T1092
focus strategy: T577, T595, T893,
T915
create mental images: T166, T348,
T350, T492, T496, T498, T504,
T854, T860, T1204, T1342
focus strategy: T343, T359, T489,
T511, T849, T871
make and confirm predictions: T304,
T306, T310, T732, T734, T1002,
T1004, T1008, T1046
focus strategy: T301, T321, T729,
T745, T999, T1019
read ahead: T264, T268, T674, T1376,
T1380, T1382
focus strategy: T261, T279, T1373,
T1395
reread: T26, T154, T156, T162, T202,
T352, T582, T772, T776, T962,
T1094, T1098, T1102, T1142, T1252
focus strategy: T151, T173, T1089,
T1115
self-question: T28, T118, T206, T266,
T308, T388, T424, T494, T620,
T624, T630, T668, T738, T770,
T774, T1050, T1210, T1254, T1330,
T1378
focus strategy: T111, T129, T617,
T635, T767, T789
summarize and paraphrase: T72, T198,
T204, T422, T426, T588, T898,
T1106
focus strategy: T195, T213, T419,
T437

use context to confirm meaning: T30,
T32, T116, T200, T312, T428, T500,
T622, T672, T778, T816, T858,
T960, T968, T970, T1056, T1140,
T1144
focus strategy: T957, T977, T1137,
T1153
use graphic aids: T538, T542, T866,
T1334, T1336
focus strategy: T533, T553, T1327,
T1349
use prior knowledge: T24, T36, T70,
T74, T80, T122, T158, T346, T502,
T852, T966, T1010, T1044, T1050,
T1096, T1200, T1202, T1206,
T1208, T1246
focus strategy: T21, T45, T67, T89,
T1041, T1065, T1197, T1219
use reference sources: T536, T662,
T664, T666, T1244, T1248, T1256
focus strategy: T659, T685, T1241,
T1267
use text structure and format: T384,
T386, T390, T814, T818, T1292,
T1294, T1296, T1332
focus strategy: T381, T397, T811,
T827, T1289, T1305
See also **Prereading Strategies; Word
Identification Strategies.**
Strategy Builder: A40–A45
Strategy, Conferences.
See **Assessment, informal.**
Strategy Reminders: T21, T67, T111,
T151, T195, T261, T301, T343, T381,
T419, T489, T533, T577, T617, T659,
T729, T767, T811, T849, T893, T957,
T999, T1041, T1089, T1137, T1197,
T1241, T1289, T1327, T1373
Structural Analysis.
See **Decoding/Phonics; Vocabulary;
Word Identification Strategies.**
Students Acquiring English.
See **Reaching All Learners, ESL.**
Student Self- and Peer Assessment.
See **Assessment.**
Student Writing Models.
See **Writing.**
Study and Research Skills
additional questions, raising: T13, T57,
T59, T101, T103, T141, T143, T185,
T187, T225, T253, T291, T293,
T333, T335, T371, T373, T409,
T411, T451, T481, T523, T525,
T567, T569, T607, T609, T649,

KEY
✔ = Tested　　Blue = Pages in this book

Index

Index

Index

Index

character development chart: T894, T1374

chart: T356, T416, T486, T614, T630, T632, T764, T866, T974, T1115, T1216

diagram: T126, T215, T574, T594, T954, T996

K-W-L chart: T262, T534, T578, T606, T660, T812, T1290, T1328

letter summary chart: T768

list: T318, T356, T432, T912, T1112, T1370

predict-o-gram: T64, T726, T1086, T1194

prediction chart/diagram: T22, T490, T958, T1086, T1138

problem/advice chart: T152

problem solution map: T850, T1042

sequence chart/diagram: T344, T530

story events map: T196

story map: T112, T302, T618, T730, T1090, T1198

story outline: T420

time line: T733, T1180, T1242

Venn diagram: T166, T323, T828

web: T18, T109, T148, T192, T258, T298, T340, T378, T656, T808, T846, T890, T1038, T1084, T1134, T1238, T1286, T1324

problem solving: T786, T1046

See **Monitor Comprehension.**

speculating: T80, T114, T204, T670, T740, T860, T1010, T1250, T1380

synthesizing: T620, T624, T625, T738

Title Page, Using.

See **Book Parts.**

Trade Book Lesson Plans

Zora Hurston and the Chinaberry Tree: T228–T229

The Black Stallion: T230–T231

Baseball in the Barrios: T454–T455

The Tarantula in My Purse: T456–T457

Volcanoes: T700–T701

Earthquake Terror: T702–T703

The Young Artist: T932–T933

Dear Benjamin Banneker: T934–T935

Frindle: T1170–T1171

A Cloak for a Dreamer: T1172–T1173

Maria's Comet: T1412–T1413

And Then What Happened, Paul Revere?: T1414–T1415

Trade Books

additional reading: R20–R22, R47–R48, R71–R72, R94–R96, R119–R120, R142–R144

multi-level books: T17, T63, T107, T147, T191, T257, T297, T339, T377, T415, T485, T529, T573, T613, T655, T725, T763, T807, T845, T889, T953, T995, T1037, T1085, T1133, T1193, T1237, T1285, T1323, T1369

Reader's Choice Library

See **Trade Book Lesson Plans.**

Typographical Cues.

See **Comprehension, text features.**

Usage

adjectives

  adjectives and articles: T796–T797, T821

  adjectives, comparing with: T878–T879, T899

adverbs

  adverbs: T1312–T1313, T1331

  adverbs, comparing with: T1358–T1359, T1377

contractions and negatives: T1274–T1275, T1293

nouns

  common and proper: T404–T405, T427

  possessive nouns (singular and plural): T518–T519, T543

  singular and plural nouns: T446–T447, T503

pronouns

  possessive pronouns: T644–T645, T663

  pronouns and antecedents: T562–T563, T585

  reflexive pronouns: T752–T753, T777

  subject and object pronouns: T602–T603, T621

verbs

  action and linking verbs: T984–T985, T1007

  main and helping verbs: T924–T925, T971

  principal parts of verbs: T1122–T1123, T1143

  regular and irregular verbs: T1162–T1163, T1205

  tenses

    past and future: T1074–T1075, T1093

    perfect: T1126–T1127, T1253

    present: T1026–T1027, T1049

See also **Daily Language Practice.**

Verbs.

See **Grammar.**

Videos.

See **Technology.**

Viewing: T44, T88, T128, T172, T212, T278, T320, T358, T396, T436, T510, T552, T594, T634, T684, T744, T788, T826, T870, T914, T976, T1018, T1064, T1114, T1152, T1218, T1266, T1304, T1348, T1394

See also **Study and Research Skills, text features, viewing.**

Visual Images, Draw or Discuss: T264, T1200

Visualizing.

See **Strategies Good Readers Use, create mental images.**

Vocabulary

antonyms: T599, T1019

Bonus Words: T18, T64, T108, T148, T192, T258, T298, T340, T378, T416, T486, T530, T574, T614, T656, T726, T764, T808, T846, T890, T954, T996, T1038, T1086, T1134, T1194, T1238, T1286, T1324, T1370

classifying and categorizing words: T443, T559, T875, T1355

compound words: T259, T321, T1267, T1341

See also **Decoding/Phonics, structural analysis; Spelling.**

KEY	
✔ = Tested	Blue = Pages in this book

Index

Index

scoring rubrics: T51, T95, T135, T179, T285, T327, T365, T403, T517, T561, T601, T643, T751, T795, T833, T877, T1161, T1225, T1273, T1311, T1357, T1403

student self- and peer assessment: T51, T95, T135, T179, T219, T285, T327, T365, T403, T445, T517, T561, T601, T643, T691, T751, T795, T833, T877, T923, T1161, T1357, T1403

capitalization and punctuation, use correctly: T179, T219, T403, T444, T643, T690, T877, T922, T1121, T1357

connect writing to reading: T50, T94, T134, T178, T284, T326, T364, T402, T516, T560, T600, T642, T750, T794, T832, T876, T982, T1024, T1072, T1120, T1160, T1224, T1272, T1310, T1356, T1402

drafts

   prewrite/draft: T51, T95, T135, T179, T219, T285, T327, T365, T403, T444, T517, T561, T601, T643, T690, T751, T795, T833, T877, T922, T982–T983, T1072–T1073, T1225, T1273, T1311, T1357, T1403

   edit/revise: T51, T95, T135, T179, T219, T285, T327, T365, T403, T444, T517, T561, T601, T643, T690, T751, T795, T833, T877, T922, T1025, T1120–T1121, T1225, T1273, T1311, T1357, T1403

evaluation

   effective features of a piece of writing, identify: T51, T95, T135, T178, T219, T285, T327, T365, T402, T445, T517, T561, T601, T642, T751, T795, T833, T877, T923, T1121, T1161, T1357, T1403

   others' writing, respond effectively to: T51, T95, T135, T179, T219, T285, T327, T365, T403, T445, T517, T561, T601, T643, T691, T751, T795, T833, T877, T923, T1161, T1357, T1403

   purpose, determine how own writing achieves: T51, T95, T135, T179, T219, T285, T327, T365, T403,

T445, T517, T561, T601, T643, T691, T751, T795, T833, T877, T923, T1025, T1121, T1161, T1225, T1273, T1311, T1357, T1403

writing growth, monitor own: T51, T95, T135, T179, T219, T285, T327, T365, T403, T445, T517, T561, T601, T643, T691, T751, T795, T833, T877, T923, T1161, T1357, T1403

writing models, use published pieces as: T9, T44, T94, T128, T249, T284, T308, T396, T540, T634, T679, T788, T870, T1018, T1120, T1272, T1346, T1391

writing, review and evaluate own collection of: T179, T219, T445, T691, T713, T877, T923, T1176, T1357

inquiry/research.

   See **Inquiry and Research.**

penmanship, gain more proficient control of: T54, T98, T138, T182, T222, T288, T330, T368, T406, T448, T520, T564, T604, T646, T694, T754, T798, T836, T880, T926, T986, T1028, T1076, T1124, T1164, T1228, T1276, T1314, T1360, T1406

process writing.

   See **Writing Process.**

publish: T16, T42, T62, T106, T146, T170, T179, T396, T403, T445, T550, T612, T643, T682, T691, T724, T806, T877, T923, T994, T1132, T1160–T1161, T1302, T1357

purposes

   audiences, communicate with a variety of: T50, T94, T134, T178, T218, T284, T326, T364, T402, T444, T516, T560, T600, T642, T690, T750, T794, T832, T876, T922, T982, T1072, T1160, T1224, T1272, T1310, T1356, T1402

   selecting form based on purpose/task

      letters, business: T600

      letters, friendly: T1310

      poems: T1224, T1402

      research report: T982, T1024, T1072

      stories, personal: T50, T178, T218

      stories, imaginative: T134, T1357

to describe: T94, T444

to entertain: T50, T134, T178, T218, T1224, T1272, T1357, T1402

to explain/inform: T284, T326, T364, T402, T444, T750, T794, T832, T876, T922, T982, T1072

to persuade: T516, T560, T600, T642, T690

rubrics

   See **Rubrics for Students; Assessment, rubrics for writing.**

student writing models, analyze

   business letter: T600

   friendly letter: T1310

   outline: T1024

   paragraphs

      that describe: T94

      that explain/inform: T284, T326, T402, T750, T794, T832, T876

      that persuade: T516, T642

   dialogue: T1272

   news story: T364

   poems

      rhymed: T1224

      unrhymed: T1402

   research report: T982, T1024, T1072, T1120, T1160

   review: T560

   stories

      imaginative: T134, T1356

      personal: T50, T178

test prep: T51, T95, T135, T179, T285, T327, T403, T517, T561, T601, T643, T751, T795, T833, T877, T1311

writing activities

   advertisement: T826

   business letter: T600–T601

   character sketch: T1152

   compare/contrast: T750–T751, T794–T795, T876–T877, T922–T923

   conversation: T945, T1272–T1273

   description: T94–T95, T444–T445, T788, T870

   dialogue: T510, T945, T1272–T1273

   diary/journal: T88, T358, T552, T744, T1266

   directions/how-to: T326–T327

   flyer: T172

Index

Acknowledgments

Grateful acknowledgment is made to Philomel Books, a division of Penguin Putnam Inc. for permission to reprint *The Emperor and the Kite* by Jane Yolen. Text copyright © 1967 by Jane Yolen.

The following is the credit list for all photos used in Harcourt *Collections* Grade 5 Theme 1:

T13, ©Lisa Quinones/BlackStar/Harcourt

T16, ©Harcourt

T16, ©Ken Karp

T26, ©Ken Karp

T28, ©Corbis/Robbie Jack

T30, ©Corbis/Wolfgang Kaehler

T36, ©Corbis/Lynn Goldsmith

T44, ©Ken Karp

T50, ©PhotDisc

T56, ©Ken Karp

T56, ©Yoav Levy/Phototake/PNI

T59, ©Tom Berthiaume/Parallel
Productions/Harcourt

T62, ©Harcourt

T74, ©PhotoDisc

T88, ©Ken Karp

T100, ©Corbis

T100, ©Ken Karp

T102, ©Joseph Rupp/BlackStar/Harcourt

T106, ©Ken Karp

T114, ©Corbis/Steve Raymer

T128, ©Ken Karp

T134, ©PhotoDisc

T140, ©Corbis/James L. amos

T143, Danny Turner

T146, ©Harcourt

T154, ©Corbis/Underwood & Underwood

T172, ©Ken Karp

T184, ©Corbis/Reuters Newsmedia Inc.

T184, ©Ken Karp

T186, ©Amy Hall

T190, ©Harcourt

T198, ©Paramount/PNI

T202, ©Corbis/Bettmann

T212, ©Ken Karp

T218, ©Ken Karp

T224, ©PhotDisc

T224, ©Ken Karp